★INFANTRY★ REGIMENTS

★ INFANTRY ★ REGIMENTS
of the United States Army

A Complete Guide to the History,
Decorations, Honors and Colors
of each Infantry Regiment
in the Regular Army

edited by

KENNETH S. GALLAGHER
and
ROBERT L. PIGEON

MILITARY PRESS
New York

PREFACE

The history of the Infantry in the United States Army is long and proud. Since the establishment of the Continental Army in 1775, the Infantry has served as the backbone of the United States Army. However, in recent decades the role of the infantry component in warfare has changed dramatically. Each new change in the battle-field function of the infantry unit necessitated a change in Army organization. Invariably reorganizations were coincident to a new military conflict in which American troops participated. Units were raised to fight, and, when the conflict was over, units were inactivated. With each new reorganization some, or many, units went out of existence, and new units were formed.

In 1957 a new system of reorganization was approved which was designed to meet a modern army's need for a flexible regimental structure and provide a coherent historical lineage for each unit. This organizational structure is known as CARS (Combat Arms Regimental System).

This book presents the historical lineage, official campaign participation credit, and honors and decorations for each infantry regiment of the United States Army (Regular Army) organized under CARS. In addition, the approved coats of arms including motto and distinctive insignia of each regiment is described. A full-color presentation of each regiment's heraldic items is included in a separate signature of the book.

Most of the material of this book was compiled by The U.S. Army Center of Military History (*Infantry, Part I: Regular Army*, Army Lineage Series. Mahon, John K. and Romana Danysh; Government Printing Office, Washington: Center of Military History, 1972.). We have endeavored to render correctly this official material, and we have updated the campaign participation credit of each unit to include the entire Vietnam conflict. Medal of Honor winners for each regiment, as well as a special presentation of the 24th and 25th Infantry, are included at the end of the book.

We are grateful to The Center of Military History for its encouragement, especially Romana Danysh, who is co-author of The Center's infantry lineage book, and John Wilson. They both were very cooperative and helpful in answering questions. Special thanks are given to Antoinette Bauer, Tracey Burke, Robert Fanelli, James Howland and Lizbeth Nauta. We are, of course, solely responsible for the accuracy of the material; and we apologize in advance for any and all errors.

KENNETH S. GALLAGHER
ROBERT L. PIGEON
August 1986

Prepared and produced by
Combined Books
26 Summit Grove Avenue
Bryn Mawr, PA 19010
and
Wieser & Wieser, Inc.
118 East 25th Street
New York, NY 10010

This 1986 edition published by
Military Press, distributed by
Crown Publishers, Inc.
ISBN 0-517-61494-4

★ CONTENTS ★

1st INFANTRY

COAT OF ARMS

Motto: *Semper Primus* (Always First)

Symbolism: The regiment's campaigns and wars are represented by the notches on the diagonal band across the shield. The upper part of the shield is red; this was the color of the old 2d Sub-Legion. The lower part is blue, the infantry color.

The crest with the numeral within the laurel wreath of victory and the motto long in use by the regiment are self-explanatory.

DISTINCTIVE INSIGNIA

This distinctive insignia is the shield of the coat of arms surmounting a gold oval belt with three blue stripes parallel to the edges of the oval and surmounted by a plain gold buckle in base and a gold band on each side of the shield bearing the motto, *Semper* on the dexter band and *Primus* on the sinister band, in red letters.

LINEAGE

1791	Constituted 3 March as the 2d Infantry, Regular Army
1792	Redesignated as Infantry of the 2d Sub-Legion
1796	Redesignated 31 October as 2d Infantry
1815	Consolidated May–October with 3d, 7th and 44th Infantry to form 1st Infantry
1869	Consolidated April with 43d Infantry, Veteran Reserve Corps, again as 1st Infantry
1918	Assigned 11 September to 13th Division
1919	Relieved 8 March from assignment to 13th Division
1921	Assigned 27 July to 2d Division
1939	Relieved 16 October from assignment to 2d Division and assigned to 6th Division
1949	Inactivated 10 January in Korea
1950	Activated 4 October at Ford Ord, California
1956	Relieved 3 April from assignment to 6th Infantry Division and assigned 15 May to United States Military Academy (U.S.M.A.) at West Point
1958	Relieved from assignment to U.S.M.A. and reorganized as parent regiment under Combat Arms Regimental System (hereafter abbreviated as CARS)

DECORATIONS

Presidential Unit Citation (Army), Streamer embroidered **MAFFIN BAY** (3rd Battalion, 1st Infantry cited)

Philippine Presidential Unit Citation, Streamer embroidered **17 OCTOBER 1944 TO 4 JULY 1945** (6th Infantry Division cited)

CAMPAIGN PARTICIPATION

War of 1812
Canada
Lundy's Lane
New Orleans
Florida 1814
Alabama 1814
Alabama 1815
Louisiana 1815

Mexican War
Monterey
Vera Cruz

Civil War
Mississippi River
Vicksburg
Texas 1861
Missouri 1861
Mississippi 1862

Indian Wars
Miami
Creeks
Seminoles
Black Hawk
Apaches
Pine Ridge
Texas 1850

War With Spain
Santiago

Philippine Insurrection
Samar 1901

World War II
New Guinea (with arrowhead)
Luzon (with arrowhead)

Vietnam
Counteroffensive, Phase II
Counteroffensive, Phase III
Tet Counteroffensive
Counteroffensive, Phase IV
Counteroffensive, Phase V
Counteroffensive, Phase VI
Tet 69 Counteroffensive
Summer–Fall 1969
Winter–Spring 1970
Sanctuary Counteroffensive
Counteroffensive, Phase VII
Consolidation I
Consolidation II
Cease-Fire

1ST BATTALION, 1ST INFANTRY

LINEAGE

1791	Constituted 3 March as a company of the 2d Infantry, organized in New England
1792	Redesignated as a company of the Infantry of the 2d Sub-Legion
1796	Redesignated 31 October as a company of the 2d Infantry
1815	Consolidated May–October with company each from the 3d, 7th and 44th Infantry to form a company of the 1st Infantry

1816	Designated 21 August Company A, 1st Infantry
1869	Consolidated in April with Company A, 43d Infantry, Veteran Reserve Corps, and designated Company A, 1st Infantry

Company lineage follows that of 1st Infantry from 1869 Consolidation to 1956 assignment to United States Military Academy (U.S.M.A.), West Point, NY

1958	Reorganized and redesignated 15 May as Headquarters and Headquarters Company, 1st Battle Group, 1st Infantry, remaining assigned to U.S.M.A.
1964	Redesignated as 1st Battalion, 1st Infantry

CAMPAIGN PARTICIPATION

War of 1812
Canada
Lundy's Lane
New Orleans
Florida 1814
Alabama 1814
Alabama 1815
Louisiana 1815

Mexican War
Monterey
Vera Cruz

Civil War
Mississippi River
Vicksburg
Texas 1861

Missouri 1861
Mississippi 1862

Indian Wars
Miami
Creeks
Seminoles
Black Hawk
Apaches
Pine Ridge
Texas 1850

War With Spain
Santiago

Philippine Insurrection
Samar 1901

World War II
New Guinea (with arrowhead)
Luzon (with arrowhead)

DECORATIONS

Presidential Unit Citation (Army), Streamer embroidered **MAFFIN BAY.**

Philippine Presidential Unit Citation, Streamer embroidered **17 OCTOBER 1944 TO 4 JULY 1945** (6th Infantry Division cited)

2D BATTALION, 1ST INFANTRY

LINEAGE

1791	Constituted 3 March as a company of the 2d Infantry, Regular Army
1792	Redesignated as a company of the Infantry of the 2d Sub-Legion
1796	Redesignated 31 October as a company of the 2d Infantry
1815	Consolidated May–October with company each from 3d, 7th and 44th Infantry to form a company of the 1st Infantry
1816	Designated 21 August as Company B, 1st Infantry

Company lineage follows that of 1st Infantry from 1869 consolidation to 1956 assignment to United States Military Academy (U.S.M.A.) West Point, NY.

1958	Relieved from assignment to the U.S.M.A., and redesignated as Headquarters and Headquarters Company, 2d Battle Group, 1st Infantry; assigned to 2d Infantry Division 14 June at Fort Benning, GA
1963	Inactivated 10 May and relieved from assignment to 2d Infantry Division
1965	Redesignated 10 September as 2d Battalion, 1st Infantry, and assigned to the 196th Infantry Brigade
1969	Relieved 15 February from assignment to 196th Infantry Brigade and assigned to 23d Infantry Division

CAMPAIGN PARTICIPATION

War of 1812

Canada
Lundy's Lane
New Orleans
Florida 1814
Alabama 1814
Alabama 1815
Louisiana 1815

Mexican War

Monterey
Vera Cruz

Civil War

Mississippi River
Vicksburg
Texas 1861
Missouri 1861
Mississippi 1862

Indian Wars

Miami
Creeks
Seminoles
Black Hawk
Apaches
Pine Ridge
Texas 1850

War With Spain

Santiago

Philippine Insurrection

Samar 1901

World War II

New Guinea (with arrowhead)
Luzon (with arrowhead)

Vietnam

Counteroffensive, Phase II
Counteroffensive, Phase III
Tet Counteroffensive
Counteroffensive, Phase IV
Counteroffensive, Phase V
Counteroffensive, Phase VI
Tet 69 Counteroffensive
Summer–Fall 1969
Winter–Spring 1970
Sanctuary Counteroffensive
Counteroffensive, Phase VII
Consolidation I
Consolidation II
Cease-Fire

DECORATIONS

Presidential Unit Citations (Army), Streamer embroidered **MAFFIN BAY**

Philippine Presidential Unit Citation, Streamer embroidered **17 OCTOBER 1944 TO 4 JULY 1945** (6th Infantry Division cited)

3D BATTALION, 1ST INFANTRY

LINEAGE

1791	Constituted 3 March as a company of 2d Infantry, Regular Army
1792	Redesignated as a company of the Infantry of the 2d Sub-Legion
1796	Redesignated 31 October as a company of the 2d Infantry
1815	Consolidated May–October with company each from 3d, 7th, and 44th Infantry to form company of the 1st Infantry
1816	Designated 21 August as Company C, 1st Infantry

Company lineage follows that of 1st Infantry from 1869 consolidation to 1956 assignment to United States Military Academy, West Point, N.Y.

1959	Redesignated 7 April as Headquarters and Headquarters Company, 3d Battle Group, 1st Infantry; reassigned to Army Reserve 77th Infantry Division and Battle Group activated 1 May with Headquarters in New York, NY
1963	Inactivated 26 March and relieved from assignment to 77th Infantry Division
1966	Redesignated 15 April as 3d Battalion, 1st Infantry, allotted to Regular Army from Army Reserve; activated 1 July in Hawaii and assigned to 11th Infantry Brigade
1969	Relieved 15 February from 11th Infantry Brigade and assigned to 23rd Infantry Division

CAMPAIGN PARTICIPATION

War of 1812

Canada
Lundy's Lane
New Orleans
Florida 1814
Alabama 1814
Alabama 1815
Louisiana 1815

Mexican War

Monterey
Vera Cruz

Civil War

Mississippi River
Vicksburg
Texas 1861

Missouri 1861
Mississippi 1862

Indian Wars

Miami
Creeks
Seminoles
Black Hawk
Apaches
Pine Ridge
Texas 1850

War With Spain

Santiago

Philippine Insurrection

Samar 1901

World War II

New Guinea (with
  arrowhead)
Luzon (with arrowhead)

Vietnam

Counteroffensive,
  Phase III
Tet Counteroffensive
Counteroffensive,
  Phase IV
Counteroffensive,
  Phase V
Counteroffensive,
  Phase VI
Tet 69 Counteroffensive
Summer–Fall 1969
Winter–Spring 1970
Sanctuary
  Counteroffensive
Counteroffensive,
  Phase VII
Consolidation I

DECORATIONS

Presidential Unit Citation (Army), Streamer embroidered **MAFFIN BAY**

Philippine Presidential Unit Citation, Streamer embroidered **17 OCTOBER 1944 TO 4 JULY 1945** (6th Infantry Division cited)

Vietnamese Cross of Gallantry with Palm, Streamer embroidered **VIETNAM 1968–1969** (3d Battalion, 1st Infantry cited)

Company C additionally entitled to: Valorous Unit Award, Streamer embroidered **QUANG NGAI PROVINCE** (Company C, 3d Battalion, 1st Infantry cited)

4TH BATTALION, 1ST INFANTRY

LINEAGE

1791   Constituted as a company of the 2d Infantry, Regular Army

1792   Redesignated as a company of the Infantry of the 2d Sub-Legion

1796   Redesignated 31 October as a company of the 2d Infantry

1815   Consolidated May–October with a company each of 3d, 7th and 44th Infantry to form 1st Infantry

1816   Designated 21 August as Company D, 1st Infantry

        Company lineage follows that of 1st Infantry from 1869 consolidation to 1956 assignment to United States Military Academy (U.S.M.A.), West Point, NY.

1958   Inactivated 15 May; relieved from assignment to U.S.M.A. and redesignated as Headquarters and Headquarters Company, 4th Battle Group, 1st Infantry

1967   Redesignated 24 November as Headquarters and

Headquarters Company, 4th Battalion, 1st Infantry, and assigned to 6th Infantry Division, Fort Campbell, KY

1968   Relieved 24 July from assignment to 6th Infantry Division

1969   Inactivated 21 July at Fort Campbell, KY

CAMPAIGN PARTICIPATION

War of 1812

Canada
Lundy's Lane
New Orleans
Florida 1814
Alabama 1814
Alabama 1815
Louisiana 1815

Mexican War

Monterey
Vera Cruz

Civil War

Mississippi River
Vicksburg
Texas 1861
Missouri 1861
Mississippi 1862

11

Indian Wars

Miami
Creeks
Seminoles
Black Hawk
Apaches
Pine Ridge
Texas 1850

War With Spain

Santiago

Philippine Insurrection

Samar 1901

World War II

New Guinea (with
arrowhead)
Luzon (with arrowhead)

DECORATIONS

Presidential Unit Citation (Army), Streamer embroidered **MAFFIN BAY.**

Philippine Presidential Unit Citation, Streamer embroidered **17 OCTOBER 1944 TO 4 JULY 1945** (6th Infantry Division cited)

5TH BATTALION, 1ST INFANTRY

LINEAGE

1791 Constituted 3 March as a company of the 2d Infantry, Regular Army

1792 Redesignated as a company of the Infantry of the 2d Sub-Legion

1796 Redesignated 31 October as a company of the 2d Infantry

1815 Consolidated May–October with a company each of the 3d, 7th and 44th Infantry to form 1st Infantry

1816 Designated 21 August as Company E, 1st Infantry

Company lineage follows that of 1st Infantry from 1869 consolidation to 1956 assignment to United States Military Academy (U.S.M.A.), West Point, NY.

1958 Inactivated 15 May; relieved from assignment to U.S.M.A. and redesignated as Headquarters and Headquarters Company, 5th Battle Group, 1st Infantry

1967 Redesignated 24 November as Headquarters and Headquarters Company, 5th Battalion, 1st Infantry; assigned to 6th Infantry Division, Fort Campbell, KY

1968 Relieved 24 July from assignment to 6th Infantry Division

1969 Inactivated 21 July at Fort Campbell, KY

CAMPAIGN PARTICIPATION

War of 1812

Canada
Lundy's Lane
New Orleans
Florida 1814
Alabama 1814
Alabama 1815
Louisiana 1815

Mexican War

Monterey
Vera Cruz

Civil War

Mississippi River
Vicksburg
Texas 1861
Missouri 1861
Mississippi 1862

Indian Wars

Miami
Creeks
Seminoles
Black Hawk
Apaches
Pine Ridge
Texas 1850

War With Spain

Santiago

Philippine Insurrection

Samar 1901

World War II

New Guinea (with
arrowhead)
Luzon (with arrowhead)

DECORATIONS

Presidential Unit Citation (Army), Streamer embroidered **MAFFIN BAY.**

Philippine Presidential Unit Citation, Streamer embroidered **17 OCTOBER 1944 TO 4 JULY 1945** (6th Infantry Division cited)

6TH BATTALION, 1ST INFANTRY

LINEAGE

1791	Constituted 3 March as a company of the 2d Infantry, Regular Army
1792	Redesignated as a company of the Infantry of the 2d Sub-Legion
1796	Redesignated 31 October as a company of the 2d Infantry
1815	Consolidated May–October with a company each of 3d, 7th and 44th Infantry to form 1st Infantry
1816	Designated 21 August as Company F, 1st Infantry

Company lineage follows that of 1st Infantry from 1869 consolidation to 1956 assignment to United States Military Academy (U.S.M.A.), West Point, NY.

1958	Inactivated 15 May; relieved from assignment to U.S.M.A. and redesignated as Headquarters and Headquarters Company, 6th Battle Group, 1st Infantry
1967	Redesignated 24 November as Headquarters and Headquarters Company, 6th Battalion, 1st Infantry; assigned to 6th Infantry Division, Fort Campbell, KY
1968	Relieved 24 July from assignment to 6th Infantry Division
1969	Inactivated 21 July at Fort Campbell, KY

CAMPAIGN PARTICIPATION

War of 1812
Canada
Lundy's Lane
New Orleans
Florida 1814
Alabama 1814
Alabama 1815
Louisiana 1815

Mexican War
Monterey
Vera Cruz

Civil War
Mississippi River
Vicksburg
Texas 1861
Missouri 1861
Mississippi 1862

Indian Wars
Miami
Creeks
Seminoles
Black Hawk
Apaches
Pine Ridge
Texas 1850

War With Spain
Santiago

Philippine Insurrection
Samar 1901

World War II
New Guinea (with arrowhead)
Luzon (with arrowhead)

DECORATIONS

Presidential Unit Citation (Army), Streamer embroidered **MAFFIN BAY.**

Philippine Presidential Unit Citation, Streamer embroidered **17 OCTOBER 1944 TO 4 JULY 1945** (6th Infantry Division cited)

2ND INFANTRY

COAT OF ARMS

Motto: *Noli Me Tangere* (Do Not Touch Me).

Symbolism: Service in the Civil War is shown by the blue cross from the Confederate flag and the red cross pattée, the badge of the 18th Division, V Corps, in which the regiment served during the greater part of that war. Service in the Mexican War is shown by the cactus; in the War with Spain by the five-bastioned fort, the badge of the V Corps in Cuba. The Indian campaigns of the regiment are shown by the arrows and quiver, and the bolo is for service in the Philippine Insurrection.

The lion in the crest represents the Canadian campaigns of the War of 1812

DISTINCTIVE INSIGNIA

The distinctive insignia is the shield and the motto of the coat of arms.

LINEAGE

1808	Constituted 12 April as 6th Infantry, Regular Army and organized May–July in Pennsylvania, New York, and New Jersey
1815	Consolidated May–October with 16th, 22d, 23d and 32d Infantry to form 2d Infantry
1861	Constituted 3 May as the 1st Battalion, 16th Infantry, Regular Army and organized 21 August at Camp Slemmer, IL
1866	Reorganized and redesignated 21 September as 16th Infantry
1869	Consolidated 18 April with 16th Infantry to form 2d Infantry
1918	Assigned 27 July to 19th Division
1919	Relieved 14 February from assignment to 19th Division
1923	Assigned 24 March to 6th Division
1939	Relieved 16 October from assignment to 6th Division and reassigned to 5th Division
1946	Inactivated 20 September at Camp Campbell, Kentucky
1947	Reactivated 15 July at Fort Jackson, SC
1950	Inactivated 30 April 1950 at Fort Jackson, SC
1951	Reactivated 1 March at Indiantown Gap Military Reservation, PA
1953	Inactivated 1 September at Indiantown Gap
1954	Reactivated 25 May at Munich, Germany
1957	Relieved 1 June from assignment to 5th Infantry Division and reorganized as a parent regiment under Combat Arms Regimental System

DECORATIONS

Valorous Unit Award, Streamer embroidered **BINH DOUNG** (2d Battalion, 2d Infantry cited)

Valorous Unit Award, Streamer embroidered **AP BAU BANG** (2d Battalion, 2d Infantry cited)

Valorous Unit Award, Streamer embroidered **BINH LONG PROVINCE 1969** (2d Battalion, 2d Infantry cited)

CAMPAIGN PARTICIPATION

War of 1812

Canada
Chippewa
Lundy's Lane
Alabama 1814

Mexican War

Vera Cruz
Cerro Gordo
Contreras
Churubusco
Molino del Rey
Chapultepec

Civil War

Bull Run
Peninsula
Shiloh
Manassas
Antietam
Fredericksburg
Murfreesborough
Chancellorsville
Gettysburg
Chickamauga
Chattanooga
Wilderness
Atlanta
Spotsylvania
Cold Harbor
Petersburg
Missouri 1861
Mississippi 1862
Virginia 1862
Kentucky 1862
Virginia 1863
Tennessee 1863
Georgia 1984

Indian Wars

Miami
Seminoles
Nez Perces
Bannocks
Pine Ridge
California 1850
California 1851
California 1852

War With Spain

Santiago

Philippine Insurrection

Without inscription

World War II

Normandy
Northern France
Rhineland
Ardennes-Alsace
Central Europe

Vietnam

Defense
Counteroffensive
Counteroffensive, Phase II
Counteroffensive, Phase III
Tet Counteroffensive
Counteroffensive, Phase IV
Counteroffensive, Phase V
Counteroffensive, Phase VI
Tet 69 Counteroffensive
Summer–Fall 1969
Winter–Spring 1970

1ST BATTALION, 2ND INFANTRY

LINEAGE

1808 — Constituted 12 April as company of the 6th Infantry Regular Army

1815 — Consolidated May–October with companies from the 16th, 22d, 23d and 32d Infantry to form a company of the 2d Infantry

1816 — Designated 22 May as Company A, 2d Infantry

1861 — Constituted 3 May as Company A, 1st Battalion, 16th Infantry, Regular Army; organized 21 August at Camp Slemmer, IL

1866 — Reorganized and redesignated 21 September as Company A, 16th Infantry

1869 — Consolidated 18 April with Company A, 2d Infantry to form Company A, 2d Infantry

Company lineage follows that of 2d Infantry from 1869 Consolidation to 1954 reactivation in Munich, Germany

1957 — Inactivated 1 June at Fort Ord, CA; relieved from assignment with 5th Infantry Division and redesignated Headquarters and Headquarters Company, 1st Battle Group, 2d Infantry

1962 — Redesignated 19 February as Headquarters and Headquarters Company, 1st Battalion, 2d Infantry; assigned to the 5th Infantry Division, Fort Devens, MA

1965 — Relieved 12 July from assignment to 5th Infantry Division and assigned to 1st Infantry Division

DECORATIONS

Vietnamese Cross of Gallantry with Palm, Streamer embroidered **VIETNAM 1965–1968** (1st Battalion, 2d Infantry cited)

Vietnamese Cross of Gallantry with Palm, Streamer embroidered **VIETNAM 1969–1970** (1st Battalion, 2d Infantry cited)

Vietnamese Civil Action Honor Medal, First Class, Streamer embroidered **VIETNAM 1965–1970** (1st Battalion, 2d Infantry cited)

Company A additionally entitled to: Valorous Unit Award, Streamer embroidered **AN LOC** (Company A, 1st Battalion, 2d Infantry cited)

CAMPAIGN PARTICIPATION

War of 1812
Canada
Chippewa
Lundy's Lane
Alabama 1814

Mexican War
Vera Cruz
Cerro Gordo
Contreras
Churubusco
Molino del Rey
Chapultepec

Civil War
Bull Run
Peninsula
Shiloh
Manassas
Antietam
Fredericksburg
Murfreesborough
Chancellorsville
Gettysburg
Chickamauga
Chattanooga
Wilderness
Atlanta
Spotsylvania
Cold Harbor
Petersburg
Missouri 1861
Mississippi 1862
Virginia 1862
Kentucky 1862
Virginia 1863
Tennessee 1863
Georgia 1864

Indian Wars
Miami
Seminoles
Nez Perces
Bannocks
Pine Ridge
California 1850
California 1851
California 1852

War With Spain
Santiago

Philippine Insurrection
Without inscription

World War II
Normandy
Northern France
Rhineland
Ardennes-Alsace
Central Europe

Vietnam
Defense
Counteroffensive
Counteroffensive, Phase II
Counteroffensive, Phase III
Counteroffensive, Phase IV
Counteroffensive, Phase V
Counteroffensive, Phase VI
Tet 69 Counteroffensive
Summer–Fall 1969
Winter–Spring 1970

2D BATTALION, 2ND INFANTRY

LINEAGE

1808	Constituted 12 April as a company of the 6th Infantry, Regular Army
1815	Consolidated May–October with companies from the 16th, 22d, 23d and 32d Infantry to form a company of the 2d Infantry
1816	Designated 22 May as Company B, 2d Infantry
1861	Constituted 3 May as Company B, 1st Battalion, 16th Infantry, Regular Army; organized at Camp Slemmer, IL
1866	Reorganized and redesignated 21 September as Company B, 16th Infantry
1869	Consolidated 18 April with Company B, 2d Infantry, into Company B, 2d Infantry

Company lineage follows that of 2d Infantry from 1869 consolidation to 1954 reactivation in Munich, Germany

1957	Reorganized and redesignated 15 February as Headquarters and Headquarters Company, 2d Battle Group, 2d Infantry; relieved from assignment to the 5th Infantry Division and assigned to 1st Infantry Division
1959	Relieved 28 January from assignment to 1st Infantry Division and reassigned to 24th Infantry Division
1962	Reorganized and redesignated 19 February as 2d Battalion, 2d Infantry; relieved from assignment to 24th Infantry Division and assigned to 5th Infantry Division
1965	Relieved 12 July from assignment to 5th Infantry Division and assigned to 1st Infantry Division
1970	Inactivated 15 April 1970 at Fort Riley, KS

CAMPAIGN PARTICIPATION

War of 1812
Canada
Chippewa
Lundy's Lane
Alabama 1814

Mexican War
Vera Cruz
Cerro Gordo
Contreras
Churubusco
Molino del Rey
Chapultepec

Civil War
Bull Run
Peninsula
Shiloh
Manassas
Antietam
Fredericksburg
Murfreesborough
Chancellorsville
Gettysburg
Chickamauga
Chattanooga
Wilderness
Atlanta
Spotsylvania
Cold Harbor
Petersburg
Missouri 1861
Mississippi 1862
Virginia 1862
Kentucky 1862
Virginia 1863
Tennessee 1863
Georgia 1864

Indian Wars
Miami
Seminoles
Nez Perces
Bannocks
Pine Ridge
California 1850
California 1851
California 1852

War With Spain
Santiago

Philippine Insurrection
Without inscription

World War II
Normandy
Northern France
Rhineland
Ardennes-Alsace
Central Europe

Vietnam
Defense
Counteroffensive
Counteroffensive,
    Phase II
Counteroffensive,
    Phase III
Tet Counteroffensive
Counteroffensive,
    Phase IV
Counteroffensive,
    Phase V
Counteroffensive,
    Phase VI
Tet 69 Counteroffensive
Summer–Fall 1969
Winter Spring 1970

DECORATIONS

Valorous Unit Award, Streamer embroidered **BINH DOUNG** (2d Battalion, 2d Infantry cited)

Valorous Unit Award, Streamer embroidered **AP BAU BANG** (2d Battalion, 2d Infantry cited)

Valorous Unit Award, Streamer embroidered **BINH LONG PROVINCE 1969** (2d Battalion, 2d Infantry cited)

Vietnamese Cross of Gallantry with Palm, Streamer embroidered **VIETNAM 1965–1968** (2d Battalion, 2d Infantry cited)

Vietnamese Cross of Gallantry with Palm, Streamer embroidered **VIETNAM 1969** (2d Battalion, 2d Infantry cited)

Vietnamese Civil Action Honor Medal, First Class, Streamer embroidered **VIETNAM 1965–1970** (2d Battalion, 2d Infantry cited)

Company C additionally entitled to: Valorous Unit Award, Streamer embroidered **BINH LONG PROVINCE** (Company C, 2d Battalion, 2d Infantry cited)

3D BATTALION, 2ND INFANTRY

LINEAGE

1808   Constituted 12 April as a company of the 6th Infantry, Regular Army

1815   Consolidated May–October with companies from the 16th, 22d, 23d and 32d Infantry to form a company of the 2d Infantry

1816   Designated 22 May as Company C, 2d Infantry

1861   Constituted 3 May as Company C, 1st Battalion, 16th Infantry, Regular Army; organized at Camp Slemmer, IL

1866   Reorganized and redesignated 21 September as Company C, 16th Infantry

1869   Consolidated 18 April with Company C, 2d Infantry, to form Company C, 2d Infantry

1917   Constituted 5 August in the National Army as Headquarters and Headquarters Company, 332d Infantry, an element of the 83d Division and organized at Camp Sherman, OH

1919   Demobilized 1 July at Camp Sherman, OH

1921   Reconstituted 24 June as element of 83d Division of the Organized Reserves

1942   Relieved 30 January from assignment to 83d Division and allotted to Army of the United States as an inactive unit

1952   Allotted 15 May to Organized Reserve Corps as an element of 83d Infantry Division

1954   Activated 22 January at Youngstown, OH

1955   Location changed 15 April to Warren, OH

1956   Location changed 4 January to Columbus, OH

1959   Consolidated 20 March with Headquarters and Headquarters Company, 3d Battle Group, 2d Infantry into Headquarters and Headquarters Company, 3d Battle Group, 2d Infantry

1963   Reorganized and redesignated 15 April as 3d Battalion, 2d Infantry

1965   Inactivated 31 December at Columbus, OH

CAMPAIGN PARTICIPATION

War of 1812
   Canada
   Chippewa
   Lundy's Lane
   Alabama 1814

Mexican War
   Vera Cruz
   Cerro Gordo
   Contreras
   Churubusco
   Molino del Rey
   Chapultepec

Civil War
   Bull Run
   Peninsula
   Shiloh
   Manassas
   Antietam
   Fredericksburg
   Murfreesborough
   Chancellorsville
   Gettysburg
   Chickamauga
   Chattanooga
   Wilderness
   Atlanta
   Spotsylvania
   Cold Harbor
   Petersburg
   Missouri 1861
   Mississippi 1862

   Virginia 1862
   Kentucky 1862
   Virginia 1863
   Tennessee 1863
   Georgia 1864

Indian Wars
   Miami
   Seminoles
   Nez Perces
   Bannocks
   Pine Ridge
   California 1850
   California 1851
   California 1852

War With Spain
   Santiago

Philippine Insurrection
   Without inscription

World War I
   Vittorio-Veneto
   Venetia 1918

World War II
   Normandy
   Northern France
   Rhineland
   Ardennes-Alsace
   Central Europe

DECORATIONS

None.

4TH BATTALION, 2ND INFANTRY

LINEAGE

1808	Constituted 12 April as the 6th Infantry, Regular Army
1815	Consolidated May–October with 16th, 22d, 23d and 32d Infantry to form 2d Infantry
1816	Designated Company D, 2d Infantry
1861	Constituted 3 May as Company D, 1st Battalion, 16th Infantry, Regular Army; organized at Camp Slemmer, IL
1866	Reorganized and redesignated 21 September as Company D, 16th Infantry
1869	Consolidated with Company D, 2d Infantry, to form Company D, 2d Infantry
	Company lineage follows that of 2d Infantry from 1869 Consolidation to 1954 reactivation in Munich, Germany
1957	Inactivated 1 June at Fort Ord, CA; relieved from assignment to 5th Infantry Division, and redesignated Headquarters and Headquarters Company, 4th Battle Group, 2d Infantry
1963	Redesignated 27 March as Headquarters and Headquarters Company, 4th Battalion, 2d Infantry, Army Reserve; assigned to the 83d Infantry Division and activated 15 April in Newark, OH
1965	Inactivated 31 December

DECORATIONS

None.

CAMPAIGN PARTICIPATION

War of 1812
Canada
Chippewa
Lundy's Lane
Alabama 1814

Mexican War
Vera Cruz
Cerro Gordo
Contreras
Churubusco
Molino del Rey
Chapultepec

Civil War
Bull Run
Peninsula
Shiloh
Manassas
Antietam
Fredericksburg
Murfreesborough
Chancellorsville
Gettysburg
Chickamauga
Chattanooga
Wilderness
Atlanta
Spotsylvania
Cold Harbor
Petersburg

Missouri 1861
Mississippi 1862
Virginia 1862
Kentucky 1862
Virginia 1863
Tennessee 1863
Georgia 1864

Indian Wars
Miami
Seminoles
Nez Perces
Bannocks
Pine Ridge
California 1850
California 1851
California 1852

War With Spain
Santiago

Philippine Insurrection
Without Inscription

World War II
Normandy
Northern France
Rhineland
Ardennes-Alsace
Central Europe

3D INFANTRY
(The Old Guard)

COAT OF ARMS

Motto: *Noli Me Tangere*

Symbolism: Because of its direct descent from the First American Regiment, the 3d Infantry is accorded the singular honor of having the shield of the coat of arms of the United States as the basis for its arms. The thirteen stripes, in this instance, commemorate the unit's service in the campaigns of Resaca de la Palma, Monterey, Cerro Gordo, Churubusco, Chapultepec, Bull Run, Peninsula, Manassas, Fredericksburg, Chancellorsville, Gettysburg, Santiago, and Luzon (1899–1900); the alternating colors of silver and red symbolize a constancy of honor and courage. The chief, blue for valor and loyalty, represents the regiment's outstanding record in the Civil War; the white Maltese cross, the badge of Sykes' Division in which the 3d served, in triple form alludes to the regiment's numerical designation. The ines-

(continued on next page)

DISTINCTIVE INSIGNIA

On a wreath an infantry officer's cocked hat of 1784 with plume, all brass. (The insignia is the crest of the coat of arms of the regiment, without color.)

(continued from previous page)

cutcheon, in the national colors of Mexico, symbolizes the unit's distinguished service during the Mexican War.

The cocked hat of the crest commemorates the founding of the First American Regiment in 1784.

The Chapultepec baton is made from the wood of the flagpole which in 1847 stood in front of the cathedral in the Grand Plaza in Mexico City. The head and ferrule are of Mexican silver. The baton was presented to the regiment in 1848 and is still in the possession of the 3d Infantry. The bayonet represents the regiment's outstanding service during the Civil War and also its tradition to "pass in review" with bayonets fixed in commemoration of the gallant charge at Cerro Gordo. The officer's dress belt symbolizes the regiment's additional role as the honor and ceremonial unit in the nation's capital (currently performed by the 1st Battalion, 3d Infantry).

DISTINCTIVE TRIMMING

(Authorized for all personnel of the 3d Infantry in addition to the distinctive insignia.)

A black leather strap 1/2 inch wide with buff leather strap 1/4 inch wide "woven" in the middle—a simulation of the old buff and black knapsack strap. (Worn on left shoulder only of coat and overcoat at the junction of the sleeve and shoulder with two buff sections showing in front.)

When this unit was under the command of General Anthony Wayne (1792–96), the special markings on the uniform were buff piping and black hair plumes. From this combination the regimental colors became buff and black, and for many years the unit was nicknamed the "Buff Sticks." It is related that men of the 3d Infantry, proud of their distinctive colors, at one time displayed these colors by weaving a broad strip of rawhide (natural buff color) in the broad black shoulder strap of the knapsack carried at that time. This buff and black knapsack strap effect is perpetuated in the distinctive trimming.

LINEAGE

1784	Constituted 3 June, First American Regiment of companies from Connecticut, New York, New Jersey, and Pennsylvania
1789	Redesignated 29 September as Regiment of Infantry
1791	Redesignated 3 March as 1st Infantry
1792	Redesignated as Infantry of the 1st Sub-Legion
1796	Redesignated 31 October as 1st Infantry
1815	Consolidated May–October with 5th, 17th, 19th, and 28th Infantry to form 3d Infantry
1861	Constituted 3 May as 3d Battalion, 19th Infantry, Regular Army
1865	Organization began at Fort Wayne, MI, Newport Barracks, KY, and Fort Columbus, NY
1866	Reorganized and redesignated 23 November as 37th Infantry
1869	One-half of 37th Infantry consolidated with 3d Infantry to form 3d Infantry and the other half consolidated with 5th Infantry to form 5th Infantry
1923	Assigned to 7th Division
1927	Relieved 15 August from assignment to 7th Division, reassigned to 6th Division
1933	Relieved 1 October from assignment to 6th Division and reassigned to 7th Division
1939	Relieved 16 October from assignment to 7th Division and reassigned May 10 to 6th Division
1941	Relieved from assignment to 6th Division
1946	Inactivated 20 November in Germany
1948	Activated 6 April at Fort Myer, VA
1957	Reorganized 1 July as parent regiment under CARS

CAMPAIGN PARTICIPATION

War of 1812
Canada
Chippewa
Lundy's Lane

Mexican War
Palo Alto
Resaca de la Palma
Monterey
Vera Cruz
Cerro Gordo
Contreras
Churubusco
Chapultepec

Civil War
Bull Run
Peninsula
Manassas
Antietam
Fredericksburg
Chancellorsville
Gettysburg
Appomattox
Texas 1861
Florida 1861
Florida 1862
Virginia 1863

Indian Wars

Miami
Semioles
Comanches
New Mexico 1856
New Mexico 1857
New Mexico 1858
New Mexico 1860
Montana 1887

War With Spain

Santiago

Philippine Insurrection

Malolos
San Isidro
Luzon 1899
Luzon 1900
Jolo 1911

World War II

American Theater
without inscription
Northern France

Vietnam

Counteroffensive,
Phase II
Counteroffensive,
Phase III
Tet Counteroffensive
Counteroffensive,
Phase IV
Counteroffensive,
Phase V
Counteroffensive,
Phase VI
Tet 69 Counteroffensive
Summer–Fall 1969
Winter–Spring 1970
Sanctuary
Counteroffensive
Counteroffensive,
Phase VII
Consolidation I

DECORATIONS

Valorous Unit Award, Streamer embroidered **SAIGON-LONG BINH** (2d Battalion, 3d Infantry cited)

1ST BATTALION, 3D INFANTRY
(The Old Guard)

LINEAGE

1784	Constituted as company of First American Regiment
1789	Redesignated 29 September as a company of the Regiment of Infantry
1791	Redesignated 3 March as a company of 1st Infantry
1792	Redesignated as company of Infantry of the 1st Sub-Legion
1796	Redesignated 31 October as company of the 1st Infantry
1815	Consolidated May–October with companies from 17th, 19th, and 28th Infantry to form a company of the 3d Infantry
1816	Designated 22 May as Company A, 3d Infantry
1861	Constituted 3 May as Company C, 3d Battalion, 19th Infantry, Regular Army
1865	Organized 19 December Newport Barracks, KY
1866	Reorganized and redesignated 23 November as Company C, 37th Infantry
1869	Consolidated 9 September with Company A and Company H, 3d Infantry to form Company A and Company H, 3d Infantry

Company lineage follows that of 3d Infantry from 1869 consolidation to 1941 assignment to 6th Division

1941	Inactivated 1 June at Fort Leonard Wood, MO
1942	Activated 14 February in Newfoundland
1946	Inactivated 20 November in Germany
1948	Activated 6 April at Fort Myer, VA
1957	Reorganized and redesignated 1 July as Headquarters and Headquarters Company, 1st Battle Group, 3d Infantry
1963	Reorganized and redesignated 20 September as 1st Battalion, 3d Infantry

CAMPAIGN PARTICIPATION

War of 1812

Canada
Chippewa
Lundy's Lane

Mexican War

Palo Alto
Resaca de la Palma
Monterey
Vera Cruz
Cerro Gordo
Contreras
Churubusco
Chapultepec

Civil War

Bull Run
Peninsula
Manassas
Antietam
Fredericksburg
Chancellorsville

Gettysburg
Appomattox
Texas 1861
Florida 1861
Florida 1862
Virginia 1863

New Mexico 1858
New Mexico 1860
Montana 1887

World War II

American Theater
without inscription
Northern France

Indian Wars

Miami
Semioles
Comanches
New Mexico 1856
New Mexico 1857

War With Spain

Santiago

Philippine Insurrection

Malolos
San Isidro
Luzon 1899
Luzon 1900
Jolo 1911

DECORATIONS

None.

2D BATTALION, 3D INFANTRY
(The Old Guard)

LINEAGE

1784   Constituted 3 June as a company of the First American Regiment

1789   Redesignated 29 September as a company of the Regiment of Infantry

1791   Redesignated 3 March as a company of 1st Infantry

1792   Redesignated as a company of the Infantry of the 1st Sub-Legion

1796   Redesignated 31 October as a company of the 1st Infantry

1815   Consolidated May–October with companies of 5th, 17th, 19th, and 28th Infantry to form 3d Infantry

1861   Constituted 3 May as Company E, 3d Battalion, 19th Infantry, Regular Army

1866   Organized at Newport Barracks, KY; reorganized and redesignated 23 November as Company E, 37th Infantry

1869   Consolidated 19 November with Company B and Company E, 3d Infantry to form Company B and Company E, 3d Infantry

Company lineage follows that of 3d Infantry from 1869 consolidation to 1941 assignment to 6th Division

1941   Inactivated 1 June at Fort Leonard Wood, MO

1942   Activated 14 February in Newfoundland

1946   Inactivated 20 November in Germany

1948   Activated 6 April at Fort Myer, VA

1957   Reorganized and redesignated 1 July as Headquarters and Headquarters Company, 2d Battle Group, 3d Infantry; assigned to 7th Infantry Division

1963   Inactivated 1 July in Korea and relieved from assignment to 7th Infantry Division

1966   Redesignated 23 March 1966 as 2d Battalion, 3d Infantry; assigned to 199th Infantry Brigade and activated 1 June at Fort Benning, GA

1970   Inactivated 15 October at Fort Benning, GA

CAMPAIGN PARTICIPATION

War of 1812

Canada
Chippewa
Lundy's Lane

Mexican War

Palo Alto
Resaca de la Palma
Monterey
Vera Cruz
Cerro Gordo
Contreras
Churubusco

Chapultepec

Civil War

Bull Run
Peninsula
Manassas
Antietam
Fredericksburg
Chancellorsville
Gettysburg
Appomattox
Texas 1861
Florida 1861

Florida 1862
Virginia 1863

Indian Wars

Miami
Seminoles
Comanches
New Mexico 1856
New Mexico 1857
New Mexico 1858
New Mexico 1860
Montana 1887

War With Spain

Santiago

Philippine Insurrection

Malolos
San Isidro
Luzon 1899
Luzon 1900
Jolo 1911

World War II

American Theater
  without inscription
Northern France

Vietnam

Counteroffensive,
  Phase II

Counteroffensive,
  Phase III
Tet Counteroffensive
Counteroffensive,
  Phase IV
Counteroffensive,
  Phase V
Counteroffensive,
  Phase VI

Tet 69 Counteroffensive
Summer–Fall 1969
Winter–Spring 1970
Sanctuary
  Counteroffensive
Counteroffensive,
  Phase VII

DECORATIONS

Valorous Unit Award, Streamer embroidered **SAIGON–LONG BINH** (2d Battalion, 3d Infantry cited)

Vietnamese Cross of Gallantry with Palm, Streamer embroidered **VIETNAM 1968** (2d Battalion, 3d Infantry cited)

3D BATTALION, 3D INFANTRY
(The Old Guard)

LINEAGE

1784	Constituted as a company of the First American Regiment
1789	Redesignated 29 September as a company of the Regiment of Infantry
1791	Redesignated 3 March as a company of 1st Infantry
1792	Redesignated as company of the Infantry of the 1st Sub-Legion
1796	Redesignated 31 October as a company of the 1st Infantry
1815	Consolidated May–October with companies of the 5th, 17th, 19th, and 28th Infantry to form a company of the 3d Infantry
1816	Designated 22 May as Company C, 3d Infantry
	Company lineage follows that of 3d Infantry from 1816 to 1941 assignment to 6th Division
1941	Inactivated 1 June at Fort Leonard Wood, MO
1942	Activated 14 February in Newfoundland
1946	Inactivated 20 November in Germany
1948	Activated 6 April at Fort Myer, VA
1957	Inactivated 1 July at Fort Myer, VA; redesignated as Headquarters and Headquarters Company, 3d Battle Group, 3d Infantry
1959	Allotted to Army Reserve 20 April; Battle Group activated 18 May at Fort Snelling, MN, and assigned to 103d Infantry Division
1963	Reorganized and redesignated 15 February as 3d Battalion, 3d Infantry; relieved 15 March from assignment to 103d Infantry Division and assigned to 205th Infantry Brigade

CAMPAIGN PARTICIPATION

War of 1812

Canada
Chippewa
Lundy's Lane

Mexican War

Palo Alto
Resaca de la Palma
Monterey
Vera Cruz
Cerro Gordo
Contreras
Churubusco
Chapultepec

Civil War

Bull Run
Peninsula
Manassas
Antietam
Fredericksburg
Chancellorsville
Gettysburg
Appomattox
Texas 1861
Florida 1861
Florida 1862
Virginia 1863

Indian Wars

Miami
Seminoles
Comanches
New Mexico 1856
New Mexico 1857
New Mexico 1858
New Mexico 1860
Montana 1887

War With Spain

Santiago

Philippine Insurrection

Malolos
San Isidro
Luzon 1899
Luzon 1900
Jolo 1911

World War II

American Theater
without inscription
Northern France

DECORATIONS

None.

4TH BATTALION, 3D INFANTRY
(The Old Guard)

LINEAGE

1784   Constituted 3 June as a company of the First American Regiment

1789   Redesignated 29 September as a company of the Regiment of Infantry

1791   Redesignated 3 March as a company of 1st Infantry

1792   Redesignated as a company of the Infantry of the 1st Sub-Legion

1796   Redesignated 31 October as a company of the 1st Infantry

1815   Consolidated May–October with companies of the 5th, 17th, 19th, and 28th Infantry to form 3d Infantry

1816   Redesignated 22 May as Company D, 3d Infantry

1861   Constituted 3 May as Company A, 3d Battalion, 19th Infantry, Regular Army

1865   Organized 6 May at Fort Wayne, MI

1866   Reorganized and redesignated 23 November as Company A, 37th Infantry

1869   Consolidated 16 December with Company D and Company K; 3d Infantry to form Company D and Company K, 3d Infantry

Company lineage follows that of 3d Infantry from 1869 consolidation to 1941 assignment to 6th Division

1941   Inactivated 1 June at Fort Leonard Wood, MO

1942   Activated 15 February in Newfoundland

1946   Inactivated 20 November in Germany

1948   Activated 6 April at Fort Myer, VA

1957   Inactivated 1 July at Fort Myer, VA, and redesignated Headquarters and Headquarters Company, 4th Battle Group, 3d Infantry

1966   Resignated 15 April as Headquarters and Headquarters Company, 4th Battalion, 3d Infantry; battalion activated 1 July in Hawaii; assigned to the 11th Infantry Brigade

1969   Relieved 15 February from assignment to 11th Infantry Brigade and assigned to 23d Infantry Division

CAMPAIGN PARTICIPATION

War of 1812

Canada
Chippewa
Lundy's Lane

Mexican War

Palo Alto
Resaca de la Palma
Monterey
Vera Cruz
Cerro Gordo
Contreras
Churubusco
Chapultepec

Civil War

Bull Run
Peninsula

Manassas
Antietam
Fredericksburg
Chancellorsville
Gettysburg
Appomattox
Texas 1861
Florida 1861
Florida 1862
Virginia 1863

Indian Wars

Miami
Seminoles
Comanches
New Mexico 1856
New Mexico 1857
New Mexico 1858

New Mexico 1860
Kansas 1868
Montana 1887

War With Spain

Santiago

World War II

American Theater
without inscription
Northern France

Vietnam

Counteroffensive,
Phase III
Tet Counteroffensive
Counteroffensive,
Phase IV
Counteroffensive,
Phase V
Counteroffensive,
Phase VI

Tet 69 Counteroffensive
Summer–Fall 1969
Winter–Spring 1970
Sanctuary
Counteroffensive

Counteroffensive,
Phase VII
Consolidation I

DECORATIONS

Vietnamese Cross of Gallantry with Palm, Streamer embroidered **VIETNAM 1968–1969** (4th Battalion, 3d Infantry cited)

5TH BATTALION, 3D INFANTRY
(The Old Guard)

LINEAGE

1784	Constituted 3 June as a company of the First American Regiment
1785	Organized in New York or Connecticut
1789	Redesignated 29 September as a company of the Regiment of Infantry
1791	Redesignated 3 March as a company of 1st Infantry
1792	Redesignated as a company of the Infantry of the 1st Sub-Legion
1796	Redesignated 31 October as a company of the 1st Infantry
1815	Consolidated May–October with companies of 5th, 17th, 19th, and 28th Infantry to form 3d Infantry
1816	Designated 22 May as Company E, 3d Infantry
1861	Constituted 3 May as Company E, 3d Battalion, 19th Infantry, Regular Army
1866	Organized 7 February at Newport Barracks, KY; reorganized and redesignated 23 November at Company E, 37th Infantry
1869	Consolidated 19 November with Company B and Company E, 3d Infantry; consolidated unit designated Company B and Company E, 3rd Infantry

Company lineage follows that of 3d Infantry from 1869 consolidation to 1941 assignment to 6th Division

1942	*Inactivated 1 September at Fort Snelling, MN*
1943	*Activated 22 October at Camp Butner, NC*
1946	*Inactivated 20 November in Germany*
1948	*Activated 6 April at Fort Lesley J. McNair, Washington, DC*
1957	*Inactivated 1 July and redesignated as Headquarters and Headquarters Company, 5th Battle Group, 3d Infantry*
1967	*Redesignated 24 November as Headquarters and Headquarters Company, 5th Battalion, 3d Infantry; assigned to the 6th Infantry Division, Fort Campbell, KY*
1968	*Relieved 24 July from assignment to the 6th Infantry Division*
1969	*Inactivated 21 July 1969*

CAMPAIGN PARTICIPATION

War of 1812

Canada
Chippewa
Lundy's Lane

Mexican War

Palo Alto

Resaca de la Palma
Monterey
Vera Cruz
Cerro Gordo
Contreras
Churubusco
Chapultepec

Civil War	Indian Wars	Philippine Insurrection	World War II
Bull Run	Miami	Malolos	American Theater
Peninsula	Seminoles	San Isidro	without inscription
Manassas	Comanches	Luzon 1899	Northern France
Antietam	New Mexico 1856	Luzon 1900	
Fredericksburg	New Mexico 1857	Jolo 1911	
Chancellorsville	New Mexico 1858		
Gettysburg	New Mexico 1860		
Appomattox	Montana 1887		
Texas 1861			
Florida 1861	War With Spain		
Florida 1862	Santiago		
Virginia 1863			

DECORATIONS

None.

6TH BATTALION, 3D INFANTRY
(The Old Guard)

LINEAGE

1784 Constituted 3 June as a company of the First American Regiment

1789 Redesignated 29 September as a company of the Regiment of Infantry

1791 Redesignated 3 March as a company of 1st Infantry

1792 Redesignated as a company of the Infantry of the 1st Sub-Legion

1796 Redesignated 31 October as a company of the 1st Infantry

1815 Consolidated May–October with companies from the 5th, 17th, 19th, and 28th Infantry to form a company of the 3d Infantry

1816 Designated 22 May as Company F, 3d Infantry

1861 Constituted 3 May as Company F, 3d Battalion, 19th Infantry, Regular Army

1866 Organized at Newport Barracks, KY; reorganized and designated 23 November as Company F, 37th Infantry

1869 Conslidated 13 October with Company F and Company H, 3d Infantry, to form Company F and Company H, 3d Infantry

Company lineage follows that of 3d Infantry from 1869 consolidation of 1941 assignment to 6th Division

1942 Inactivated 1 September at Fort Snelling, MN

1943 Activated 22 October at Camp Butner, NC

1946 Inactivated 20 November in Germany

1948 Activated 6 April at Fort Lesley J. McNair, Washington, DC

1957 Inactivated 1 July and redesignated as Headquarters and Headquarters Company, 6th Battle Group, 3d Infantry

1967 Redesignated 24 November as Headquarters and Headquarters Company, 6th Battalion, 3d Infantry; assigned to the 6th Division and activated at Fort Campbell, KY

1968 Relieved 24 July from assignment to the 6th Infantry Division

1969 Inactivated 1 February at Fort Campbell, KY

CAMPAIGN PARTICIPATION

War of 1812
Canada
Chippewa
Lundy's Lane

Mexican War
Palo Alto
Resaca de la Palma
Monterey
Vera Cruz
Cerro Gordo
Contreras

Churubusco
Chapultepec

Civil War
Bull Run
Peninsula
Manassas
Antietam
Fredericksburg
Chancellorsville
Gettysburg
Appomattox

Texas 1861
Florida 1861
Florida 1862
Virginia 1863

New Mexico 1860
Montana 1887

World War II

American Theater
without inscription
Northern France

Indian Wars

Miami
Seminoles
Comanches
New Mexico 1856
New Mexico 1857
New Mexico 1858

War With Spain

Santiago

Philippine Insurrection

Malolos
San Isidro
Luzon 1899
Luzon 1900
Jolo 1911

DECORATIONS

None.

7TH BATTALION, 3D INFANTRY
(The Old Guard)

LINEAGE

1784	Constituted 3 June as a company of the First American Regiment
1789	Redesignated 29 September as a company of the Regiment of Infantry
1791	Redesignated 3 March as a company of the 1st Infantry
1792	Redesignated as a company of the Infantry of the 1st Sub-Legion
1796	Redesignated 31 October as a company of the 1st Infantry
1815	Consolidated May-October with companies of 5th, 17th, 19th and 28th Infantry to form 3d Infantry
1816	Designated 22 May as Company G, 3d Infantry
1861	Constituted 3 May as Company I, 3d Battalion, 19th Infantry Regular Army
1866	Organized 25 September at Fort Columbus, NY; reorganized and redesignated 23 November as Company I, 37th Infantry
1869	Consolidated 18 August with Company G and Company I, 3d Infantry; consolidated unit designated Company G, and Company I, 3d Infantry

Company lineage follows that of 3d Infantry from 1869 consolidation to 1941 assignment to 6th Division

1942	Inactivated 1 September at Fort Snelling, MN
1943	Activated 22 October at Camp Butner, NC
1946	Inactivated 20 November in Germany
1948	Activated 6 April at Fort Lesley J. McNair, Washington, DC
1957	Inactivated 1 July; redesignated as Headquarters and Headquarters Company, 7th Battle Group, 3d Infantry
1967	Redesignated 24 November as Headquarters and Headquarters Company, 7th Battalion, 3d Infantry; assigned to the 6th Infantry Division, Fort Campbell, KY
1968	Inactivated 25 July

CAMPAIGN PARTICIPATION

War of 1812

Canada
Chippewa
Lundy's Lane

Mexican War

Palo Alto
Resaca de la Palma
Monterey
Vera Cruz
Cerro Gordo
Contreras
Churubusco
Chapultepec

Civil War

Bull Run
Peninsula
Manassas
Antietam
Fredericksburg
Chancellorsville
Gettysburg
Appomattox
Texas 1861
Florida 1861
Florida 1862
Virginia 1863

Indian Wars

Miami
Seminoles
Comanches
New Mexico 1856
New Mexico 1857
New Mexico 1858
New Mexico 1860
Montana 1887

War With Spain

Santiago

Philippine Insurrection

Malolos
San Isidro
Luzon 1899
Luzon 1900
Jolo 1911

World War II

American Theater
  without inscription
Northern France

DECORATIONS

None.

4TH INFANTRY
(Warriors)

COAT OF ARMS

Motto: *Noli Me Tangere* (Don't Tread on Me).

Symbolism: The green shield recalls the Mexican War. The national flag bore fifteen stars during the War of 1812. The white Maltese cross represents the service of the regiment in the Civil War; the arrow, the Indian Wars; the castle, the War with Spain; the bolo, the Philippine Insurrection; and the fleur-de-lis, World War I.

Previous to the approval of the coat of arms, the crest and motto were in use by the regiment for many years.

DISTINCTIVE INSIGNIA

The distinctive insignia is a strip of scarlet cloth or ribbon 1½ inches in width with a green stripe ½ inch in width in the center thereof; to be made into a band to fit the shoulder loop of coat.

Subsequent to the Mexican War and until the blue uniform was abolished, the Band of the 4th Infantry was authorized to wear a scarlet piping on the chevrons and trousers stripes in commemoration of distinguished service in the battle of Monterey in serving a captured battery against the enemy. The scarlet is to perpetuate this distinguished service of an element of the regiment. Green is the predominating color of the regimental coat of arms; it also symbolizes the service of the 4th Infantry in the Mexican War.

LINEAGE

1812	Constituted 11 January as the 14th Infantry, Regular Army and organized in Virginia, Maryland, Delaware, and Pennsylvania
1815	Consolidated May–October with the 18th, 20th, 36th, and 38th Infantry to form the 4th Infantry
1861	A new company constituted 3 May as the 3d Battalion, 12th Infantry, Regular Army
1865	Organized 23 December at Fort Hamilton, NY
1866	Reorganized and redesignated 7 December as 30th Infantry
1869	Consolidated in March with 4th Infantry; consolidated unit designated 4th Infantry
1917	Assigned 1 October to the 3d Division
1940	Relieved 15 May from assignment to the 3d Division
1945	Assigned 1 November to the 25th Infantry Division
1947	Inactivated 31 January at Osaka, Japan, and relieved 1 February from assignment to 25th Infantry Division
1948	Activated 1 October at Fort Lewis, WA
1954	Assigned 10 October to 71st Infantry Division
1956	Relieved 15 September from assignment to 71st Infantry Division
1958	Reorganized 15 February as a parent regiment under CARS

CAMPAIGN PARTICIPATION

War of 1812
Canada
Bladensburg
McHenry

Mexican War
Palo Alto
Resaca de la Palma
Monterey
Vera Cruz
Cerro Gordo
Churubusco
Molino del Rey
Chapultepec
Puebla 1847
Tlaxcala 1847

Civil War
Peninsula
Manassas
Antietam
Fredericksburg
Chancellorsville
Gettysburg
Wilderness
Spotsylvania
Cold Harbor
Petersburg
Appomattox
Virginia 1863

Indian Wars
Tippecanoe
Seminoles
Black Hawk
Little Big Horn
Utes
Washington 1855
Oregon 1855
Washington 1856
Oregon 1856

War With Spain
Santiago

Philippine Insurrection
Manila
Malolos
Cavite
Luzon 1899

World War I
Aisne
Champagne-Marne
Aisne-Marne
St. Mihiel
Meuse-Argonne
Champagne 1918

World War II
Aleutian Islands

DECORATIONS

French Croix de Guerre with Gilt Star, World War I, Streamer embroidered **CHAMPAGNE-MARNE AISNE-MARNE** (4th Infantry cited)

1st Battalion, 4th Infantry
(Warriors)

LINEAGE

1812	Constituted 11 January as a company of the 14th Infantry, Regular Army
1815	Consolidated May–October with a company each from 18th, 20th, 36th, and 38th Infantry to form a company of the 4th Infantry

1816	Designated 21 August as Company A, 4th Infantry
1861	A new company constituted 3 May as Company A, 3d Battalion, 12th Infantry, Regular Army
1865	Organized 23 December at Fort Hamilton, NY
1866	Reorganized and redesignated 7 December as Company A, 30th Infantry
1869	Consolidated 31 March with Company A, 4th Infantry, to form Company A, 4th Infantry

Company lineage follows that of 4th Infantry from 1869 consolidation to 1956 relief from assignment to 71st Brigade

1958	Reorganized and redesignated as Headquarters and Headquarters Company, 1st Battle Group, 4th Infantry, and assigned to 2d Infantry Brigade
1962	Inactivated 2 April at Fort Devens, MA
1963	Redesignated 18 April as 1st Battalion, 4th Infantry; relieved from assignment to 2d Infantry Brigade and assigned to 3d Infantry Division; activated 5 June in Germany

CAMPAIGN PARTICIPATION

War of 1812

Canada
Bladensburg
McHenry

Mexican War

Palo Alto
Resaca de la Palma
Monterey

Vera Cruz
Cerro Gordo
Churubusco
Molino del Rey
Chapultepec
Puebla 1847
Tlaxcala 1847

Civil War

Peninsula
Manassas
Antietam
Fredericksburg
Chancellorsville
Gettysburg
Wilderness
Spotsylvania
Cold Harbor
Petersburg
Appomattox
Virginia 1863

Indian Wars

Tippecanoe
Seminoles
Black Hawk
Little Big Horn

Utes
Washington 1855
Oregon 1855
Washington 1856
Oregon 1856

War With Spain

Santiago

Philippine Insurrection

Manila
Malolos
Cavite
Luzon 1899

World War I

Aisne
Champagne-Marne
Aisne-Marne
St. Mihiel
Meuse-Argonne
Champagne 1918

World War II

Aleutian Islands

DECORATIONS

Presidential Unit Citation (Army), Streamer embroidered **CHICAGOF VALLEY** (Company A, 4th Infantry cited)

French Croix de Guerre with Gilt Star, World War I, Streamer embroidered **CHAMPAGNE-MARNE AISNE-MARNE** (4th Infantry cited)

2D BATTALION, 4TH INFANTRY
(Warriors)

LINEAGE

1812	Constituted 11 January as a company of the 14th Infantry, Regular Army
1815	Consolidated May–October with a company each of the 18th, 20th, 36th, and 38th Infantry to form a company of the 4th Infantry
1816	Designated 21 August as Company B, 4th Infantry
1861	A new company constituted 3 May as Company B, 3d Battalion, 12th Infantry, Regular Army
1865	Organized 23 December at Fort Hamilton, NY
1866	Reorganized and redesignated 7 December as Company B, 30th Infantry
1869	Consolidated 31 March with Company B, 4th Infantry to form Company B, 4th Infantry

Company lineage follows that of 4th Infantry from 1869 consolidation to 1956 relief from assignment to 71st Infantry Division

1958   Reorganized and redesignated 15 February as Headquarters and Headquarters Company, 2d Battle Group, 4th Infantry, and assigned to 3d Infantry Division

1963   Relieved 18 April from assignment to the 3d Infantry Division and inactivated 3 June in Germany

1969   Redesignated 21 July as the 2d Battalion, 4th Infantry; activated at Fort Campbell, KY

CAMPAIGN PARTICIPATION

War of 1812
Canada
Bladensburg
McHenry

Molino del Rey
Chapultepec
Puebla 1847
Tlaxcala 1847

Mexican War
Palo Alto
Resaca de la Palma
Monterey
Vera Cruz
Cerro Gordo
Churubusco

Civil War
Peninsula
Manassas
Antietam
Fredericksburg
Chancellorsville
Gettysburg

Wilderness
Spotsylvania
Cold Harbor
Petersburg
Appomattox
Virginia 1863

Indian Wars
Tippecanoe
Seminoles
Black Hawk
Little Big Horn
Utes
Washington 1855
Oregon 1855
Washington 1856
Oregon 1856
California 1861

War With Spain
Santiago

Philippine Insurrection
Manila
Malolos
Cavite
Luzon 1899

World War I
Aisne
Champagne-Marne
Aisne-Marne
St. Mihiel
Meuse-Argonne
Champagne 1918

World War II
Aleutian Islands

DECORATIONS

French Croix de Guerre with Gilt Star, World War I, Streamer embroidered **CHAMPAGNE-MARNE AISNE-MARNE** (4th Infantry cited)

3D BATTALION, 4TH INFANTRY
(Warriors)

LINEAGE

1812   Constituted 11 January 1812 as a company of the 14th Infantry, Regular Army

1815   Consolidated May–October with a company each from the 18th, 20th, 36th, and 38th Infantry to form a company of the 4th Infantry

1816   Designated 21 August as Company C, 4th Infantry

1861   A new company constituted 3 May as Company C, 3d Battalion, 12th Infantry, Regular Army

1865   Organized 23 December at Fort Hamilton, NY

1866   Reorganized and redesignated 7 December as Company C, 30th Infantry

1869   Consolidated 31 March with Company C, 4th Infantry, to form Company C, 4th Infantry

Company lineage follows that of 4th Infantry from 1869 consolidation to 1956 relief from assignment to 71st Infantry Division

1917   A new company constituted 23 July as Headquarters and Headquarters Company, 3d Battalion, 405th Infantry, an element of the 102d Division and demobilized 30 November

This Company lineage differs from that of 4th Infantry from its constitution to 1 June 1959 consolidation as follows:

1921   Reconstituted 24 June as an element of the 102d Division Organized Reserves, organized at Little Rock, AR

1942	Ordered into active military service 15 September and reorganized at Camp Maxey, TX
1946	Inactivated 1 June in Germany and reactivated 12 November in the Organized Reserves at Mankato, MN
1947	Inactivated 3 January and reactivated 25 April at St. Louis, MO
1948	Inactivated 12 March
1950	Activated 18 December at Flora, IL
1951	Location changed 15 March to Fairfield, IL
1959	Consolidated 1 June with Headquarters and Headquarters Company, 3d Battle Group, 4th Infantry to form Headquarters and Headquarters Company, 3d Battle Group, 4th Infantry
1963	Reorganized and redesignated 1 April as 3d Battalion, 4th Infantry
1965	Inactivated 31 December at Fairfield, IL

CAMPAIGN PARTICIPATION

War of 1812

Canada
Bladensburg
McHenry

Mexican War

Palo Alto
Resaca de la Palma
Monterey

Vera Cruz
Cerro Gordo
Churubusco
Molino del Rey
Chapultepec
Puebla 1847
Tlaxcala 1847

Civil War

Peninsula
Manassas
Antietam
Fredericksburg
Chancellorsville
Gettysburg
Wilderness
Spotsylvania
Cold Harbor
Petersburg
Appomattox
Virginia 1863

Indian Wars

Tippecanoe
Seminoles
Black Hawk
Little Big Horn
Utes
Washington 1855
Oregon 1855
Washington 1856
Oregon 1856

War With Spain

Santiago

Philippine Insurrection

Manila
Malolos
Cavite
Luzon 1899

World War I

Aisne
Champagne-Marne
Aisne-Marne
St. Mihiel
Meuse-Argonne
Champagne 1918

World War II

Aleutian Islands
Rhineland
Central Europe

DECORATIONS

Presidential Unit Citation (Army), Streamer embroidered **ROER RIVER** (405th Infantry cited)

French Croix de Guerre with Gilt Star, World War I, Streamer embroidered **CHAMPAGNE-MARNE AISNE-MARNE** (4th Infantry cited)

5TH INFANTRY

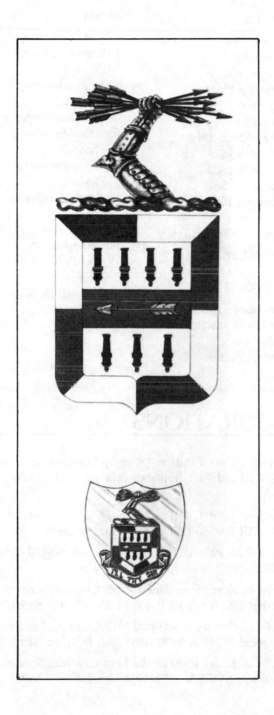

COAT OF ARMS

Motto: I'll try, Sir.

Symbolism: The shield is white, the color of infantry facings when the regiment was organized. The red fess with arrow commemorates the battle of Tippecanoe; the battle of Lundy's Lane is shown by the seven cannon captured there; and the border of green, white, and red is for the Mexican War.

The crest is a modification of the crest of General Nelson A. Miles, who was for many years Colonel of the 5th Infantry and who led it in several notable Indian engagements. His crest is an arm in armor grasping an anchor; arrows, to symbolize Indian campaigns, are substituted for the anchor in the regimental crest.

DISTINCTIVE INSIGNIA

The distinctive insignia is the shield, crest, and motto of the coat of arms, all superimposed on a silver shield with two concave arcs at top.

LINEAGE

1808	Constituted 12 April as the 4th Infantry, Regular Army; organized in New England
1815	Consolidated May–June with the 9th, 13th, 21st, 40th, and 46th Infantry to form the 5th Infantry
1861	A new company constituted 3 May as the 3d Battalion, 19th Infantry, Regular Army
1865	Organized at Fort Wayne, MI; Newport Barracks, KY; and Fort Columbus, NY
1866	Reorganized and redesignated 23 November as the 37th Infantry
1869	One half of the 37th Infantry consolidated in June with 5th Infantry to form the 5th Infantry; the remaining half consolidated with the 3d Infantry to form the 3d Infantry
1918	Assigned 27 July to the 17th Division
1919	Relieved 10 February from assignment to the 17th Division
1923	Assigned 24 March to the 9th Division
1927	Relieved 15 August from assignment to the 9th Division and assigned to the 5th Division
1933	Relieved 1 October from assignment to the 5th Division and assigned to the 9th Division
1940	Relieved 15 July from assignment to the 9th Division
1943	Assigned 10 July to the 71st Light Division
1946	Relieved 1 May from assignment to the 71st Infantry Division and inactivated 15 November at Salzburg, Austria
1949	Activated 1 January in Korea
1954	Assigned 10 October to the 71st Infantry Division
1956	Relieved 25 August from assignment to the 71st Infantry Division and assigned 1 September to the 8th Infantry Division
1957	Relieved 1 August from assignment to the 8th Infantry Division and reorganized as a parent regiment under CARS

CAMPAIGN PARTICIPATION

War of 1812

Canada
Chippewa
Lundy's Lane

Mexican War

Palo Alto
Resaca de la Palma
Monterey
Churubusco
Molino del Rey
Chapultepec
Vera Cruz 1847

Civil War

New Mexico 1862

Indian Wars

Tippecanoe
Seminoles
Comanches
Little Big Horn
Nez Perces
Bannocks
New Mexico 1860
Montana 1879
Montana 1880
Montana 1881
Montana 1887

Philippine Insurrection

Without inscription

World War II

American Theater
without inscription
Rhineland
Central Europe

Korean War

UN defensive
UN offensive
CCF intervention
First UN counteroffensive
CCF spring offensive
UN summer-fall offensive
Second Korean winter
Korea, summer-fall 1952
Third Korean winter
Korea, summer 1953

Vietnam

Counteroffensive
Counteroffensive,
  Phase II
Counteroffensive,
  Phase III
Tet Counteroffensive
Counteroffensive,
  Phase IV
Counteroffensive,
  Phase V
Counteroffensive,
  Phase VI
Tet 69 Counteroffensive
Summer-Fall 1969
Winter-Spring 1970
Sanctuary
  Counteroffensive
Counteroffensive,
  Phase VII

DECORATIONS

Presidential Unit Citation (Army), Streamer embroidered **CHIN JU** (3d Battalion, 5th Infantry and attached units cited)

Presidential Unit Citation (Army), Streamer embroidered **BEN CUI** (1st Battalion, 5th Infantry cited)

Valorous Unit Award, Streamer embroidered **CU CHI DISTRICT** (1st Battalion, 5th Infantry cited)

Republic of Korea Presidential Unit Citation, Streamer embroidered **KOREA 1950–1952** (5th Infantry cited)

Republic of Korea Presidential Unit Citation, Streamer embroidered **KOREA 1950–1953** (5th Infantry cited)

Republic of Korea Presidential Unit Citation, Streamer embroidered **KOREA 1952–1954** (5th Infantry cited)

1st Battalion, 5th Infantry

LINEAGE

1808   Constituted 12 April as a company of the 4th Infantry, Regular Army

1815   Consolidated May–October with a company each of the 9th, 13th, 21st, 40th, and 46th Infantry to form a company of the 5th Infantry

1816   Designated 22 May as Company A, 5th Infantry

1861   A new company constituted 3 May as Company K, 3d Battalion, 19th Infantry, Regular Army

1866   Organized 25 September at Fort Columbus, NY; reorganized and redesignated 23 November as Company K, 37th Infantry

1869   Consolidated in June with Company A and Company B, 5th Infantry to form Company A and Company B, 5th Infantry

Company lineage follows that of 5th Infantry from 1869 consolidation to 1956 assignment to the 8th Infantry Division

1957   Reorganized and redesignated 1 August as Headquarters and Headquarters Company, 1st Battle Group, 5th Infantry; assigned to the 8th Infantry Division

1959   Relieved from assignment to the 8th Infantry Division and assigned to the 1st Infantry Division

1963   Relieved 1 February from assignment to the 1st Infantry Division; assigned to the 25th Infantry Division; reorganized and redesignated 12 August as 1st Battalion, 5th Infantry

CAMPAIGN PARTICIPATION

War of 1812
Canada
Chippewa
Lundy's Lane

Mexican War
Palo Alto
Resaca de la Palma
Monterey
Churubusco
Molino del Rey
Chapultepec
Vera Cruz 1847

Civil War
New Mexico 1862

Indian Wars
Tippecanoe
Seminoles
Comanches
Little Big Horn
Nez Perces
Bannocks
New Mexico 1860
Montana 1879
Montana 1880
Montana 1881
Montana 1887

Philippine Insurrection
Without inscription

World War II
American Theater
  without inscription
Rhineland
Central Europe

Korean War
UN defensive
UN offensive
CCF intervention
First UN counteroffensive
CCF spring offensive
UN summer-fall offensive
Second Korean winter
Korea, summer-fall 1952
Third Korean winter
Korea, summer 1953

Vietnam
Counteroffensive
Counteroffensive,
  Phase II
Counteroffensive,
  Phase III
Tet Counteroffensive
Counteroffensive,
  Phase IV
Counteroffensive,
  Phase V
Counteroffensive,
  Phase VI
Tet 69 Counteroffensive
Summer-Fall 1969
Winter-Spring 1970
Sanctuary
  Counteroffensive
Counteroffensive,
  Phase VII

DECORATIONS

Presidential Unit Citation (Army), Streamer embroidered SONGNAEDONG (Company A, 5th Infantry cited)

Presidential Unit Citation (Army), Streamer embroidered CHIN JU

Presidential Unit Citation (Army), Streamer embroidered BEN CUI (1st Battalion, 5th Infantry cited)

Valorous Unit Award, Streamer embroidered CU CHI DISTRICT (1st Battalion, 5th Infantry cited)

Republic of Korea Presidential Unit Citation, Streamer embroidered KOREA 1950–1952 (5th Infantry cited)

Republic of Korea Presidential Unit Citation, Streamer embroidered KOREA 1950–1953 (5th Infantry cited)

Republic of Korea Presidential Unit Citation, Streamer embroidered KOREA 1952–1954 (5th Infantry cited)

Vietnamese Cross of Gallantry with Palm, Streamer embroidered VIETNAM 1966–1968 (1st Battalion, 5th Infantry cited)

2D BATTALION, 5TH INFANTRY

LINEAGE

1808 Constituted 12 April as a company of the 4th Infantry, Regular Army

1815 Consolidated May–October with a company each from the 9th, 13th, 21st, 40th, and 46th Infantry to form a company of the 5th Infantry

1816 Designated 22 May as Company B, 5th Infantry

1861 A new company constituted 3 May as Company K, 3d Battalion, 19th Infantry, Regular Army

1866 Organized 25 September at Fort Columbus, NY; reorganized and redesignated 23 November as Company K, 37th Infantry

1869 Consolidated in June with Company A and Company B, 5th Infantry, to form Company A and Company B, 5th Infantry

Company lineage follows that of 5th Infantry from 1869 consolidation to 1956 assignment to the 8th Infantry Division

1957 Inactivated 1 August in Germany and relieved from assignment to 8th Infantry Division; redesignated 19 November as Headquarters and Headquarters Company, 2d Battle Group, 5th Infantry; activated 1 December and assigned to the 9th Infantry Division

1962 Inactivated 31 January at Fort Carson, CO, and relieved from assignment to the 9th Infantry Division

1969 Redesignated 6 December as the 2d Battalion, 5th Infantry, and activated in Hawaii as an element of the 25th Infantry Division

CAMPAIGN PARTICIPATION

War of 1812
Canada
Chippewa
Lundy's Lane

Mexican War
Palo Alto
Resaca de la Palma
Monterey
Churubusco
Molino del Rey
Chapultepec
Vera Cruz 1847

Civil War
New Mexico 1862

Indian Wars
Tippecanoe
Seminoles
Comanches
Little Big Horn
Nez Perces
Bannocks
New Mexico 1860

Montana 1879
Montana 1880
Montana 1881
Montana 1887

Philippine Insurrection
Without inscription

World War II
American Theater
    without inscription
Rhineland
Central Europe

Korean War
UN defensive
UN offensive
CCF intervention
First UN counteroffensive
CCF spring offensive
UN summer-fall offensive
Second Korean winter
Korea, summer-fall 1952
Third Korean winter
Korea, summer 1953

DECORATIONS

Presidential Unit Citation (Army), Streamer embroidered **CHIN JU**

Republic of Korea Presidential Unit Citation, Streamer embroidered **KOREA 1950–1952** (5th Infantry cited)

Republic of Korea Presidential Unit Citation, Streamer embroidered **KOREA 1950–1953** (5th Infantry cited)

Republic of Korea Presidential Unit Citation, Streamer embroidered **KOREA 1952–1954** (5th Infantry cited)

3D BATTALION, 5TH INFANTRY

LINEAGE

1808 Constituted 12 April as a company of the 4th Infantry, Regular Army

1815 Consolidated May–October with a company each from the 9th, 13th, 21st, 40th, and 46th Infantry to form a company of the 5th Infantry

1816	Designated 22 May as Company C, 5th Infantry
1861	A new company constituted 3 May as Company G, 3d Battalion, 19th Infantry, Regular Army
1866	Organized April–May at Newport Barracks, KY; reorganized and redesignated 23 November as Company G, 37th Infantry
1869	Consolidated in June with Company C and Company D, 5th Infantry, to form Company C and Company D, 5th Infantry

Company lineage follows that of 5th Infantry from 1869 consolidation to 1956 assignment to 8th Infantry Division

1957	Inactivated 1 August in Germany and relieved from assignment to 8th Infantry Division; redesignated as Headquarters and Headquarters Company, 3d Battle Group, 5th Infantry
1959	Withdrawn from Regular Army and allotted to Army Reserve; assigned to the 94th Infantry Division; Battle Group activated 1 May with Headquarters at Boston, MA
1963	Inactivated 1 March and relieved of assignment to 94th Infantry Division
1968	Redesignated 26 June as 3d Battalion, 5th Infantry; allotted to Regular Army and assigned to 193d Infantry Brigade; activated at Fort Kobbe, Canal Zone

CAMPAIGN PARTICIPATION

War of 1812
Canada
Chippewa
Lundy's Lane

Mexican War
Palo Alto
Resaca de la Palma
Monterey
Churubusco
Molino del Rey
Chapultepec
Vera Cruz 1847

Civil War
New Mexico 1862

Indian Wars
Tippecanoe
Seminoles
Comanches
Little Big Horn
Nez Perces
Bannocks
New Mexico 1860
Montana 1879
Montana 1880
Montana 1881
Montana 1887

Philippine Insurrection
Luzon 1900
Luzon 1901

World War II
American Theater without inscription
Rhineland
Central Europe

Korean War
UN defensive
UN offensive
CCF intervention
First UN counteroffensive
CCF spring offensive
UN summer-fall offensive
Second Korean winter
Korea, summer-fall 1952
Third Korean winter
Korea, summer 1953

DECORATIONS

Presidential Unit Citation (Army), Streamer embroidered **CHIN JU**

Republic of Korea Presidential Unit Citation, Streamer embroidered **KOREA 1950–1952** (5th Infantry cited)

Republic of Korea Presidential Unit Citation, Streamer embroidered **KOREA 1950–1953** (5th Infantry cited)

Republic of Korea Presidential Unit Citation, Streamer embroidered **KOREA 1952–1954** (5th Infantry cited)

6TH INFANTRY
(The Regulars)

COAT OF ARMS

Motto: Unity is Strength.

Symbolism: The alligator symbolizes service in several Indian campaigns, notably in the Second Seminole War, when the regiment bore the brunt of the fighting at the battle of Lake Okeechobee on 25 December 1837. Service in the Mexican War with General Scott, especially at Churubusco and at the assault on the citadel of Chapultepec, is commemorated with a scaling ladder (in green, the Mexican color), by means of which the walls of Chapultepec were stormed. The chief, symbolic of the crossing of the Meuse near Dun during World War I, is the arms of the ancient Lords of Dun—a silver cross on a red field. The wavy partition line represents the river. The shield is white, the color of infantry facings when the regiment was organized.

The crest represents service in the Canadian campaigns of 1813 and 1814 during the War of 1812.

DISTINCTIVE INSIGNIA

The distinctive insignia is the shield and motto of the coat of arms.

LINEAGE

1812	Constituted 11 January as the 11th Infantry, Regular Army; organized in Vermont, New Hampshire, and Connecticut
1815	Consolidated May–October with the 25th, 27th, 29th, and 37th Infantry to form the 6th Infantry
1869	Consolidated 1 May with the 42d Infantry, Veteran Reserve Corps to form the 6th Infantry
1917	Assigned 18 November to the 5th Division
1921	Relieved in August from assignment to the 5th Division
1923	Assigned 24 March to the 6th Division
1939	Relieved 16 October from assignment to the 6th Division
1940	Reorganized 15 July as the 6th Infantry (Armored) and assigned to the 1st Armored Division
1942	Redesignated 1 January as the 6th Armored Infantry
1944	Regiment broken up 20 July and redesignated as elements of the 1st Armored Division
1950	Redesignated 10 October as 6th Infantry and activated at Grafenwohr, Germany
1958	Reorganized 1 June as a parent regiment under CARS

CAMPAIGN PARTICIPATION

War of 1812

Canada
Chippewa
Lundy's Lane

Mexican War

Vera Cruz
Cerro Gordo
Churubusco
Molino del Rey
Chapultepec

Civil War

Peninsula
Manassas
Antietam
Fredericksburg
Chancellorsville
Gettysburg
Virginia 1862

Indian Wars

Seminoles
Black Hawk
Little Big Horn
Cheyennes
Utes
South Dakota 1823
Kansas 1829
Nebraska 1855
Kansas 1857
North Dakota 1872
North Dakota 1873
Montana 1879

War With Spain

Santiago

Philippine Insurrection

Jolo
Negros 1899
Panay 1900

Mexican Expedition

Mexico 1916–1917

World War I

St. Mihiel
Meuse-Argonne
Alsace 1918
Lorraine 1918

World War II

Algeria-French Morocco (with arrowhead)
Tunisia
Naples-Foggia
Anzio
Rome-Arno
North Apennines
Po Valley

Vietnam

Counteroffensive, Phase III
Tet Counteroffensive
Counteroffensive, Phase IV
Counteroffensive, Phase V
Counteroffensive, Phase VI
Tet 69 Counteroffensive
Summer-Fall 1969
Winter-Spring 1970
Sanctuary Counteroffensive
Counteroffensive, Phase VII
Consolidation I

DECORATIONS

Presidential Unit Citation (Army), Streamer embroidered **MT. PORCHIA** (6th Armored Infantry cited)

Presidential Unit Citation (Army), Streamer embroidered **ORAN, ALGERIA** (3d Battalion, 6th Armored Infantry cited)

Valorous Unit Award, Streamer embroidered **LO GIANG** (1st Battalion, 6th Infantry cited)

1ST BATTALION, 6TH INFANTRY
(The Regulars)

LINEAGE

1812   Constituted 11 January as a company of the 11th Infantry, Regular Army

1815   Consolidated May–October with a company each from the 25th, 27th, 29th, and 37th Infantry to form a company of the 6th Infantry

1816   Designated 22 May as Company A, 6th Infantry

1869   Consolidated 1 May with Company A, 42d Infantry, Veteran Reserve Corps to form Company A, 6th Infantry

Company lineage follows that of 6th Infantry from 1869 consolidation to 1939 relief from assignment to 6th Division

1940   Reorganized 15 July as Company A, 6th Infantry (Armored), an element of the 1st Armored Division

1942   Redesignated 1 January as Company A, 6th Armored Infantry

1944   Reorganized and redesignated 20 July as Company A, 6th Armored Infantry Battalion, an element of the 1st Armored Division

1946   Converted and redesignated 1 May as Troop A, 12th Constabulary Squadron, an element of the 1st Constabulary Regiment

1947   Inactivated 20 September at Fritzlar, Germany

1950   Converted and redesignated 10 October as Company A, 6th Infantry, activated 16 October at Grafenwohr, Germany (concurrently 12th Constabulary Squadron relieved from assignment to 1st Constabulary Squadron)

1957   Reorganized and redesignated 15 February as Headquarters and Headquarters Company, 1st Armored Rifle Battalion, 6th Infantry, an element of the 1st Armored Division

1962   Reorganized and redesignated 3 February as the 1st Battalion, 6th Infantry

1967   Relieved 12 May from assignment to the 1st Armored Division and assigned to the 198th Infantry Brigade

1969   Relieved 15 February from assignment to the 198th Infantry Brigade and assigned to the 23d Infantry Division

CAMPAIGN PARTICIPATION

War of 1812
Canada
Chippewa
Lundy's Lane

Mexican War
Vera Cruz
Cerro Gordo
Churubusco
Molino del Rey
Chapultepec

Civil War
Peninsula
Manassas
Antietam
Fredericksburg
Chancellorsville
Gettysburg
Virginia 1862

Indian Wars
Seminoles
Black Hawk
Little Big Horn
Cheyennes
Utes
South Dakota 1823
Kansas 1829
Nebraska 1855
Kansas 1857
Nevada 1860
North Dakota 1872
North Dakota 1873
Montana 1879

War With Spain
Santiago

Philippine Insurrection
Jolo
Negros 1899
Panay 1900

Mexican Expedition
Mexico 1916–1917

World War I
St. Mihiel
Meuse-Argonne
Alsace 1918
Lorraine 1918

World War II
Algeria-French Morocco (with arrowhead)
Tunisia
Naples-Foggia
Anzio
Rome-Arno
North Apennines
Po Valley

Vietnam
Counteroffensive, Phase III
Tet Counteroffensive
Counteroffensive, Phase IV
Counteroffensive, Phase V
Counteroffensive, Phase VI
Tet 69 Counteroffensive
Summer-Fall 1969
Winter-Spring 1970
Sanctuary Counteroffensive
Counteroffensive, Phase VII
Consolidation I

DECORATIONS

Presidential Unit Citation (Army), Streamer embroidered **MT. PORCHIA** (6th Armored Infantry cited)

Presidential Unit Citation (Army), Streamer embroidered **ORAN, ALGERIA**

Valorous Unit Award, Streamer embroidered **LO GIANG** (1st Battalion, 6th Infantry cited)

2D BATTALION, 6TH INFANTRY
(The Regulars)

LINEAGE

1812	Constituted 11 January as a company of the 11th Infantry, Regular Army
1815	Consolidated May–October with a company each of the 25th, 27th, 29th, and 37th Infantry to form a company of the 6th Infantry
1816	Designated 22 May as Company B, 6th Infantry
1869	Consolidated 1 May with Company B, 42d Infantry, Veteran Reserve Corps to form Company B, 6th Infantry
	Company lineage follows that of 6th Infantry from 1869 consolidation to 1939 relief from assignment to 6th Division
1940	Reorganized 15 July as Company B, 6th Infantry (Armored), an element of the 1st Armored Division
1942	Redesignated 1 January as Company B, 6th Armored Infantry
1944	Reorganized and redesignated 20 July as Company B, 6th Armored Infantry Battalion, an element of the 1st Armored Division
1946	Converted and redesignated 1 May as Troop B, 12th Constabulary Squadron, an element of the 1st Constabular Regiment
1947	Inactivated 20 September at Fritzlar, Germany
1950	Converted and redesignated 10 October as Company B, 6th Infantry, activated 16 October at Grafenwohr, Germany (concurrently 12th Constabulary Squadron relieved from assignment to 1st Constabulary Regiment)
1958	Reorganized and redesignated 1 June as Headquarters and Headquarters Company, 2d Battle Group, 6th Infantry
1963	Reorganized and redesignated 1 September as 2d Battalion, 6th Infantry and assigned to the United States Army Berlin Brigade

CAMPAIGN PARTICIPATION

War of 1812
Canada
Chippewa
Lundy's Lane

Mexican War
Vera Cruz
Cerro Gordo
Churubusco
Molino del Rey
Chapultepec

Civil War
Peninsula
Manassas
Antietam
Fredericksburg
Chancellorsville
Gettysburg
Virginia 1862

Indian Wars
Seminoles
Black Hawk
Little Big Horn
Cheyennes
Utes
South Dakota 1823
Kansas 1829
Nebraska 1855
Kansas 1857

North Dakota 1872
North Dakota 1873
Montana 1879

War With Spain
Santiago

Philippine Insurrection
Jolo
Negros 1899
Panay 1900

Mexican Expedition
Mexico 1916–1917

World War I
St. Mihiel
Meuse-Argonne
Alsace 1918
Lorraine 1918

World War II
Algeria-French Morocco (with arrowhead)
Tunisia
Naples-Foggia
Anzio
Rome-Arno
North Apennines
Po Valley

DECORATIONS

Presidential Unit Citation (Army), Streamer embroidered **MT. PORCHIA** (6th Armored Infantry cited)

Presidential Unit Citation (Army), Streamer embroidered **ORAN, ALGERIA**

3D BATTALION, 6TH INFANTRY
(The Regulars)

LINEAGE

1812   Constituted 11 January as a company of the 11th Infantry, Regular Army

1815   Consolidated May–October with a company each from the 25th, 27th, 29th, and 37th Infantry to form a company of the 6th Infantry

1816   Designated 22 May as Company C, 6th Infantry

1869   Consolidated 1 May with Company C, 42d Infantry, Veteran Reserve Corps to form Company C, 6th Infantry

Company lineage follows that of 6th Infantry from 1869 consolidation to 1939 relief from assignment to 6th Division

1940   Reorganized 15 July as Company C, 6th Infantry (Armored), an element of the 1st Armored Division

1942   Redesignated 1 January as Company C, 6th Armored Infantry

1944   Reorganized and redesignated 20 July as Company C, 6th Armored Infantry Battalion, an element of the 1st Armored Division

1946   Converted and redesignated 1 May as Troop C, 12th Constabulary Squadron, an element of the 1st Constabulary Regiment

1947   Inactivated 20 September at Fritzlar, Germany

1950   Converted and redesignated 10 October as Company C, 6th Infantry; activated 16 October at Grafenwohr, Germany (concurrently 12th Constabulary Squadron relieved from assignment to 1st Constabulary Regiment)

1958   Reorganized and redesignated 1 June as Headquarters and Headquarters Company, 3d Battle Group, 6th Infantry

1963   Reorganized and redesignated 1 September as 3d Battalion, 6th Infantry; assigned to the United States Berlin Brigade

CAMPAIGN PARTICIPATION

War of 1812
Canada
Chippewa
Lundy's Lane

Mexican War
Vera Cruz
Cerro Gordo
Churubusco
Molino del Rey
Chapultepec

Civil War
Peninsula
Manassas
Antietam
Fredericksburg
Chancellorsville
Gettysburg
Virginia 1862

Indian Wars
Seminoles
Black Hawk
Little Big Horn
Cheyennes
Utes
South Dakota 1823
Kansas 1829
Nebraska 1855
Kansas 1857

North Dakota 1872
North Dakota 1873
Montana 1879

War With Spain
Santiago

Philippine Insurrection
Jolo
Negros 1899
Panay 1900

Mexican Expedition
Mexico 1916–1917

World War I
St. Mihiel
Meuse-Argonne
Alsace 1918
Lorraine 1918

World War II
Algeria-French Morocco
(with arrowhead)
Tunisia
Naples-Foggia
Anzio
Rome-Arno
North Apennines
Po Valley

DECORATIONS

Presidential Unit Citation (Army), Streamer embroidered **MT. PORCHIA** (6th Armored Infantry cited)

Presidential Unit Citation (Army), Streamer embroidered **ORAN, ALGERIA**

4TH BATTALION, 6TH INFANTRY
(The Regulars)

LINEAGE

1812	Constituted 11 January as a company of the 11th Infantry, Regular Army
1815	Consolidated May–October with a company each from the 25th, 27th, 29th, and 37th Infantry to form a company of the 6th Infantry
1816	Designated 22 May as Company D, 6th Infantry
1869	Consolidated 1 May with Company D, 42d Infantry, Veteran Reserve Corps to form Company D, 6th Infantry

Company lineage follows that of 6th Infantry from 1869 consolidation to 1959 consolidation with 407th Infantry

1918	A new company constituted 23 July as Headquarters and Headquarters Company, 407th Infantry, an element of the 102d Division, National Army

This Company lineage differs from that of 6th Infantry from its constitution to 1 June 1959 consolidation as follows:

1921	*Reconstituted 24 June in the Organized Reserves as an element of the 102d Division organized at St. Louis, MO*
1942	*Ordered into active service 15 September and reorganized at Camp Maxey, TX*
1946	*Inactivated 16 March at Camp Kilmer, NJ*
1947	*Activated 7 April in the Organized Reserves at Danville, IL*
1948	*Location changed 15 March to St. Louis, MO*
1959	*Consolidated 1 June with Headquarters and Headquarters Company, 4th Battle Group, 6th Infantry, to form Headquarters and Headquarters Company, 4th Battle Group, 6th Infantry*
1963	Reorganized and redesignated 1 April as 4th Battalion, 6th Infantry
1965	Inactivated 31 December at St. Louis, MO

CAMPAIGN PARTICIPATION

War of 1812
Canada
Chippewa
Lundy's Lane

Mexican War
Vera Cruz
Cerro Gordo
Churubusco
Molino del Rey
Chapultepec

Civil War
Peninsula
Manassas
Antietam
Fredericksburg
Chancellorsville
Gettysburg
Virginia 1862

Indian Wars
Seminoles
Black Hawk
Little Big Horn
Cheyennes
Utes
South Dakota 1823
Kansas 1829
Nebraska 1855
Kansas 1857
North Dakota 1872
North Dakota 1873
Montana 1879

War With Spain
Santiago

Philippine Insurrection
Jolo
Negros 1899
Panay 1900

Mexican Expedition
Mexico 1916–1917

World War I
St. Mihiel
Meuse-Argonne
Alsace 1918
Lorraine 1918

World War II
Algeria-French Morocco (with arrowhead)
Tunisia
Naples-Foggia
Anzio
Rome-Arno
North Apennines
Po Valley
Rhineland
Central Europe

DECORATIONS

Presidential Unit Citation (Army), Streamer embroidered **MT. PORCHIA** (6th Armored Infantry cited)

Presidential Unit Citation (Army), Streamer embroidered **ORAN, ALGERIA**

5TH BATTALION, 6TH INFANTRY
(The Regulars)

LINEAGE

1812   Constituted 11 January as a company of the 11th Infantry, Regular Army

1815   Consolidated May–October with a company each from 25th, 27th, 29th, and 37th Infantry to form a company of the 6th Infantry

1816   Designated 22 May as Company E, 6th Infantry

1869   Consolidated 1 May with Company E, 42d Infantry, Veteran Reserve Corps to form Company E, 6th Infantry

Company lineage follows that of 6th Infantry from 1869 consolidation to 1939 relief from assignment to 6th Division

1940   Reorganized 15 July as Company E, 6th Infantry (Armored), an element of the 1st Armored Infantry

1942   Redesignated 1 January as Company E, 6th Armored Infantry

1944   Reorganized and redesignated 20 July as Company B, 11th Armored Infantry Battalion, an element of the 1st Armored Division

1946   Converted and redesignated 1 May as Troop B, 11th Constabulary Squadron, an element of the 1st Constabulary Regiment

1947   Inactivated 20 September at Fritzlar, Germany

1949   Converted and redesignated 7 April as Company B, 11th Armored Infantry Battalion, and relieved from assignment to 1st Constabulary Regiment

1950   Redesignated 10 October as Company E, 6th Infantry, and activated 16 October at Grafenwohr, Germany

1958   Inactivated 1 June in Germany and redesignated as Headquarters and Headquarters Company, 5th Battle Group, 6th Infantry

1962   Redesignated 3 February as Headquarters and Headquarters Company, 5th Battalion, 6th Infantry; assigned to the 1st Armored Division activated at Fort Hood, TX

CAMPAIGN PARTICIPATION

War of 1812
   Canada
   Chippewa
   Lundy's Lane

Mexican War
   Vera Cruz
   Cerro Gordo
   Churubusco
   Molino del Rey
   Chapultepec

Civil War
   Peninsula
   Manassas
   Antietam
   Fredericksburg
   Chancellorsville
   Gettysburg
   Virginia 1862

Indian Wars
   Seminoles
   Black Hawk
   Little Big Horn
   Cheyennes
   Utes
   South Dakota 1823
   Kansas 1829
   Nebraska 1855
   Kansas 1857

Kansas 1857
North Dakota 1872
North Dakota 1873
Montana 1879

War With Spain
   Santiago

Philippine Insurrection
   Jolo
   Negros 1899
   Panay 1900

Mexican Expedition
   Mexico 1916–1917

World War I
   St. Mihiel
   Meuse-Argonne
   Alsace 1918
   Lorraine 1918

World War II
   Algeria-French Morocco (with arrowhead)
   Tunisia
   Naples-Foggia
   Anzio
   Rome-Arno
   North Apennines
   Po Valley

DECORATIONS

Presidential Unit Citation (Army), Streamer embroidered **MT. PORCHIA** (6th Armored Infantry cited)

Presidential Unit Citation (Army), Streamer embroidered **ORAN, ALGERIA**

Presidential Unit Citation (Army), Streamer embroidered **PALAZZO** (Company B, 11th Armored Infantry Battalion cited)

6TH BATTALION, 6TH INFANTRY
(The Regulars)

LINEAGE

1812	Constituted 11 January as a company of the 11th Infantry, Regular Army
1815	Consolidated May–October with a company each from the 25th, 27th, 29th, and 37th Infantry to form a company of the 6th Infantry
1816	Designated 22 May as Company F, 6th Infantry
1869	Consolidated 1 May with Company F, 42d Infantry, Veteran Reserve Corps, to form Company F, 6th Infantry

Company lineage follows that of 6th Infantry from 1869 consolidation to 1939 relief from assignment with 6th Division

1940	Reorganized 15 July as Company F, 6th Infantry (Armored), an element of the 1st Armored Division
1942	Redesignated 1 January as Company F, 6th Armored Infantry
1944	Reorganized and redesignated 20 July as Company C, 11th Armored Infantry Battalion, an element of the 1st Armored Division
1946	Converted and redesignated 1 May as Troop C, 11th Constabulary Squadron, an element of the 1st Constabulary Regiment
1947	Inactivated 20 September at Fritzlar, Germany
1949	Converted and redesignated 7 April as Company C, 11th Armored Infantry Battalion; relieved from assignment to 1st Constabulary Regiment
1950	Redesignated 10 October as Company F, 6th Infantry; activated at Grafenwohr, Germany
1958	Inactivated 1 June in Germany and redesignated as Headquarters and Headquarters Company, 6th Battle Group, 6th Infantry
1963	Redesignated 26 March as Headquarters and Headquarters Company, 6th Battalion, 6th Infantry; withdrawn from Regular Army and allotted to the Army Reserve; assigned to the 102d Infantry Division
1963	Activated 1 April with Headquarters at St. Louis, MO
1965	Inactivated 31 December at St. Louis, MO

CAMPAIGN PARTICIPATION

War of 1812
  Canada
  Chippewa
  Lundy's Lane

Mexican War
  Vera Cruz
  Cerro Gordo
  Churubusco
  Molino del Rey
  Chapultepec

Civil War
  Peninsula
  Manassas
  Antietam
  Fredericksburg
  Chancellorsville
  Gettysburg
  Virginia 1862

Indian Wars
  Seminoles
  Black Hawk
  Little Big Horn
  Cheyennes
  Utes
  South Dakota 1823
  Kansas 1829
  Nebraska 1855
  Kansas 1857
  North Dakota 1872
  North Dakota 1873
  Montana 1879

War With Spain
  Santiago

Philippine Insurrection
  Jolo
  Negros 1899
  Panay 1900

Mexican Expedition
  Mexico 1916–1917

World War I
  St. Mihiel
  Meuse-Argonne
  Alsace 1918
  Lorraine 1918

World War II
  Algeria-French Morocco
    (with arrowhead)
  Tunisia
  Naples-Foggia
  Anzio
  Rome-Arno
  North Apennines
  Po Valley

DECORATIONS

Presidential Unit Citation (Army), Streamer embroidered **MT. PORCHIA** (6th Armored Infantry cited)

Presidential Unit Citation (Army), Streamer embroidered **ORAN, ALGERIA**

7TH BATTALION, 6TH INFANTRY
(The Regulars)

LINEAGE

1812   Constituted 11 January as a company of the 11th Infantry, Regular Army

1815   Consolidated May–October with a company each from the 25th, 27th, 29th, and 37th Infantry to form a company of the 6th Infantry

1816   Designated 22 May as Company G, 6th Infantry

1869   Consolidated 1 May with Company G, 42d Infantry, Veteran Reserve Corps, to form Company G, 6th Infantry

Company lineage follows that of 6th Infantry from 1869 consolidation to 1939 relief from assignment with 6th Division

1940   Reorganized 15 July as Company G, 6th Infantry (Armored), an element of the 1st Armored Division

1942   Redesignated 1 January as Company G, 6th Armored Infantry

1944   Reorganized and redesignated 20 July as Company A, 14th Armored Infantry Battalion, an element of the 1st Armored Division

1946   Converted and redesignated 1 May as Troop A, 14th Constabulary Squadron, an element of the 15th Constabulary Regiment

1948   Inactivated 20 December at Blaufelden, Germany; converted and redesignated as Company A, 14th Armored Infantry Battalion, an element of the 1st Armored Division

1950   Redesignated 10 October as Company G, 6th Infantry; activated 16 October at Grafenwohr, Germany (concurrently relieved from assignment to 1st Armored Division)

1958   Inactivated 1 June and redesignated as Headquarters and Headquarters Company, 7th Battle Group, 6th Infantry

1967   Redesignated 9 May as Headquarters and Headquarters Company, 7th Battalion, 6th Infantry; assigned to the 1st Armored Division; activated 12 May at Fort Hood, TX; relieved 20 October from assignment to 1st Armored Division and assigned to 2d Armored Division

1970   Inactivated 16 December at Fort Hood, TX

CAMPAIGN PARTICIPATION

War of 1812
Canada
Chippewa
Lundy's Lane

Mexican War
Vera Cruz
Cerro Gordo
Churubusco
Molino del Rey
Chapultepec

Civil War
Peninsula
Manassas
Antietam
Fredericksburg
Chancellorsville
Gettysburg
Virginia 1862

Indian Wars
Seminoles
Black Hawk
Little Big Horn
Cheyennes
Utes
South Dakota 1823
Kansas 1829
Nebraska 1855
Kansas 1857
North Dakota 1872
North Dakota 1873
Montana 1879

War With Spain
Santiago

Philippine Insurrection
Jolo
Negros 1899
Panay 1900

Mexican Expedition
Mexico 1916–1917

World War I
St. Mihiel
Meuse-Argonne
Alsace 1918
Lorraine 1918

World War II
Algeria-French Morocco (with arrowhead)
Tunisia
Naples-Foggia
Anzio
Rome-Arno
North Apennines
Po Valley

DECORATIONS

Presidential Unit Citation (Army), Streamer embroidered **MT. PORCHIA** (6th Armored Infantry cited)

Presidential Unit Citation (Army), Streamer embroidered **ORAN, ALGERIA**

7TH INFANTRY
(Cottonbalers)

COAT OF ARMS

Motto: *Volens et Potens* (Willing and Able).

Symbolism: The shield is white and blue, the old and present infantry colors. The field gun is for the battle of Cerro Gordo, where the 7th participated in the decisive attack by an assault on Telegraph Hill, a strongly fortified point. This portion of the shield is in the Mexican colors—red, white, and green. The wall is for the battle of Fredericksburg in which the regiment held for twelve hours a position only eighty yards in front of a stone wall protecting the enemy. The base alludes to the shoulder sleeve insignia of the 3d Division with which the 7th Infantry served during World War I. The French Croix de Guerre with Gilt Star was awarded to the regiment for action in the Aisne-Marne campaign of that war.

The cotton bale and bayonets in the crest are taken from the arms of the 7th Infantry adopted in 1912.

DISTINCTIVE INSIGNIA

The distinctive insignia is the crest of the coat of arms encircled by a ribbon bearing the motto of the coat of arms.

LINEAGE

1812	Constituted 11 January as the 8th Infantry Regular Army and organized in Tennessee, Georgia and adjacent territories
1815	Consolidated May–October with the 24th Infantry and the 39th Infantry to form the 7th Infantry
1861	A new company constituted 3 May as the 3d Battalion, 18th Infantry, Regular Army; organized 16 October at Camp Thomas, OH
1866	Reorganized and redesignated 26 December as 36th Infantry
1869	Consolidated May–June with the 7th Infantry to form the 7th Infantry
1917	Assigned 21 November to 3d Division
1957	Relieved 1 July from assignment to the 3d Infantry Division and reorganized as a parent regiment under CARS

CAMPAIGN PARTICIPATION

War of 1812

Canada
New Orleans
Florida 1814
Louisiana 1815

Mexican War

Monterey
Vera Cruz
Cerro Gordo
Contreras
Churubusco
Molino del Rey
Chapultepec
Texas 1846

Civil War

Fredericksburg
Murfreesborough
Chancellorsville
Gettysburg
Chickamauga
Chattanooga
Atlanta
New Mexico 1861
New Mexico 1862
Tennessee 1862
Mississippi 1862
Kentucky 1862
Tennessee 1863
Georgia 1864

Indian Wars

Creeks
Seminoles
Little Big Horn
Nez Perces
Utes
Pine Ridge
New Mexico 1860
Wyoming 1866
Montana 1872

War With Spain

Santiago

Philippine Insurrection

Samar 1901
Samar 1902

World War I

Aisne
Champagne-Marne
Aisne-Marne
St. Mihiel
Meuse-Argonne
Ile de France 1918
Champagne 1918

World War II

Algeria-French Morocco
(with arrowhead)
Tunisia
Sicily (with arrowhead)
Naples-Foggia
Anzio (with arrowhead)
Rome-Arno
Southern France (with arrowhead)
Rhineland
Ardennes-Alsace
Central Europe

Korean War

CCF intervention
First UN counteroffensive
CCF spring offensive
UN summer-fall offensive
Second Korean winter
Korea, summer–fall 1952
Third Korean winter
Korea, summer 1953

Vietnam

Counteroffensive, Phase II
Counteroffensive, Phase III
Tet Counteroffensive
Counteroffensive, Phase IV
Counteroffensive, Phase V
Counteroffensive, Phase VI
Tet 69 Counteroffensive
Summer–Fall 1969
Winter–Spring 1970
Sanctuary Counteroffensive
Counteroffensive, Phase VII

DECORATIONS

Presidential Unit Citation (Army), Streamer embroidered **COLMAR** (3d Infantry Division cited)

Presidential Unit Citation (Army), Streamer embroidered **CHOKSONG** (1st Battalion, 7th Infantry cited)

Presidential Unit Citation (Army), Streamer embroidered **SEGOK** (3d Battalion, 7th Infantry cited)

Presidential Unit Citation (Army), Streamer embroidered **KOWANG-NI** (2d Battalion, 7th Infantry and attached units cited)

Valorous Unit Award, Streamer embroidered **SAIGON-LONG BINH** (3d Battalion, 7th Infantry cited)

French Croix de Guerre with Gilt Star, World War I, Streamer embroidered **AISNE-MARNE** (7th Infantry cited)

French Croix de Guerre with Palm, World War II, Streamer embroidered **COLMAR** (7th Infantry cited)

French Croix de Guerre, World War II, Fourragere (7th Infantry cited)

Republic of Korea Presidential Unit Citation, Streamer embroidered **UIJONGBU CORRIDOR** (7th Infantry cited)

Republic of Korea Presidential Unit Citation, Streamer embroidered **IRON TRIANGLE** (7th Infantry cited)

Chryssoun Aristion Andrias (Bravery Gold Medal of Greece), Streamer embroidered **KOREA** (7th Infantry cited)

1ST BATTALION, 7TH INFANTRY
(Cottonbalers)

LINEAGE

1812	Constituted 11 January as a company of the 8th Infantry, Regular Army
1815	Consolidated May–October with a company each from the 24th and 39th Infantry to form a company of the 7th Infantry
1816	Designated 21 August as Company A, 7th Infantry
1861	A new company constituted 3 May as Company A, 3d Battalion, 18th Infantry, Regular Army; organized at Camp Thomas, OH
1866	Reorganized and redesignated 26 December as Company A, 36th Infantry
1869	Consolidated 26 May with Company A, 7th Infantry; consolidated unit designated Company A, 7th Infantry
1917	Assigned 21 November to 3d Division
1957	Reorganized and redesignated 1 July as Headquarters and Headquarters Company, 1st Battle Group, 7th Infantry; remained assigned to the 3d Infantry division
1963	Reorganized and redesignated 20 June as 1st Battalion, 7th Infantry

Indian Wars

Creeks
Seminoles
Little Big Horn
Nez Perces
Utes
Pine Ridge
New Mexico 1860
Wyoming 1866
Montana 1872

War With Spain

Santiago

Philippine Insurrection

Samar 1901
Samar 1902

World War I

Aisne
Champagne-Marne
Aisne-Marne
St. Mihiel
Meuse-Argonne
Ile de France 1918
Champagne 1918

World War II

Algeria-French Morocco (with arrowhead)
Tunisia
Sicily (with arrowhead)
Naples-Foggia
Anzio (with arrowhead)
Rome-Arno
Southern France (with arrowhead)
Rhineland
Ardennes-Alsace
Central Europe

Korean War

CCF intervention
First UN counteroffensive
CCF spring offensive
UN summer-fall offensive
Second Korean winter
Korea, summer–fall 1952
Third Korean winter
Korea, summer 1953

CAMPAIGN PARTICIPATION

War of 1812

Canada
New Orleans
Florida 1814
Louisiana 1815

Mexican War

Monterey
Vera Cruz
Cerro Gordo
Contreras
Churubusco
Molino del Rey
Chapultepec
Texas 1846

Civil War

Fredericksburg
Murfreesborough
Chancellorsville
Gettysburg
Chickamauga
Chattanooga
Atlanta
New Mexico 1861
New Mexico 1862
Tennessee 1862
Mississippi 1862
Kentucky 1862
Tennessee 1863
Georgia 1864

DECORATIONS

Presidential Unit Citation (Army), Streamer embroidered **COLMAR** (3d Infantry Division cited)

Presidential Unit Citation (Army), Streamer embroidered **CHOKSONG** (1st Battalion, 7th Infantry cited)

Presidential Unit Citation (Army), Streamer embroidered **SEGOK**

Presidential Unit Citation (Army), Streamer embroidered **KOWANG-NI**

French Croix de Guerre with Gilt Star, World War I, Streamer embroidered **AISNE-MARNE** (7th Infantry cited)

French Croix de Guerre with Palm, World War II, Streamer embroidered **COLMAR** (7th Infantry cited)

French Croix de Guerre, World War II, Fourragere (7th Infantry cited)

Republic of Korea Presidential Unit Citation, Streamer embroidered **UIJONGBU CORRIDOR** (7th Infantry cited)

Republic of Korea Presidential Unit Citation, Streamer embroidered **IRON TRIANGLE** (7th Infantry cited)

Chryssoun Aristion Andrias (Bravery Gold Medal of Greece), Streamer embroidered **KOREA** (7th Infantry cited)

2D BATTALION, 7TH INFANTRY
(Cottonbalers)

LINEAGE

1812	Constituted 11 January as a company of the 8th Infantry, Regular Army
1815	Consolidated May–October with a company each from the 24th and 39th Infantry to form a company of the 7th Infantry
1816	Designated 21 August as Company B, 7th Infantry
1861	A new company constituted 3 May as Company B, 3d Battalion, 18th Infantry, Regular Army; organized at Camp Thomas, OH
1866	Reorganized and redesignated 26 December as Company B, 36th Infantry
1869	Consolidated 4 June with Company B, 7th Infantry; consolidated unit designated Company B, 7th Infantry
1917	Assigned 21 November to 3d Division
1957	Reorganized and redesignated 1 July as Headquarters and Headquarters Company, 2d Battle Group, 7th Infantry; relieved from assignment to 3d Infantry Division and assigned to the 10th Infantry Division
1958	Inactivated 14 June at Fort Benning, GA
1963	Redesignated 18 April as 2d Battalion, 7th Infantry; relieved from assignment to the 10th Infantry Division and assigned to the 3d Infantry Division; activated 20 June in Germany
1966	Inactivated 1 May in Germany

CAMPAIGN PARTICIPATION

War of 1812

Canada
New Orleans
Florida 1814
Louisiana 1815

Mexican War

Monterey
Vera Cruz
Cerro Gordo
Contreras
Churubusco
Molino del Rey
Chapultepec
Texas 1846

Civil War

Fredericksburg
Murfreesborough
Chancellorsville
Gettysburg
Chickamauga
Chattanooga
Atlanta
New Mexico 1861
New Mexico 1862
Tennessee 1862
Mississippi 1862
Kentucky 1862
Tennessee 1863
Georgia 1864

Indian Wars

Creeks
Seminoles
Little Big Horn
Nez Perces
Utes
Pine Ridge
New Mexico 1860
Wyoming 1866
Montana 1872

War With Spain

Santiago

Philippine Insurrection

Samar 1901
Samar 1902

World War I

Aisne
Champagne-Marne
Aisne-Marne
St. Mihiel
Meuse-Argonne
Ile de France 1918
Champagne 1918

World War II

Algeria-French Morocco (with arrowhead)
Tunisia
Sicily (with arrowhead)
Naples-Foggia
Anzio (with arrowhead)
Rome-Arno
Southern France (with arrowhead)
Rhineland
Ardennes-Alsace
Central Europe

Korean War

CCF intervention
First UN counteroffensive
CCF spring offensive
UN summer-fall offensive
Second Korean winter
Korea, summer–fall 1952
Third Korean winter
Korea, summer 1953

DECORATIONS

Presidential Unit Citation (Army), Streamer embroidered **COLMAR** (3d Infantry Division cited)

Presidential Unit Citation (Army), Streamer embroidered **CHOKSONG** (1st Battalion, 7th Infantry cited)

Presidential Unit Citation (Army), Streamer embroidered **SEGOK**

Presidential Unit Citation (Army), Streamer embroidered **KOWANG-NI**

French Croix de Guerre with Gilt Star, World War I, Streamer embroidered **AISNE-MARNE** (7th Infantry cited)

French Croix de Guerre with Palm, World War II, Streamer embroidered **COLMAR** (7th Infantry cited)

French Croix de Guerre, World War II, Fourragere (7th Infantry cited)

Republic of Korea Presidential Unit Citation, Streamer embroidered **UIJONGBU CORRIDOR** (7th Infantry cited)

Republic of Korea Presidential Unit Citation, Streamer embroidered **IRON TRIANGLE** (7th Infantry cited)

Chryssoun Aristion Andrias (Bravery Gold Medal of Greece), Streamer embroidered **KOREA** (7th Infantry cited)

3D BATTALION, 7TH INFANTRY
(Cottonbalers)

LINEAGE

1812	Constituted 11 January as a company of the 8th Infantry, Regular Army
1815	Consolidated May–October with a company each from the 24th and 39th Infantry to form a company of the 7th Infantry
1816	Designated 21 August as Company C, 7th Infantry
1861	A new company constituted 3 May as Company C, 3d Battalion, 18th Infantry, Regular Army; organized at Camp Thomas, OH
1866	Reorganized and redesignated 26 December as Company C, 36th Infantry
1869	Consolidated 26 May with Company C, 7th Infantry; consolidated unit designated Company C, 7th Infantry
1917	Assigned 21 November to the 3d Division
1957	Inactivated 1 July at Fort Benning, GA, and relieved from assignment to the 3d Infantry Division; redesignated as Headquarters and Headquarters Company, 3d Battle Group, 7th Infantry
1959	Withdrawn 11 May from Regular Army, allotted to the Army Reserve and assigned to the 102d Infantry Division; Battle Group activated 1 June with Headquarters at Danville, IL
1963	Inactivated 1 April and relieved from assignment to 102d Infantry Division
1966	Redesignated 23 March as the 3d Battalion, 7th Infantry; withdrawn from the Army Reserve and allotted to Regular Army; assigned to 199th Infantry Brigade and activated 1 June at Fort Benning, GA
1970	Inactivated 15 October at Fort Benning, GA

CAMPAIGN PARTICIPATION

War of 1812

Canada
New Orleans
Florida 1814
Louisiana 1815

Mexican War

Monterey
Vera Cruz
Cerro Gordo
Contreras
Churubusco
Molino del Rey
Chapultepec
Texas 1846

Civil War

Fredericksburg
Murfreesborough
Chancellorsville
Gettysburg
Chickamauga
Chattanooga
Atlanta
New Mexico 1861
New Mexico 1862
Tennessee 1862
Mississippi 1862
Kentucky 1862
Tennessee 1863
Georgia 1864

Indian Wars

Creeks
Seminoles
Little Big Horn
Nez Perces
Utes
Pine Ridge
New Mexico 1860
Wyoming 1866
Montana 1872

War With Spain

Santiago

Philippine Insurrection

Samar 1901
Samar 1902

World War I

Aisne
Champagne-Marne
Aisne-Marne
St. Mihiel
Meuse-Argonne
Ile de France 1918
Champagne 1918

World War II

Algeria-French Morocco
(with arrowhead)
Tunisia
Sicily (with arrowhead)
Naples-Foggia
Anzio (with arrowhead)
Rome-Arno
Southern France (with
arrowhead)
Rhineland
Ardennes-Alsace
Central Europe

Korean War

CCF intervention
First UN counteroffensive
CCF spring offensive
UN summer-fall offensive
Second Korean winter
Korea, summer–fall 1952
Third Korean winter
Korea, summer 1953

Vietnam

Counteroffensive,
Phase II
Counteroffensive,
Phase III
Tet Counteroffensive
Counteroffensive,
Phase IV
Counteroffensive,
Phase V
Counteroffensive,
Phase VI
Tet 69 Counteroffensive
Summer–Fall 1969
Winter–Spring 1970
Sanctuary
Counteroffensive
Counteroffensive,
Phase VII

DECORATIONS

Presidential Unit Citation (Army), Streamer embroidered **COLMAR** (3d Infantry Division cited)

Presidential Unit Citation (Army), Streamer embroidered **CHOKSONG** (1st Battalion, 7th Infantry cited)

Presidential Unit Citation (Army), Streamer embroidered **SEGOK**

Presidential Unit Citation (Army), Streamer embroidered **KOWANG-NI**

Valorous Unit Award, Streamer embroidered **SAIGON-LONG BINH** (3d Battalion, 7th Infantry cited)

French Croix de Guerre with Gilt Star, World War I, Streamer embroidered **AISNE-MARNE** (7th Infantry cited)

French Croix de Guerre with Palm, World War II, Streamer embroidered **COLMAR** (7th Infantry cited)

French Croix de Guerre, World War II, Fourragere (7th Infantry cited)

Republic of Korea Presidential Unit Citation, Streamer embroidered **UIJONGBU CORRIDOR** (7th Infantry cited)

Republic of Korea Presidential Unit Citation, Streamer embroidered **IRON TRIANGLE** (7th Infantry cited)

Chryssoun Aristion Andrias (Bravery Gold Medal of Greece), Streamer embroidered **KOREA** (7th Infantry cited)

Vietnamese Cross of Gallantry with Palm, Streamer embroidered **VIETNAM 1968** (3d Battalion, 7th Infantry cited)

4TH BATTLE GROUP, 7TH INFANTRY
(Cottonbalers)

LINEAGE

1812	Constituted 11 January as a company of the 8th Infantry, Regular Army
1815	Consolidated May–October with a company each from the 24th and 39th Infantry to form a company of the 7th Infantry
1816	Designated 21 August as Company D, 7th Infantry

1861	A new company constituted 3 May as Company D, 3d Battalion, 18th Infantry, Regular Army; organized at Camp Thomas, OH
1866	Reorganized and redesignated 26 December as Company D, 36th Infantry
1869	Consolidated 4 June with Company D, 7th Infantry, to form Company D, 7th Infantry

1917	Assigned 21 November to 3d Division
1957	Inactivated 1 July at Fort Benning, GA, and relieved from assignment to 3d Infantry Division; redesignated as Headquarters and Headquarters Company, 4th Battle Group, 7th Infantry
1962	Battle Group activated 24 September at Fort Benning, GA
1963	Inactivated 15 February

CAMPAIGN PARTICIPATION

War of 1812

Canada
New Orleans
Florida 1814
Louisiana 1815

Mexican War

Monterey
Vera Cruz
Cerro Gordo
Contreras
Churubusco
Molino del Rey
Chapultepec
Texas 1846

Civil War

Fredericksburg
Murfreesborough
Chancellorsville
Gettysburg
Chickamauga
Chattanooga
Atlanta
New Mexico 1861
New Mexico 1862
Tennessee 1862
Mississippi 1862
Kentucky 1862
Tennessee 1863
Georgia 1864

Indian Wars

Creeks
Seminoles
Little Big Horn
Nez Perces
Utes
Pine Ridge
New Mexico 1860
Wyoming 1866
Montana 1872

War With Spain

Santiago

Philippine Insurrection

Samar 1901
Samar 1902

World War I

Aisne
Champagne-Marne
Aisne-Marne
St. Mihiel
Meuse-Argonne
Ile de France 1918
Champagne 1918

World War II

Algeria-French Morocco (with arrowhead)
Tunisia
Sicily (with arrowhead)
Naples-Foggia
Anzio (with arrowhead)
Rome-Arno
Southern France (with arrowhead)
Rhineland
Ardennes-Alsace
Central Europe

Korean War

CCF intervention
First UN counteroffensive
CCF spring offensive
UN summer-fall offensive
Second Korean winter
Korea, summer–fall 1952
Third Korean winter
Korea, summer 1953

DECORATIONS

Presidential Unit Citation (Army), Streamer embroidered **COLMAR** (3d Infantry Division cited)

Presidential Unit Citation (Army), Streamer embroidered **CHOKSONG** (1st Battalion, 7th Infantry cited)

Presidential Unit Citation (Army), Streamer embroidered **SEGOK**

Presidential Unit Citation (Army), Streamer embroidered **KOWANG-NI**

French Croix de Guerre with Gilt Star, World War I, Streamer embroidered **AISNE-MARNE** (7th Infantry cited)

French Croix de Guerre with Palm, World War II, Streamer embroidered **COLMAR** (7th Infantry cited)

French Croix de Guerre, World War II, Fourragere (7th Infantry cited)

Republic of Korea Presidential Unit Citation, Streamer embroidered **UIJONGBU CORRIDOR** (7th Infantry cited)

Republic of Korea Presidential Unit Citation, Streamer embroidered **IRON TRIANGLE** (7th Infantry cited)

Chryssoun Aristion Andrias (Bravery Gold Medal of Greece), Streamer embroidered **KOREA** (7th Infantry cited)

8TH INFANTRY

COAT OF ARMS

Motto: *Patriae Fidelitas* (Loyalty to Country)

Symbolism: The shield is white with a blue bend, the old and present infantry colors. The three heraldic flowers on the bend are symbolic of: first, the rose, the flower of the state of New York, where the regimental headquarters was first organized; second, the hispida, the flower of the Philippines, where the regiment saw service during the Insurrection; and third, the temple flower, which is the flower of Cuba, where the 8th served during the War with Spain. The arrow and tomahawk represent the Indian campaigns in which the regiment has participated. The claw representing the maimed strength of the Prussian eagle alludes to the regiment's part in the occupation of Germany after World War I.

The crest symbolizes service in the Mexican War; the 8th was the first U.S. regiment to plant its colors on the fort at Churubusco.

DISTINCTIVE INSIGNIA

The distinctive insignia is the shield of the coat of arms surmounted by a mural crown, the shield and crown mounted on a heavy Roman gold boss figured in high relief.

LINEAGE

1838	Constituted 5 July as the 8th Infantry, Regular Army; organized in New York, Vermont, and Michigan
1861	A new company constituted 3 May as 3d Battalion, 15th Infantry, Regular Army
1864	Organized by March at Fort Adams, RI
1866	Reorganized and redesignated 21 September as 33d Infantry
1869	Consolidated in May with 8th Infantry to form the 8th Infantry
1917	Assigned to the 8th Division
1923	Relieved from assignment to 8th Division and assigned to the 4th Division
1946	Inactivated 25 February at Camp Butner, NC
1947	Activated 15 July at Fort Ord, CA
1957	Relieved 1 April from assignment to 4th Infantry Division and reorganized as a parent regiment under CARS

CAMPAIGN PARTICIPATION

Mexican War

Palo Alto
Resaca de la Palma
Monterey
Vera Cruz
Cerro Gordo
Churubusco
Molino del Rey
Chapultepec

Antietam
Fredericksburg
Chancellorsville
Gettysburg
Wilderness
Atlanta
Spotsylvania
Cold Harbor
Petersburg
Texas 1861

Civil War

Peninsula
Manassas

Indian Wars

Seminoles
Apaches
New Mexico 1858
New Mexico 1860
Montana 1872
Arizona 1876

War With Spain

Santiago

Philippine Insurrection

Luzon 1901

World War I

Without inscription

World War II

Normandy (with arrowhead)
Northern France
Rhineland

Ardennes-Alsace
Central Europe

Vietnam

Counteroffensive, Phase II
Counteroffensive, Phase III
Tet Counteroffensive
Counteroffensive, Phase IV
Counteroffensive, Phase V
Counteroffensive, Phase VI
Tet 69 Counteroffensive
Summer–Fall 1969
Winter–Spring 1970
Sanctuary Counteroffensive
Counteroffensive, Phase VII

DECORATIONS

Presidential Unit Citation (Army), Streamer embroidered **BEACHES OF NORMANDY** (8th Infantry cited)

Presidential Unit Citation (Army), Streamer embroidered **PLEIKU PROVINCE** (1st and 3rd Battalions, 8th Infantry cited)

Belgian Fourragere 1940 (8th Infantry cited)

Cited in the Order of the Day of the Belgian Army for action in **BELGIUM** (8th Infantry cited)

Cited in the Order of the Day of the Belgian Army for action in the **ARDENNES** (8th Infantry cited)

1st Battalion, 8th Infantry

LINEAGE

1838	Organized 1 July as a detachment of recruits at Detroit, MI; designated 5 July as Company A, 8th Infantry, a newly constituted unit in Regular Army
1861	Constituted 3 May as Company A, 3d Battalion, 15th Infantry, Regular Army
1864	Organized by March at Fort Adams, RI

1866	Reorganized and redesignated 21 September as Company A, 33d Infantry
1869	Consolidated in May with Company A, 8th Infantry; consolidated unit designated Company A, 8th Infantry
1917	Assigned 17 December to 8th Division
1923	Relieved 24 March from assignment to 8th Division and assigned to 4th Division
1946	Inactivated 25 February at Camp Butner, NC
1947	Activated 15 July at Fort Ord, CA
1957	Reorganized and redesignated 1 April as Headquarters and Headquarters Company, 1st Battle Group, 8th Infantry; remained assigned to 4th Infantry Division
1963	Reorganized and redesignated 1 October as 1st Battalion, 8th Infantry
1970	Inactivated 10 April at Fort Lewis, WA

CAMPAIGN PARTICIPATION

Mexican War

Palo Alto
Resaca de la Palma
Monterey
Vera Cruz
Cerro Gordo
Churubusco
Molino del Rey
Chapultepec

Civil War

Peninsula
Manassas
Antietam
Fredericksburg
Chancellorsville
Gettysburg
Wilderness
Atlanta
Spotsylvania
Cold Harbor
Petersburg
Texas 1861

Indian Wars

Seminoles
Apaches
New Mexico 1858
New Mexico 1860
Montana 1872
Arizona 1876

War With Spain

Santiago

Philippine Insurrection

Luzon 1901

World War I

Without inscription

World War II

Normandy (with arrowhead)
Northern France
Rhineland
Ardennes-Alsace
Central Europe

Vietnam

Counteroffensive, Phase II
Counteroffensive, Phase III
Tet Counteroffensive
Counteroffensive, Phase IV
Counteroffensive, Phase V
Counteroffensive, Phase VI
Tet 69 Counteroffensive
Summer–Fall 1969
Winter–Spring 1970

DECORATIONS

Presidential Unit Citation (Army), Streamer embroidered **BEACHES OF NORMANDY** (8th Infantry cited)

Presidential Unit Citation (Army), Streamer embroidered **PLEIKU PROVINCE** (1st Battalion, 8th Infantry cited)

Belgian Fourragere 1940 (8th Infantry cited)

Cited in the Order of the Day of the Belgian Army for action in **BELGIUM** (8th Infantry cited)

Cited in the Order of the Day of the Belgian Army for action in the **ARDENNES** (8th Infantry cited)

Vietnamese Cross of Gallentry with Palm, Streamer embroidered **VIETNAM 1966–1969** (1st Battalion, 8th Infantry cited)

Vietnamese Civil Action Honor Medal, First Class, Streamer embroidered **VIETNAM 1966–1969** (1st Battalion, 8th Infantry cited)

Company A and Company C, each additionally entitled to: Presidential Unit Citation (Army), Streamer embroidered **KONTUM PROVINCE** (Company A and Company C, 1st Battalion, 8th Infantry cited)

2D BATTALION, 8TH INFANTRY

LINEAGE

1838	Constituted 5 July as Company B, 8th Infantry, Regular Army, in Detroit MI

1861	A new company constituted 3 May as Company B, 3d Battalion, 15th Infantry, Regular Army
1864	Organized by March at Fort Adams, RI

1866	Reorganized and redesignated 21 September as Company B, 33d Infantry
1869	Consolidated in May with Company B, 8th Infantry; consolidated unit designated Company B, 8th Infantry
1917	Assigned 17 December to 8th Division
1923	Relieved 24 March from assignment to 8th Division and assigned to 4th Division
1946	Inactivated 25 February at Camp Butner, NC
1947	Activated 15 July at Fort Ord, CA
1957	Inactivated 1 April at Fort Lewis, WA, and relieved from assignment to 4th Infantry Division; redesignated 1 August as Headquarters and Headquarters Company, 2d Battle Group, 8th Infantry; assigned to the 8th Infantry Division and activated in Germany
1959	Relieved 1 January from assignment to the 8th Infantry Division and assigned to the 1st Infantry Division
1963	Reorganized and redesignated 1 October as 2d Battalion, 8th Infantry; relieved from assignment to 1st Infantry Division and assigned to the 4th Infantry Division

CAMPAIGN PARTICIPATION

Mexican War

Palo Alto
Resaca de la Palma
Monterey
Vera Cruz
Cerro Gordo
Churubusco
Molino del Rey
Chapultepec

Civil War

Peninsula

Manassas
Antietam
Fredericksburg
Chancellorsville
Gettysburg
Wilderness
Atlanta
Spotsylvania
Cold Harbor
Petersburg
Texas 1861

Indian Wars

Seminoles
Apaches
New Mexico 1858
New Mexico 1860
Montana 1872
Arizona 1876

War With Spain

Santiago

Philippine Insurrection

Luzon 1901

World War I

Without inscription

World War II

Normandy (with arrowhead)
Northern France
Rhineland
Ardennes-Alsace
Central Europe

Vietnam

Counteroffensive, Phase II
Counteroffensive, Phase III
Tet Counteroffensive
Counteroffensive, Phase IV
Counteroffensive, Phase V
Counteroffensive, Phase VI
Tet 69 Counteroffensive
Summer–Fall 1969
Winter–Spring 1970
Sanctuary Counteroffensive
Counteroffensive, Phase VII

DECORATIONS

Presidential Unit Citation (Army), Streamer embroidered **BEACHES OF NORMANDY** (8th Infantry cited)

Belgian Fourragere 1940 (8th Infantry cited)

Cited in the Order of the Day of the Belgian Army for action in **BELGIUM** (8th Infantry cited)

Cited in the Order of the Day of the Belgian Army for action in the **ARDENNES** (8th Infantry cited)

Vietnamese Cross of Gallantry with Palm, Streamer embroidered **VIETNAM 1966–1969** (2d Battalion, 8th Infantry cited)

Vietnamese Civil Action Honor Medal, First Class, Streamer embroidered **VIETNAM 1966–1969** (2d Battalion, 8th Infantry cited)

3D BATTALION, 8TH INFANTRY

LINEAGE

1838	Constituted 5 July as Company C, 8th Infantry, Regular Army; organized 9 July at Buffalo, NY
1861	A new company constituted 3 May as Company C, 3d Battalion, 15th Infantry, Regular Army

1864	Organized by March at Fort Adams, RI
1866	Reorganized and redesignated 21 September as Company C, 33d Infantry
1869	Consolidated in May with Company C, 8th Infantry; consolidated unit designated Company C, 8th Infantry
1917	Assigned 17 December to 8th Division
1923	Relieved 24 March from assignment to 8th Division and assigned to 4th Division
1946	Inactivated 25 February at Camp Butner, NC
1947	Activated 15 July at Fort Ord, CA
1957	Inactivated 1 April at Fort Lewis, WA and relieved from assignment to 4th Infantry Division; redesignated as Headquarters and Headquarters Company, 3d Battle Group, 8th Infantry
1963	Redesignated 21 August as Headquarters and Headquarters Company, 3d Battalion, 8th Infantry; assigned to 4th Infantry Division and Battalion activated 1 October at Fort Lewis, WA
1970	Inactivated 15 December at Fort Carson, CO

CAMPAIGN PARTICIPATION

Mexican War

Palo Alto
Resaca de la Palma
Monterey
Vera Cruz
Cerro Gordo
Churubusco
Molino del Rey
Chapultepec

Antietam
Fredericksburg
Chancellorsville
Gettysburg
Wilderness
Atlanta
Spotsylvania
Cold Harbor
Petersburg
Texas 1861

Civil War

Peninsula
Manassas

Indian Wars

Seminoles
Apaches
New Mexico 1858
New Mexico 1860
Montana 1872
Arizona 1876

War With Spain

Santiago

Philippine Insurrection

Luzon 1901

World War I

Without inscription

World War II

Normandy (with arrowhead)
Northern France

Rhineland
Ardennes-Alsace
Central Europe

Vietnam

Counteroffensive, Phase II
Counteroffensive, Phase III
Tet Counteroffensive
Counteroffensive, Phase IV
Counteroffensive, Phase V
Counteroffensive, Phase VI
Tet 69 Counteroffensive
Summer–Fall 1969
Winter–Spring 1970
Sanctuary Counteroffensive
Counteroffensive, Phase VII

DECORATIONS

Presidential Unit Citation (Army), Streamer embroidered **BEACHES OF NORMANDY** (8th Infantry cited)

Presidential Unit Citation (Army), Streamer embroidered **PLEIKU PROVINCE** (3d Battalion, 8th Infantry cited)

Belgian Fourragere 1940 (8th Infantry cited)

Cited in the Order of the Day of the Belgian Army for action in **BELGIUM** (8th Infantry cited)

Cited in the Order of the Day of the Belgian Army for action in the **ARDENNES** (8th Infantry cited)

Vietnamese Cross of Gallantry with Palm, Streamer embroidered **VIETNAM 1966–1969** (3d Battalion, 8th Infantry cited)

Vietnamese Civil Action Honor Medal, First Class, Streamer embroidered **VIETNAM 1966–1969** (3d Battalion, 8th Infantry cited)

COMPANY E, 8TH INFANTRY

LINEAGE

1838	Constituted 5 July as Company E, 8th Infantry, Regular Army; organized in July at Buffalo, NY

1861	A new company constituted 3 May as Company E, 3d Battalion, 15th Infantry, Regular Army

1864	Organized by March at Fort Adams, RI
1866	Reorganized and redesignated 21 September as Company E, 33d Infantry
1869	Consolidated in May with Company E, 8th Infantry; consolidated unit designated Company E, 8th Infantry
1917	Assigned 17 December to 8th Division
1923	Relieved 24 March from assignment to 8th Division and assigned to 4th Division
1946	Inactivated 25 February at Camp Butner, NC
1947	Activated 15 July at Fort Ord, CA
1957	Inactivated 1 April at Fort Lewis, WA and relieved from assignment to the 4th Infantry Division; redesignated as Headquarters and Headquarters Company, 5th Battle Group, 8th Infantry
1962	Redesignated 5 November as Company E, 8th Infantry; withdrawn from Regular Army and allotted to Army Reserve
1963	Activated 22 March at Roslinde, MA
1965	Inactivated 17 December

CAMPAIGN PARTICIPATION

Mexican War

Palo Alto
Resaca de la Palma
Monterey
Vera Cruz
Cerro Gordo
Churubusco
Molino del Rey
Chapultepec

Civil War

Chancellorsville
Gettysburg
Wilderness
Spotsylvania
Cold Harbor
Petersburg
Texas 1861

Indian Wars

Apaches
New Mexico 1858
New Mexico 1860
Arizona 1876

War With Spain

Santiago

World War II-EAME

Normandy (with arrowhead)
Northern France
Rhineland
Ardennes-Alsace
Central Europe

DECORATIONS

Presidential Unit Citation (Army), Streamer embroidered **BEACHES OF NORMANDY** (8th Infantry cited)

Belgian Fourragere 1940 (8th Infantry cited)

Cited in the Order of the Day of the Belgian Army for action in **BELGIUM** (8th Infantry cited)

Cited in the Order of the Day of the Belgian Army for action in the **ARDENNES** (8th Infantry cited)

9TH INFANTRY
(Manchu)

COAT OF ARMS

Motto: Keep up the Fire

Symbolism: The field of the shield is blue, the infantry color. The regiment's Indian campaigns are commemorated by the wigwam. Service in the Philippine Insurrection and China Relief Expedition is shown by the sun in splendor, a device used by the Filipino insurrectos, and by the imperial Chinese dragon, respectively. In 1898 the regiment took part in the battle of Santiago, crossing the San Juan River at the "bloody angle"; this is represented by the wavy chevron.

The crest is the insignia used by the division with which the regiment served in World War I, surrounded by a Fourragere awarded by the French government for distinguished services rendered.

DISTINCTIVE INSIGNIA

The distinctive insignia is an imperial five-toed Chinese dragon, head to chief facing the dexter, encircling a disc bearing the numeral "9" all or; the motto "Keep up the Fire" around edge of disc. The design commemorates the campaigns in China.

LINEAGE

1855	Constituted as 9th Infantry, Regular Army; organized at Fort Monroe, VA
1861	A new company constituted 3 May as 2d Battalion, 18th Infantry, Regular Army; organized at Camp Thomas, OH
1866	Reorganized and redesignated 21 September as 27th Infantry
1869	Consolidated in June with 9th Infantry to form 9th Infantry
1917	Assigned 22 September to 2d Division
1957	Relieved 20 June from assignment to 2d Infantry Division and reorganized as a parent regiment under CARS

CAMPAIGN PARTICIPATION

Civil War

Murfreesborough
Chickamauga
Chattanooga
Atlanta
Mississippi 1862
Kentucky 1862
Tennessee 1863
Georgia 1864

Indian Wars

Little Big Horn
Washington 1856
Washington 1858
Wyoming 1866
Wyoming 1867

War With Spain

Santiago

China Relief Expedition

Tientsin
Yang-tsun
Peking

Philippine Insurrection

San Isidro
Zapote River
Malolos
Tarlac
Luzon 1899
Luzon 1900
Samar 1901

World War I

Aisne
Aisne-Marne
St. Mihiel
Meuse-Argonne
Lorraine 1918
Ile de France 1918

World War II

Normandy (with arrowhead)
Northern France
Rhineland
Ardennes-Alsace
Central Europe

Korean War

UN defensive
UN offensive
CCF intervention
First UN counteroffensive
CCF spring offensive
UN summer–fall offensive
Second Korean winter
Korea, summer–fall 1952
Third Korean winter
Korea, summer 1953

Vietnam

Counteroffensive
Counteroffensive, Phase II
Counteroffensive, Phase III
Tet Counteroffensive
Counteroffensive, Phase IV
Counteroffensive, Phase V
Counteroffensive, Phase VI
Tet 69 Counteroffensive
Summer–Fall 1969
Winter–Spring 1970
Sanctuary Counteroffensive
Counteroffensive, Phase VII

DECORATIONS

Presidential Unit Citation (Army), Streamer embroidered **BREST, FRANCE** (3d Battalion, 9th Infantry cited)

Presidential Unit Citation (Army), Streamer embroidered **SIEGFRIED LINE** (2d Battalion, 9th Infantry cited)

Presidential Unit Citation (Army), Streamer embroidered **ARDENNES** (1st Battalion, 9th Infantry cited)

Presidential Unit Citation (Army), Streamer embroidered **HONGCHON** (2d Infantry Division cited)

Presidential Unit Citation (Navy), Streamer embroidered **HWACHON RESERVOIR** (1st Battalion, 9th Infantry cited)

Navy Unit Commendation, Streamer embroidered **PANMUNJOM** (1st Battalion, 9th Infantry cited)

French Croix de Guerre with Palm, World War I, Streamer embroidered **AISNE-MARNE** (9th Infantry cited)

French Croix de Guerre with Palm, World War I, Streamer embroidered **MEUSE-ARGONNE** (9th Infantry cited)

French Croix de Guerre with Palm, World War I, Streamer embroidered **CHATEAU THIERRY** (9th Infantry cited)

French Croix de Guerre, World War I, Fourragere (9th Infantry cited)

Republic of Korea Presidential Unit Citation, Streamer embroidered **NAKTONG RIVER LINE** (9th Infantry cited)

Republic of Korea Presidential Unit Citation, Streamer embroidered **KOREA** (9th Infantry cited)

Luxembourg Croix de Guerre, Streamer embroidered **LUXEMBOURG** (9th Infantry cited)

Belgian Fourragere 1940 (9th Infantry cited)

Cited in the Order of the Day of the Belgian Army for action in the **ARDENNES** (9th Infantry cited)

Cited in the Order of the Day of the Belgian Army for action at **ELSENBORN CREST** (9th Infantry cited)

1ST BATTALION, 9TH INFANTRY
(Manchu)

LINEAGE

1855   Constituted 3 March as Company A, 9th Infantry, Regular Army; organized 26 March at Fort Monroe, VA

1861   A new company constituted 3 May as Company A, 2d Battalion, 19th Infantry; organized in October at Camp Thomas, OH

1866   Reorganized and redesignated 21 September as Company A, 27th Infantry

1869   Consolidated in June with Company A, 9th Infantry; consolidated unit designated Company A, 9th Infantry

1917   Assigned 22 September to 2d Division

1957   Reorganized and redesignated 20 June as Headquarters and Headquarters Company, 1st Battle Group, 9th Infantry; 16 December relieved from assignment to 2d Infantry Division

1963   Reorganized and redesignated 25 January as 1st Battalion, 9th Infantry and assigned to 2d Infantry Division

CAMPAIGN PARTICIPATION

Civil War

Murfreesborough
Chickamauga
Chattanooga
Atlanta
Mississippi 1862
Kentucky 1862
Tennessee 1863
Georgia 1864

Indian Wars

Little Big Horn
Washington 1856
Washington 1858
Wyoming 1866
Wyoming 1867

War With Spain

Santiago

China Relief Expedition

Tientsin
Yang-tsun
Peking

Philippine Insurrection

San Isidro
Zapote River
Malolos
Tarlac
Luzon 1899
Luzon 1900
Samar 1901

World War I

Aisne
Aisne-Marne
St. Mihiel
Meuse-Argonne
Lorraine 1918
Ile de France 1918

World War II

Normandy (with arrowhead)
Northern France
Rhineland
Ardennes-Alsace
Central Europe

Korean War

UN defensive
UN offensive
CCF intervention
First UN counteroffensive
CCF spring offensive
UN summer–fall offensive
Second Korean winter
Korea, summer–fall 1952
Third Korean winter
Korea, summer 1953

DECORATIONS

Presidential Unit Citation (Army), Streamer embroidered **BREST, FRANCE**

Presidential Unit Citation (Army), Streamer embroidered **SIEGFRIED LINE**

Presidential Unit Citation (Army), Streamer embroidered **ARDENNES** (1st Battalion, 9th Infantry cited)

Presidential Unit Citation (Army), Streamer embroidered **HONGCHON** (2d Infantry Division cited)

Presidential Unit Citation (Navy), Streamer embroidered **HWACHON RESERVOIR** (1st Battalion, 9th Infantry cited)

Navy Unit Commendation, Streamer embroidered **PANMUNJOM** (1st Battalion, 9th Infantry cited)

French Croix de Guerre with Palm, World War I, Streamer embroidered **AISNE-MARNE** (9th Infantry cited)

French Croix de Guerre with Palm, World War I, Streamer embroidered **MEUSE-ARGONNE** (9th Infantry cited)

French Croix de Guerre with Palm, World War I, Streamer embroidered **CHATEAU THIERRY** (9th Infantry cited)

French Croix de Guerre, World War I, Fourragere (9th Infantry cited)

Republic of Korea Presidential Unit Citation, Streamer embroidered **NAKTONG RIVER LINE** (9th Infantry cited)

Republic of Korea Presidential Unit Citation, Streamer embroidered **KOREA** (9th Infantry cited)

Luxembourg Croix de Guerre, Streamer embroidered **LUXEMBOURG** (9th Infantry cited)

Belgian Fourragere 1940 (9th Infantry cited)

Cited in the Order of the Day of the Belgian Army for action in the **ARDENNES** (9th Infantry cited)

Cited in the Order of the Day of the Belgian Army for action at **ELSENBORN CREST** (9th Infantry cited)

2D BATTALION, 9TH INFANTRY
(Manchu)

LINEAGE

1855   Constituted as Company B, 9th Infantry, Regular Army; organized 26 March at Fort Monroe, VA

1861   A new company constituted 3 May as Company B, 2d Battalion, 18th Infantry, Regular Army; organized in October at Camp Thomas, OH

1866   Reorganized and redesignated 21 September as Company B, 27th Infantry

1869   Consolidated in June with Company B, 9th Infantry, to form Company B, 9th Infantry

1917   Assigned 22 September to 2d Division

1957   Inactivated 20 June in Alaska and relieved from assignment to 2d Infantry Division; redesignated as Headquarters and Headquarters Company, 2d Battle Group, 9th Infantry

1958   Assigned 17 March to 2d Infantry Division and Battle Group activated 14 June at Fort Benning, GA

1963   Reorganized and redesignated 1 February as 2d Battalion, 9th Infantry

CAMPAIGN PARTICIPATION

Civil War
Murfreesborough
Chickamauga
Chattanooga
Atlanta
Mississippi 1862
Kentucky 1862
Tennessee 1863
Georgia 1864

Indian Wars
Little Big Horn
Washington 1856
Washington 1858
Wyoming 1866
Wyoming 1867

War With Spain
Santiago

China Relief Expedition
Tientsin
Yang-tsun
Peking

Philippine Insurrection
San Isidro
Zapote River
Malolos
Tarlac
Luzon 1899
Luzon 1900
Samar 1901

World War I
Aisne
Aisne-Marne
St. Mihiel
Meuse-Argonne
Lorraine 1918
Ile de France 1918

World War II
Normandy (with arrowhead)
Northern France
Rhineland
Ardennes-Alsace
Central Europe

Korean War
UN defensive
UN offensive
CCF intervention
First UN counteroffensive
CCF spring offensive
UN summer–fall offensive
Second Korean winter
Korea, summer–fall 1952
Third Korean winter
Korea, summer 1953

DECORATIONS

Presidential Unit Citation (Army), Streamer embroidered **BREST, FRANCE**

Presidential Unit Citation (Army), Streamer embroidered **SIEGFRIED LINE**

Presidential Unit Citation (Army), Streamer embroidered **ARDENNES** (1st Battalion, 9th Infantry cited)

Presidential Unit Citation (Army), Streamer embroidered **HONGCHON** (2d Infantry Division cited)

Presidential Unit Citation (Navy), Streamer embroidered **HWACHON RESERVOIR** (1st Battalion, 9th Infantry cited)

Navy Unit Commendation, Streamer embroidered **PANMUNJOM** (1st Battalion, 9th Infantry cited)

French Croix de Guerre with Palm, World War I, Streamer embroidered **AISNE-MARNE** (9th Infantry cited)

French Croix de Guerre with Palm, World War I, Streamer embroidered **MEUSE-ARGONNE** (9th Infantry cited)

French Croix de Guerre with Palm, World War I, Streamer embroidered **CHATEAU THIERRY** (9th Infantry cited)

French Croix de Guerre, World War I, Fourragere (9th Infantry cited)

Republic of Korea Presidential Unit Citation, Streamer embroidered **NAKTONG RIVER LINE** (9th Infantry cited)

Republic of Korea Presidential Unit Citation, Streamer embroidered **KOREA** (9th Infantry cited)

Luxembourg Croix de Guerre, Streamer embroidered **LUXEMBOURG** (9th Infantry cited)

Belgian Fourragere 1940 (9th Infantry cited)

Cited in the Order of the Day of the Belgian Army for action in the **ARDENNES** (9th Infantry cited)

Cited in the Order of the Day of the Belgian Army for action
at **ELSENBORN CREST** (9th Infantry cited)

3D BATTALION, 9TH INFANTRY
(Manchu)

LINEAGE

1855 Constituted 3 March as Company C, 9th Infantry, Regular Army; organized 26 March at Fort Monroe, VA

1861 A new company constituted 3 May as Company C, 2d Battalion, 18th Infantry, Regular Army; organized in October at Camp Thomas, OH

1866 Reorganized and redesignated 21 September as Company C, 27th Infantry

1869 Consolidated in June with Company C, 9th Infantry, to form Company C, 9th Infantry

1917 Assigned 22 September to 2d Division

1918 A new company constituted 23 July as Headquarters and Headquarters Company, 405th Infantry, an element of the 102d Division National Army; demobilized 30 November

Company lineage differs from that of 9th Infantry from its constitution to 1 June 1959 consolidation as follows:

1921 *Reconstituted 24 June in the Organized Reserves as an element of the 102d Division organized in November at Little Rock, AK*

1942 *Ordered into active military service 15 September and reorganized at Camp Maxey, TX*

1946 *Inactivated 1 June in Germany and activated 31 October in the Organized Reserves at Minneapolis, MN*

1947 *Inactivated 3 January and activated 24 January at St. Louis, MO*

1957 *Company C, 9th Infantry, inactivated 20 June in Alaska and relieved from assignment to 2d Infantry Division; redesignated Headquarters and Headquarters Company, 3d Battle Group, 9th Infantry*

1959 Withdrawn 11 May from Regular Army, allotted to Army Reserve, and assigned to 102d Infantry Division; activated 1 June and consolidated with Headquarters and Headquarters Company, Battle Group 3, 405th Infantry, to form Headquarters and Headquarters Company, 3d Battle Group, 9th Infantry

1963 Reorganized and redesignated 1 April as 3d Battalion, 9th Infantry

1965 Inactivated 31 December at Quincy, IL

CAMPAIGN PARTICIPATION

Civil War
  Murfreesborough
  Chickamauga
  Chattanooga
  Atlanta
  Mississippi 1862
  Kentucky 1862
  Tennessee 1863
  Georgia 1864

Indian Wars
  Little Big Horn
  Washington 1856
  Washington 1858
  Wyoming 1866
  Wyoming 1867

War With Spain
  Santiago

China Relief Expedition
  Tientsin
  Yang-tsun
  Peking

Philippine Insurrection
  San Isidro
  Zapote River
  Malolos

  Tarlac
  Luzon 1899
  Luzon 1900
  Samar 1901

World War I
  Aisne
  Aisne-Marne
  St. Mihiel
  Meuse-Argonne
  Lorraine 1918
  Ile de France 1918

World War II
  Normandy (with arrowhead)
  Northern France
  Rhineland
  Ardennes-Alsace
  Central Europe

Korean War
  UN defensive
  UN offensive
  CCF intervention
  First UN counteroffensive
  CCF spring offensive
  UN summer–fall offensive

Second Korean winter
Korea, summer–fall 1952
Third Korean winter
Korea, summer 1953

DECORATIONS

Presidential Unit Citation (Army), Streamer embroidered **BREST, FRANCE**

Presidential Unit Citation (Army), Streamer embroidered **ROER RIVER** (405th Infantry cited)

Presidential Unit Citation (Army), Streamer embroidered **SIEGFRIED LINE**

Presidential Unit Citation (Army), Streamer embroidered **ARDENNES** (1st Battalion, 9th Infantry cited)

Presidential Unit Citation (Army), Streamer embroidered **HONGCHON** (2d Infantry Division cited)

Presidential Unit Citation (Navy), Streamer embroidered **HWACHON RESERVOIR** (1st Battalion, 9th Infantry cited)

Navy Unit Commendation, Streamer embroidered **PANMUNJOM** (1st Battalion, 9th Infantry cited)

French Croix de Guerre with Palm, World War I, Streamer embroidered **AISNE-MARNE** (9th Infantry cited)

French Croix de Guerre with Palm, World War I, Streamer embroidered **MEUSE-ARGONNE** (9th Infantry cited)

French Croix de Guerre with Palm, World War I, Streamer embroidered **CHATEAU THIERRY** (9th Infantry cited)

French Croix de Guerre, World War I, Fourragere (9th Infantry cited)

Republic of Korea Presidential Unit Citation, Streamer embroidered **NAKTONG RIVER LINE** (9th Infantry cited)

Republic of Korea Presidential Unit Citation, Streamer embroidered **KOREA** (9th Infantry cited)

Luxembourg Croix de Guerre, Streamer embroidered **LUXEMBOURG** (9th Infantry cited)

Belgian Fourragere 1940 (9th Infantry cited)

Cited in the Order of the Day of the Belgian Army for action in the **ARDENNES** (9th Infantry cited)

Cited in the Order of the Day of the Belgian Army for action at **ELSENBORN CREST** (9th Infantry cited)

4TH BATTALION, 9TH INFANTRY
(Manchu)

LINEAGE

1855   Constituted 3 March as Company D, 9th Infantry, Regular Army; organized 17 March at Fort Monroe, VA

1861   A new company constituted 3 May as Company D, 2d Battalion, 18th Infantry, Regular Army; organized in October at Camp Thomas, OH

1866   Reorganized and redesignated 21 September as Company D, 27th Infantry

1869   Consolidated in June with Company D, 9th Infantry; consolidated unit designated Company D, 9th Infantry

1917   Assigned 22 September to 2d Division

1957   Inactivated 20 June in Alaska and relieved from assignment to 2d Division; redesignated as Headquarters and Headquarters Company, 4th Battle Group, 9th Infantry

1963   Activated 25 January in Alaska and assigned 20 May to the 171st Infantry Brigade; reorganized

and redesignated 1 July as 4th Battalion, 9th Infantry

1966   Relieved 14 January from assignment to 171st Infantry Brigade and assigned to 25th Infantry Brigade

CAMPAIGN PARTICIPATION

Civil War

Murfreesborough
Chickamauga
Chattanooga
Atlanta
Mississippi 1862
Kentucky 1862
Tennessee 1863
Georgia 1864

Indian Wars

Little Big Horn

Washington 1856
Washington 1858
Wyoming 1866
Wyoming 1867

War With Spain

Santiago

China Relief Expedition

Tientsin
Yang-tsun
Peking

Philippine Insurrection

San Isidro
Zapote River
Malolos
Tarlac
Luzon 1899
Luzon 1900
Samar 1901

World War I

Aisne
Aisne-Marne
St. Mihiel
Meuse-Argonne
Lorraine 1918
Ile de France 1918

World War II

Normandy (with arrowhead)
Northern France
Rhineland
Ardennes-Alsace
Central Europe

Korean War

UN defensive
UN offensive
CCF intervention

First UN counteroffensive
CCF spring offensive
UN summer–fall offensive
Second Korean winter
Korea, summer–fall 1952
Third Korean winter
Korea, summer 1953

Vietnam

Counteroffensive
Counteroffensive, Phase II
Counteroffensive, Phase III
Tet Counteroffensive
Counteroffensive, Phase IV
Counteroffensive, Phase V
Counteroffensive, Phase VI
Tet 69 Counteroffensive
Summer–Fall 1969
Winter–Spring 1970
Sanctuary Counteroffensive
Counteroffensive, Phase VII

DECORATIONS

Presidential Unit Citation (Army), Streamer embroidered **BREST, FRANCE**

Presidential Unit Citation (Army), Streamer embroidered **SIEGFRIED LINE**

Presidential Unit Citation (Army), Streamer embroidered **ARDENNES** (1st Battalion, 9th Infantry cited)

Presidential Unit Citation (Army), Streamer embroidered **HONGCHON** (2d Infantry Division cited)

Presidential Unit Citation (Navy), Streamer embroidered **HWACHON RESERVOIR** (1st Battalion, 9th Infantry cited)

Navy Unit Commendation, Streamer embroidered **PAN-MUNJOM** (1st Battalion, 9th Infantry cited)

French Croix de Guerre with Palm, World War I, Streamer embroidered **AISNE-MARNE** (9th Infantry cited)

French Croix de Guerre with Palm, World War I, Streamer embroidered **MEUSE-ARGONNE** (9th Infantry cited)

French Croix de Guerre with Palm, World War I, Streamer embroidered **CHATEAU THIERRY** (9th Infantry cited)

French Croix de Guerre, World War I, Fourragere (9th Infantry cited)

Republic of Korea Presidential Unit Citation, Streamer embroidered **NAKTONG RIVER LINE** (9th Infantry cited)

Republic of Korea Presidential Unit Citation, Streamer embroidered **KOREA** (9th Infantry cited)

Luxembourg Croix de Guerre, Streamer embroidered **LUXEMBOURG** (9th Infantry cited)

Belgian Fourragere 1940 (9th Infantry cited)

Cited in the Order of the Day of the Belgian Army for action in the **ARDENNES** (9th Infantry cited)

Cited in the Order of the Day of the Belgian Army for action at **ELSENBORN CREST** (9th Infantry cited)

Vietnamese Cross of Gallantry with Palm, Streamer embroidered **VIETNAM 1966–1968**

5TH BATTALION, 9TH INFANTRY
(Manchu)

LINEAGE

1855	Constituted 3 March as Company E, 9th Infantry; organized 17 March at Fort Monroe, VA
1861	A new company constituted 3 May as Company E, 2d Battalion, 18th Infantry; organized in October at Camp Thomas, OH
1866	Reorganized and redesignated 21 September as Company E, 27th Infantry
1869	Consolidated in June with Company E, 9th Infantry; consolidated unit designated Company E, 9th Infantry

1917	Assigned 22 September to 2d Division
1957	Inactivated 20 June in Alaska and relieved from assignment to 2d Infantry Division; redesignated as Headquarters and Headquarters Company, 5th Battle Group, 9th Infantry
1963	Redesignated 26 March as Headquarters and Headquarters Company, 5th Battalion, 9th Infantry; withdrawn from Regular Army and allotted to Army Reserve; assigned to 102d Infantry Division; Battalion activated 1 April with Headquarters at Danville, IL
1965	Inactivated 31 December

CAMPAIGN PARTICIPATION

Civil War

Murfreesborough
Chickamauga
Chattanooga
Atlanta
Mississippi 1862
Kentucky 1862
Tennessee 1863
Georgia 1864

Indian Wars

Little Big Horn
Washington 1856
Washington 1858
Wyoming 1866
Wyoming 1867

War With Spain

Santiago

China Relief Expedition

Tientsin
Yang-tsun
Peking

Philippine Insurrection

San Isidro
Zapote River
Malolos
Tarlac
Luzon 1899

Luzon 1900
Samar 1901

World War I

Aisne
Aisne-Marne
St. Mihiel
Meuse-Argonne
Lorraine 1918
Ile de France 1918

World War II

Normandy (with arrowhead)
Northern France
Rhineland
Ardennes-Alsace
Central Europe

Korean War

UN defensive
UN offensive
CCF intervention
First UN counteroffensive
CCF spring offensive
UN summer–fall offensive
Second Korean winter
Korea, summer–fall 1952
Third Korean winter
Korea, summer 1953

DECORATIONS

Presidential Unit Citation (Army), Streamer embroidered **BREST, FRANCE**

Presidential Unit Citation (Army), Streamer embroidered **SIEGFRIED LINE**

Presidential Unit Citation (Army), Streamer embroidered **ARDENNES**

Presidential Unit Citation (Army), Streamer embroidered **HONGCHON** (2d Infantry Division cited)

Presidential Unit Citation (Navy), Streamer embroidered **HWACHON RESERVOIR**

Navy Unit Commendation, Streamer embroidered **PANMUNJOM**

French Croix de Guerre with Palm, World War I, Streamer embroidered **AISNE-MARNE** (9th Infantry cited)

French Croix de Guerre with Palm, World War I, Streamer embroidered **MEUSE-ARGONNE** (9th Infantry cited)

French Croix de Guerre with Palm, World War I, Streamer embroidered **CHATEAU THIERRY** (9th Infantry cited)

French Croix de Guerre, World War I, Fourragere (9th Infantry cited)

Republic of Korea Presidential Unit Citation, Streamer embroidered **NAKTONG RIVER LINE** (9th Infantry cited)

Republic of Korea Presidential Unit Citation, Streamer embroidered **KOREA** (9th Infantry cited)

Luxembourg Croix de Guerre, Streamer embroidered **LUXEMBOURG** (9th Infantry cited)

Belgian Fourragere 1940 (9th Infantry cited)

Cited in the Order of the Day of the Belgian Army for action in the **ARDENNES** (9th Infantry cited)

Cited in the Order of the Day of the Belgian Army for action at **ELSENBORN CREST** (9th Infantry cited)

6TH BATTALION, 9TH INFANTRY
(Manchu)

LINEAGE

1855   Constituted 3 March as Company F, 9th Infantry, Regular Army; organized 22 May at Fort Monroe, VA

1861   A new company constituted 3 May as Company F, 2d Battalion, 18th Infantry, Regular Army; organized in October at Camp Thomas, OH

1866   Reorganized and redesignated 21 September as Company F, 27th Infantry

1869   Consolidated in June with Company F, 9th Infantry; consolidated unit designated Company F, 9th Infantry

1917   Assigned 22 September to 2d Division

1957   Inactivated 20 June in Alaska and relieved from assignment to 2d Division; redesignated as Headquarters and Headquarters Company, 6th Battle Group, 9th Infantry

1965   Redesignated 17 December as Headquarters and Headquarters Company, 6th Battalion, 9th Infantry; assigned to 171st Infantry Brigade and Battalion activated 20 December in Alaska

CAMPAIGN PARTICIPATION

Civil War
Murfreesborough
Chickamauga
Chattanooga
Atlanta
Mississippi 1862
Kentucky 1862
Tennessee 1863
Georgia 1864

Indian Wars
Little Big Horn
Washington 1856
Washington 1858
Wyoming 1866
Wyoming 1867

War With Spain
Santiago

China Relief Expedition
Tientsin
Yang-tsun
Peking

Philippine Insurrection
San Isidro
Zapote River
Malolos
Tarlac
Luzon 1899
Luzon 1900
Samar 1901

World War I
Aisne
Aisne-Marne
St. Mihiel
Meuse-Argonne
Lorraine 1918
Ile de France 1918

World War II
Normandy (with arrowhead)
Northern France
Rhineland
Ardennes-Alsace
Central Europe

Korean War
UN defensive
UN offensive
CCF intervention
First UN counteroffensive
CCF spring offensive
UN summer–fall offensive
Second Korean winter
Korea, summer–fall 1952
Third Korean winter
Korea, summer 1953

DECORATIONS

Presidential Unit Citation (Army), Streamer embroidered **BREST, FRANCE**

Presidential Unit Citation (Army), Streamer embroidered **SIEGFRIED LINE** (2d Battalion, 9th Infantry cited)

Presidential Unit Citation (Army), Streamer embroidered **ARDENNES**

Presidential Unit Citation (Navy), Streamer embroidered **HONGCHON** (2d Infantry Division cited)

Presidential Unit Citation (Navy), Streamer embroidered **HWACHON RESERVOIR**

Navy Unit Commendation, Streamer embroidered **PANMUNJOM**

French Croix de Guerre with Gilt Star, World War I, Streamer embroidered **ILE DE FRANCE** (Company F, 9th Infantry cited)

French Croix de Guerre with Palm, World War I, Streamer embroidered **AISNE-MARNE** (9th Infantry cited)

French Croix de Guerre with Palm, World War I, Streamer embroidered **MEUSE-ARGONNE** (9th Infantry cited)

French Croix de Guerre with Palm, World War I, Streamer embroidered **CHATEAU THIERRY** (9th Infantry cited)

French Croix de Guerre, World War I, Fourragere (9th Infantry cited)

Republic of Korea Presidential Unit Citation, Streamer embroidered **NAKTONG RIVER LINE** (9th Infantry cited)

Republic of Korea Presidential Unit Citation, Streamer embroidered **KOREA** (9th Infantry cited)

Luxembourg Croix de Guerre, Streamer embroidered **LUXEMBOURG** (9th Infantry cited)

Belgian Fourragere 1940 (9th Infantry cited)

Cited in the Order of the Day of the Belgian Army for action in the **ARDENNES** (9th Infantry cited)

Cited in the Order of the Day of the Belgian Army for action at **ELSENBORN CREST** (9th Infantry cited)

10TH INFANTRY

BADGE (Regimental badge in lieu of coat of arms)

Symbolism: The Roman numeral "X" signifies the numerical designation of the regiment; the sword is representative of the dress sabers carried by the officers of the regiment when it was organized; the circular band is indicative of the knapsack straps and waist belts, like those of the French *chasseurs-à-pied*, worn by the 10th Infantry in the late 1850's. The motto is taken from an address made by Colonel Edmund B. Alexander, first colonel of the regiment, upon the occasion of the presentation of the regimental colors at Carlisle Barracks, Pennsylvania, in September 1855. The Roman numerals "MDCCCLV" signify the year the regiment was constituted and organized.

DISTINCTIVE INSIGNIA

The distinctive insignia is the badge of the regiment.

LINEAGE

1855	Constituted 3 March as the 10th Infantry, Regular Army; organized in April at Carlisle Barracks, PA
1861	A new company constituted 3 May as 2d Battalion, 17th Infantry, Regular Army; organized in June at Fort Preble, ME
1866	Reorganized and redesignated 16 December as 26th Infantry
1869	Consolidated June–July with 10th Infantry to form 10th Infantry
1918	Assigned 5 July to 14th Division
1919	Relieved from assignment to 14th Division
1923	Assigned 24 March to the 5th Division
1946	Inactivated 20 September at Camp Campbell, KY
1947	Activated 15 July at Fort Jackson, SC
1950	Inactivated 30 April
1951	Activated 1 March at Indiantown Gap, PA
1953	Inactivated 1 September
1954	Activated 25 May at Galingen, Germany
1957	Relieved 1 June from assignment to the 5th Infantry Division and reorganized as a parent regiment under CARS

CAMPAIGN PARTICIPATION

Civil War

Peninsula
Manassas
Antietam
Fredericksburg
Chancellorsville
Gettysburg
Wilderness
Spotsylvania
Cold Harbor
Petersburg
New Mexico 1862
Virginia 1862
Virginia 1863

Indian Wars

Comanches
Apaches

War With Spain

Santiago

Philippine Insurrection

Without Inscription

World War II

Normandy
Northern France
Rhineland
Ardennes-Alsace
Central Europe

DECORATIONS

French Croix de Guerre with Palm, World War II, Streamer embroidered **MOSELLE RIVER** (10th Infantry cited)

1ST BATTALION, 10TH INFANTRY

LINEAGE

1855	Constituted 3 March as Company A, 10th Infantry, Regular Army; organized at Carlisle Barracks, PA
1861	A new company constituted 3 May as Company A, 2d Battalion, 17th Infantry
1862	Organized in June at Fort Preble, ME
1866	Reorganized and redesignated 16 December as Company A, 26th Infantry
1869	Consolidated 10 June with Company A, 10th Infantry; consolidated unit designated Company A, 10th Infantry
	Company lineage follows that of 10th Infantry from 1869 consolidation to 1923 assignment to 5th Division
1929	Inactivated 31 October at Fort Thomas, KY
1933	Activated 1 October at Fort Hayes, OH
1946	Inactivated 20 September at Camp Campbell, KY
	Company lineage follows that for 10th Infantry from 1946 inactivation to 1954 reactivation in Galingen, Germany
1957	Reorganized and redesignated 1 June as Headquarters and Headquarters Company, 1st Battle Group, 10th Infantry; relieved from assignment to 5th Infantry Division
1961	Inactivated 25 April at Fort Ord, CA

1962	Redesignated 3 February as the 1st Battalion, 10th Infantry and activated at Fort Carson, CO; assigned to 5th Infantry Division
1970	Relieved 15 December from assignment to 5th Infantry Division and assigned to 4th Infantry Division

CAMPAIGN PARTICIPATION

Civil War

Peninsula
Manassas
Antietam
Fredericksburg
Chancellorsville
Gettysburg
Wilderness
Spotsylvania
Cold Harbor
Petersburg
New Mexico 1862
Virginia 1862
Virginia 1863

Indian Wars

Comanches
Apaches
New Mexico 1860
New Mexico 1861

War With Spain

Santiago

Philippine Insurrection

Mindanao

World War II

Normandy
Northern France
Rhineland
Ardennes-Alsace
Central Europe

DECORATIONS

French Croix de Guerre with Palm, World War II, Streamer embroidered **MOSELLE RIVER** (10th Infantry cited)

2D BATTALION, 10TH INFANTRY

LINEAGE

1855	Constituted 3 March as Company B, 10th Infantry, Regular Army; organized at Carlisle Barracks, PA
1861	A new company constituted 3 May as Company B, 2d Battalion, 17th Infantry, Regular Army
1862	Organized in June at Fort Preble, ME
1866	Reorganized and redesignated 16 December as Company B, 26th Infantry
1869	Consolidated 23 June with Company B, 10th Infantry; consolidated unit designated Company B, 10th Infantry
	Company lineage follows that of 10th Infantry from 1869 consolidation to 1923 assignment to 5th Division
1929	Inactivated 31 October at Fort Thomas, KY
1933	Activated 1 October at Fort Hayes, OH
1946	Inactivated 20 September at Camp Campbell, KY
1947	Activated 25 July at Fort Jackson, SC
1950	Inactivated 30 April
1951	Activated 1 March at Indiantown Gap Military Reservation, PA
1953	Inactivated 1 September
1954	Activated 25 May at Galingen, Germany
1957	Inactivated 1 June at Fort Ord, CA and relieved from assignment to 5th Infantry Division; redesignated 1 July as Headquarters and Headquarters Company, 2d Battle Group, 10th Infantry and assigned to 10th Infantry Division and activated in Germany
1958	Inactivated 14 June at Fort Benning, GA, and relieved from assignment to 10th Infantry Division
1960	Activated 23 April at Fort William D. Davis, Canal Zone
1962	Reorganized and redesignated 19 February as 2d Battalion, 10th Infantry, and assigned to 5th Infantry Division
1970	Relieved 15 December from assignment to 5th Infantry Division and assigned to 4th Infantry Division

CAMPAIGN PARTICIPATION

Civil War

Peninsula
Manassas
Antietam
Fredericksburg
Chancellorsville
Gettysburg
Wilderness
Spotsylvania

Cold Harbor
Petersburg
New Mexico 1862
Virginia 1862
Virginia 1863

Indian Wars

Comanches
Apaches

War With Spain

Santiago

Philippine Insurrection

Without inscription

World War II

Normandy
Northern France
Rhineland
Ardennes-Alsace
Central Europe

DECORATIONS

French Croix de Guerre with Palm, World War II, Streamer embroidered **MOSELLE RIVER** (10th Infantry cited)

3D BATTALION, 10TH INFANTRY

LINEAGE

1855	Constituted 3 May as Company C, 10th Infantry, Regular Army; organized at Carlisle Barracks, PA
1861	A new company constituted 3 May as Company C, 2d Battalion, 17th Infantry, Regular Army
1862	Organized in June at Fort Preble, ME
1866	Reorganized and redesignated 16 December as Company C, 26th Infantry
1869	Consolidated 25 July with Company C, 10th Infantry; consolidated unit designated Company C, 10th Infantry
1917	A new company constituted 5 August as Headquarters and Headquarters Company, 1st Battalion, 331st Infantry, an element of the 83d Division, National Army; organized 30 August at Camp Sherman, OH

Company lineage differs from that of 10th Infantry from its constitution to 20 March 1959 consolidation as follows:

1919	Demobilized 9 February at Camp Sherman, OH
1921	Reconstituted 24 June in the Organized Reserves as an element of the 83d Division; organized in November at Cleveland, OH
1942	Ordered into active military service 15 August and reorganized at Camp Atterbury, IN
1946	Inactivated 30 March at Camp Kilmer, NJ and activated 26 December in the Organized Reserves at Columbus, OH
1959	Consolidated 20 March with Headquarters and Headquarters Company, 3d Battle Group, 10th Infantry to form Headquarters and Headquarters Company, 3d Battle Group, 10th Infantry; Battle Group activated 20 March
1963	Reorganized and redesignated 15 April as 3d Battalion, 10th Infantry
1965	Inactivated 31 December at Cleveland, OH
1967	Withdrawn 10 May from Army Reserve and allotted to Regular Army; relieved from assignment to 83d Infantry Division and assigned to 5th Infantry Division; activated 26 May at Fort Carson, CO
1970	Inactivated at Fort Carson, CO

CAMPAIGN PARTICIPATION

Civil War

Peninsula
Manassas
Antietam
Fredericksburg
Chancellorsville
Gettysburg
Wilderness
Spotsylvania
Cold Harbor
Petersburg
New Mexico 1862
Virginia 1862
Virginia 1863

Indian Wars

Comanches
Apaches

War With Spain

Santiago

Philippine Insurrection

Without inscription

World War I

Without inscription

World War II
Normandy
Northern France
Rhineland
Ardennes-Alsace
Central Europe

DECORATIONS

French Croix de Guerre with Palm, World War II, Streamer embroidered **MOSELLE RIVER** (10th Infantry cited)

4TH BATTALION, 10TH INFANTRY

LINEAGE

1855	Constituted 3 March as Company D, 10th Infantry, Regular Army; organized at Carlisle Barracks, PA
1861	A new company constituted 3 May as Company D, 2d Battalion, 17th Infantry, Regular Army
1862	Organized in June at Fort Preble, ME
1866	Reorganized and redesignated 16 December as Company D, 26th Infantry
1869	Consolidated 25 July with Company D, 10th Infantry; consolidated unit designated Company D, 10th Infantry

Company lineage follows that of 10th Infantry from 1869 consolidation to 1923 assignment to 5th Division

1923	Assigned 24 March to 5th Division
1929	Inactivated 31 October at Fort Thomas, KY
1933	Activated 1 October at Fort Hayes, OH
1946	Inactivated 20 September at Camp Campbell, KY
1947	Activated 15 July at Fort Jackson, SC
1950	Inactivated 30 April
1951	Activated 1 March at Indiantown Gap Military Reservation, PA
1953	Inactivated 1 September
1954	Activated 25 May at Galingen, Germany
1957	Inactivated 1 June at Fort Ord, CA and relieved from assignment to 5th Infantry Division; redesignated Headquarters and Headquarters Company, 4th Battle Group, 10th Infantry
1962	Activated 19 February at Fort William D. Davis, Canal Zone; reorganized and redesignated 1 October as 4th Battalion, 10th Infantry, and assigned to 193d Infantry Brigade

CAMPAIGN PARTICIPATION

Civil War
Peninsula
Manassas
Antietam
Fredericksburg
Chancellorsville
Gettysburg
Wilderness
Spotsylvania
Cold Harbor
Petersburg
New Mexico 1862
Virginia 1862
Virginia 1863

Indian Wars
Comanches
Apaches

War With Spain
Santiago

Philippine Insurrection
Without inscription

World War II
Normandy
Northern France
Rhineland
Ardennes-Alsace
Central Europe

DECORATIONS

French Croix de Guerre with Palm, World War II, Streamer embroidered **MOSELLE RIVER** (10th Infantry cited)

5TH BATTALION, 10TH INFANTRY

LINEAGE

1855   Constituted 3 March as Company E, 10th Infantry, Regular Army; organized at Carlisle Barracks, PA

1861   A new company constituted 3 May as Company E, 2d Battalion, 17th Infantry, Regular Army

1862   Organized in June at Fort Preble, ME

1866   Reorganized and redesignated 16 December as Company E, 26th Infantry

1869   Consolidated 25 July with Company E, 10th Infantry, to form Company E, 10th Infantry

1918   Assigned 5 July to 14th Division

1919   Relieved in February from assignment to 14th Division

1921   Inactivated 16 December at Camp Sherman, OH

1922   Activated 7 June at Camp Knox, KY

1923   Assigned 24 March to 5th Division

1946   Inactivated 20 September at Camp Campbell, KY

1947   Activated 15 July at Fort Jackson, SC

1950   Inactivated 30 April

1951   Activated 1 March at Indiantown Gap Military Reservation, PA

1953   Inactivated 1 September

1954   Activated 25 May at Galingen, Germany

1957   Reorganized and redesignated 1 June as Company E, 1st Battle Group, 10th Infantry, and relieved from assignment to 5th Infantry Division

1961   Inactivated 25 April at Fort Ord, CA, and redesignated as Headquarters and Headquarters Company, 5th Battle Group, 10th Infantry

1969   Redesignated 15 November as Headquarters and Headquarters Company, 5th Battalion, 10th Infantry, and activated as an element of the 5th Infantry Division

1970   Inactivated at Fort Carson, CO

CAMPAIGN PARTICIPATION

Civil War
Peninsula
Manassas
Antietam
Fredericksburg
Chancellorsville
Gettysburg
Wilderness
Spotsylvania
Cold Harbor
Petersburg
New Mexico 1862
Virginia 1862
Virginia 1863

Indian Wars
Comanches
Apaches
Nebraska 1855

War With Spain
Santiago

Philippine Insurrection
Without inscription

World War II
Normandy
Northern France
Rhineland
Ardennes-Alsace
Central Europe

DECORATIONS

French Croix de Guerre with Palm, World War II, Streamer embroidered **MOSELLE RIVER** (10th Infantry cited)

11TH INFANTRY

COAT OF ARMS

Motto: *Semper Fidelis* (Always Faithful)

Symbolism: The shield is blue, the infantry color, and carries the castle from the arms of Spain for the War with Spain and Satanta's "arrow" for the regiment's campaign against the Comanches, Cheyennes, and Kiowas in 1874. Satanta was a noted Kiowa Indian chief whose "arrow" was really a spear with feathers on the end and a handle. The crossed kampilan and bolo show engagements against the Moros of Mindanao and the Filipinos of the Visayas, respectively. A chief of honorable augmentation bearing the cross of the ancient Lords of Dun commemorates the crossing of the Meuse River near Dun during World War I. The embattled partition represents the siege of Chattanooga in 1863.

During the Civil War the predecessors of the 11th Infantry served in the 1st Division, XIV Corps and the 2d Division, V Corps, whose badges were a red acorn and a white Maltese cross, respectively. In World War I and regiment was an element of the 5th Division, with a red lozenge as the shoulder sleeve insignia. A combination of these three insignia forms the crest.

DISTINCTIVE INSIGNIA

The distinctive insignia is the shield of the coat of arms.

LINEAGE

1861	Constituted 3 May as 2d Battalion, 15th Infantry and 3d Battalion, 11th Infantry
1862	2d Battalion, 15th Infantry organized 6 May at Newport Barracks, KY
1863	3d Battalion, 11th Infantry organized 20 August at Fort Independence, MA
1866	2d Battalion, 15th Infantry reorganized and re-designated 1 December as 24th Infantry
	3d Battalion, 11th Infantry reorganized and re-designated 1 December as 29th Infantry
1869	24th Infantry and 29th Infantry consolidated 25 April to form 11th Infantry
1917	Assigned 17 November to 5th Division
1946	Inactivated 20 September at Camp Campbell, KY
1947	Activated 15 July at Fort Jackson, SC
1950	Inactivated 30 April
1951	Activated 1 March at Indiantown Gap Military Reservation, PA
1953	Inactivated 1 September
1954	Activated 25 May in Germany
1957	Relieved 1 June from assignment to 5th Infantry Division and reorganized as a parent regiment under CARS

CAMPAIGN PARTICIPATION

Civil War

Shiloh
Murfreesborough
Chickamauga
Chattanooga
Atlanta
Mississippi 1862
Kentucky 1862
Tennessee 1863
Georgia 1864

Indian Wars

Comanches

War With Spain

Puerto Rico

Philippine Insurrection

Mindanao

World War I

St. Mihiel
Meuse-Argonne
Alsace 1918
Lorraine 1918

World War II

Normandy
Northern France
Rhineland
Ardennes-Alsace
Central Europe

Vietnam

Counteroffensive, Phase V
Counteroffensive, Phase VI
Tet 69 Counteroffensive
Summer-Fall 1969
Winter-Spring 1970
Sanctuary Counteroffensive
Counteroffensive, Phase VII
Consolidation I

DECORATIONS

None.

1ST BATTALION, 11TH INFANTRY

LINEAGE

1861	Constituted 3 May as Company A, 2d Battalion, 15th Infantry, and Company A, 3d Battalion, 11th Infantry
1862	Company A, 2d Battalion, 15th Infantry organized 6 May at Newport Barracks, KY
1863	Company A, 3d Battalion, 11th Infantry organized 20 August at Fort Independence, MA
1866	Company A, 2d Battalion, 15th Infantry reorganized and redesignated 1 December as Company A, 24th Infantry
	Company A, 3d Battalion, 11th Infantry reorganized and redesignated 1 December as Company A, 29th Infantry
1869	Company A, 24th Infantry and Company A, 19th Infantry consolidated 25 April to form Company A, 11th Infantry
1917	Assigned 17 November to 5th Division
1946	Inactivated 20 September at Camp Campbell, KY
1947	Activated 15 July at Fort Jackson, SC
1950	Inactivated 30 April

1951	Activated 1 March at Indiantown Gap Military Reservation, PA
1953	Inactivated 1 September
1954	Activated 25 May in Germany
1957	Inactivated 1 June at Fort Ord, CA
1958	Redesignated 4 March as Headquarters and Headquarters Company, 1st Battle Group, 11th Infantry and relieved from assignment to 5th Infantry Division; Battle Group activated 14 June at Fort Benning, GA as an element of 2d Infantry Division
1962	Reorganized and redesignated 19 February as 1st Battalion, 11th Infantry and relieved from assignment to 2d Infantry Division; assigned to 5th Infantry Division

CAMPAIGN PARTICIPATION

Civil War

Shiloh
Murfreesborough
Chickamauga
Chattanooga
Atlanta
Mississippi 1862
Kentucky 1862

Tennessee 1863
Georgia 1864

Indian Wars

Comanches

War With Spain

Puerto Rico

Philippine Insurrection

Mindanao

World War I

St. Mihiel
Meuse-Argonne
Alsace 1918
Lorraine 1918

World War II

Normandy
Northern France
Rhineland
Ardennes-Alsace
Central Europe

Vietnam

Counteroffensive,
   Phase V
Counteroffensive,
   Phase VI
Tet 69 Counteroffensive
Summer-Fall 1969
Winter-Spring 1970
Sanctuary
   Counteroffensive
Counteroffensive,
   Phase VII
Consolidation I

DECORATIONS

Vietnamese Cross of Gallantry with Palm, Streamer embroidered **VIETNAM 1968** (1st Battalion, 11th Infantry cited)

2D BATTALION, 11TH INFANTRY

LINEAGE

1861	Constituted 3 May as Company B, 2d Battalion, 15th Infantry, and Company B, 3d Battalion, 11th Infantry
1862	Company B, 2d Battalion, 15th Infantry organized 6 May at Newport Barracks, KY
1863	Company B, 3d Battalion, 11th Infantry organized 20 August at Fort Independence, MA
1866	Company B, 2d Battalion, 15th Infantry reorganized and redesignated 1 December as Company B, 24th Infantry
	Company B, 3d Battalion, 11th Infantry reorganized and redesignated 1 December as Company B, 29th Infantry
1869	Company B, 24th Infantry, and Company B, 29th Infantry consolidated 25 April to form Company B, 11th Infantry
1917	Assigned 17 November to 5th Division
1946	Inactivated 20 September at Camp Campbell, KY
1947	Activated 15 July at Fort Jackson, SC
1950	Inactivated 30 April
1951	Activated 1 March at Indiantown Gap Military Reservation, PA
1953	Inactivated 1 September
1954	Activated 25 May in Germany

1957	Inactivated 1 June at Fort Ord, CA and relieved from assignment to 5th Infantry Division; redesignated as Headquarters and Headquarters Company, 2d Battle Group, 11th Infantry
1962	Redesignated 19 February as Headquarters and Headquarters Company, 2d Battalion, 11th Infantry and assigned to 5th Infantry Division; activated at Fort Carson, CO
1970	Relieved 15 December from assignment to 5th Infantry Division and assigned to 4th Infantry Division

CAMPAIGN PARTICIPATION

Civil War

Shiloh
Murfreesborough
Chickamauga
Chattanooga
Atlanta
Mississippi 1862

Kentucky 1862
Tennessee 1863
Georgia 1864

Indian Wars

Comanches

War With Spain

Puerto Rico

Philippine Insurrection

Mindanao

World War I

St. Mihiel
Meuse-Argonne
Alsace 1918
Lorraine 1918

World War II

Normandy
Northern France
Rhineland
Ardennes-Alsace
Central Europe

DECORATIONS

None.

3D BATTALION, 11TH INFANTRY

LINEAGE

1861	Constituted 3 May as Company C, 2d Battalion, 15th Infantry, and Company C, 3d Battalion, 11th Infantry
1862	Company C, 2d Battalion, 15th Infantry organized 19 May at Newport Barracks, KY
1863	Company C, 3d Battalion, 11th Infantry organized 20 August at Fort Independence, MA
1866	Company C, 2d Battalion, 15th Infantry reorganized and redesignated 1 December as Company C, 24th Infantry
	Company C, 3d Battalion, 11th Infantry reorganized and redesignated 1 December as Company C, 29th Infantry
1869	Company C, 24th Infantry, and Company C, 29th Infantry consolidated 25 April to form Company C, 11th Infantry
	Company lineage follows that of 11th Infantry from 1869 consolidation to 1959 consolidation

1917	A new company constituted 5 August as Headquarters and Headquarters Company, 336th Infantry, an element of the 84th Division National Army organized 25 August at Camp Zachary Taylor, KY
	Company lineage differs from that of 11th Infantry from its constitution to 1959 consolidation as follows:
1919	*Demobilized 18 February*
1921	*Reconstituted 24 June in the Organized Reserves as an element of the 84th Division; organized in November at Culver, IN*
1942	*Inactivated 30 January and relieved from assignment to 84th Division*
1955	*Activated 5 December in Army Reserve at Fort Thomas, KY, as an element of 83d Infantry Division*
1959	*336th Infantry and 3d Battle Group, 11th Infantry, consolidated 20 March to form Headquarters and Headquarters Group, 3d Battle Group, 11th Infantry*

1963	Reorganized and redesignated 15 April as 3d Battalion, 11th Infantry
1965	Inactivated 31 December at Cincinnati, OH
1967	Withdrawn 10 May from Army Reserve and allotted to Regular Army; relieved from assignment to 83d Infantry Division and assigned to 5th Infantry Division; activated 26 May at Fort Carson, CO
1970	Relieved 15 December from assignment to 5th Infantry Division and assigned to 4th Infantry Division

CAMPAIGN PARTICIPATION

Civil War

Shiloh
Murfreesborough
Chickamauga
Chattanooga
Atlanta

Mississippi 1862
Kentucky 1862
Tennessee 1863
Georgia 1864

Indian Wars

Comanches

War With Spain

Puerto Rico

Philippine Insurrection

Mindanao

World War I

St. Mihiel
Meuse-Argonne

Alsace 1918
Lorraine 1918

World War II

Normandy
Northern France
Rhineland
Ardennes-Alsace
Central Europe

DECORATIONS

None.

4TH BATTALION, 11TH INFANTRY

LINEAGE

1861	Constituted 3 May as Company D, 2d Battalion, 15th Infantry, and Company D, 3d Battalion, 11th Infantry
1862	Company D, 2d Battalion, 15th Infantry organized in May at Newport Barracks, KY
1863	Company D, 3d Battalion, 11th Infantry organized 20 August at Fort Independence, MA
1866	Company D, 2d Battalion, 15th Infantry reorganized and redesignated 1 December as Company D, 24th Infantry
	Company D, 3d Battalion, 11th Infantry reorganized and redesignated 1 December as Company D, 29th Infantry
1869	Company D, 24th Infantry and Company D, 29th Infantry consolidated to form Company D, 11th Infantry
1917	Assigned 17 November to 5th Division
1946	Inactivated 20 September at Camp Campbell, KY

1947	Activated 15 July at Fort Jackson, SC
1950	Inactivated 30 April
1951	Activated 1 March at Indiantown Gap Military Reservation, PA
1953	Inactivated 1 September
1954	Activated 25 May in Germany
1957	Inactivated 1 June at Fort Ord, CA and relieved from assignment to 5th Infantry Division; redesignated Headquarters and Headquarters Company, 4th Battle Group, 11th Infantry
1963	Redesignated 27 March as Headquarters and Headquarters Company, 4th Battalion, 11th Infantry and withdrawn from Regular Army; allotted to Army Reserve and assigned to 83d Infantry Division; Battalion activated 15 April with Headquarters at South Charleston, WV
1965	Inactivated 31 December

CAMPAIGN PARTICIPATION

Civil War

Shiloh
Murfreesborough
Chickamauga
Chattanooga
Atlanta
Mississippi 1862
Kentucky 1862

Tennessee 1863
Georgia 1864

Indian Wars

Comanches

War With Spain

Puerto Rico

Philippine Insurrection

Mindanao
Samar 1901

World War I

St. Mihiel
Meuse-Argonne
Alsace 1918

Lorraine 1918

World War II

Normandy
Northern France
Rhineland
Ardennes-Alsace
Central Europe

DECORATIONS

None.

5TH BATTALION, 11TH INFANTRY

LINEAGE

1861	Constituted 3 May as Company E, 2d Battalion, 15th Infantry, and Company E, 3d Battalion, 11th Infantry
1862	Company E, 2d Battalion, 11th Infantry organized in May at Newport Barracks, KY
1863	Company E, 3d Battalion, 11th Infantry organized 20 August at Fort Independence, MA
1866	Company E, 2d Battalion, 15th Infantry reorganized and redesignated 1 December as Company E, 24th Infantry
	Company E, 3d Battalion, 11th Infantry reorganized and redesignated 1 December as Company E, 29th Infantry
1869	Company E, 24th Infantry, and Company E, 29th Infantry consolidated 25 April to form Company E, 11th Infantry
1917	Assigned 17 November to 5th Division
1946	Inactivated 20 September at Camp Campbell, KY
1947	Activated 15 July at Fort Jackson, SC
1950	Inactivated 30 April
1951	Activated 1 March at Indiantown Gap Military Reservation, PA
1953	Inactivated 1 September
1954	Activated 25 May in Germany
1957	Inactivated 1 June at Fort Ord, CA and relieved from assignment to 5th Infantry Division; redesignated Headquarters and Headquarters Company, 5th Battle Group, 11th Infantry
1969	Redesignated 15 November as Headquarters and Headquarters Company, 5th Battalion, 11th Infantry and activated at Fort Carson, CO as an element of the 5th Infantry Division
1970	Inactivated 15 December

CAMPAIGN PARTICIPATION

Civil War

Shiloh
Murfreesborough
Chickamauga
Chattanooga
Atlanta
Mississippi 1862
Kentucky 1862
Tennessee 1863
Georgia 1864

Indian Wars

Comanches

War With Spain

Puerto Rico

Philippine Insurrection

Mindanao

World War I

St. Mihiel
Meuse-Argonne
Alsace 1918
Lorraine 1918

World War II

Normandy
Northern France
Rhineland
Ardennes-Alsace
Central Europe

DECORATIONS

French Croix de Guerre with Palm, World War II, Streamer embroidered **FONTAINEBLEAU** (2d Battalion, 11th Infantry cited)

12TH INFANTRY

COAT OF ARMS

Motto: *Ducti Amore Patriae* (Having Been Led by Love of Country)

Symbolism: The field is blue for infantry. This regiment took part in the Civil War; its great achievement was its first engagement at Gaines' Mill, Virginia, on 27 and 28 June 1862, where its losses were almost 50 percent. This is shown by the moline crosses which represent the iron fastening of a millstone and recall the crushing losses sustained. The wigwam stands for the Indian campaigns in which the regiment took part. The chief is for the War with Spain and the Philippine Insurrection, yellow and red being the Spanish colors, red and blue the Katipunan colors; the embattled partition line is for the capture of the blockhouse at El Caney, Cuba, and the sea lion is from the arms of the Philippine Islands.

The crest in the Spanish colors commemorates the capture of a Spanish flag at El Caney.

DISTINCTIVE INSIGNIA

The distinctive insignia is a modified version of the shield of the coat of arms.

LINEAGE

1861	Constituted 3 May as 1st Battalion, 12th Infantry, Regular Army; organized 20 October at Fort Hamilton, NY
1866	Redesignated 7 December as 12th Infantry
1917	Assigned 17 December to 8th Division
1927	Relieved 15 August from 8th Division and assigned to 4th Division
1933	Relieved 1 October from 4th Division and assigned to 8th Division
1941	Relieved 10 October from assignment to 8th Division and assigned to 4th Division
1946	Inactivated 27 February at Camp Butner, NC
1947	Activated 15 July at Fort Ord, CA
1957	Relieved 1 April from assignment to 4th Infantry Division and reorganized as a parent regiment under CARS

CAMPAIGN PARTICIPATION

Civil War

Peninsula
Manassas
Antietam
Fredericksburg
Chancellorsville
Gettysburg
Wilderness
Spotsylvania
Cold Harbor

Petersburg
Virginia 1862
Virginia 1863

Indian Wars

Modocs
Bannocks
Pine Ridge

War With Spain

Santiago

Philippine Insurrection

Malolos
Tarlac
Luzon 1899

World War II

Normandy (with arrowhead)
Northern France
Rhineland
Ardennes-Alsace
Central Europe

Vietnam

Counteroffensive, Phase II
Counteroffensive, Phase III
Tet Counteroffensive
Summer-Fall 1969
Winter-Spring 1970
Sanctuary Counteroffensive
Counteroffensive, Phase VII

DECORATIONS

Presidential Unit Citation (Army), Streamer embroidered **LUXEMBOURG** (12th Infantry cited)

Presidential Unit Citation (Army), Streamer embroidered **SUOI TRE, VIETNAM** (2d Battalion, 12th Infantry cited)

Presidential Unit Citation (Army), Streamer embroidered **PLEIKU PROVINCE** (3d Battalion, 12th Infantry cited)

Valorous Unit Award, Streamer embroidered **PLEIKU PROVINCE** (1st Battalion, 12th Infantry cited)

Valorous Unit Award, Streamer embroidered **SAIGON—LONG BINH** (4th Battalion, 12th Infantry cited)

Valorous Unit Award, Streamer embroidered **CENTRAL HIGHLANDS** (1st Battalion, 12th Infantry cited)

Belgian Fourragere 1940 (12th Infantry cited)

Cited in the Order of the Day of the Belgian Army for action in **BELGIUM** (12th Infantry cited)

Cited in the Order of the Day of the Belgian Army for action in the **ARDENNES** (12th Infantry cited)

1ST BATTALION, 12TH INFANTRY

LINEAGE

1861	Constituted 3 May as Company A, 1st Battalion, 12th Infantry, Regular Army; organized 20 October at Fort Hamilton, NY
1866	Reorganized and redesignated 7 December as Company A, 12th Infantry

Company lineage follows that of the 12th Infantry from 1866 through 1946 activation at Fort Ord, CA

1957	Reorganized and redesignated 1 April as Headquarters and Headquarters Company, 1st Battle Group, 12th Infantry and assigned to 4th Infantry Division

1963 Reorganized and redesignated 1 October as 1st Battalion, 12th Infantry

CAMPAIGN PARTICIPATION

Civil War

Peninsula
Manassas
Antietam
Fredericksburg
Chancellorsville
Gettysburg
Wilderness
Spotsylvania
Cold Harbor
Petersburg
Virginia 1862
Virginia 1863

Indian Wars

Modocs
Bannocks
Pine Ridge

War With Spain

Santiago

Philippine Insurrection

Malolos
Tarlac
Luzon 1899

World War II

Normandy (with arrowhead)
Northern France
Rhineland
Ardennes-Alsace
Central Europe

Vietnam

Counteroffensive, Phase II
Counteroffensive, Phase III
Tet Counteroffensive
Counteroffensive, Phase IV
Counteroffensive, Phase V
Counteroffensive, Phase VI
Tet 69 Counteroffensive
Summer-Fall 1969
Winter-Spring 1970
Sanctuary Counteroffensive
Counteroffensive, Phase VII

DECORATIONS

Presidential Unit Citation (Army), Streamer embroidered **LUXEMBOURG** (12th Infantry cited)

Valorous Unit Award, Streamer embroidered **PLEIKU PROVINCE** (1st Battalion, 12th Infantry cited)

Valorous Unit Award, Streamer embroidered **CENTRAL HIGHLANDS** (1st Battalion, 12th Infantry cited)

Belgian Fourragere 1940 (12th Infantry cited)

Cited in the Order of the Day of the Belgian Army for action in **BELGIUM** (12th Infantry cited)

Cited in the Order of the Day of the Belgian Army for action in the **ARDENNES** (12th Infantry cited)

Vietnamese Cross of Gallantry with Palm, Streamer embroidered **VIETNAM 1966–1969** (1st Battalion, 12th Infantry cited)

Vietnamese Civil Action Honor Medal, First Class, Streamer embroidered **VIETNAM 1966–1969** (1st Battalion, 12th Infantry cited)

Company B and Company C each additionally entitled to: Valorous Unit Award, Streamer embroidered **KONTUM** (Company B and Company C, 1st Battalion, 12th Infantry cited)

2D BATTALION, 12TH INFANTRY

LINEAGE

1861 Constituted 3 May as Company B, 1st Battalion, 12th Infantry, Regular Army; organized 20 October at Fort Hamilton, NY

1866 Reorganized and redesignated 7 December as Company B, 12th Infantry

Company lineage follows that of the 12th Infantry from 1866 through 1946 activation at Fort Ord, CA

1957 Inactivated 1 April at Fort Lewis, WA, and relieved from assignment to 4th Infantry Division; redesignated 1 August as Headquarters and Headquarters Company, 2d Battle Group, 12th Infantry; assigned to the 8th Infantry Division and activated in Germany

1959 Relieved 24 March from assignment to 8th Infantry Division and assigned to 1st Infantry Division

1963 Reorganized and redesignated 1 October as 2d Battalion, 12th Infantry; relieved from 1st Infantry Division and assigned to 4th Infantry Division

CAMPAIGN PARTICIPATION

Civil War

Peninsula
Manassas
Antietam
Fredericksburg
Chancellorsville
Gettysburg
Wilderness
Spotsylvania
Cold Harbor
Petersburg
Virginia 1862
Virginia 1863

Indian Wars

Modocs
Bannocks
Pine Ridge

War With Spain

Santiago

Philippine Insurrection

Malolos
Tarlac
Luzon 1899

World War II

Normandy (with arrowhead)
Northern France
Rhineland
Ardennes-Alsace
Central Europe

Vietnam

Counteroffensive, Phase II
Counteroffensive, Phase III
Tet Counteroffensive
Counteroffensive, Phase IV
Counteroffensive, Phase V
Counteroffensive, Phase VI
Tet 69 Counteroffensive
Summer-Fall 1969
Winter-Spring 1970
Sanctuary Counteroffensive
Counteroffensive, Phase VII

DECORATIONS

Presidential Unit Citation (Army), Streamer embroidered **LUXEMBOURG** (12th Infantry cited)

Presidential Unit Citation (Army), Streamer embroidered **SUOI TRE, VIETNAM** (2d Battalion, 12th Infantry cited)

Belgian Fourragere 1940 (12th Infantry cited)

Cited in the Order of the Day of the Belgian Army for action in **BELGIUM** (12th Infantry cited)

Cited in the Order of the Day of the Belgian Army for action in the **ARDENNES** (12th Infantry cited)

Vietnamese Cross of Gallantry with Palm, Streamer embroidered **VIETNAM 1966–1967** (2d Battalion, 12th Infantry cited)

Vietnamese Cross of Gallantry with Palm; Streamer embroidered **VIETNAM 1967–1968** (2d Battalion, 12th Infantry cited)

3D BATTALION, 12TH INFANTRY

LINEAGE

1861   Constituted 3 May as Company C, 1st Battalion, 12th Infantry, Regular Army; organized 20 October at Fort Hamilton, NY

1866   Reorganized and redesignated 7 December as Company C, 12th Infantry

Company lineage follows that of the 12th Infantry from 1866 through 1946 activation at Fort Ord, CA

1957   Inactivated 1 April at Fort Lewis, WA, and relieved from assignment to 4th Infantry Division; redesignated as Headquarters and Headquarters Company, 3d Battle Group, 12th Infantry

1959   Withdrawn 17 March from Regular Army and allotted to Army Reserve; assigned to 79th Infantry Division; Battle Group activated 23 March at Baltimore, MD

1963   Inactivated 28 February at Baltimore, MD, and relieved 28 March from assignment to 79th Infantry Division

1965   Redesignated 16 September as 3d Battalion, 12th Infantry, withdrawn from Army Reserve and allotted to Regular Army; assigned to 4th Infantry Division and activated 1 November at Fort Lewis, WA

1970   Inactivated 15 December at Fort Carson, CO

CAMPAIGN PARTICIPATION

Civil War

Peninsula
Manassas
Antietam
Fredericksburg
Chancellorsville
Gettysburg
Wilderness
Spotsylvania
Cold Harbor
Petersburg
Virginia 1862
Virginia 1863

Indian Wars

Modocs
Bannocks
Pine Ridge

War With Spain

Santiago

Philippine Insurrection

Malolos
Tarlac
Luzon 1899

World War II

Normandy (with
arrowhead)
Northern France
Rhineland
Ardennes-Alsace
Central Europe

Vietnam

Counteroffensive,
Phase II

Counteroffensive,
Phase III
Tet Counteroffensive
Counteroffensive,
Phase IV
Counteroffensive,
Phase V
Counteroffensive,
Phase VI
Tet 69 Counteroffensive
Summer-Fall 1969
Winter-Spring 1970
Sanctuary
Counteroffensive
Counteroffensive,
Phase VII

DECORATIONS

Presidential Unit Citation (Army), Streamer embroidered **LUXEMBOURG** (12th Infantry cited)

Presidential Unit Citation (Army), Streamer embroidered **PLEIKU PROVINCE** (3d Battalion, 12th Infantry cited)

Belgian Fourragere 1940 (12th Infantry cited)

Cited in the Order of the Day of the Belgian Army for action in **BELGIUM** (12th Infantry cited)

Cited in the Order of the Day of the Belgian Army for action in the **ARDENNES** (12th Infantry cited)

Vietnamese Cross of Gallantry with Palm, Streamer embroidered **VIETNAM 1966–1969** (3d Battalion, 12th Infantry cited)

Vietnamese Civil Action Honor Medal, First Class, Streamer embroidered **VIETNAM 1966–1969** (3d Battalion, 12th Infantry cited)

4TH BATTALION, 12TH INFANTRY

LINEAGE

1861   Constituted 3 May as Company D, 1st Battalion, 12th Infantry, Regular Army; organized at Fort Hamilton, NY

1866   Reorganized and redesignated 7 December as Company D, 12th Infantry

Company lineage follows that of the 12th Infantry from 1866 through 1946 activation at Fort Ord, CA

1957   Inactivated 1 April at Fort Lewis, WA, and relieved from assignment to 4th Infantry Division; redesignated as Headquarters and Headquarters Company, 4th Battle Group, 12th Infantry

1966   Redesignated 23 March as Headquarters and Headquarters Company, 4th Battalion, 12th Infantry, and assigned to 199th Infantry Brigade; activated 1 June at Fort Benning, GA

1970   Inactivated 15 October at Fort Benning, GA

CAMPAIGN PARTICIPATION

Civil War

Peninsula

Manassas
Antietam

Fredericksburg
Chancellorsville
Gettysburg
Wilderness
Spotsylvania
Cold Harbor
Petersburg
Virginia 1862
Virginia 1863

Indian Wars

Modocs
Bannocks
Pine Ridge
Arizona 1881

War With Spain

Santiago

Philippine Insurrection

Malolos
Tarlac
Luzon 1899

World War II

Normandy (with
arrowhead)

Northern France
Rhineland
Ardennes-Alsace
Central Europe

Vietnam

Counteroffensive,
Phase II
Counteroffensive,
Phase III
Tet Counteroffensive
Counteroffensive,
Phase IV
Counteroffensive,
Phase V
Counteroffensive,
Phase VI
Tet 69 Counteroffensive
Summer-Fall 1969
Winter-Spring 1970
Sanctuary
Counteroffensive
Counteroffensive,
Phase VII

DECORATIONS

Presidential Unit Citation (Army), Streamer embroidered **LUXEMBOURG** (12th Infantry cited)

Valorous Unit Award, Streamer embroidered **SAIGON— LONG BINH** (4th Battalion, 12th Infantry cited)

Belgian Fourragere 1940 (12th Infantry cited)

Cited in the Order of the Day of the Belgian Army for action in **BELGIUM** (12th Infantry cited)

Cited in the Order of the Day of the Belgian Army for action in the **ARDENNES** (12th Infantry cited)

Vietnamese Cross of Gallantry with Palm, Streamer embroidered **VIETNAM 1968** (4th Battalion, 12th Infantry cited)

Company D additionally entitled to: Presidential Unit Citation (Army), Streamer embroidered **SAIGON** (Company D, 4th Battalion, 12th Infantry cited)

5TH BATTALION, 12TH INFANTRY

LINEAGE

1861   Constituted 3 May as Company E, 1st Battalion, 12th Infantry, Regular Army; organized 20 October at Fort Hamilton, NY

1866   Reorganized and redesignated 7 December as Company E, 12th Infantry

         Company lineage follows that of the 12th Infantry from 1866 through 1946 activation at Fort Ord, CA

1957   Inactivated 1 April at Fort Lewis, WA, and relieved from assignment to 4th Infantry Division; redesignated as Headquarters and Headquarters Company, 5th Battle Group, 12th Infantry

1967   Redesignated 1 November as Headquarters and Headquarters Company, 5th Battalion, 12th Infantry, and activated at Fort Lewis, WA

1968   Assigned 7 April to 199th Infantry Brigade

1970   Inactivated 15 October at Fort Benning, GA

CAMPAIGN PARTICIPATION

Civil War

Peninsula
Manassas
Antietam
Fredericksburg
Chancellorsville
Gettysburg
Wilderness
Spotsylvania
Cold Harbor
Petersburg
Virginia 1862
Virginia 1863

Indian Wars

Modocs
Bannocks
Pine Ridge

War With Spain

Santiago

Philippine Insurrection

Malolos
Tarlac
Luzon 1899

World War II

Normandy (with arrowhead)
Northern France
Rhineland
Ardennes-Alsace
Central Europe

Vietnam

Counteroffensive, Phase IV
Counteroffensive, Phase V
Counteroffensive, Phase VI
Tet 69 Counteroffensive
Summer-Fall 1969
Winter-Spring 1970
Sanctuary Counteroffensive
Counteroffensive, Phase VII

DECORATIONS

Presidential Unit Citation (Army), Streamer embroidered **LUXEMBOURG** (12th Infantry cited)

Belgian Fourragere 1940 (12th Infantry cited)

Cited in the Order of the Day of the Belgian Army for action in **BELGIUM** (12th Infantry cited)

Cited in the Order of the Day of the Belgian Army for action in the **ARDENNES** (12th Infantry cited)

13TH INFANTRY
(First at Vicksburg)

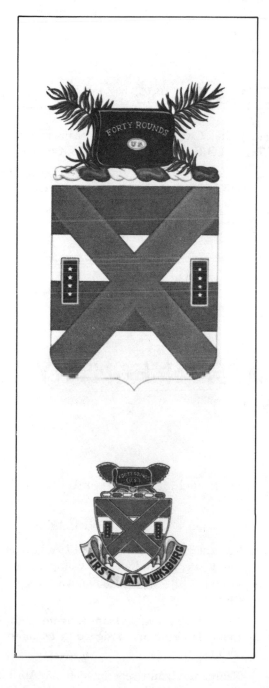

COAT OF ARMS

Motto: First at Vicksburg

Symbolism: The four blue and white bars of the shield are in the present and old infantry colors and indicate service in the Civil War, the War with Spain, the Indian Wars, and the Philippine Insurrection. The saltire cross is from the Confederate battle flag with the color changed from blue to red. The billets are the shoulder straps of the two generals which this regiment has produced, Generals Sherman and Sheridan. (When the 13th Infantry was organized in 1861–62, Sherman was its first colonel and Sheridan was one of its original captains.)

The crest is the badge of the XV Corps of the Civil War and the motto is the proud designation given the regiment by General Grant.

DISTINCTIVE INSIGNIA

The distinctive insignia is the shield, crest, and motto of the coat of arms.

LINEAGE

1861	Constituted 3 May as 1st Battalion, 13th Infantry, Regular Army
1862	Organized at Jefferson Barracks, MO, and Alton, IL
1866	Reorganized and redesignated 21 September as 13th Infantry
1917	Assigned 17 December to 8th Division
1923	Relieved 24 March from 8th Division and assigned to 9th Division
1927	Relieved 15 August from 9th Division and assigned to 5th Division
1933	Relieved 1 October from 5th Division and assigned to 9th Division
1940	Inactivated 14 June in the Canal Zone and relieved 22 June from assignment to 9th Division; assigned to 8th Division and activated 14 July at Camp Jackson, SC
1945	Inactivated 18 November at Fort Leonard Wood, MO
1950	Activated 17 August at Fort Jackson, SC
1957	Relieved 1 August from assignment to 8th Infantry Division and reorganized as a parent regiment under CARS

CAMPAIGN PARTICIPATION

Civil War
Mississippi River
Vicksburg
Chattanooga
Mississippi 1863
Tennessee 1863

Indian Wars
North Dakota 1866
Montana 1868

War With Spain
Santiago

Philippine Insurrection
Cavite
San Fabian
Luzon 1899
Luzon 1900

World War II
Normandy
Northern France
Rhineland
Central Europe

DECORATIONS

Presidential Unit Citation (Army), Streamer embroidered **HURTGEN FOREST** (1st Battalion, 13th Infantry cited)

French Croix de Guerre with Palm, World War II, Streamer embroidered **NORMANDY** (13th Infantry cited)

Luxembourg Croix de Guerre, Streamer embroidered **LUXEMBOURG** (8th Infantry Division cited)

1st Battalion, 13th Infantry
(First at Vicksburg)

LINEAGE

1861	Constituted 3 May as Company A, 1st Battalion, 13th Infantry; organized 8 October at Jefferson Barracks, MO
1866	Reorganized and redesignated 21 September as Company A, 13th Infantry
1917	Assigned 17 December to 8th Division
1923	Relieved 24 March from 8th Division and assigned to 9th Division
1927	Relieved 15 August from 9th Division and assigned to 5th Division
1929	Inactivated 31 October at Fort Strong, MA
1940	Activated 14 July at Camp Jackson, SC
1945	Inactivated 18 November at Fort Leonard Wood, MO
1950	Activated 17 August at Fort Jackson, SC
1957	Reorganized and redesignated 1 August as Headquarters and Headquarters Company, 1st Battle Group, 13th Infantry; remained assigned to 8th Infantry Division
1959	Relieved 28 February from assignment to 8th Infantry Division and assigned to 1st Infantry Division
1963	Reorganized and redesignated 25 April as 1st Battalion, 13th Infantry, and relieved from assignment to 1st Infantry Division, assigned to 8th Infantry Division

CAMPAIGN PARTICIPATION

Civil War

Mississippi River
Vicksburg
Chattanooga
Mississippi 1863
Tennessee 1863

Indian Wars

North Dakota 1866
Montana 1868

War With Spain

Santiago

Philippine Insurrection

Cavite
San Fabian
Luzon 1899
Luzon 1900

World War II

Normandy
Northern France
Rhineland
Central Europe

DECORATIONS

Presidential Unit Citation (Army), Streamer embroidered **HURTGEN FOREST** (1st Battalion, 13th Infantry cited)

French Croix de Guerre with Palm, World War II, Streamer embroidered **NORMANDY** (13th Infantry cited)

Luxembourg Croix de Guerre, Streamer embroidered **LUXEMBOURG** (8th Infantry Division cited)

2D BATTALION, 13TH INFANTRY
(First at Vicksburg)

LINEAGE

1861	Constituted 3 May as Company B, 1st Battalion, 13th Infantry; organized 13 November at Jefferson Barracks, MO
1866	Reorganized and redesignated 21 September as Company B, 13th Infantry
1917	Assigned 17 December to 8th Division
1923	Relieved 24 March from 8th Division and assigned to 9th Division
1927	Relieved 15 August from assignment to 9th Division and assigned to 5th Division
1929	Inactivated 31 October at Fort Strong, MA
1940	Activated 14 July at Camp Jackson, SC
1945	Inactivated 18 November at Fort Leonard Wood, MO
1950	Activated 17 August at Fort Jackson, SC
1957	Inactivated 1 August in Germany and relieved from assignment to 8th Infantry Division; redesignated 1 December as Headquarters and Headquarters Company, 2d Battle Group, 13th Infantry; assigned to 9th Infantry Division and activated at Fort Carson, CO
1962	Inactivated 31 January at Fort Carson, CO
1963	Redesignated 27 March as 2d Battalion, 13th Infantry, and relieved from assignment to 9th Infantry Division; assigned to 8th Infantry Division and activated 1 April in Germany

CAMPAIGN PARTICIPATION

Civil War

Mississippi River
Vicksburg
Chattanooga
Mississippi 1863
Tennessee 1863

Indian Wars

North Dakota 1866
Montana 1868

War With Spain

Santiago

Philippine Insurrection

Cavite
San Fabian
Luzon 1899
Luzon 1900

World War II

Normandy
Northern France
Rhineland
Central Europe

DECORATIONS

Presidential Unit Citation (Army), Streamer embroidered **HURTGEN FOREST** (1st Battalion, 13th Infantry cited)

French Croix de Guerre with Palm, World War II, Streamer embroidered **NORMANDY** (13th Infantry cited)

French Croix de Guerre with Silver Star, World War II, Streamer embroidered **VESLEY, FRANCE** (Company B, 13th Infantry cited)

Luxembourg Croix de Guerre, Streamer embroidered **LUXEMBOURG** (8th Infantry Division cited)

3D BATTALION, 13TH INFANTRY
(First at Vicksburg)

LINEAGE

1861	Constituted 3 May as Company C, 1st Battalion, 13th Infantry; organized 13 November at Jefferson Barracks, MO
1866	Reorganized and redesignated 21 September as Company C, 13th Infantry
1917	Assigned 17 December to 8th Division
1923	Relieved 24 March from 8th Division and assigned to 9th Division
1927	Relieved 15 August from assignment to 9th Division and assigned to 5th Division
1929	Inactivated 31 October at Fort Strong, MA
1940	Activated 14 July at Camp Jackson, SC
1945	Inactivated 18 November at Fort Leonard Wood, MO
1950	Activated 17 August at Fort Jackson, SC
1957	Inactivated 1 August in Germany and relieved from assignment to 8th Infantry Division; redesignated 1 December as Headquarters and Headquarters Company, 3d Battle Group, 13th Infantry
1959	Withdrawn 6 April from Regular Army and allotted to Army Reserve; assigned to 94th Infantry Division and activated 1 May at Roslindale, MA
1963	Inactivated 1 March and relieved from assignment to 9th Infantry Division

CAMPAIGN PARTICIPATION

Civil War
Mississippi River
Vicksburg
Chattanooga
Mississippi 1863
Tennessee 1863

Indian Wars
North Dakota 1866
Montana 1868

War With Spain
Santiago

Philippine Insurrection
Cavite
San Fabian
Luzon 1899
Luzon 1900

World War II
Normandy
Northern France
Rhineland
Central Europe

DECORATIONS

Presidential Unit Citation (Army), Streamer embroidered **HURTGEN FOREST** (1st Battalion, 13th Infantry cited)

French Croix de Guerre with Palm, World War II, Streamer embroidered **NORMANDY** (13th Infantry cited)

Luxembourg Croix de Guerre, Streamer embroidered **LUXEMBOURG** (8th Infantry Division cited)

4TH BATTALION, 13TH INFANTRY
(First at Vicksburg)

LINEAGE

1861   Constituted 3 May as Company D, 1st Battalion, 13th Infantry

1862   Organized 1 April at Alton, IL

1866   Reorganized and redesignated 21 September as Company D, 13th Infantry

1917   Assigned 17 December to 8th Division

1923   Relieved 24 March from 8th Division and assigned to 9th Division

1927   Relieved 15 August from assignment to 9th Division and assigned to 5th Division

1929   Inactivated 31 October at Fort Strong, MA

1940   Activated 14 July at Camp Jackson, SC

1945   Inactivated 18 November at Fort Leonard Wood, MO

1950   Activated 17 August at Fort Jackson, SC

1957   Inactivated 1 August in Germany and relieved from assignment to 8th Infantry Division; redesignated Headquarters and Headquarters Company, 4th Battle Group, 13th Infantry

1959   Redesignated 10 May as Headquarters and Headquarters Company, 4th Battalion, 13th Infantry and assigned to 198th Infantry Brigade at Fort Hood, TX; inactivated 12 May and relieved from assignment to 198th Infantry Brigade

CAMPAIGN PARTICIPATION

Civil War

Mississippi River
Vicksburg
Chattanooga
Mississippi 1863
Tennessee 1863

Indian Wars

North Dakota 1866
Montana 1868

War With Spain

Santiago

Philippine Insurrection

Cavite
San Fabian
Luzon 1899
Luzon 1900

World War II

Normandy
Northern France
Rhineland
Central Europe

DECORATIONS

French Croix de Guerre with Palm, World War II, Streamer embroidered **NORMANDY** (13th Infantry cited)

Luxembourg Croix de Guerre, Streamer embroidered **LUXEMBOURG** (8th Infantry Division cited)

14TH INFANTRY
(Golden Dragons)

COAT OF ARMS

Motto: The Right of the Line

Symbolism: Service in the Civil War is shown by the white cross pattée, the badge of Sykes' Regular division of the V Corps of the Army of the Potomac. Indian campaigns are indicated by the arrows. The 14th Infantry was at the capture of Manila during the War with Spain, symbolized by the castle, and in the fighting around the same city in 1899 during the Philippine Insurrection, indicated by the palm.

The dragon in the crest symbolizes service in the China Relief Expedition. The motto is the much prized remark made by General Meade directing the station of the regiment in the review just after the Civil War.

DISTINCTIVE INSIGNIA

The distinctive insignia is a gold imperial Chinese dragon placed against a red conventionalized Spanish castle with the motto "The Right of the Line" in gold letters on a blue ribbon scroll. The dragon is the crest of the coat of arms and the castle is one of the charges on the regimental shield.

LINEAGE

1861	Constituted 3 May as 2d Battalion, 14th Infantry, Regular Army; organized 1 July at Fort Trumbull, CT
1862	Reorganized and redesignated 30 April as 1st Battalion, 14th Infantry
1866	Reorganized and redesignated 21 September as 14th Infantry
1869	Consolidated 26 July with 45th Infantry, Veteran Reserve Corps, to form 14th Infantry
1918	Assigned 27 July to 19th Division
1919	Relieved 14 February from assignment to 19th Division
1943	Assigned 10 July to 71st Light Division
1946	Relieved 1 May from assignment to 71st Infantry Division and inactivated 1 September in Germany
1948	Activated 1 October at Camp Carson, CO
1951	Assigned 1 August to 25th Infantry Division
1957	Relieved 1 February from assignment to 25th Infantry Division and reorganized as a parent regiment under CARS

Indian Wars

Little Big Horn
Bannocks
Arizona 1866
Wyoming 1874

War With Spain

Manila

China Relief Expedition

Yang-tsun
Peking

Philippine Insurrection

Manila
Laguna de Bay
Zapote River
Cavite
Luzon 1899

World War II

Rhineland
Central Europe

Korean War

UN summer–fall
offensive
Second Korean winter

Korea, summer–fall 1952
Third Korean winter
Korea, summer 1953

Vietnam

Counteroffensive
Counteroffensive,
Phase II
Counteroffensive,
Phase III
Tet Counteroffensive
Counteroffensive,
Phase IV
Counteroffensive,
Phase V
Counteroffensive,
Phase VI
Tet 69 Counteroffensive
Summer–Fall 1969
Winter–Spring 1970
Sanctuary
Counteroffensive
Counteroffensive,
Phase VII
Consolidation I
Consolidation II
Cease-Fire

CAMPAIGN PARTICIPATION

Civil War

Peninsula
Manassas
Antietam
Fredericksburg
Chancellorsville

Gettysburg
Wilderness
Spotsylvania
Cold Harbor
Petersburg
Virginia 1862
Virginia 1863

DECORATIONS

Presidential Unit Citation (Navy), Streamer embroidered **CHU LAI** (1st Battalion, 14th Infantry cited)

Republic of Korea Presidential Unit Citation, Streamer embroidered **MUNSAN-NI** (14th Infantry cited)

1st Battalion, 14th Infantry
(Golden Dragons)

LINEAGE

1861	Constituted 3 May as Company A, 2d Battalion, 14th Infantry, Regular Army; organized 8 July at Fort Trumbull, CT
1862	Reorganized and redesignated 30 April as Company A, 1st Battalion, 14th Infantry

1866	Reorganized and redesignated 21 September as Company A, 14th Infantry
1869	Consolidated 26 July with Company G, 45th Infantry, Veteran Reserve Corps, to form Company A, 14th Infantry

Company lineage follows that of 14th Infantry from 1869 consolidation to 1951 assignment to 25th Infantry Division

1957   Reorganized and redesignated 1 February as Headquarters and Headquarters Company, 1st Battle Group, 14th Infantry; remained assigned to 25th Infantry Division

1963   Reorganized and redesignated 26 August as 1st Battalion, 14th Infantry

1967   Relieved 1 August from assignment to 25th Infantry Division and assigned to 4th Infantry Division

1970   Relieved 15 December from assignment to 4th Infantry Division and assigned to 25th Infantry Division

CAMPAIGN PARTICIPATION

Civil War

Peninsula
Manassas
Antietam
Fredericksburg
Chancellorsville
Gettysburg
Wilderness
Spotsylvania
Cold Harbor
Petersburg
Virginia 1862
Virginia 1863

Indian Wars

Little Big Horn
Bannocks
Arizona 1866
Wyoming 1874

War With Spain

Manila

China Relief Expedition

Yang-tsun
Peking

Philippine Insurrection

Manila
Laguna de Bay
Zapote River
Cavite
Luzon 1899

World War II

Rhineland
Central Europe

Korean War

UN summer–fall offensive
Second Korean winter
Korea, summer–fall 1952
Third Korean winter
Korea, summer 1953

Vietnam

Counteroffensive
Counteroffensive, Phase II
Counteroffensive, Phase III
Tet Counteroffensive
Counteroffensive, Phase IV
Counteroffensive, Phase V
Counteroffensive, Phase VI
Tet 69 Counteroffensive
Summer–Fall 1969
Winter–Spring 1970
Sanctuary Counteroffensive
Counteroffensive, Phase VII

DECORATIONS

Presidential Unit Citation (Navy), Streamer embroidered **CHU LAI** (1st Battalion, 14th Infantry cited)

Republic of Korea Presidential Unit Citation, Streamer embroidered **MUNSAN-NI** (14th Infantry cited)

Vietnamese Cross of Gallantry with Palm, Streamer embroidered **VIETNAM 1966–1967** (1st Battalion, 14th Infantry cited)

Vietnamese Cross of Gallantry with Palm, Streamer embroidered **VIETNAM 1967–1969** (1st Battalion, 14th Infantry cited)

Vietnamese Civil Action Honor Medal, First Class, Streamer embroidered **VIETNAM 1967–1969** (1st Battalion, 14th Infantry cited)

2D BATTALION, 14TH INFANTRY
(Golden Dragons)

LINEAGE

1861   Constituted 3 May as Company B, 2d Battalion, 14th Infantry, organized 8 July at Fort Trumbull, CT

1862   Reorganized and redesignated 30 April as Company B, 1st Battalion, 14th Infantry

1866   Reorganized and redesignated 21 September as Company B, 14th Infantry

1869	Consolidated 15 August with Company A, 45th Infantry, Veteran Reserve Corps, to form Company B, 14th Infantry
	Company lineage follows that of 14th Infantry from 1869 consolidation to 1951 assignment to 25th Infantry Division
1957	Redesignated 17 May as Headquarters and Headquarters Company, 2d Battle Group, 14th Infantry, and activated 25 May at Fort Benning, GA
1958	Assigned 1 July to 1st Infantry Brigade
1960	Inactivated 16 May at Fort Benning, GA, and relieved from assignment to 1st Infantry Brigade
1963	Redesignated 21 June as 2d Battalion, 14th Infantry, and assigned to 25th Infantry Division; activated 26 August in Hawaii

CAMPAIGN PARTICIPATION

Civil War

Peninsula
Manassas
Antietam
Fredericksburg
Chancellorsville
Gettysburg
Wilderness
Spotsylvania
Cold Harbor
Petersburg
Virginia 1862
Virginia 1863

Indian Wars

Little Big Horn
Bannocks
Arizona 1866
Wyoming 1874

War With Spain

Manila

China Relief Expedition

Yang-tsun
Peking

Philippine Insurrection

Manila
Laguna de Bay
Zapote River
Cavite
Luzon 1899

World War II

Rhineland
Central Europe

Korean War

UN summer–fall offensive
Second Korean winter
Korea, summer–fall 1952
Third Korean winter
Korea, summer 1953

Vietnam

Counteroffensive
Counteroffensive, Phase II
Counteroffensive, Phase III
Tet Counteroffensive
Counteroffensive, Phase IV
Counteroffensive, Phase V
Counteroffensive, Phase VI
Tet 69 Counteroffensive
Summer–Fall 1969
Winter–Spring 1970
Sanctuary Counteroffensive
Counteroffensive, Phase VII

DECORATIONS

Republic of Korea Presidential Unit Citation, Streamer embroidered **MUNSAN-NI** (14th Infantry cited)

Vietnamese Cross of Gallantry with Palm, Streamer embroidered **VIETNAM 1966–1968** (2d Battalion, 14th Infantry cited)

3D BATTALION, 14TH INFANTRY
(Golden Dragons)

LINEAGE

1861	Constituted 3 May as Company F, 2d Battalion, 14th Infantry, Regular Army; organized 8 July at Fort Trumbull, CT
1862	Reorganized and redesignated 30 April as Company F, 1st Battalion, 14th Infantry
1866	Reorganized and redesignated 21 September as Company F, 14th Infantry
1869	Consolidated 26 July with Company C, 45th Infantry, Veteran Reserve Corps, to form Company C, 14th Infantry
	Company lineage follows that of 14th Infantry from 1869 consolidation to 1 June 1959 consolidation
1918	A new company constituted 23 July as Headquarters and Headquarters Company, 406th Infantry, an element of the 102d Division, demobilized 30 November

406th Infantry lineage differs from that of 14th Infantry from its constitution to 1 June 1959 consolidation as follows:

1921   Reconstituted 24 June in Organized Reserves as an element of 102d Division; organized in October at Springfield, MO

1942   Ordered into active military service 15 September and reorganized at Camp Maxey, TX

1946   Inactivated 16 March at Camp Kilmer, NJ

1947   Activated 3 January in Organized Reserves at Kansas City, MO

1959   Consolidated 1 June with Headquarters and Headquarters Company, 3d Battle Group, 14th Infantry, to form Headquarters and Headquarters Company, 3d Battle Group, 14 Infantry

1963   Reorganized and redesignated 1 April as 3d Battalion, 14th Infantry

1965   Inactivated 31 December and relieved from assignment to 102d Infantry Division

1969   Withdrawn 6 December from the Army Reserve and allotted to Regular Army; activated in Hawaii as an element of 25th Infantry Division

1970   Inactivated 15 December in Hawaii

CAMPAIGN PARTICIPATION

Civil War
Peninsula
Manassas
Antietam
Fredericksburg
Chancellorsville
Gettysburg
Wilderness
Spotsylvania
Cold Harbor
Petersburg
Virginia 1862
Virginia 1863

Indian Wars
Little Big Horn
Bannocks
Arizona 1866
Wyoming 1874

War With Spain
Manila

China Relief Expedition
Yang-tsun
Peking

Philippine Insurrection
Manila
Laguna de Bay
Zapote River
Cavite
Luzon 1899

World War II
Rhineland
Central Europe

Korean War
UN summer–fall offensive
Second Korean winter
Korea, summer–fall 1952
Third Korean winter
Korea, summer 1953

DECORATIONS

Republic of Korea Presidential Unit Citation, Streamer embroidered **MUNSAN-NI** (14th Infantry cited)

COMPANY D, 14TH INFANTRY
(Golden Dragons)

LINEAGE

1861   Constituted 3 May as Company D, 2d Battalion, 14th Infantry; organized 8 July at Fort Trumbull, CT

1862   Reorganized and redesignated 30 April as Company D, 1st Battalion, 14th Infantry

1866   Reorganized and redesignated 21 September as Company D, 14th Infantry

Company lineage follows that of 14th Infantry from 1869 consolidation through 1948 activation at Camp Carson, CO)

1957   Inactivated 1 February in Hawaii and relieved from assignment to 25th Infantry Division

1959   Withdrawn 3 June from Regular Army and allotted to the Army Reserve; activated 17 August at St. Thomas, Virgin Islands

1968   Inactivated 31 March at St. Thomas, Virgin Islands

CAMPAIGN PARTICIPATION

Civil War

Peninsula
Manassas
Antietam
Fredericksburg
Chancellorsville
Gettysburg
Wilderness
Spotsylvania
Cold Harbor
Petersburg
Virginia 1862
Virginia 1863

Indian Wars

Bannocks

War With Spain

Manila

China Relief Expedition

Yang-tsun
Peking

Philippine Insurrection

Manila
Laguna de Bay
Zapote River
Luzon 1899

World War II

Rhineland
Central Europe

Korean War

UN summer–fall
offensive
Second Korean winter
Korea, summer–fall 1952
Third Korean winter
Korea, summer 1953

DECORATIONS

Republic of Korea Presidential Unit Citation, Streamer embroidered **MUNSAN-NI** (14th Infantry cited)

COMPANY E, 14TH INFANTRY
(Golden Dragons)

LINEAGE

1861	Constituted 3 May as Company E, 2d Battalion, 14th Infantry; organized 8 July at Fort Trumbull, CT
1862	Reorganized and redesignated 30 April as Company E, 1st Battalion, 14th Infantry
1866	Reorganized and redesignated 21 September as Company E, 14th Infantry

Company lineage follows that of 14th Infantry from 1869 consolidation through 1948 activities at Camp Carson, CO

1957	Inactivated 1 February in Hawaii, relieved from assignment to 25th Infantry Division and redesignated as Headquarters and Headquarters Company, 5th Battle Group, 14 Infantry
1960	Redesignated 21 December as Company E, 14th Infantry, and activated 24 December in Korea
1966	Inactivated 1 January in Korea

CAMPAIGN PARTICIPATION

Civil War

Peninsula
Manassas
Antietam
Fredericksburg
Chancellorsville
Gettysburg
Wilderness
Spotsylvania
Cold Harbor
Petersburg
Virginia 1862
Virginia 1863

Indian Wars

Bannocks

War With Spain

Manila

China Relief Expedition

Yang-tsun
Peking

Philippine Insurrection

Manila
Laguna de Bay
Zapote River
Cavite
Luzon 1899

World War II

Rhineland
Central Europe

Korean War

UN summer–fall
offensive
Second Korean winter
Korea, summer–fall 1952
Third Korean winter
Korea, summer 1953

Vietnam

Counteroffensive,
Phase VII
Consolidation I
Consolidation II
Cease-Fire

DECORATIONS

Republic of Korea Presidential Unit Citation, Streamer embroidered **MUNSAN-NI** (14th Infantry cited)

15TH INFANTRY

COAT OF ARMS

Motto: Can Do

Symbolism: The shield is blue and white, the present and former infantry colors. On the lower part is the Chinese dragon, and in the white chief the badge of the XIV Corps in the Civil War is repeated four times for four major campaigns: Murfreesboro, Chickamauga, Chattanooga, and Atlanta. Chickamauga, where the regiment fought and held so gallantly, is further emphasized by the rock.

The crest is the triangle and devices from the Katipunan flag of the Philippine Insurrection. The motto is the watchword of the regiment in "pidgin English," in recollection of the regiment's long service in China.

DISTINCTIVE INSIGNIA

The distinctive insignia is the shield and motto of the coat of arms.

LINEAGE

1861	Constituted 3 May as the 1st Battalion, 15th Infantry, Regular Army; organized September–October at Newport Barracks, KY
	Another company constituted 3 May as the 3d Battalion, 17th Infantry, Regular Army
1865	3d Battalion, 17th Infantry organized 29 October at Hart Island, NY
1866	1st Battalion, 15th Infantry reorganized and redesignated 21 September as 15th Infantry
	3d Battalion, 17th Infantry reorganized and redesignated 21 September as 35th Infantry
1869	15th Infantry and 35th Infantry consolidated 12 August to form 15th Infantry
1922	Assigned 17 July to Philippine Division
1923	Relieved 1 April from assignment to Philippine Division and assigned to American Forces in China
1938	Relieved 2 March from assignment to United States Army Troops in China
1940	Assigned 12 January to 3d Division
1957	Relieved 1 July from assignment to 3d Infantry Division and reorganized as a parent regiment under CARS

CAMPAIGN PARTICIPATION

Civil War
Shiloh
Murfreesborough
Chickamauga
Chattanooga
Atlanta
Mississippi 1862
Alabama 1862
Tennessee 1862
Kentucky 1862
Tennesssee 1863
Georgia 1864

Indian Wars
Utes
New Mexico 1880

China Relief Expedition
Without inscription

Philippine Insurrection
Luzon 1900
Luzon 1901

World War II
Algeria–French Morocco (with arrowhead)
Tunisia
Sicily (with arrowhead)
Naples–Foggia
Anzio (with arrowhead)
Rome–Arno
Southern France (with arrowhead)
Rhineland
Ardennes–Alsace
Central Europe

Korean War
CCF intervention
First UN counteroffensive
CCF spring offensive
UN summer–fall offensive
Second Korean winter
Korea, summer–fall 1952
Third Korean winter
Korea, summer 1953

DECORATIONS

Presidential Unit Citation (Army), Streamer embroidered **COLMAR** (3d Infantry Division cited)

Presidential Unit Citation (Army), Streamer embroidered **MONTELIMAR** (1st Battalion, 15th Infantry cited)

Presidential Unit Citation (Army), Streamer embroidered **SAN FRATELLO** (3rd Battalion, 15th Infantry cited)

Presidential Unit Citation (Army), Streamer embroidered **KOWANG-NI** (2d Battalion, 15th Infantry and attached units cited)

Presidential Unit Citation (Navy), Streamer embroidered **HWACHON RESERVOIR** (1st Battalion, 15th Infantry cited)

Navy Unit Commendation, Streamer embroidered **PANMUNJOM** (1st Battalion, 15th Infantry cited)

French Croix de Guerre with Palm, World War II, Streamer embroidered **COLMAR** (15th Infantry cited)

French Croix de Guerre, World War II, Fourragere (15th Infantry cited)

Republic of Korea Presidential Unit Citation, Streamer embroidered **UIJONGBU CORRIDOR** (15th Infantry cited)

Republic of Korea Presidential Unit Citation, Streamer embroidered **IRON TRIANGLE** (15th Infantry cited)

Chryssoun Aristion Andrias (Bravery Gold Medal of Greece), Streamer embroidered **KOREA** (15th Infantry cited)

1st Battalion, 15th Infantry

LINEAGE

1861   Constituted 3 May as Company A, 1st Battalion, 15th Infantry, Regular Army; organized 21 September at Newport Barracks, KY

Another company constituted 3 May as Company A, 3d Battalion, 17th Infantry

1865   Company A, 3d Battalion, 17th Infantry; organized 29 October at Hart Island, NY

1866   Company A, 1st Battalion, 15th Infantry reorganized and redesignated 21 September as Company A, 15th Infantry

Company A, 3d Battalion, 17th Infantry reorganized and redesignated 21 September as Company A 35th Infantry

1869   Company A, 15th Infantry and Company A, 35th Infantry consolidated 12 August; consolidated unit designated Company A, 15th Infantry

1922   Assigned 17 July to Philippine Division

1929   Inactivated 1 April at Fort William McKinley, Philippine Islands

1931   Relieved from assignment to Philippine Division

1940   Assigned 12 January to 3d Division and activated 23 May at Fort Lewis, WA

1957   Reorganized and redesignated 1 July as Headquarters and Headquarters Company, 1st Battle Group, 15th Infantry, and remained assigned to 3d Infantry Division

1963   Reorganized and redisgnated 15 July as 1st Battalion, 15th Infantry

CAMPAIGN PARTICIPATION

Civil War
Shiloh
Murfreesborough
Chickamauga
Chattanooga
Atlanta
Mississippi 1862
Alabama 1862
Tennessee 1862
Kentucky 1862
Tennessee 1863
Georgia 1864

Indian Wars
Utes
New Mexico 1880

China Relief Expedition
Without inscription

Philippine Insurrection
Luzon 1900
Luzon 1901

World War II
Algeria–French Morocco (with arrowhead)
Tunisia
Sicily (with arrowhead)
Naples–Foggia
Anzio (with arrowhead)
Rome–Arno
Southern France (with arrowhead)
Rhineland
Ardennes–Alsace
Central Europe

Korean War
CCF intervention
First UN counteroffensive
CCF spring offensive
UN summer–fall offensive
Second Korean winter
Korea, summer–fall 1952
Third Korean winter
Korea, summer 1953

DECORATIONS

Presidential Unit Citation (Army), Streamer embroidered **COLMAR** (3d Infantry Division cited)

Presidential Unit Citation (Army), Streamer embroidered **MONTELIMAR** (1st Battalion, 15th Infantry cited)

Presidential Unit Citation (Army), Streamer embroidered **SAN FRATELLO**

Presidential Unit Citation (Army), Streamer embroidered **KOWANG-NI**

Presidential Unit Citation (Navy), Streamer embroidered **HWACHON RESERVOIR** (1st Battalion, 15th Infantry cited)

Navy Unit Commendation, Streamer embroidered **PANMUNJOM** (1st Battalion, 15th Infantry cited)

French Croix de Guerre with Palm, World War II, Streamer embroidered **COLMAR** (15th Infantry cited)

French Croix de Guerre, World War II, Fourragere (15th Infantry cited)

Republic of Korea Presidential Unit Citation, Streamer embroidered **UIJONGBU CORRIDOR** (15th Infantry cited)

Republic of Korea Presidential Unit Citation, Streamer embroidered **IRON TRIANGLE** (15th Infantry cited)

Republic of Korea Presidential Unit Citation, Streamer embroidered **KOREA** (1st Battalion, 15th Infantry cited)

Chryssoun Aristion Andrias (Bravery Gold Medal of Greece), Streamer embroidered **KOREA** (15th Infantry cited)

2D BATTALION, 15TH INFANTRY

LINEAGE

1861   Constituted 3 May as Company B, 1st Battalion, 15th Infantry, Regular Army; organized in September at Newport Barracks, KY

Another company constituted 3 May as Company B, 3d Battalion, 17th Infantry

1865   Company B, 3d Battalion, 17th Infantry; organized 29 October at Hart Island, NY

1866   Company B, 1st Battalion, 15th Infantry reorganized and redesignated 21 September as Company B, 15th Infantry

Company B, 3d Battalion, 17th Infantry reorganized and redesignated 21 September as Company B, 35th Infantry

1869   Company B, 15th Infantry and Company B, 35th Infantry consolidated 12 August; consolidated unit designated Company B, 15th Infantry

1922   Assigned 17 July to Philippine Division

1929   Inactivated 1 April at Fort William McKinley, Philippine Islands

1940   Activated 23 May at Fort Lewis, WA

1957   Reorganized and redesignated 1 July as Headquarters and Headquarters Company, 2d Battle Group, 15th Infantry, and relieved from assignment to 3d Infantry Division; assigned to 10th Infantry Division

1958   Inactivated 19 June at Fort Benning, GA

1963   Redesignated 23 May as 2d Battalion, 15th Infantry, and relieved from assignment to 10th Infantry Division; assigned to 3d Infantry Division and activated 3 June in Germany

CAMPAIGN PARTICIPATION

Civil War
Shiloh
Murfreesborough
Chickamauga
Chattanooga
Atlanta
Mississippi 1862
Alabama 1862
Tennessee 1862
Kentucky 1862
Tennesssee 1863
Georgia 1864

Indian Wars
Utes
New Mexico 1880

China Relief Expedition
Without inscription

Philippine Insurrection
Luzon 1900
Luzon 1901

World War II
Algeria-French Morocco (with arrowhead)
Tunisia
Sicily (with arrowhead)
Naples-Foggia
Anzio (with arrowhead)
Rome-Arno
Southern France (with arrowhead)
Rhineland
Ardennes-Alsace
Central Europe

Korean War
CCF intervention
First UN counteroffensive
CCF spring offensive
UN summer-fall offensive
Second Korean winter
Korea, summer-fall 1952
Third Korean winter
Korea, summer 1953

DECORATIONS

Presidential Unit Citation (Army), Streamer embroidered **COLMAR** (3d Infantry Division cited)

Presidential Unit Citation (Army), Streamer embroidered **MONTELIMAR** (1st Battalion, 15th Infantry cited)

Presidential Unit Citation (Army), Streamer embroidered **SURANG-NI** (Company B, 15th Infantry cited)

Presidential Unit Citation (Army), Streamer embroidered **SAN FRATELLO**

Presidential Unit Citation (Army), Streamer embroidered **KOWANG-NI**

Presidential Unit Citation (Navy), Streamer embroidered **HWACHON RESERVOIR** (1st Battalion, 15th Infantry cited)

Navy Unit Commendation, Streamer embroidered **PANMUNJOM** (1st Battalion, 15th Infantry cited)

French Croix de Guerre with Palm, World War II, Streamer embroidered **COLMAR** (15th Infantry cited)

French Croix de Guerre, World War II, Fourragere (15th Infantry cited)

Republic of Korea Presidential Unit Citation, Streamer embroidered **UIJONGBU CORRIDOR** (15th Infantry cited)

Republic of Korea Presidential Unit Citation, Streamer embroidered **IRON TRIANGLE** (15th Infantry cited)

Republic of Korea Presidential Unit Citation, Streamer embroidered **KOREA** (1st Battalion, 15th Infantry cited)

Chryssoun Aristion Andrias (Bravery Gold Medal of Greece), Streamer embroidered **KOREA** (15th Infantry cited)

3D BATTALION, 15TH INFANTRY

LINEAGE

1861   Constituted 3 May as Company C, 1st Battalion, 15th Infantry, Regular Army; organized 17 October at Newport Barracks, KY

Another company constituted 3 May as Company C, 3d Battalion, 17th Infantry, Regular Army

1865   Company C, 3d Battalion, 17th Infantry; organized 29 October at Hart Island, NY

1866   Company C, 1st Battalion, 15th Infantry reorganized and redesignated 21 September as Company C, 15th Infantry

Company C, 3d Battalion, 17th Infantry reorganized and redesignated 21 September as Company C, 35th Infantry

1869   Company C, 15th Infantry and Company C, 35th Infantry consolidated 12 August; consolidated unit designated Company C, 15th Infantry

1922   Assigned 17 July to Philippine Division

1929   Inactivated 1 April at Fort William McKinley, Philippine Islands

1940   Activated 23 May at Fort Lewis, WA, and assigned to 3d Division

Company lineage follows that of 15th Infantry from 1940 activation to 1959 consolidation

1943   A new company constituted 18 January as Headquarters and Headquarters Company, 2d Battalion, 245th Infantry, an element of the 63d Infantry Division and activated 15 June at Camp Blanding, FL

This company lineage differs from that of 15th Infantry from its constitution to 1959 consolidation as follows:

1945   Inactivated 29 September at Camp Kilmer, NJ

1952   Allotted with 63d Infantry Division to Organized Reserve Corps and activated 1 March at Santa Ana, CA

1959   Consolidated 1 May with Headquarters and Headquarters Company, 3d Battle Group, 15th Infantry to form Headquarters and Headquarters Company, 3d Battle Group, 15th Infantry

1959   Withdrawn 31 March from Regular Army, and allotted to Army Reserve, and assigned to 63d Infantry Division; Battle Group activated 1 May at Santa Ana, CA

1963   Reorganized and redesignated 1 April as 3d Battalion, 15th Infantry

1965   Inactivated 31 December at Santa Ana, CA

CAMPAIGN PARTICIPATION

Civil War
Shiloh
Murfreesborough
Chickamauga
Chattanooga
Atlanta
Mississippi 1862
Alabama 1862
Tennessee 1862
Kentucky 1862
Tennesssee 1863
Georgia 1864

Indian Wars
Utes
New Mexico 1880

China Relief Expedition
Without inscription

Philippine Insurrection
Luzon 1900
Luzon 1901

World War II
Algeria–French Morocco (with arrowhead)
Tunisia
Sicily (with arrowhead)
Naples–Foggia
Anzio (with arrowhead)
Rome–Arno
Southern France (with arrowhead)
Rhineland
Ardennes–Alsace
Central Europe

Korean War
CCF intervention
First UN counteroffensive
CCF spring offensive
UN summer–fall offensive
Second Korean winter
Korea, summer–fall 1952
Third Korean winter
Korea, summer 1953

DECORATIONS

Presidential Unit Citation (Army), Streamer embroidered **COLMAR** (3d Infantry Division cited)

Presidential Unit Citation (Army), Streamer embroidered **MONTELIMAR** (1st Battalion, 15th Infantry cited)

Presidential Unit Citation (Army), Streamer embroidered **JEBSHEIM, FRANCE** (2d Battalion, 254th Infantry cited)

Presidential Unit Citation (Army), Streamer embroidered **SAN FRATELLO**

Presidential Unit Citation (Army), Streamer embroidered **KOWANG-NI**

Presidential Unit Citation (Navy), Streamer embroidered **HWACHON RESERVOIR** (1st Battalion, 15th Infantry cited)

Navy Unit Commendation, Streamer embroidered **PAN-MUNJOM** (1st Battalion, 15th Infantry cited)

French Croix de Guerre with Palm, World War II, Streamer embroidered **COLMAR** (15th Infantry cited)

French Croix de Guerre, World War II, Fourragere (15th Infantry cited)

Republic of Korea Presidential Unit Citation, Streamer embroidered **UIJONGBU CORRIDOR** (15th Infantry cited)

Republic of Korea Presidential Unit Citation, Streamer embroidered **IRON TRIANGLE** (15th Infantry cited)

Republic of Korea Presidential Unit Citation, Streamer embroidered **KOREA** (1st Battalion, 15th Infantry cited)

Chryssoun Aristion Andrias (Bravery Gold Medal of Greece), Streamer embroidered **KOREA** (15th Infantry cited)

4TH BATTALION, 15TH INFANTRY

LINEAGE

1861	Constituted 3 May as Company D, 1st Battalion, 15th Infantry, Regular Army; organized 17 October at Newport Barracks, KY
	Another company constituted 3 May as Company D, 3d Battalion, 17th Infantry, Regular Army
1865	Company D, 3d Battalion, 17th Infantry organized 29 October at Hart Island, NY
1866	Company D, 1st Battalion, 15th Infantry reorganized and redesignated 21 September as Company D, 15th Infantry
	Company D, 3d Battalion, 17th Infantry reorganized and redesignated 21 September as Company D, 35th Infantry
1869	Company D, 15th Infantry and Company D, 35th Infantry consolidated 12 August; consolidated unit designated Company D, 15th Infantry
1922	Assigned 17 July to Philippine Division
1929	Inactivated 1 April at Fort William McKinley, Philippine Islands
1940	Activated 23 May at Fort Lewis, WA, and assigned to 3d Division
1957	Inactivated 1 July at Fort Benning, GA, relieved from assignment to 3rd Infantry Division, and redesignated Headquarters and Headquarters Company, 4th Battle Group, 15th Infantry
1963	Redesignated 27 March as Headquarters and Headquarters Company, 4th Battalion, 15th Infantry, and withdraws from Regular Army, and allotted to Army Reserve; assigned to 63d Infantry Division and activated 1 April at Santa Barbara, CA
1965	Inactivated 31 December

CAMPAIGN PARTICIPATION

Civil War
Shiloh
Murfreesborough
Chickamauga
Chattanooga
Atlanta
Mississippi 1862
Alabama 1862
Tennessee 1862
Kentucky 1862
Tennessee 1863
Georgia 1864

Indian Wars
Utes
New Mexico 1880

China Relief Expedition
Without inscription

Philippine Insurrection
Luzon 1900
Luzon 1901

World War II
Algeria–French Morocco (with arrowhead)
Tunisia
Sicily (with arrowhead)
Naples–Foggia
Anzio (with arrowhead)
Rome–Arno
Southern France (with arrowhead)
Rhineland
Ardennes–Alsace
Central Europe

Korean War
CCF intervention
First UN counteroffensive
CCF spring offensive
UN summer–fall offensive
Second Korean winter
Korea, summer–fall 1952
Third Korean winter
Korea, summer 1953

DECORATIONS

Presidential Unit Citation (Army), Streamer embroidered **COLMAR** (3d Infantry Division cited)

Presidential Unit Citation (Army), Streamer embroidered **MONTELIMAR** (1st Battalion, 15th Infantry cited)

Presidential Unit Citation (Army), Streamer embroidered **SAN FRATELLO**

Presidential Unit Citation (Army), Streamer embroidered **KOWANG-NI**

Presidential Unit Citation (Navy), Streamer embroidered **HWACHON RESERVOIR** (1st Battalion, 15th Infantry cited)

Navy Unit Commendation, Streamer embroidered **PAN-MUNJOM** (1st Battalion, 15th Infantry cited)

French Croix de Guerre with Palm, World War II, Streamer embroidered **COLMAR** (15th Infantry cited)

French Croix de Guerre, World War II, Fourragere (15th Infantry cited)

Republic of Korea Presidential Unit Citation, Streamer embroidered **UIJONGBU CORRIDOR** (15th Infantry cited)

Republic of Korea Presidential Unit Citation, Streamer embroidered **IRON TRIANGLE** (15th Infantry cited)

Republic of Korea Presidential Unit Citation, Streamer embroidered **KOREA** (1st Battalion, 15th Infantry cited)

Chryssoun Aristion Andrias (Bravery Gold Medal of Greece), Streamer embroidered **KOREA** (15th Infantry cited)

16TH INFANTRY

COAT OF ARMS

Motto: *Semper Paratus* (Always Prepared)

Symbolism: The shield is the fur vair, white and blue, from the arms of Fléville, France. This town was captured by the 16th Infantry on 4 October 1918 after very heavy fighting in the Meuse-Argonne campaign of World War I. The crossed arrow and bolo recall the Indian and Philippine fighting and the five-bastioned fort was the badge of the V Corps in Cuba.

The crest is the white Maltese cross of the V Corps in the Civil War and represents the desperate fighting in the Wheatfield and Devil's Den at Gettysburg where the regiment lost approximately 50 percent of its effective strength. The motto, "Always Prepared," has been used by the regiment since 1907.

DISTINCTIVE INSIGNIA

The distinctive insignia is the shield of the coat of arms.

LINEAGE

1861	Constituted 3 May as 1st Battalion, 11th Infantry, Regular Army
	Another company constituted 3 May as 3d Battalion, 16th Infantry, Regular Army
1862	1st Battalion, 11th Infantry organized at Fort Independence, MA, and Perryville, MD
1864	3d Battalion, 16th Infantry organized April at Madison Barracks, NY
1866	1st Battalion, 11th Infantry reorganized and redesignated 5 December as the 11th Infantry
	3d Battalion, 16th Infantry reorganized and redesignated 21 September as 34th Infantry
1869	11th Infantry and 34th Infantry consolidated 28 March–6 April to form 16th Infantry
1917	Assigned 8 June to 1st Expeditionary Division (later designated 1st Division)
1957	Relieved 15 February from assignment to 1st Infantry Division and reorganized as a parent regiment under CARS

CAMPAIGN PARTICIPATION

Civil War

Peninsula
Manassas
Antietam
Fredericksburg
Chancellorsville
Gettysburg
Wilderness
Spotsylvania
Cold Harbor
Petersburg
Virginia 1862
Virginia 1863

Indian Wars

Cheyennes
Utes
Pine Ridge

War With Spain

Santiago

Philippine Insurrection

Luzon 1899

Mexican Expedition

Mexico 1916–1917

World War I

Montdidier-Noyon
Aisne-Marne
St. Mihiel
Meuse-Argonne
Lorraine 1917
Lorraine 1918
Picardy 1918

World War II

Algeria-French Morocco
   (with arrowhead)
Tunisia
Sicily (with arrowhead)
Normandy (with
   arrowhead)
Northern France
Rhineland
Ardennes-Alsace
Central Europe

Vietnam

Defense
Counteroffensive
Counteroffensive,
   Phase II
Counteroffensive,
   Phase III
Tet Counteroffensive
(other campaigns to be
determined)

DECORATIONS

Presidential Unit Citation (Army), Streamer embroidered **NORMANDY** (16th Infantry cited)

Presidential Unit Citation (Army), Streamer embroidered **MATEUR, TUNISIA** (1st Battalion, 16th Infantry cited)

Presidential Unit Citation (Army), Streamer embroidered **SICILY** (1st and 2d Battalions, 16th Infantry cited)

Presidential Unit Citation (Army), Streamer embroidered **HURTGEN FOREST** (1st and 2d Battalions, 16th Infantry cited)

Presidential Unit Citation (Army), Streamer embroidered **HAMICH, GERMANY** (3d Battalion, 16th Infantry cited)

French Croix de Guerre with Palm, World War I, Streamer embroidered **AISNE-MARNE** (16th Infantry cited)

French Croix de Guerre with Palm, World War I, Streamer embroidered **MEUSE-ARGONNE** (16th Infantry cited)

French Croix de Guerre with Palm, World War I, Streamer embroidered **KASSERINE** (16th Infantry cited)

French Croix de Guerre with Palm, World War I, Streamer embroidered **NORMANDY** (16th Infantry cited)

French Medaille Militaire, Streamer embroidered **FRANCE** (16th Infantry cited)

French Medaille Militaire, Fourragere (16th Infantry cited)

Belgian Fourragere 1940 (16th Infantry cited)

Cited in the Order of the Day of the Belgian Army for action at **EUPEN-MALMEDY** (16th Infantry cited)

Cited in the Order of the Day of the Belgian Army for action at the **MONS** (16th Infantry cited)

1st Battalion, 16th Infantry

LINEAGE

1861　Constituted 3 May as Company A, 1st Battalion, 11th Infantry, Regular Army; organized in September at Fort Independence, MA

　　　Another company constituted 3 May as Company A, 3d Battalion, 16th Infantry

1864　Company A, 3d Battalion, 16th Infantry; organized in April at Madison Barracks, NY

1866　Company A, 1st Battalion, 11th Infantry reorganized and redesignated 5 December as Company A, 11th Infantry

　　　Company A, 3d Battalion, 16th Infantry reorganized and redesignated 5 December as Company A, 34th Infantry

1869　Company A, 11th Infantry and Company A, 34th Infantry consolidated 6 April to form Company A, 16th Infantry

1917　Assigned 8 June to 1st Expeditionary Division (later designated 1st Division)

1957　Reorganized and redesignated 15 February as Headquarters and Headquarters Company, 1st Battle Group, 16th Infantry; remained assigned to 1st Infantry Division

1959　Relieved 13 March from assignment to 1st Infantry Division and assigned to 8th Infantry Division

1963　Reorganized and redesignated 1 April as 1st Battalion, 16th Infantry; relieved 25 April from assignment to 8th Infantry Division and assigned to 1st Infantry Division

CAMPAIGN PARTICIPATION

Civil War
Peninsula
Manassas
Antietam
Fredericksburg
Chancellorsville
Gettysburg
Wilderness
Spotsylvania
Cold Harbor
Petersburg
Virginia 1862
Virginia 1863

Indian Wars
Cheyennes
Utes
Pine Ridge

War With Spain
Santiago

Philippine Insurrection
Luzon 1899

Mexican Expedition
Mexico 1916–1917

World War I
Montdidier-Noyon
Aisne-Marne
St. Mihiel
Meuse-Argonne
Lorraine 1917
Lorraine 1918
Picardy 1918

World War II
Algeria-French Morocco (with arrowhead)
Tunisia
Sicily (with arrowhead)
Normandy (with arrowhead)
Northern France
Rhineland
Ardennes-Alsace
Central Europe

Vietnam
Defense
Counteroffensive
Counteroffensive, Phase II
Counteroffensive, Phase III
Tet Counteroffensive
Counteroffensive, Phase IV
Counteroffensive, Phase V
Counteroffensive, Phase VI
Tet 69 Counteroffensive
Summer-Fall 1969
Winter-Spring 1970

DECORATIONS

Presidential Unit Citation (Army), Streamer embroidered **NORMANDY** (16th Infantry cited)

Presidential Unit Citation (Army), Streamer embroidered **MATEUR, TUNISIA** (1st Battalion, 16th Infantry cited)

Presidential Unit Citation (Army), Streamer embroidered **SICILY** (1st Battalion, 16th Infantry cited)

Presidential Unit Citation (Army), Streamer embroidered **HURTGEN FOREST** (1st Battalion, 16th Infantry cited)

Presidential Unit Citation (Army), Streamer embroidered **HAMICH, GERMANY**

French Croix de Guerre with Palm, World War I, Streamer embroidered **AISNE-MARNE** (16th Infantry cited)

French Croix de Guerre with Palm, World War I, Streamer embroidered **MEUSE-ARGONNE** (16th Infantry cited)

French Croix de Guerre with Palm, World War II, Streamer embroidered **KASSERINE** (16th Infantry cited)

French Croix de Guerre with Palm, World War II, Streamer embroidered **NORMANDY** (16th Infantry cited)

French Medaille Militaire, Streamer embroidered **FRANCE** (16th Infantry cited)

French Medaille Militaire, Fourragere (16th Infantry cited)

Belgian Fourragere 1940 (16th Infantry cited)

Cited in the Order of the Day of the Belgian Army for action in **EUPEN-MALMEDY** (16th Infantry cited)

Cited in the Order of the Day of the Belgian Army for action in the **MONS** (16th Infantry cited)

Vietnamese Cross of Gallantry with Palm, Streamer embroidered **VIETNAM 1965–1968** (1st Battalion, 16th Infantry cited)

Vietnamese Cross of Gallantry with Palm, Streamer embroidered **VIETNAM 1965–1968** (1st Battalion, 16th Infantry cited)

Vietnamese Civil Action Honor Medal, First Class, Streamer embroidered **VIETNAM 1965–1970** (1st Battalion, 16th Infantry cited)

2D BATTALION, 16TH INFANTRY

LINEAGE

1861   Constituted 3 May as Company B, 1st Battalion, 11th Infantry, Regular Army; organized in September at Fort Independence, MA

Another company constituted 3 May as Company B, 3d Battalion, 16th Infantry, Regular Army

1864   Company B, 3d Battalion, 16th Infantry organized in April at Madison Barracks, NY

1966   Company B, 1st Battalion, 11th Infantry reorganized and redesignated 5 December as Company B, 11th Infantry

Company B, 3d Battalion, 16th Infantry reorganized and redesignated 21 September as Company B, 34th Infantry

1869   Company B, 11th Infantry and Company B, 34th Infantry consolidated 31 March to form Company B, 16th Infantry

1917   Assigned 8 June to 1st Expeditionary Division (later 1st Division)

1957   Inactivated 15 February at Fort Riley, KS, and relieved from assignment to 1st Infantry Division; redesignated as Headquarters and Headquarters Company, 2d Battle Group, 16th Infantry

1963   Activated 1 October at Fort Riley, KS, and assigned to 1st Infantry Division

1964   Reorganized and redesignated 2 March as 2d Battalion, 16th Infantry

CAMPAIGN PARTICIPATION

Civil War

Peninsula
Manassas
Antietam
Fredericksburg
Chancellorsville
Gettysburg
Wilderness
Spotsylvania
Cold Harbor
Petersburg
Virginia 1862
Virginia 1863

Indian Wars

Cheyennes
Utes
Pine Ridge

War With Spain

Santiago

Philippine Insurrection

Luzon 1899

Mexican Expedition

Mexico 1916–1917

World War I

Montdidier-Noyon
Aisne-Marne
St. Mihiel
Meuse-Argonne
Lorraine 1917
Lorraine 1918
Picardy 1918

World War II

Algeria-French Morocco
   (with arrowhead)
Tunisia
Sicily (with arrowhead)
Normandy (with
   arrowhead)
Northern France
Rhineland
Ardennes-Alsace
Central Europe

Vietnam

Defense
Counteroffensive
Counteroffensive,
   Phase II
Counteroffensive,
   Phase III
Tet Counteroffensive
Counteroffensive,
   Phase IV
Counteroffensive,
   Phase V
Counteroffensive,
   Phase VI
Tet 69 Counteroffensive
Summer-Fall 1969
Winter-Spring 1970

DECORATIONS

Presidential Unit Citation (Army), Streamer embroidered **NORMANDY** (16th Infantry cited)

Presidential Unit Citation (Army), Streamer embroidered **MATEUR, TUNISIA** (1st Battalion, 16th Infantry cited)

Presidential Unit Citation (Army), Streamer embroidered **SICILY** (1st Battalion, 16th Infantry cited)

Presidential Unit Citation (Army), Streamer embroidered **HURTGEN FOREST** (1st Battalion, 16th Infantry cited)

Presidential Unit Citation (Army), Streamer embroidered **HAMICH, GERMANY**

French Croix de Guerre with Palm, World War I, Streamer embroidered **AISNE-MARNE** (16th Infantry cited)

French Croix de Guerre with Palm, World War I, Streamer embroidered **MEUSE-ARGONNE** (16th Infantry cited)

French Croix de Guerre with Palm, World War II, Streamer embroidered **KASSERINE** (16th Infantry cited)

French Croix de Guerre with Palm, World War II, Streamer embroidered **NORMANDY** (16th Infantry cited)

French Medaille Militaire, Streamer embroidered **FRANCE** (16th Infantry cited)

French Medaille Militaire, Fourragere (16th Infantry cited)

Belgian Fourragere 1940 (16th Infantry cited)

Cited in the Order of the Day of the Belgian Army for action in **EUPEN-MALMEDY** (16th Infantry cited)

Cited in the Order of the Day of the Belgian Army for action at **MONS** (16th Infantry cited)

Vietnamese Cross of Gallantry with Palm, Streamer embroidered **VIETNAM 1965-1968** (2d Battalion, 16th Infantry cited)

Vietnamese Civil Action Honor Medal, First Class, Streamer embroidered **VIETNAM 1965-1970** (2d Battalion, 16th Infantry cited)

Company C additionally entitled to: Valorous Unit Award, Streamer embroidered **COURTENAY PLANTATION** (Company C, 2d Battalion, 16 Infantry cited)

3D BATTALION, 16TH INFANTRY

LINEAGE

1861   Constituted 3 May as Company C, 1st Battalion, 11th Infantry, Regular Army

Another company constituted 3 May as Company C, 3d Battalion, 16th Infantry

1862   Company C, 1st Battalion, 11th Infantry organized 15 February at Perryville, MD

1864   Company C, 3d Battalion, 16th Infantry organized in April at Madison Barracks, NY

1866   Company C, 1st Battalion, 11th Infantry reorganized and redesignated 5 December as Company C, 11th Infantry

Company C, 3d Battalion, 16th Infantry reorganized and redesignated 21 September as Company C, 34th Infantry

1869   Company C, 11th Infantry and Company C, 34th Infantry consolidated 4 April to form Company C, 16th Infantry

1917   Assigned 8 June to 1st Expeditionary Division (later designated 1st Division)

1957   Inactivated 15 February at Fort Riley, KS, and relieved from assignment to 1st Infantry Division; redesignated as Headquarters and Headquarters Company, 3d Battle Group, 16th Infantry

1959   Withdrawn 6 April from Regular Army; allotted to the Army Reserve and assigned to 94th Infantry Division and Battle Group activated 1 May at Worcester, MA

1963   Reorganized and redesignated 7 January as 3d Battalion, 16th Infantry and relieved from assignment to 94th Infantry Division; assigned to 187th Infantry Brigade

CAMPAIGN PARTICIPATION

Civil War

Peninsula
Manassas
Antietam
Fredericksburg
Chancellorsville
Gettysburg
Wilderness

Spotsylvania
Cold Harbor
Petersburg
Virginia 1862
Virginia 1863

Indian Wars

Cheyennes
Utes
Pine Ridge

War With Spain

Santiago

Philippine Insurrection

Luzon 1899

Mexican Expedition

Mexico 1916–1917

World War I

Montdidier-Noyon
Aisne-Marne
St. Mihiel
Meuse-Argonne
Lorraine 1917
Lorraine 1918
Picardy 1918

World War II

Algeria-French Morocco
(with arrowhead)
Tunisia
Sicily (with arrowhead)
Normandy (with
arrowhead)
Northern France
Rhineland
Ardennes-Alsace
Central Europe

DECORATIONS

Presidential Unit Citation (Army), Streamer embroidered **NORMANDY** (16th Infantry cited)

Presidential Unit Citation (Army), Streamer embroidered **MATEUR, TUNISIA** (1st Battalion, 16th Infantry cited)

Presidential Unit Citation (Army), Streamer embroidered **SICILY** (1st Battalion, 16th Infantry cited)

Presidential Unit Citation (Army), Streamer embroidered **HURTGEN FOREST** (1st Battalion, 16th Infantry cited)

Presidential Unit Citation (Army), Streamer embroidered **HAMICH, GERMANY**

French Croix de Guerre with Palm, World War I, Streamer embroidered **AISNE-MARNE** (16th Infantry cited)

French Croix de Guerre with Palm, World War I, Streamer embroidered **MEUSE-ARGONNE** (16th Infantry cited)

French Croix de Guerre with Palm, World War II, Streamer embroidered **KASSERINE** (16th Infantry cited)

French Croix de Guerre with Palm, World War II, Streamer embroidered **NORMANDY** (16th Infantry cited)

French Medaille Militaire, Streamer embroidered **FRANCE** (16th Infantry cited)

French Medaille Militaire, Fourragere (16th Infantry cited)

Belgian Fourragere 1940 (16th Infantry cited)

Cited in the Order of the Day of the Belgian Army for action in **EUPEN-MALMEDY** (16th Infantry cited)

Cited in the Order of the Day of the Belgian Army for action at **MONS** (16th Infantry cited)

17TH INFANTRY

COAT OF ARMS

Motto: Truth and Courage.

Symbolism: The shield is blue for infantry. Service in the Civil War is shown by the white cross pattée, the badge of the V Corps in the Army of the Potomac, and by the wall which symbolizes the famous stone wall at Fredericksburg. The five-bastioned fort was the badge of the V Corps in Cuba. The buffalo represents service in Korea.

The crest is a sea lion taken from the Spanish arms of Manila, and the arrows represent Indian campaigns.

DISTINCTIVE INSIGNIA

The distinctive insignia is the shield of the coat of arms.

LINEAGE

1861	Constituted 3 May as 1st Battalion, 17th Infantry, Regular Army; organized 6 July at Fort Preble, ME
1866	Reorganized and redesignated 13 December as 17th Infantry
1869	Consolidated 1 June with 44th Infantry, Veteran Reserve Corps to form 17th Infantry
1918	Assigned 5 July to 11th Division
1923	Relieved 24 March from assignment to 11th Division and assigned to 7th Division
1927	Relieved 15 August from assignment to 7th Division and assigned to 6th Division
1933	Relieved 1 October from assignment to 6th Division and assigned to 7th Division
1957	Relieved 1 July from assignment to 7th Division and reorganized as a parent regiment under CARS

CAMPAIGN PARTICIPATION

Civil War

Peninsula
Manassas
Antietam
Fredericksburg
Chancellorsville
Gettysburg
Wilderness
Spotsylvania
Cold Harbor
Petersburg
Virginia 1862
Virginia 1863

Indian Wars

Little Big Horn
Pine Ridge
North Dakota 1872

War With Spain

Santiago

Philippine Insurrection

Manila
Malolos
San Isidro

Tarlac
Mindanao
Luzon 1899
Luzon 1900

Mexican Expedition

Mexico 1916–1917

World War II

Aleutian Islands (with arrowhead)
Eastern Mandates (with arrowhead)
Leyte
Ryukyus (with arrowhead)

Korean War

UN defensive
UN offensive
CCF intervention
First UN counteroffensive
CCF spring offensive
UN summer-fall objective
Second Korean winter
Korea, summer-fall 1952
Third Korean winter
Korea, summer 1953

Vietnam

Counteroffensive,
   Phase VII
Consolidation I
Consolidation II
Cease-Fire

DECORATIONS

Presidential Unit Citation (Army), Streamer embroidered **LEYTE** (17th Infantry cited)

Philippine Presidential Unit Citation, Streamer embroidered **17 OCTOBER 1944 TO 4 JULY 1945** (17th Infantry cited)

Republic of Korea Presidential Unit Citation, Streamer embroidered **INCHON** (17th Infantry cited)

Republic of Korea Presidential Unit Citation, Streamer embroidered **KOREA 1952–1953** (17th Infantry cited)

Republic of Korea Presidential Unit Citation, Streamer embroidered **KOREA 1950–1953** (17th Infantry cited)

1ST BATTALION, 17TH INFANTRY

LINEAGE

1861	Constituted 3 May as Company A, 1st Battalion, 17th Infantry, Regular Army; organized 6 July at Fort Preble, ME
1866	Reorganized and redesignated 13 December as Company A, 17th Infantry
1869	Consolidated 1 June with Company A, 44th Infantry, Veteran Reserve Corps to form Company A, 17th Infantry

Company lineage follows that of 17th Infantry from 1869 consolidation to 1933 assignment to 7th Division

1957	Reorganized and redesignated 1 July as Headquarters and Headquarters Company, 1st Battle Group, 17th Infantry and remained assigned to 7th Infantry Division
1963	Reorganized and redesignated 1 July as 1st Battalion, 17th Infantry

CAMPAIGN PARTICIPATION

Civil War

Peninsula
Manassas
Antietam
Fredericksburg
Chancellorsville
Gettysburg
Wilderness
Spotsylvania
Cold Harbor
Petersburg
Virginia 1862
Virginia 1863

Indian Wars

Little Big Horn
Pine Ridge
North Dakota 1872

War With Spain

Santiago

Philippine Insurrection

Manila
Malolos
San Isidro
Tarlac
Mindanao
Luzon 1899
Luzon 1900

Mexican Expedition

Mexico 1916–1917

World War II

Aleutian Islands (with arrowhead)
Eastern Mandates (with arrowhead)
Leyte
Ryukyus (with arrowhead)

Korean War

UN defensive
UN offensive
CCF intervention
First UN counteroffensive
CCF spring offensive
UN summer-fall objective
Second Korean winter
Korea, summer-fall 1952
Third Korean winter
Korea, summer 1953

DECORATIONS

Presidential Unit Citation (Army), Streamer embroidered **LEYTE** (17th Infantry cited)

Philippine Presidential Unit Citation, Streamer embroidered **17 OCTOBER 1944 TO 4 JULY 1945** (17th Infantry cited)

Republic of Korea Presidential Unit Citation, Streamer embroidered **INCHON** (17th Infantry cited)

Republic of Korea Presidential Unit Citation, Streamer embroidered **KOREA 1952–1953** (17th Infantry cited)

Republic of Korea Presidential Unit Citation, Streamer embroidered **KOREA 1950–1953** (17th Infantry cited)

2D BATTALION, 17TH INFANTRY

LINEAGE

1861	Constituted 3 May as Company B, 1st Battalion, 17th Infantry, Regular Army; organized 6 July at Fort Preble, ME
1866	Reorganized and redesignated 13 December as Company B, 17th Infantry
1869	Consolidated 1 June with Company B, 44th Infantry, Veteran Reserve Corps to form Company B, 17th Infantry
	Company lineage follows that of 17th Infantry from 1869 consolidation to 1933 assignment to 7th Division
1957	Inactivated 1 July in Korea, relieved from assignment to 7th Infantry Division, and redesignated as Headquarters and Headquarters Company, 2d Battle Group, 17th Infantry
1963	Assigned 1 February to 7th Infantry Division, activated in Korea, and reorganized and redesignated 1 July as 2d Battalion, 17th Infantry

CAMPAIGN PARTICIPATION

Civil War

Peninsula
Manassas
Antietam
Fredericksburg
Chancellorsville
Gettysburg
Wilderness
Spotsylvania
Cold Harbor
Petersburg
Virginia 1862
Virginia 1863

Indian Wars

Little Big Horn
Pine Ridge
North Dakota 1872

War With Spain

Santiago

Philippine Insurrection

Manila
Malolos
San Isidro
Tarlac
Mindanao
Luzon 1899
Luzon 1900

Mexican Expedition

Mexico 1916–1917

World War II

Aleutian Islands (with arrowhead)

Eastern Mandates (with arrowhead)
Leyte
Ryukyus (with arrowhead)

Korean War

UN defensive
UN offensive
CCF intervention
First UN counteroffensive
CCF spring offensive
UN summer-fall objective
Second Korean winter
Korea, summer-fall 1952
Third Korean winter
Korea, summer 1953

DECORATIONS

Presidential Unit Citation (Army), Streamer embroidered **ATTU** (Company B, 17th Infantry cited)

Presidential Unit Citation (Army), Streamer embroidered **LEYTE** (17th Infantry cited)

Philippine Presidential Unit Citation, Streamer embroidered **17 OCTOBER 1944 TO 4 JULY 1945** (17th Infantry cited)

Republic of Korea Presidential Unit Citation, Streamer embroidered **INCHON** (17th Infantry cited)

Republic of Korea Presidential Unit Citation, Streamer embroidered **KOREA 1952–1953** (17th Infantry cited)

Republic of Korea Presidential Unit Citation, Streamer embroidered **KOREA 1950–1953** (17th Infantry cited)

3D BATTALION, 17TH INFANTRY

LINEAGE

1861   Constituted 3 May as Company C, 1st Battalion, 17th Infantry, Regular Army; organized 6 July at Fort Preble, ME

1866   Reorganized and redesignated 13 December as Company C, 17th Infantry

1869   Consolidated 1 June with Company C, 44th Infantry, Veteran Reserve Corps to form Company C, 17th Infantry

   Company lineage follows that of 17th Infantry from 1869 consolidation to 1933 assignment to 7th Division

1957   Inactivated 1 July in Korea, relieved from assignment to 7th Infantry Division, and redesignated as Headquarters and Headquarters Company, 3d Battle Group, 17th Infantry

1959   Withdrawn 20 April from Regular Army and allotted to Army Reserve; Battle Group activated 18 May at Council Bluffs, IA and assigned to 103d Infantry Division

1963   Reorganized and redesignated 15 February as 3d Battalion, 17th Infantry, relieved 15 March from assignment to 103d Infantry Division, and assigned to 205th Infantry Brigade

1968   Inactivated 31 January at Council Bluffs, IA

CAMPAIGN PARTICIPATION

Civil War

Peninsula
Manassas
Antietam
Fredericksburg
Chancellorsville
Gettysburg
Wilderness
Spotsylvania
Cold Harbor
Petersburg
Virginia 1862
Virginia 1863

Indian Wars

Little Big Horn
Pine Ridge
North Dakota 1872

War With Spain

Santiago

Philippine Insurrection

Manila
Malolos
San Isidro

Tarlac
Mindanao
Luzon 1899
Luzon 1900

Mexican Expedition

Mexico 1916–1917

World War II

Aleutian Islands (with arrowhead)
Eastern Mandates (with arrowhead)
Leyte
Ryukyus (with arrowhead)

Korean War

UN defensive
UN offensive
CCF intervention
First UN counteroffensive
CCF spring offensive
UN summer-fall objective
Second Korean winter
Korea, summer-fall 1952
Third Korean winter
Korea, summer 1953

DECORATIONS

Presidential Unit Citation (Army), Streamer embroidered **LEYTE** (17th Infantry cited)

Philippine Presidential Unit Citation, Streamer embroidered **17 OCTOBER 1944 TO 4 JULY 1945** (17th Infantry cited)

Republic of Korea Presidential Unit Citation, Streamer embroidered **INCHON** (17th Infantry cited)

Republic of Korea Presidential Unit Citation, Streamer embroidered **KOREA 1952–1953** (17th Infantry cited)

Republic of Korea Presidential Unit Citation, Streamer embroidered **KOREA 1950–1953** (17th Infantry cited)

COMPANY D, 17TH INFANTRY

LINEAGE

1861   Constituted 3 May as Company D, 1st Battalion, 17th Infantry, Regular Army; organized 6 July at Fort Preble, ME

1866   Reorganized and redesignated 13 December as Company D, 17th Infantry

1869   Consolidated 1 June with Company D, 44th Infantry, Veteran Reserve Corps to form Company D, 17th Infantry

Company lineage follows that of 17th Infantry from 1869 consolidation to 1933 assignment to 7th Division

1957   Inactivated 1 July in Korea, relieved from assignment to 7th Infantry Division, and redesignated as Headquarters and Headquarters Company, 4th Battle Group, 17th Infantry

1960   Redesignated 22 June as Company D, 17th Infantry and activated 24 June in Korea

1964   Inactivated 26 December in Korea

1965   Activated 15 May in Germany

1969   Inactivated 21 February at Fort Benning, GA

CAMPAIGN PARTICIPATION

Civil War

Peninsula
Manassas
Antietam
Fredericksburg
Chancellorsville
Gettysburg
Wilderness
Spotsylvania
Cold Harbor
Petersburg
Virginia 1862
Virginia 1863

War With Spain

Santiago

Philippine Insurrection

Malolos
San Isidro
Tarlac
Luzon 1899
Luzon 1900

Mexican Expedition

Mexico 1916–1917

World War II-AP

Aleutian Islands (with arrowhead)
Eastern Mandates (with arrowhead)
Leyte
Ryukyus (with arrowhead)

Korean War

UN defensive
UN offensive
CCF intervention
First UN counteroffensive
CCF spring offensive
UN summer-fall objective
Second Korean winter
Korea, summer-fall 1952
Third Korean winter
Korea, summer 1953

Vietnam

Counteroffensive, Phase VII
Consolidation I
Consolidation II
Cease-Fire

DECORATIONS

Presidential Unit Citation (Army), Streamer embroidered **LEYTE** (17th Infantry cited)

Philippine Presidential Unit Citation, Streamer embroidered **17 OCTOBER 1944 TO 4 JULY 1945** (17th Infantry cited)

Republic of Korea Presidential Unit Citation, Streamer embroidered **INCHON** (17th Infantry cited)

Republic of Korea Presidential Unit Citation, Streamer embroidered **KOREA 1952–1953** (17th Infantry cited)

Republic of Korea Presidential Unit Citation, Streamer embroidered **KOREA 1950–1953** (17th Infantry cited)

18TH INFANTRY

COAT OF ARMS

Motto: *In Omnia Paratus* (In All Things Prepared)

Symbolism: Civil War service is shown by the saltire cross from the Confederate flag. The crossed arrows represent the regiment's Indian campaigns; the VIII Corps badge recalls service in the 2d Brigade, 2d Division of that corps in the War with Spain and the bolo stands for operations in the Visayas during the Philippine Insurrection. In World War I the regiment was awarded two French Croix de Guerre with Palm and the French Fourragere for its part in the Soissons offensive on 18 July 1918 and the operations of early October 1918 around Exermont and Hill 240 in the old province of Lorraine. The chief bears the bend of the arms of Lorraine between the fleurs-de-lis of the arms of Soissons.

The crest is the badge of the 1st Division of the XIV Corps of the Army of the Cumberland, with which the regiment served during most of its operations in the Civil War.

DISTINCTIVE INSIGNIA

The distinctive insignia is the shield and motto of the coat of arms.

LINEAGE

1861 Constituted 3 May as 1st Battalion, 18th Infantry, Regular Army; organized 22 July at Camp Thomas, OH

Another company constituted 3 May as 2d Battalion, 16th Infantry

1866 1st Battalion, 18th Infantry reorganized and redesignated 31 December as 18th Infantry

2d Battalion, 16th Infantry reorganized and redesignated 21 September as 25th Infantry

1869 18th Infantry and 25th Infantry consolidated 28 April to form 18th Infantry

1917 Assigned 8 June to 1st Expeditionary Division (later 1st Infantry Division)

1957 Relieved 15 February from assignment to 1st Infantry Division and reorganized as a parent regiment under CARS

CAMPAIGN PARTICIPATION

Civil War

Murfreesborough
Chickamauga
Chattanooga
Atlanta
Mississippi 1862
Kentucky 1862
Tennessee 1863
Georgia 1864

Indian Wars

Wyoming 1867
Dakota 1867
Montana 1881
Montana 1882

War With Spain

Manila

Philippine Insurrection

Iloilo
Panay 1899
Panay 1900

World War I

Montdidier-Noyon
Aisne-Marne
St. Mihiel
Meuse-Argonne
Lorraine 1917
Lorraine 1918
Picardy 1918

World War II

Algeria-French Morocco (with arrowhead)
Tunisia
Sicily (with arrowhead)
Normandy (with arrowhead)
Northern France
Rhineland
Ardennes-Alsace
Central Europe

Vietnam

Defense
Counteroffensive
Counteroffensive, Phase II
Counteroffensive, Phase III
Tet Counteroffensive
Counteroffensive, Phase IV
Counteroffensive, Phase V
Counteroffensive, Phase VI
Tet 69 Counteroffensive
Summer-Fall 1969
Winter-Spring 1970

DECORATIONS

Presidential Unit Citation (Army), Streamer embroidered **NORMANDY** (18th Infantry cited)

Presidential Unit Citation (Army), Streamer embroidered **AACHEN, GERMANY** (1st and 3d Battalions, 18th Infantry cited)

Presidential Unit Citation (Army), Streamer embroidered **BEJA, TUNISIA** (2d Battalion, 18th Infantry cited)

French Croix de Guerre with Palm, World War I, Streamer embroidered **AISNE-MARNE** (18th Infantry cited)

French Croix de Guerre with Palm, World War I, Streamer embroidered **MEUSE-ARGONNE** (18th Infantry cited)

French Croix de Guerre with Palm, World War II, Streamer embroidered **KASSERINE** (18th Infantry cited)

French Croix de Guerre with Palm, World War II, Streamer embroidered **NORMANDY** (18th Infantry cited)

French Medaille Militaire, Streamer embroidered **FRANCE** (18th Infantry cited)

French Medaille Militaire, Fourragere (18th Infantry cited)

Belgian Fourragere 1940 (18th Infantry cited)

Cited in the Order of the Day of the Belgian Army for action at **MONS** (18th Infantry cited)

Cited in the Order of the Day of the Belgian Army for action at **EUPEN-MALMEDY** (18th Infantry cited)

1st Battalion, 18th Infantry

LINEAGE

1861   Constituted 3 May as Company B, 2d Battalion, 18th Infantry, Regular Army; organized 17 September at Camp Thomas, OH, and redesignated 20 September as Company H, 1st Battalion, 18th Infantry; redesignated 19 October as Company A, 1st Battalion, 10th Infantry

1866   Reorganized and redesignated 31 December as Company A, 18th Infantry

1869   Consolidated 28 April with Company A, 25th Infantry to form Company A, 18th Infantry

1917   Assigned 8 June to 1st Expeditionary Division (later 1st Infantry Division)

1957   Reorganized and redesignated 15 February as Headquarters and Headquarters Company, 1st Battle Group, 18th Infantry; remained assigned to 1st Infantry Division

1959   Relieved 14 April from assignment to 1st Infantry Division and assigned to 8th Infantry Division

1963   Relieved 1 April from assignment to 8th Infantry Division and assigned to 1st Infantry Division

1964   Reorganized and redesignated 2 January as 1st Battalion, 18th Infantry

CAMPAIGN PARTICIPATION

Civil War

Murfreesborough
Chickamauga
Chattanooga
Atlanta
Mississippi 1862
Kentucky 1862
Tennessee 1863
Georgia 1864

Indian Wars

Wyoming 1867
Dakota 1867
Montana 1881
Montana 1882

War With Spain

Manila

Philippine Insurrection

Iloilo
Panay 1899
Panay 1900

World War I

Montdidier-Noyon
Aisne-Marne
St. Mihiel
Meuse-Argonne
Lorraine 1917
Lorraine 1918
Picardy 1918

World War II

Algeria-French Morocco (with arrowhead)
Tunisia
Sicily (with arrowhead)
Normandy (with arrowhead)
Northern France
Rhineland
Ardennes-Alsace
Central Europe

Vietnam

Defense
Counteroffensive
Counteroffensive, Phase II
Counteroffensive, Phase III
Tet Counteroffensive
Counteroffensive, Phase IV
Counteroffensive, Phase V
Counteroffensive, Phase VI
Tet 69 Counteroffensive
Summer-Fall 1969
Winter-Spring 1970

DECORATIONS

Presidential Unit Citation (Army), Streamer embroidered **NORMANDY** (18th Infantry cited)

Presidential Unit Citation (Army), Streamer embroidered **AACHEN, GERMANY** (1st Battalion, 18th Infantry cited)

Presidential Unit Citation (Army), Streamer embroidered **BEJA, TUNISIA**

French Croix de Guerre with Palm, World War I, Streamer embroidered **AISNE-MARNE** (18th Infantry cited)

French Croix de Guerre with Palm, World War I, Streamer embroidered **MEUSE-ARGONNE** (18th Infantry cited)

French Croix de Guerre with Palm, World War II, Streamer embroidered **KASSERINE** (18th Infantry cited)

French Croix de Guerre with Palm, World War II, Streamer embroidered **NORMANDY** (18th Infantry cited)

French Medaille Militaire, Streamer embroidered **FRANCE** (18th Infantry cited)

French Medaille Militaire, Fourragere (18th Infantry cited)

Belgian Fourragere 1940 (18th Infantry cited)

Cited in the Order of the Day of the Belgian Army for action at **MONS** (18th Infantry cited)

Cited in the Order of the Day of the Belgian Army for action at **EUPEN-MALMEDY** (18th Infantry cited)

Vietnamese Cross of Gallantry with Palm, Streamer embroidered **VIETNAM 1965-1968** (1st Battalion, 18th Infantry cited)

Vietnamese Cross of Gallantry with Palm, Streamer embroidered **VIETNAM 1969-1970** (1st Battalion, 18th Infantry cited)

Vietnamese Civil Action Honor Medal, First Class, Streamer embroidered **VIETNAM 1965–1970** (1st Battalion, 18th Infantry cited)

2D BATTALION, 18TH INFANTRY

LINEAGE

1861   Constituted 3 May as Company B, 1st Battalion, 18th Infantry, Regular Army; organized 9 September at Camp Thomas, OH

1866   Reorganized and redesignated 31 December as Company B, 18th Infantry

1869   Consolidated 28 April with Company B, 25th Infantry to form Company B, 18th Infantry

1917   Assigned 8 June to 1st Expeditionary Division (later designated 1st Infantry Division)

1957   Inactivated 15 February at Fort Riley, KS, relieved from assignment to 1st Infantry Division, and redesignated as Headquarters and Headquarters Company, 2d Battle Group, 18th Infantry

1963   Activated 1 October at Fort Riley, KS and assigned to 1st Infantry Division

1964   Reorganized and redesignated 2 March as 2d Battalion, 18th Infantry and inactivated 15 April at Fort Riley, KS

CAMPAIGN PARTICIPATION

Civil War

Murfreesborough
Chickamauga
Chattanooga
Atlanta
Mississippi 1862
Kentucky 1862
Tennessee 1863
Georgia 1864

Indian Wars

Wyoming 1867
Dakota 1867
Montana 1881
Montana 1882

War With Spain

Manila

Philippine Insurrection

Iloilo
Panay 1899
Panay 1900

World War I

Montdidier-Noyon
Aisne-Marne
St. Mihiel
Meuse-Argonne
Lorraine 1917
Lorraine 1918
Picardy 1918

World War II

Algeria-French Morocco (with arrowhead)
Tunisia
Sicily (with arrowhead)
Normandy (with arrowhead)
Northern France
Rhineland
Ardennes-Alsace
Central Europe

Vietnam

Defense
Counteroffensive
Counteroffensive, Phase II
Counteroffensive, Phase III
Tet Counteroffensive
Counteroffensive, Phase IV
Counteroffensive, Phase V
Counteroffensive, Phase VI
Tet 69 Counteroffensive
Summer-Fall 1969
Winter-Spring 1970

DECORATIONS

Presidential Unit Citation (Army), Streamer embroidered **NORMANDY** (18th Infantry cited)

Presidential Unit Citation (Army), Streamer embroidered **AACHEN, GERMANY** (1st Battalion, 18th Infantry cited)

Presidential Unit Citation (Army), Streamer embroidered **BEJA, TUNISIA**

French Croix de Guerre with Palm, World War I, Streamer embroidered **AISNE-MARNE** (18th Infantry cited)

French Croix de Guerre with Palm, World War I, Streamer embroidered **MEUSE-ARGONNE** (18th Infantry cited)

French Croix de Guerre with Palm, World War II, Streamer embroidered **KASSERINE** (18th Infantry cited)

French Croix de Guerre with Palm, World War II, Streamer embroidered **NORMANDY** (18th Infantry cited)

French Medaille Militaire, Streamer embroidered **FRANCE** (18th Infantry cited)

French Medaille Militaire, Fourragere (18th Infantry cited)

Belgian Fourragere 1940 (18th Infantry cited)

Cited in the Order of the Day of the Belgian Army for action at **MONS** (18th Infantry cited)

Cited in the Order of the Day of the Belgian Army for action at **EUPEN-MALMEDY** (18th Infantry cited)

Vietnamese Cross of Gallantry with Palm, Streamer embroidered **VIETNAM 1965–1968** (2d Battalion, 18th Infantry cited)

Vietnamese Civil Action Honor Medal, First Class, Streamer embroidered **VIETNAM 1965–1970** (1st Battalion, 18th Infantry cited)

3D BATTALION, 18TH INFANTRY

LINEAGE

1861 Constituted 3 May as Company B, 1st Battalion, 18th Infantry, Regular Army; organized 15 August at Camp Thomas, OH; redesignated 9 September as Company C, 1st Battalion, 18th Infantry

1866 Reorganized and redesignated 31 December as Company C, 18th Infantry

1869 Consolidated 18 April with Company C, 25th Infantry to form Company C, 18th Infantry

Company lineage follows that of 18th Infantry from 1869 consolidation to 1959 consolidation

1917 A new company constituted 5 August as Headquarters and Headquarters Company, 3d Battalion, 301st Infantry, an element of the 76th Division organized in August at Camp Devens, MA

The 301st Infantry lineage differs from that of 18th Infantry from its constitution to 1 May 1959 consolidation as follows:

1919 Demobilized in January at Camp Devens, MA

1921 Reconstituted 24 June in the Organized Reserves as an element of the 94th Division organized in November in Massachusetts

1942 Ordered into active military service 15 September and reorganized at Fort Custer, MI

1946 Inactivated 29 January at Camp Kilmer, NJ

1947 Activated 13 February in the Organized Reserves at Lawrence, MA

1959 Consolidated 1 May with Headquarters and Headquarters Company, 3d Battle Group, 18th Infantry to form Headquarters and Headquarters Company, 3d Battle Group, 18th Infantry

1963 Reorganized and redesignated 7 January as 3d Battalion, 18th Infantry, relieved from assignment to 94th Division, and assigned to 187th Infantry Brigade at Lowell, MA

CAMPAIGN PARTICIPATION

Civil War

Murfreesborough
Chickamauga
Chattanooga
Atlanta
Mississippi 1862
Kentucky 1862
Tennessee 1863
Georgia 1864

Indian Wars

Wyoming 1867
Dakota 1867
Montana 1881
Montana 1882

War With Spain

Manila

Philippine Insurrection

Iloilo
Panay 1899
Panay 1900

World War I

Montdidier-Noyon
Aisne-Marne
St. Mihiel
Meuse-Argonne
Lorraine 1917
Lorraine 1918
Picardy 1918

World War II

Algeria-French Morocco (with arrowhead)
Tunisia
Sicily (with arrowhead)
Normandy (with arrowhead)
Northern France
Rhineland
Ardennes-Alsace
Central Europe

DECORATIONS

Presidential Unit Citation (Army), Streamer embroidered **NORMANDY** (18th Infantry cited)

Presidential Unit Citation (Army), Streamer embroidered **AACHEN, GERMANY** (1st Battalion, 18th Infantry cited)

Presidential Unit Citation (Army), Streamer embroidered **BEJA, TUNISIA**

French Croix de Guerre with Palm, World War I, Streamer embroidered **AISNE-MARNE** (18th Infantry cited)

French Croix de Guerre with Palm, World War I, Streamer embroidered **MEUSE-ARGONNE** (18th Infantry cited)

French Croix de Guerre with Palm, World War II, Streamer embroidered **KASSERINE** (18th Infantry cited)

French Croix de Guerre with Palm, World War II, Streamer embroidered **NORMANDY** (18th Infantry cited)

French Medaille Militaire, Streamer embroidered **FRANCE** (18th Infantry cited)

French Medaille Militaire, Fourragere (18th Infantry cited)

Belgian Fourragere 1940 (18th Infantry cited)

Cited in the Order of the Day of the Belgian Army for action at **MONS** (18th Infantry cited)

Cited in the Order of the Day of the Belgian Army for action at **EUPEN-MALMEDY** (18th Infantry cited)

4TH BATTALION, 18TH INFANTRY

LINEAGE

1861 Organized 19 September at Camp Thomas, OH, as Company D, 1st Battalion, 18th Infantry, Regular Army

1866 Reorganized and redesignated 31 December as Company D, 18th Infantry

1869 Consolidated in April with Company D, 25th Infantry to form Company D, 18th Infantry

1917 Assigned 8 June to 1st Expeditionary Division (later designated 1st Infantry Division)

1957 Inactivated 15 February at Fort Riley, KS, relieved from assignment to 1st Infantry Division, and redesignated as Headquarters and Headquarters Company, 4th Battle Group, 18th Infantry

1963 Redesignated 23 August as Headquarters and Headquarters Company, 4th Battalion, 18th Infantry, activated 1 September in Germany, and assigned to U.S. Army Berlin Brigade

CAMPAIGN PARTICIPATION

Civil War

Murfreesborough
Chickamauga
Chattanooga
Atlanta
Mississippi 1862
Kentucky 1862
Tennessee 1863
Georgia 1864

Indian Wars

Wyoming 1867
Dakota 1867

Montana 1881
Montana 1882

War With Spain

Manila

Philippine Insurrection

Iloilo
Panay 1899
Panay 1900

World War I

Montdidier-Noyon
Aisne-Marne
St. Mihiel
Meuse-Argonne
Lorraine 1917
Lorraine 1918
Picardy 1918

World War II

Algeria-French Morocco (with arrowhead)
Tunisia
Sicily (with arrowhead)
Normandy (with arrowhead)
Northern France
Rhineland
Ardennes-Alsace
Central Europe

DECORATIONS

Presidential Unit Citation (Army), Streamer embroidered **NORMANDY** (18th Infantry cited)

Presidential Unit Citation (Army), Streamer embroidered **AACHEN, GERMANY** (1st Battalion, 18th Infantry cited)

Presidential Unit Citation (Army), Streamer embroidered **BEJA, TUNISIA**

French Croix de Guerre with Palm, World War I, Streamer embroidered **AISNE-MARNE** (18th Infantry cited)

French Croix de Guerre with Palm, World War I, Streamer embroidered **MEUSE-ARGONNE** (18th Infantry cited)

French Croix de Guerre with Palm, World War II, Streamer embroidered **KASSERINE** (18th Infantry cited)

French Croix de Guerre with Palm, World War II, Streamer embroidered **NORMANDY** (18th Infantry cited)

French Medaille Militaire, Streamer embroidered **FRANCE** (18th Infantry cited)

French Medaille Militaire, Fourragere (18th Infantry cited)

Belgian Fourragere 1940 (18th Infantry cited)

Cited in the Order of the Day of the Belgian Army for action at **MONS** (18th Infantry cited)

Cited in the Order of the Day of the Belgian Army for action at **EUPEN-MALMEDY** (18th Infantry cited)

19TH INFANTRY
(The Rock of Chickamauga)

COAT OF ARMS

Motto: The Rock of Chickamauga

Symbolism: The 19th Infantry was organized in 1861 and the principal charge on the shield is a reproduction of the regimental insignia of that period. The three stars commemorate service in the Civil War, the War with Spain, and the Philippine Insurrection.

The crest symbolizes the great achievement of the regiment at the battle of Chickamauga on 19-20 September 1863, when it formed part of General Thomas' command and earned its nickname and motto, "The Rock of Chickamauga." At the end of the second day, there were only four officers and fifty-one enlisted men on duty and the regiment was commanded by a second lieutenant. The strap of a second lieutenant is shown on the rock.

DISTINCTIVE INSIGNIA

The distinctive insignia is the shield and motto of the coat of arms.

LINEAGE

1861	Constituted 3 May as 1st Battalion, 19th Infantry, Regular Army; organized 9 July at Indianapolis, IN
	Another company constituted 3 May as 2d Battalion, 19th Infantry, Regular Army
1863	2d Battalion, 19th Infantry organized 3 March at Fort Wayne, MI
1866	1st Battalion, 19th Infantry reorganized and redesignated 1 October as 19th Infantry
	2d Battalion, 19th Infantry reorganized and redesignated 1 October as 28th Infantry
1869	19th Infantry and 28th Infantry consolidated 25 March to form 19th Infantry
1918	Assigned 29 July to 18th Division
1919	Relieved 14 February from assignment to 18th Division
1922	Assigned 17 October to Hawaiian Division
1941	Relieved 26 August from assignment to Hawaiian Division and assigned to 24th Division
1958	Relieved 5 June from assignment to 24th Infantry Division and reorganized as a parent regiment under CARS

CAMPAIGN PARTICIPATION

Civil War

Shiloh
Murfreesborough
Chickamauga
Chattanooga
Atlanta
Mississipi 1862
Kentucky 1862
Tennessee 1863
Georgia 1864

Indian Wars

Utes

War With Spain

Puerto Rico

Philippine Insurrection

Panay 1899
Cebu 1899
Panay 1900
Cebu 1900
Cebu 1901
Bohol 1901

World War II

Central Pacific
New Guinea (with arrowhead)

Leyte (with arrowhead)
Luzon (with arrowhead)
Southern Philippines (with arrowhead)

Korean War

UN defensive
UN offensive
CCF intervention
First UN counteroffensive
CCF spring offensive
UN summer-fall offensive
Second Korean winter
Korea, summer 1953

DECORATIONS

Presidential Unit Citation (Army), Streamer embroidered **DAVAO** (19th Infantry cited)

Presidential Unit Citation (Army), Streamer embroidered **LEYTE** (2d Battalion, 19th Infantry cited)

Presidential Unit Citation (Army), Streamer embroidered **DEFENSE OF KOREA** (24th Infantry Division cited)

Philippine Presidential Unit Citation, Streamer embroidered **17 OCTOBER 1944 TO 4 JULY 1945** (19th Infantry cited)

Republic of Korea Presidential Unit Citation, Streamer embroidered **PYONGTAEK** (19th Infantry cited)

Republic of Korea Presidential Unit Citation, Streamer embroidered **KOREA** (24th Infantry Division cited)

1ST BATTALION, 19TH INFANTRY
(The Rock of Chickamauga)

LINEAGE

1861	Constituted 3 May as Company A, 1st Battalion, 19th Infantry, Regular Army; organized 24 August at Indianapolis, IN
1866	Reorganized and redesignated 1 October as Company A, 19th Infantry
1869	Consolidated 17 April with Company A, 28th Infantry to form Company A, 19th Infantry

Company lineage follows that of 19th Infantry from 1869 consolidation through 1941 assignment to the 24th Division

1958 Redesignated 5 June as Headquarters and Headquarters Company, 1st Battle Group, 19th Infantry, and assigned to 24th Infantry Division, and activated 1 July in Germany

1963 Reorganized and redesignated 1 February as 1st Battalion, 19th Infantry

1970 Inactivated 15 April at Fort Riley, KS

World War II
Central Pacific
New Guinea (with arrowhead)
Leyte (with arrowhead)
Luzon (with arrowhead)
Southern Philippines (with arrowhead)

Korean War
UN defensive
UN offensive
CCF intervention
First UN counteroffensive
CCF spring offensive
UN summer-fall offensive
Second Korean winter
Korea, summer 1953

CAMPAIGN PARTICIPATION

Civil War
Shiloh
Murfreesborough
Chickamauga
Chattanooga
Atlanta
Mississipi 1862
Kentucky 1862
Tennessee 1863
Georgia 1864

Indian Wars
Utes

War With Spain
Puerto Rico

Philippine Insurrection
Jolo
Panay 1899
Cebu 1899
Panay 1900
Cebu 1900
Cebu 1901
Bohol 1901

DECORATIONS

Presidential Unit Citation (Army), Streamer embroidered **DAVAO** (19th Infantry cited)

Presidential Unit Citation (Army), Streamer embroidered **LEYTE**

Presidential Unit Citation (Army), Streamer embroidered **DEFENSE OF KOREA** (24th Infantry Division cited)

Philippine Presidential Unit Citation, Streamer embroidered **17 OCTOBER 1944 TO 4 JULY 1945** (19th Infantry cited)

Republic of Korea Presidential Unit Citation, Streamer embroidered **PYONGTAEK** (19th Infantry cited)

Republic of Korea Presidential Unit Citation, Streamer embroidered **KOREA** (24th Infantry Division cited)

2D BATTALION, 19TH INFANTRY
(The Rock of Chickamauga)

LINEAGE

1861 Constituted 3 May as Company B, 1st Battalion, 19th Infantry, Regular Army; organized 30 September at Indianapolis, IN

1866 Reorganized and redesignated 1 October as Company B, 19th Infantry

1869 Consolidated 15 April with Company B, 28th Infantry to form Company B, 19th Infantry

Company lineage follows that of 19th Infantry from 1869 consolidation through 1941 assignment to the 24th Division

1957 Reorganized and redesignated 1 February as Headquarters and Headquarters Company, 2d Battle Group, 19th Infantry, and relieved from assignment to 24th Infantry Division; assigned to 25th Infantry Division

1958 Inactivated 25 March in Hawaii

1961 Activated 1 July in Hawaii

1962 Relieved 19 February from assignment to 25th Infantry Division and assigned to 24th Infantry Division

1963 Reorganized and redesignated 1 February as 2d Battalion, 19th Infantry

1966 Inactivated 1 May in Germany

CAMPAIGN PARTICIPATION

Civil War

Shiloh
Murfreesborough
Chickamauga
Chattanooga
Atlanta
Mississipi 1862
Kentucky 1862
Tennessee 1863
Georgia 1864

Indian Wars

Utes

War With Spain

Puerto Rico

Philippine Insurrection

Jolo
Panay 1899

Cebu 1899
Panay 1900
Cebu 1900
Cebu 1901
Bohol 1901

World War II

Central Pacific
New Guinea (with
  arrowhead)
Leyte (with arrowhead)
Luzon (with arrowhead)
Southern Philippines
  (with arrowhead)

Korean War

UN defensive
UN offensive
CCF intervention
First UN counteroffensive

CCF spring offensive
UN summer-fall offensive
Second Korean winter
Korea, summer 1953

DECORATIONS

Presidential Unit Citation (Army), Streamer embroidered **DAVAO** (19th Infantry cited)

Presidential Unit Citation (Army), Streamer embroidered **LEYTE**

Presidential Unit Citation (Army), Streamer embroidered **DEFENSE OF KOREA** (24th Infantry Division cited)

Philippine Presidential Unit Citation, Streamer embroidered **17 OCTOBER 1944 TO 4 JULY 1945** (19th Infantry cited)

Republic of Korea Presidential Unit Citation, Streamer embroidered **PYONGTAEK** (19th Infantry cited)

Republic of Korea Presidential Unit Citation, Streamer embroidered **KOREA** (24th Infantry Division cited)

3D BATTALION, 19TH INFANTRY
(The Rock of Chickamauga)

LINEAGE

1861   Constituted 3 May as Company C, 1st Battalion, 19th Infantry, Regular Army; organized 25 November at Indianapolis, IN

1866   Reorganized and redesignated 1 October as Company C, 19th Infantry

1869   Consolidated 15 April with Company I, 28th Infantry to form Company C, 19th Infantry

Company lineage follows that of 19th Infantry from 1869 consolidation through 1941 assignment to the 24th Division

1958   Relieved 9 April from assignment to 24th Infantry Division

1963   Reorganized and redesignated 1 February as Headquarters and Headquarters Company, 3d Battalion, 19th Infantry, and assigned to 24th Infantry Division

1970   Inactivated 15 April in Germany

CAMPAIGN PARTICIPATION

Civil War

Shiloh
Murfreesborough
Chickamauga
Chattanooga
Atlanta
Mississipi 1862
Kentucky 1862
Tennessee 1863
Georgia 1864

Indian Wars

Utes

War With Spain

Puerto Rico

Philippine Insurrection

Panay 1899
Cebu 1899
Panay 1900
Cebu 1900
Cebu 1901
Bohol 1901

World War II

Central Pacific
New Guinea (with
  arrowhead)
Leyte (with arrowhead)
Luzon (with arrowhead)
Southern Philippines
  (with arrowhead)

Korean War

UN defensive
UN offensive
CCF intervention
First UN counteroffensive

CCF spring offensive
UN summer-fall offensive
Second Korean winter
Korea, summer 1953

DECORATIONS

Presidential Unit Citation (Army), Streamer embroidered **DAVAO** (19th Infantry cited)

Presidential Unit Citation (Army), Streamer embroidered **LEYTE**

Presidential Unit Citation (Army), Streamer embroidered **DEFENSE OF KOREA** (24th Infantry Division cited)

Philippine Presidential Unit Citation, Streamer embroidered **17 OCTOBER 1944 TO 4 JULY 1945** (19th Infantry cited)

Republic of Korea Presidential Unit Citation, Streamer embroidered **PYONGTAEK** (19th Infantry cited)

Republic of Korea Presidential Unit Citation, Streamer embroidered **KOREA** (24th Infantry Division cited)

4TH BATTLE, GROUP, 19TH INFANTRY
(The Rock of Chickamauga)

LINEAGE

1861	Constituted 3 May as Company D, 1st Battalion, 19th Infantry, Regular Army; organized 25 December at Indianapolis, IN
1866	Reorganized and redesignated 1 October as Company D, 19th Infantry
1869	Consolidated 29 April with Company H, 28th Infantry to form Company D, 19th Infantry

Company lineage follows that of 19th Infantry from 1869 consolidation through 1941 assignment to the 24th Division

1958	Inactivated 5 June and relieved from assignment to 24th Division
1959	Redesignated 19 March as Headquarters and Headquarters Company, 4th Battle Group, 19th Infantry, withdrawn from Regular Army, and allotted to Army Reserve; assigned to 83d Infantry Division; Battle Group activated 20 March at South Charleston, WV
1963	Inactivated 15 April and relieved from assignment to 83d Infantry

CAMPAIGN PARTICIPATION

Civil War

Shiloh
Murfreesborough
Chickamauga
Chattanooga

Atlanta
Mississipi 1862
Kentucky 1862
Tennessee 1863
Georgia 1864

Indian Wars

Utes

War With Spain

Puerto Rico

Philippine Insurrection

Jolo
Panay 1899
Cebu 1899
Panay 1900
Cebu 1900
Cebu 1901
Bohol 1901

World War II

Central Pacific

New Guinea (with arrowhead)
Leyte (with arrowhead)
Luzon (with arrowhead)
Southern Philippines (with arrowhead)

Korean War

UN defensive
UN offensive
CCF intervention
First UN counteroffensive
CCF spring offensive
UN summer-fall offensive
Second Korean winter
Korea, summer 1953

DECORATIONS

Presidential Unit Citation (Army), Streamer embroidered **DAVAO** (19th Infantry cited)

Presidential Unit Citation (Army), Streamer embroidered **LEYTE**

Presidential Unit Citation (Army), Streamer embroidered **DEFENSE OF KOREA** (24th Infantry Division cited)

Philippine Presidential Unit Citation, Streamer embroidered **17 OCTOBER 1944 TO 4 JULY 1945** (19th Infantry cited)

Republic of Korea Presidential Unit Citation, Streamer embroidered **PYONGTAEK** (19th Infantry cited)

Republic of Korea Presidential Unit Citation, Streamer embroidered **KOREA** (24th Infantry Division cited)

COMPANY E, 19TH INFANTRY
(The Rock of Chickamauga)

LINEAGE

1861	Constituted 3 May as Company E, 1st Battalion, 19th Infantry, Regular Army
1862	Organized 15 March at Indianapolis, IN
1866	Reorganized and redesignated 1 October as Company E, 19th Infantry

Company lineage follows that of 19th Infantry from 1869 consolidation through 1941 assignment to the 24th Division

1958	Inactivated 5 June, relieved from assignment to 24th Infantry Division, and redesignated as Headquarters and Headquarters Company, 5th Battle Group, 19th Infantry
1963	Redesignated 1 February as Company E, 19th Infantry and activated in Korea
1967	Inactivated 1 December in Korea

CAMPAIGN PARTICIPATION

Civil War
Shiloh
Murfreesborough
Chickamauga
Chattanooga
Atlanta
Mississipi 1862
Kentucky 1862
Tennessee 1863
Georgia 1864

Indian Wars
Utes

War With Spain
Puerto Rico

Philippine Insurrection
Panay 1899
Panay 1900
Cebu 1901

World War II
Central Pacific
New Guinea (with arrowhead)
Leyte (with arrowhead)
Luzon (with arrowhead)
Southern Philippines (with arrowhead)

Korean War
UN defensive
UN offensive
CCF intervention
First UN counteroffensive
CCF spring offensive
UN summer-fall offensive
Second Korean winter
Korea, summer 1953

DECORATIONS

Presidential Unit Citation (Army), Streamer embroidered **DAVAO** (19th Infantry cited)

Presidential Unit Citation (Army), Streamer embroidered **LEYTE**

Presidential Unit Citation (Army), Streamer Embroidered **LEYTE** (2d Battalion, 19th Infantry cited)

Philippine Presidential Unit Citation, Streamer embroidered **17 OCTOBER 1944 TO 4 JULY 1945** (19th Infantry cited)

Republic of Korea Presidential Unit Citation, Streamer embroidered **PYONGTAEK** (19th Infantry cited)

Republic of Korea Presidential Unit Citation, Streamer embroidered **KOREA** (24th Infantry Division cited)

20TH INFANTRY
(Sykes' Regulars)

COAT OF ARMS

Motto: *Tant Que Je Puis* (To the Limit of Our Ability)

Symbolism: During the Civil War this unit served in the 2d Division of the V Corps, the badge of which was a white cross pattée. The regiment saw service in Cuba in the War with Spain as a portion of the V Corps at El Caney and San Juan. The badge of the V Corps was a five-bastioned fort. During the Philippine Insurrection it took part in the Pasig expedition of 1899, which is signified by the Katipunan device in the base.

The muskets in the crest form the Roman numeral "XX," the numerical designation of the regiment.

DISTINCTIVE INSIGNIA

The distinctive insignia is the crest of the coat of arms.

LINEAGE

1861	Constituted 3 May as 2d Battalion, 11th Infantry, Regular Army
1862	Organized 6 June at Fort Independence, MA
1866	Reorganized and redesignated 6 December as 20th Infantry
1918	Assigned 9 July to 10th Division
1919	Relieved 14 February from assignment to 10th Division
1920	Assigned 18 September to 2d Division
1939	Relieved 16 October from assignment to 2d division and assigned to 6th Division
1949	Inactivated 10 January in Korea
1950	Activated 4 October at Fort Ord, CA
1956	Relieved 3 April from assignment to 6th Infantry Division
1957	Reorganized 15 November as a parent regiment under CARS

CAMPAIGN PARTICIPATION

Civil War

Peninsula
Manassas
Antietam
Fredericksburg
Chancellorsville
Gettysburg
Wilderness
Spotsylvania
Cold Harbor
Petersburg
Virginia 1862
Virginia 1863

Indian Wars

Little Big Horn
Pine Ridge

War With Spain

Santiago

Philippine Insurrection

Manila
Luzon 1901

World War II

New Guinea
Luzon (with arrowhead)

Vietnam

Counteroffensive, Phase III
Tet Counteroffensive
Counteroffensive, Phase IV
Counteroffensive, Phase V
Counteroffensive, Phase VI
Tet 69 Counteroffensive
Summer–Fall 1969
Winter–Spring 1970
Sanctuary Counteroffensive
Counteroffensive, Phase VII
Consolidation I

DECORATIONS

Presidential Unit Citation (Army), Streamer embroidered **CABARUAN HILLS** (2d Battalion, 20th Infantry cited)

Presidential Unit Citation (Army), Streamer embroidered **MAFFIN BAY** (3d Battalion, 20th Infantry cited)

Presidential Unit Citation (Army), Streamer embroidered **MUNOZ** (3d Battalion, 20th Infantry cited)

Philippine Presidential Unit Citation, Streamer embroidered **17 OCTOBER 1944 TO 4 JULY 1945** (6th Infantry Division cited)

1ST BATTALION, 20TH INFANTRY
(Sykes' Regulars)

LINEAGE

1861	Constituted 3 May as Company A, 2d Battalion, 11th Infantry, Regular Army
1862	Organized 26 July at Fort Independence, MA
1866	Reorganized and redesignated 6 December as Company A, 20th Infantry

Company lineage follows that of 20th Infantry from 1866 through 1950 activation at Fort Ord, CA

1957	Reorganized and redesignated 15 November as Headquarters and Headquarters Company, 1st Battle Group, 20th Infantry
1962	Inactivated 8 August at Fort Kobbe, Canal Zone

1966   Redesignated 23 May as 1st Battalion, 20th Infantry, activated 1 July in Hawaii and assigned to 11th Infantry Brigade

1969   Relieved 15 February from assignment to 11th Infantry Brigade and assigned to 23d Infantry Division

CAMPAIGN PARTICIPATION

Civil War
Peninsula
Manassas
Antietam
Fredericksburg
Chancellorsville
Gettysburg
Wilderness
Spotsylvania
Cold Harbor
Petersburg
Virginia 1862
Virginia 1863

Indian Wars
Little Big Horn
Pine Ridge

War With Spain
Santiago

Philippine Insurrection
Manila
Luzon 1901

World War II
New Guinea
Luzon (with arrowhead)

Vietnam
Counteroffensive, Phase III
Tet Counteroffensive
Counteroffensive, Phase IV
Counteroffensive, Phase V
Counteroffensive, Phase VI
Tet 69 Counteroffensive
Summer–Fall 1969
Winter–Spring 1970
Sanctuary Counteroffensive
Counteroffensive, Phase VII
Consolidation I

DECORATIONS

Presidential Unit Citation (Army), Streamer embroidered **CABARUAN HILLS**

Presidential Unit Citation (Army), Streamer embroidered **MAFFIN BAY**

Presidential Unit Citation (Army), Streamer embroidered **MUNOZ**

Philippine Presidential Unit Citation, Streamer embroidered **17 OCTOBER 1944 TO 4 JULY 1945** (6th Infantry Division cited)

Vietnamese Cross of Gallantry with Palm, Streamer embroidered **VIETNAM 1968–1969** (1st Battalion, 20th Infantry cited)

2D BATTALION, 20TH INFANTRY
(Sykes' Regulars)

LINEAGE

1861   Constituted 3 May as Company B, 2d Battalion, 11th Infantry, Regular Army

1862   Organized 8 September at Fort Independence, MA

1866   Reorganized and redesignated 6 December as Company B, 20th Infantry

Company lineage follows that of 20th Infantry from 1866 through 1950 activation at Fort Ord, CA

1957   Inactivated 15 November at Fort Kobbe, Canal Zone, and redesignated as Headquarters and Headquarters Company, 2d Battle Group, 20th Infantry

1967   Redesignated 24 November as Headquarters and Headquarters Company, 2d Battalion, 20th Infantry; assigned to the 6th Infantry Division and activated at Fort Campbell, KY

1968   Inactivated 25 July in Hawaii

CAMPAIGN PARTICIPATION

Civil War
Peninsula
Manassas
Antietam
Fredericksburg
Chancellorsville
Gettysburg
Wilderness
Spotsylvania
Cold Harbor

Petersburg
Virginia 1862
Virginia 1863

Indian Wars

Little Big Horn
Pine Ridge

War With Spain

Santiago

Philippine Insurrection

Manila
Luzon 1901

World War II

New Guinea
Luzon (with arrowhead)

DECORATIONS

Presidential Unit Citation (Army), Streamer embroidered **CABARUAN HILLS**

Presidential Unit Citation (Army), Streamer embroidered **MAFFIN BAY**

Presidential Unit Citation (Army), Streamer embroidered **MUNOZ**

Philippine Presidential Unit Citation, Streamer embroidered **17 OCTOBER 1944 TO 4 JULY 1945** (6th Infantry Division cited)

3D BATTALION, 20TH INFANTRY
(Sykes' Regulars)

LINEAGE

1861   Constituted 3 May as Company C, 2d Battalion, 11th Infantry, Regular Army

1862   Organized 13 November at Fort Independence, MA

1866   Reorganized and redesignated 6 December as Company C, 20th Infantry

Company lineage follows that of 20th Infantry from 1866 through 1950 activation at Fort Ord, CA

1957   Inactivated 15 November at Fort Kobbe, Canal Zone, and redesignated Headquarters and Headquarters Company, 3d Battle Group, 20th Infantry

1959   Withdrawn 19 March from Regular Army, allotted to Army Reserve, and assigned to 90th Infantry Division; Battle Group activated 1 April at Houston, TX

1963   Inactivated 27 March and relieved from assignment to 90th Infantry Division

1967   Redesignated 10 May as 3d Battalion, 20th Infantry, withdrawn from Army Reserve, and allotted to Regular Army; assigned to 198th Infantry Brigade and activated at Fort Hood, TX; inactivated 12 May and relieved from assignment to 198th Infantry Brigade; activated 24 November at Fort Campbell, KY, and assigned to 6th Infantry Division

1968   Inactivated 25 July at Schofield Barracks, Hawaii

CAMPAIGN PARTICIPATION

Civil War

Peninsula
Manassas
Antietam
Fredericksburg
Chancellorsville
Gettysburg
Wilderness
Spotsylvania
Cold Harbor
Petersburg
Virginia 1862
Virginia 1863

Indian Wars

Little Big Horn
Pine Ridge

War With Spain

Santiago

Philippine Insurrection

Manila
Luzon 1901

World War II

New Guinea
Luzon (with arrowhead)

DECORATIONS

Presidential Unit Citation (Army), Streamer embroidered **CABARUAN HILLS**

Presidential Unit Citation (Army), Streamer embroidered **MAFFIN BAY**

Presidential Unit Citation (Army), Streamer embroidered **MUNOZ**

Philippine Presidential Unit Citation, Streamer embroidered **17 OCTOBER 1944 TO 4 JULY 1945** (6th Infantry Division cited)

4TH BATTALION, 20TH INFANTRY
(Sykes' Regulars)

LINEAGE

1861   Constituted 3 May as Company D, 11th Infantry, Regular Army

1863   Organized 26 January at Fort Independence, MA

1866   Reorganized and redesignated 6 December as Company D, 20th Infantry

Company lineage follows that of 20th Infantry from 1866 through 1950 activation at Fort Ord, CA

1957   Inactivated 15 November at Fort Kobbe, Canal Zone, and redesignated Headquarters and Headquarters Company, 4th Battle Group, 20th Infantry

1962   Redesignated 3 August as Headquarters and Headquarters Company, 4th Battalion, 20th Infantry; assigned to 193d Infantry Brigade and activated 8 August at Fort Clayton, Canal Zone

CAMPAIGN PARTICIPATION

Civil War

Peninsula	Fredericksburg
Manassas	Chancellorsville
Antietam	Gettysburg

Wilderness
Spotsylvania
Cold Harbor
Petersburg
Virginia 1862
Virginia 1863

Indian Wars

Little Big Horn
Pine Ridge

War With Spain

Santiago

Philippine Insurrection

Manila
Luzon 1901

World War II

New Guinea
Luzon (with arrowhead)

DECORATIONS

Presidential Unit Citation (Army), Streamer embroidered **CABARUAN HILLS**

Presidential Unit Citation (Army), Streamer embroidered **MAFFIN BAY**

Presidential Unit Citation (Army), Streamer embroidered **MUNOZ**

Philippine Presidential Unit Citation, Streamer embroidered **17 OCTOBER 1944 TO 4 JULY 1945** (6th Infantry Division cited)

COMPANY E, 20TH INFANTRY
(Sykes' Regulars)

LINEAGE

1861   Constituted 3 May as Company F, 2d Battalion, 11th Infantry, Regular Army

1865   Organized 8 September at camp near Richmond, VA

1866   Reorganized and redesignated 6 December as Company E, 20th Infantry

Company lineage follows that of 20th Infantry from 1866 through 1950 activation at Fort Ord, CA

1957   Inactivated 15 November at Fort Kobbe, Canal Zone, and redesignated Headquarters and Headquarters Company, 5th Battle Group, 20th Infantry

1960   Redesignated 22 June as Company E, 20th Infantry and activated 24 June in Korea

1966   Inactivated 1 January in Korea

1967   Activated 25 September in Vietnam

1969   Inactivated 1 February in Vietnam

CAMPAIGN PARTICIPATION

War With Spain

Santiago

Philippine Insurrection

Manila
Luzon 1901

World War II-AP

New Guinea
Luzon (with arrowhead)

Vietnam

Counteroffensive,
Phase III
Tet Counteroffensive
Counteroffensive,
Phase IV
Counteroffensive,
Phase V
Counteroffensive,
Phase VI

DECORATIONS

Presidential Unit Citation (Army), Streamer embroidered **CABARUAN HILLS** (2d Battalion, 20th Infantry cited)

Philippine Presidential Unit Citation, Streamer embroidered **17 OCTOBER 1944 TO 4 JULY 1945** (6th Infantry Division cited)

Vietnamese Cross of Gallantry with Palm, Streamer embroidered **VIETNAM 1967–1968** (Company E, 20th Infantry cited)

Vietnamese Civil Action Honor Medal, First Class, Streamer embroidered **VIETNAM 1967–1968** (Company E, 20th Infantry cited)

6TH BATTALION, 20TH INFANTRY
(Sykes' Regulars)

LINEAGE

1861   Constituted 3 May as Company F, 2d Battalion, 11th Infantry, Regular Army

1865   Organized in September at camp near Richmond, VA

1866   Reorganized and redesignated 6 December as Company F, 20th Infantry

Company lineage follows that of 20th Infantry from 1866 through 1950 activation at Fort Ord, CA

1957   Inactivated 15 November at Fort Kobbe, Canal Zone, and redesignated Headquarters and Headquarters Company, 6th Battle Group, 20th Infantry

1967   Redesignated 24 November as Headquarters and Headquarters Company, 6th Battalion, 20th Infantry; and assigned to 6th Infantry Division; activated at Fort Campbell, KY

1968   Inactivated 25 July at Schofield Barracks, Hawaii

CAMPAIGN PARTICIPATION

Civil War

Peninsula
Manassas
Antietam
Fredericksburg
Chancellorsville
Gettysburg
Wilderness
Spotsylvania
Cold Harbor
Petersburg
Virginia 1862
Virginia 1863

Indian Wars

Little Big Horn
Pine Ridge

War With Spain

Santiago

Philippine Insurrection

Manila
Luzon 1901

World War II

New Guinea
Luzon (with arrowhead)

DECORATIONS

Presidential Unit Citation (Army), Streamer embroidered **CABARUAN HILLS** (2d Battalion, 20th Infantry cited)

Presidential Unit Citation (Army), Streamer embroidered **MAFFIN BAY**

Presidential Unit Citation (Army), Streamer embroidered **MUNOZ**

Philippine Presidential Unit Citation, Streamer embroidered **17 OCTOBER 1944 TO 4 JULY 1945** (6th Infantry Division cited)

21ST INFANTRY
(Gimlet)

COAT OF ARMS

Motto: Duty.

Symbolism: This unit's baptism of fire was at Cedar Mountain on 9 August 1862, where it performed its mission with such success as to bring forth special mention from General Prince, the brigade commander. This incident is shown by the cedar tree. At Santiago the 21st Infantry was in the V Corps, the badge of which was a five-bastioned fort, and its Philippine Insurrection service is shown by the Katipunan sun. The colors of the shield, blue and white, have been the infantry colors during the existence of the regiment.

The arrows in the crest stand for Indian campaigns. The rattlesnake skin was an Indian emblem of war.

DISTINCTIVE INSIGNIA

The distinctive insignia is the shield, crest, and motto of the coat of arms.

LINEAGE

1861   Constituted 3 May as 2d Battalion, 12th Infantry, Regular Army

Another company constituted 3 May as 3d Battalion, 14th Infantry, Regular Army

1862   2d Battalion, 12th Infantry organized 20 May at Fort Hamilton, NY

1865   3d Battalion, 14th Infantry organized 22 July at Fort Trumbull, CT

1866   2d Battalion, 12th Infantry reorganized and redesignated 7 December as 21st Infantry

3d Battalion, 14th Infantry reorganized and redesignated 21 September as 32d Infantry

1869   21st Infantry and 32d Infantry consolidated 9–31 August to form 21st Infantry

1918   Assigned 29 July to 16th Division

1919   Relieved 8 March from assignment to 16th Division

1921   Assigned 22 October to Hawaiian Division

1941   Relieved 26 August from assignment to Hawaiian Division and assigned to 24th Division

1958   Relieved 5 June from assignment to 24th Infantry Division and reorganized as a parent regiment under CARS

CAMPAIGN PARTICIPATION

Civil War

Peninsula
Manassas
Antietam
Fredericksburg
Chancellorsville
Gettysburg
Wilderness
Spotsylvania
Cold Harbor
Petersburg
Virginia 1862
Virginia 1863

Indian Wars

Modocs
Nez Perces
Bannocks
Arizona 1866
Arizona 1867
Arizona 1868
Arizona 1869
Arizona 1870

War With Spain

Santiago

Philippine Insurrection

Zapote River
Luzon 1899
Luzon 1901
Luzon 1902

World War II

Central Pacific
New Guinea (with arrowhead)
Leyte
Luzon
Southern Philippines (with arrowhead)

Korean War

UN defensive
UN offensive
CCF intervention
First UN counteroffensive
CCF spring offensive
UN summer–fall offensive
Second Korean winter
Korea, summer 1953

Vietnam

Counteroffensive, Phase II
Counteroffensive, Phase III
Tet Counteroffensive
Counteroffensive, Phase IV
Counteroffensive, Phase V
Counteroffensive, Phase VI
Tet 69 Counteroffensive
Summer–Fall 1969
Winter–Spring 1970
Sanctuary Counteroffensive
Counteroffensive, Phase VII
Consolidation I
Consolidation II
Cease-Fire

DECORATIONS

Presidential Unit Citation (Army), Streamer embroidered **DEFENSE OF KOREA** (24th Infantry Division cited)

Presidential Unit Citation (Army), Streamer embroidered **SANGHONG JONG-NI** (Headquarters and Headquarters Company and Medical Company, 21st Infantry cited)

Philippine Presidential Unit Citation, Streamer embroidered **17 OCTOBER 1944 TO 4 JULY 1945** (21st Infantry cited)

Republic of Korea Presidential Unit Citation, Streamer embroidered **PYONGTAEK** (21st Infantry cited)

Republic of Korea Presidential Unit Citation, Streamer embroidered **KOREA** (24th Infantry Division cited)

1st Battalion, 21st Infantry
(Gimlet)

LINEAGE

1861   Constituted 3 May as Company A, 2d Battalion, 12th Infantry, Regular Army

Another company constituted 3 May as Company A, 3d Battalion, 14th Infantry, Regular Army

1862   Company A, 2d Battalion, 12th Infantry organized 20 May at Fort Hamilton, NY

1865   Company A, 3d Battalion, 14th Infantry organized in August at Fort Trumbull, CT

1866   Company A, 2d Battalion, 12th Infantry reorganized and redesignated 7 December as Company A, 21st Infantry

Company A, 3d Battalion, 14th Infantry reorganized and redesignated 21 September as Company A, 32d Infantry

1869   Company A, 21st Infantry and Company A, 32d Infantry consolidated 20 August; consolidated unit designated Company A, 21st Infantry

Company lineage follows that of 21st Infantry from 1869 consolidation through 1941 assignment to 24th Division

1958   Redesignated 5 June as Headquarters and Headquarters Company, 1st Battle Group, 21st Infantry; and assigned to 24th Division; activated 1 July in Germany

1963   Reorganized and redesignated 1 February as 1st Battalion, 21st Infantry

1970   Inactivated 15 April in Germany

CAMPAIGN PARTICIPATION

Civil War

Peninsula
Manassas
Antietam
Fredericksburg
Chancellorsville
Gettysburg
Wilderness
Spotsylvania
Cold Harbor
Petersburg
Virginia 1862
Virginia 1863

Indian Wars

Modocs
Nez Perces
Bannocks
Arizona 1866
Arizona 1867
Arizona 1868
Arizona 1869
Arizona 1870

War With Spain

Santiago

Philippine Insurrection

Zapote River
Luzon 1899
Luzon 1900
Luzon 1901
Luzon 1902

World War II

Central Pacific
New Guinea (with arrowhead)
Leyte
Luzon
Southern Philippines (with arrowhead)

Korean War

UN defensive
UN offensive
CCF intervention
First UN counteroffensive
CCF spring offensive
UN summer–fall offensive
Second Korean winter
Korea, summer 1953

DECORATIONS

Presidential Unit Citation (Army), Streamer embroidered **DEFENSE OF KOREA** (24th Infantry Division cited)

Presidential Unit Citation (Army), Streamer embroidered **SANGHONG JONG-NI**

Philippine Presidential Unit Citation, Streamer embroidered **17 OCTOBER 1944 TO 4 JULY 1945** (21st Infantry cited)

Republic of Korea Presidential Unit Citation, Streamer embroidered **PYONGTAEK** (21st Infantry cited)

Republic of Korea Presidential Unit Citation, Streamer embroidered **KOREA** (24th Infantry Division cited)

2D BATTALION, 21ST INFANTRY
(Gimlet)

LINEAGE

1861   Constituted 3 May as Company B, 2d Battalion, 12th Infantry, Regular Army

Another company constituted 3 May as Company B, 3d Battalion, 14th Infantry

1862   Company B, 2d Battalion, 12th Infantry organized 20 May at Fort Hamilton, NY

1865   Company B, 3d Battalion, 14th Infantry organized in August at Fort Trumbull, CT

1866   Company B, 2d Battalion, 12th Infantry reorganized and redesignated 7 December as Company B, 21st Infantry

Company B, 3d Battalion, 14th Infantry reorganized and redesignated 21 September as Company B, 32d Infantry

1869   Company B, 21st Infantry and Company B, 32d Infantry consolidated 26 August; consolidated unit designated Company B, 21st Infantry

Company lineage follows that of 21st Infantry from 1869 consolidation through 1941 assignment to 24th Division

1957   Reorganized and redesignated 1 February as Headquarters and Headquarters Company, 2d Battle Group, 21st Infantry, relieved from assignment to 24th Infantry Division, and assigned to 25th Infantry Division

1963   Reorganized and redesignated 1 February as 2d Battalion, 21st Infantry, relieved from assignment to 25th Infantry Division, and assigned to 24th Infantry Division

1970   Inactivated 15 April at Fort Riley, KS

CAMPAIGN PARTICIPATION

Civil War

Peninsula
Manassas
Antietam
Fredericksburg
Chancellorsville
Gettysburg
Wilderness
Spotsylvania
Cold Harbor
Petersburg
Virginia 1862
Virginia 1863

Indian Wars

Modocs
Nez Perces
Bannocks
Arizona 1866
Arizona 1867
Arizona 1868
Arizona 1869
Arizona 1870

War With Spain

Santiago

Philippine Insurrection

Zapote River
Luzon 1899
Luzon 1901
Luzon 1902

World War II

Central Pacific
New Guinea (with arrowhead)
Leyte
Luzon
Southern Philippines (with arrowhead)

Korean War

UN defensive
UN offensive
CCF intervention
First UN counteroffensive
CCF spring offensive
UN summer–fall offensive
Second Korean winter
Korea, summer 1953

DECORATIONS

Presidential Unit Citation (Army), Streamer embroidered **DEFENSE OF KOREA** (24th Infantry Division cited)

Presidential Unit Citation (Army), Streamer embroidered **SANGHONG JONG-NI**

Philippine Presidential Unit Citation, Streamer embroidered **17 OCTOBER 1944 TO 4 JULY 1945** (21st Infantry cited)

Republic of Korea Presidential Unit Citation, Streamer embroidered **PYONGTAEK** (21st Infantry cited)

Republic of Korea Presidential Unit Citation, Streamer embroidered **KOREA** (24th Infantry Division cited)

3D BATTALION, 21ST INFANTRY
(Gimlet)

LINEAGE

1861	Constituted 3 May as Company C, 2d Battalion, 12th Infantry, Regular Army
	Another company constituted 3 May as Company C, 3d Battalion, 14th Infantry
1862	Company C, 2d Battalion, 12th Infantry organized 28 May at Fort Hamilton, NY
1865	Company C, 3d Battalion, 14th Infantry organized in September at Hart Island, NY
1866	Company C, 2d Battalion, 12th Infantry reorganized and redesignated 7 December as Company C, 21st Infantry
	Company C, 3d Battalion, 14th Infantry reorganized and redesignated 21 September as Company C, 32d Infantry
1869	Company C, 21st Infantry and Company C, 32d Infantry consolidated 27 August; consolidated unit designated Company C, 21st Infantry

Company lineage follows that of 21st Infantry from 1869 consolidation through 1941 assignment to 24th Division

1958	Inactivated 5 June and relieved from assignment to 24th Infantry Division
1959	Redesignated 31 March as Headquarters and Headquarters Company, 3d Battle Group, 21st Infantry, withdrawn from Regular Army, allotted to Army Reserve, and assigned to 63d Infantry Division; Battle Group activated 1 May at Santa Barbara, CA
1963	Inactivated 1 April and relieved from assignment to 63rd Infantry Division
1965	Redesignated 10 September as 3d Battalion, 21st Infantry, withdrawn from Army Reserve, allotted to Regular Army, and assigned to 196th Infantry Brigade; activated 15 September at Fort Devens, MA
1969	Relieved 15 February from assignment to 196th Infantry Brigade and assigned to 23d Infantry Division

CAMPAIGN PARTICIPATION

Civil War

Peninsula
Manassas
Antietam
Fredericksburg
Chancellorsville
Gettysburg
Wilderness
Spotsylvania
Cold Harbor
Petersburg
Virginia 1862
Virginia 1863

Indian Wars

Modocs
Nez Perces
Bannocks
Arizona 1866
Arizona 1867
Arizona 1868
Arizona 1869
Arizona 1870

War With Spain

Santiago

Philippine Insurrection

Zapote River
Luzon 1899
Luzon 1900
Luzon 1901
Luzon 1902

World War II

Central Pacific
New Guinea (with arrowhead)

Leyte
Luzon
Southern Philippines (with arrowhead)

Korean War

UN defensive
UN offensive
CCF intervention
First UN counteroffensive
CCF spring offensive
UN summer–fall offensive
Second Korean winter
Korea, summer 1953

Vietnam

Counteroffensive, Phase II
Counteroffensive, Phase III
Tet Counteroffensive
Counteroffensive, Phase IV
Counteroffensive, Phase V
Counteroffensive, Phase VI
Tet 69 Counteroffensive
Summer–Fall 1969
Winter–Spring 1970
Sanctuary Counteroffensive
Counteroffensive, Phase VII
Consolidation I
Consolidation II
Cease-Fire

DECORATIONS

Presidential Unit Citation (Army), Streamer embroidered **DEFENSE OF KOREA** (24th Infantry Division cited)

Presidential Unit Citation (Army), Streamer embroidered **SANGHONG JONG-NI**

Philippine Presidential Unit Citation, Streamer embroidered **17 OCTOBER 1944 TO 4 JULY 1945** (21st Infantry cited)

Republic of Korea Presidential Unit Citation, Streamer embroidered **PYONGTAEK** (21st Infantry cited)

Republic of Korea Presidential Unit Citation, Streamer embroidered **KOREA** (24th Infantry Division cited)

4TH BATTALION, 21ST INFANTRY
(Gimlet)

LINEAGE

1861	Constituted 3 May as Company D, 2d Battalion, 12th Infantry, Regular Army
	Another company constituted 3 May as Company D, 3d Battalion, 14th Infantry, Regular Army
1862	Company D, 2d Battalion, 12th Infantry organized 20 August at Fort Hamilton, NY
1865	Company D, 3d Battalion, 14th Infantry organized in September at Hart Island, NY
1866	Company D, 2d Battalion, 12th Infantry reorganized and redesignated Company D, 21st Infantry
	Company D, 3d Battalion, 14th Infantry reorganized and redesignated Company D, 32d Infantry
1869	Company D, 21st Infantry and Company D, 32d Infantry consolidated 21 August; consolidated unit designated Company D, 21st Infantry

Company lineage follows that of 21st Infantry from 1869 consolidation through 1941 assignment to 24th Division

1958	Inactivated 5 June and relieved from assignment to 24th Infantry Division; redesignated as Headquarters and Headquarters Company, 4th Battalion, 21st Infantry
1965	Redesignated 11 October as Headquarters and Headquarters Company, 4th Battalion, 21st Infantry, assigned to 25th Infantry Division, and activated 6 December in Hawaii
1966	Inactivated 3 January in Hawaii and relieved from assignment to 25th Infantry Division
1967	Activated 1 November in Hawaii and assigned to 11th Infantry Brigade
1969	Relieved 15 February from assignment to 11th Infantry Brigade and assigned to 23d Infantry Division

CAMPAIGN PARTICIPATION

Civil War

Peninsula
Manassas
Antietam
Fredericksburg
Chancellorsville
Gettysburg
Wilderness
Spotsylvania
Cold Harbor
Petersburg
Virginia 1862
Virginia 1863

Indian Wars

Modocs
Nez Perces
Bannocks
Arizona 1866
Arizona 1867
Arizona 1868
Arizona 1869
Arizona 1870

War With Spain

Santiago

Philippine Insurrection

Zapote River
Luzon 1899
Luzon 1901
Luzon 1902

World War II

Central Pacific
New Guinea (with arrowhead)
Leyte
Luzon
Southern Philippines (with arrowhead)

Korean War

UN defensive
UN offensive
CCF intervention
First UN counteroffensive
CCF spring offensive
UN summer–fall offensive
Second Korean winter
Korea, summer 1953

Vietnam

Counteroffensive, Phase IV
Counteroffensive, Phase V
Counteroffensive, Phase VI
Tet 69 Counteroffensive
Summer–Fall 1969
Winter–Spring 1970
Sanctuary Counteroffensive
Counteroffensive, Phase VII

DECORATIONS

Presidential Unit Citation (Army), Streamer embroidered **DEFENSE OF KOREA** (24th Infantry Division cited)

Presidential Unit Citation (Army), Streamer embroidered **SANGHONG JONG-NI**

Philippine Presidential Unit Citation, Streamer embroidered **17 OCTOBER 1944 TO 4 JULY 1945** (21st Infantry cited)

Republic of Korea Presidential Unit Citation, Streamer embroidered **PYONGTAEK** (21st Infantry cited)

Republic of Korea Presidential Unit Citation, Streamer embroidered **KOREA** (24th Infantry Division cited)

Vietnamese Cross of Gallantry with Palm, Streamer embroidered **VIETNAM 1968–1969** (4th Battalion, 21st Infantry cited)

5TH BATTALION, 21ST INFANTRY
(Gimlet)

LINEAGE

1861   Constituted 3 May as Company E, 2d Battalion, 12th Infantry, Regular Army

Another company constituted 3 May as Company E, 3d Battalion, 14th Infantry, Regular Army

1862   Company E, 2d Battalion, 12th Infantry organized 20 May at Fort Hamilton, NY

1865   Company E, 3d Battalion, 14th Infantry organized in September at Hart Island, NY

1866   Company E, 2d Battalion, 12th Infantry reorganized and redesignated 7 December as Company E, 21st Infantry

Company E, 3d Battalion, 14th Infantry reorganized and redesignated 21 September as Company E, 32d Infantry

1869   Company E, 21st Infantry and Company E, 32d Infantry consolidated 19 August; consolidated unit designated Company E, 21st Infantry

Company lineage follows that of 21st Infantry from 1869 consolidation through 1941 assignment to 24th Division

1958   Inactivated 5 June, relieved from assignment to 24th Infantry Division, and redesignated Headquarters and Headquarters Company, 5th Battle Group, 21st Infantry

1965   Redesignated 11 October as Headquarters and Headquarters Company, 5th Battalion, 21st Infantry, assigned to 25th Infantry Division, and activated 6 December in Hawaii

1966   Inactivated 3 January in Hawaii and relieved from assignment to 25th Infantry Division

CAMPAIGN PARTICIPATION

Civil War

Peninsula
Manassas
Antietam
Fredericksburg
Chancellorsville
Gettysburg
Wilderness
Spotsylvania
Cold Harbor
Petersburg
Virginia 1862
Virginia 1863

Indian Wars

Modocs
Nez Perces
Bannocks
Arizona 1866
Arizona 1867
Arizona 1868
Arizona 1869
Arizona 1870

War With Spain

Santiago

Philippine Insurrection

Zapote River
Luzon 1899
Luzon 1901
Luzon 1902

World War II

Central Pacific
New Guinea (with arrowhead)
Leyte
Luzon
Southern Philippines (with arrowhead)

Korean War

UN defensive
UN offensive
CCF intervention
First UN counteroffensive
CCF spring offensive
UN summer–fall offensive
Second Korean winter
Korea, summer 1953

DECORATIONS

Presidential Unit Citation (Army), Streamer embroidered **DEFENSE OF KOREA** (24th Infantry Division cited)

Presidential Unit Citation (Army), Streamer embroidered **SANGHONG JONG-NI**

Philippine Presidential Unit Citation, Streamer embroidered **17 OCTOBER 1944 TO 4 JULY 1945** (21st Infantry cited)

Republic of Korea Presidential Unit Citation, Streamer embroidered **PYONGTAEK** (21st Infantry cited)

Republic of Korea Presidential Unit Citation, Streamer embroidered **KOREA** (24th Infantry Division cited)

22D INFANTRY

COAT OF ARMS

Motto: Deeds Not Words

Symbolism: The shield is white and blue, the old and present infantry colors. The embattled partition line is for the wars in which the regiment has taken part. The arrows stand for five Indian campaigns; the sun in splendor was the old Katipunan device in the Philippine Insurrection.

The crest is for the War with Spain, being the badge of the V Corps in the Spanish colors, and charged with a royal palm to commemorate the fact that the 22d Infantry was the first regiment to land on Cuban soil in that war.

DISTINCTIVE INSIGNIA

The distinctive insignia is the shield of the coat of arms.

LINEAGE

1861	Constituted 3 May as 2d Battalion, 13th Infantry, Regular Army
	Another company constituted 3 May as 3d Battalion, 13th Infantry, Regular Army
1865	2d Battalion, 13th Infantry organized 15 May at Camp Dennison, OH
	3d Battalion, 13th Infantry organized in December at Jefferson Barracks, MO
1866	2d Battalion, 13th Infantry reorganized and redesignated 21 September as 22d Infantry
	3d Battalion, 13th Infantry reorganized and redesignated 21 September as 31st Infantry
1869	22d Infantry and 31st Infantry consolidated in May to form 22d Infantry
1923	Assigned 24 March to 4th Division
1946	Inactivated 1 March at Camp Butner, NC
1947	Activated 15 July at Fort Ord, CA
1957	Relieved 1 April from assignment to 4th Infantry Division and reorganized as a parent regiment under CARS

CAMPAIGN PARTICIPATION

Indian Wars

Little Big Horn
Pine Ridge
North Dakota 1868
North Dakota 1869
Montana 1872

War With Spain

Santiago

Philippine Insurrection

Manila
Malolos
San Isidro
Mindanao
Jolo
Luzon 1900

World War II

Normandy (with arrowhead)
Northern France
Rhineland
Ardennes-Alsace
Central Europe

Vietnam

Counteroffensive, Phase II
Counteroffensive, Phase III
Tet Counteroffensive
Counteroffensive, Phase IV
Counteroffensive, Phase V
Counteroffensive, Phase VI
Tet 69 Counteroffensive
Summer–Fall 1969
Winter–Spring 1970
Sanctuary Counteroffensive
Counteroffensive, Phase VII
Consolidation I
Consolidation II

DECORATIONS

Presidential Unit Citation (Army), Streamer embroidered **HURTGEN FOREST** (22d Infantry cited)

Presidential Unit Citation (Army), Streamer embroidered **ST. GILLIS-MARIGNY** (22d Infantry cited)

Presidential Unit Citation (Army), Streamer embroidered **CARENTAN** (3d Battalion, 22d Infantry cited)

Presidental Unit Citation (Army), Streamer embroidered **SUOI TRE, VIETNAM** (2d Battalion and 3d Battalion [less Company C], 22d Infantry cited)

Valorous Unit Award, Streamer embroidered **TAY NINH PROVINCE** (3d Battalion, 22d Infantry cited)

Valorous Unit Award, Streamer embroidered **KONTUM** (1st Battalion, 22d Infantry cited)

Belgian Fourragere 1940 (22d Infantry cited)

Cited in the Order of the Day of the Belgian Army for action in **BELGIUM** (22d Infantry cited)

Cited in the Order of the Day of the Belgian Army for action in the **ARDENNES** (22d Infantry cited)

1ST BATTALION, 22D INFANTRY

LINEAGE

1861	Constituted 3 May as Company A and Company I, 2d Battalion, 13th Infantry
1865	Organized in May at Camp Dennison, OH
1866	Reorganized and redesignated 21 September as Company A and Company I, 22d Infantry
1869	Companies A and I, 22d Infantry consolidated 4 May to form Company A, 22d Infantry
1923	Assigned 24 March to 4th Division

1927	Inactivated 30 June at Fort McPherson, GA
1940	Activated 1 June at Fort McClellan, AL
1946	Inactivated 1 March at Camp Butner, NC
1947	Activated 15 July at Fort Ord, CA
1957	Reorganized and redesignated 1 April as Headquarters and Headquarters Company, 1st Battle Group, 22d Infantry, and assigned to 4th Infantry Division
1963	Reorganized and redesignated 1 October as 1st Battalion, 22d Infantry

CAMPAIGN PARTICIPATION

Indian Wars

Little Big Horn
Pine Ridge
North Dakota 1868
North Dakota 1869
Montana 1872

War With Spain

Santiago

Philippine Insurrection

Manila
Malolos
San Isidro

Mindanao
Jolo
Luzon 1900

World War II

Normandy (with arrowhead)
Northern France
Rhineland
Ardennes-Alsace
Central Europe

Vietnam

Counteroffensive, Phase II
Counteroffensive, Phase III
Tet Counteroffensive
Counteroffensive, Phase IV
Counteroffensive, Phase V
Counteroffensive, Phase VI
Tet 69 Counteroffensive
Summer–Fall 1969
Winter–Spring 1970
Sanctuary Counteroffensive
Counteroffensive, Phase VII
Consolidation I
Consolidation II

DECORATIONS

Presidential Unit Citation (Army), Streamer embroidered **HURTGEN FOREST** (22d Infantry cited)

Presidential Unit Citation (Army), Streamer embroidered **ST. GILLIS-MARIGNY** (22d Infantry cited)

Presidential Unit Citation (Army), Streamer embroidered **CARENTAN**

Valorous Unit Award, Streamer embroidered **KONTUM** (1st Battalion, 22d Infantry cited)

Belgian Fourragere 1940 (22d Infantry cited)

Cited in the Order of the Day of the Belgian Army for action in **BELGIUM** (22d Infantry cited)

Cited in the Order of the Day of the Belgian Army for action in the **ARDENNES** (22d Infantry cited)

Vietnamese Cross of Gallantry with Palm, Streamer embroidered **VIETNAM 1966–1969** (1st Battalion, 22d Infantry cited)

Vietnamese Civil Action Honor Medal, First Class, Streamer embroidered **VIETNAM 1966–1969** (1st Battalion, 22d Infantry cited)

2D BATTALION, 22D INFANTRY

LINEAGE

1861	Constituted 3 May as Company B and Company K, 2d Battalion, 13th Infantry, Regular Army
1865	Organized in May at Camp Dennison, OH
1866	Reorganized and redesignated 21 September as Company B and Company K, 22d Infantry
1869	Companies B and K, 22d Infantry consolidated 4 May; consolidated unit designated Company B, 22d Infantry
1923	Assigned 24 March to 4th Division
1927	Inactivated 30 June at Fort McPherson, GA
1940	Activated 1 June at Fort McClellan, AL
1946	Inactivated 1 March at Camp Butner, NC
1947	Activated 15 July at Fort Ord, CA

1957   Inactivated 1 April at Fort Lewis, WA, relieved from assignment to 4th Infantry Division, and redesignated Headquarters and Headquarters Company, 2d Battle Group, 22d Infantry

1963   Redesignated 21 August as Headquarters and Headquarters Company, 2d Battalion, 22d Infantry, and assigned to 4th Infantry Division; Battalion activated 1 October at Fort Lewis, WA

1967   Relieved 1 August from assignment to 4th Infantry Division and assigned to 25th Infantry Division

1970   Relieved 15 December from assignment to 25th Infantry Division and assigned to 4th Infantry Division

CAMPAIGN PARTICIPATION

Indian Wars

Little Big Horn
Pine Ridge
North Dakota 1868
North Dakota 1869
Montana 1872

War With Spain

Santiago

Philippine Insurrection

Manila
Malolos
San Isidro
Mindanao
Jolo
Luzon 1900

World War II

Normandy (with arrowhead)
Northern France
Rhineland
Ardennes-Alsace
Central Europe

Vietnam

Counteroffensive, Phase II
Counteroffensive, Phase III
Tet Counteroffensive
Counteroffensive, Phase IV
Counteroffensive, Phase V
Counteroffensive, Phase VI
Tet 69 Counteroffensive
Summer–Fall 1969
Winter–Spring 1970
Sanctuary Counteroffensive
Counteroffensive, Phase VII

DECORATIONS

Presidential Unit Citation (Army), Streamer embroidered **HURTGEN FOREST** (22d Infantry cited)

Presidential Unit Citation (Army), Streamer embroidered **ST. GILLIS-MARIGNY** (22d Infantry cited)

Presidential Unit Citation (Army), Streamer embroidered **CARENTAN**

Presidential Unit Citation (Army), Streamer embroidered **SUOI TRE, VIETNAM** (2d Battalion, 22d Infantry cited)

Belgian Fourragere 1940 (22d Infantry cited)

Cited in the Order of the Day of the Belgian Army for action in **BELGIUM** (22d Infantry cited)

Cited in the Order of the Day of the Belgian Army for action in the **ARDENNES** (22d Infantry cited)

Vietnamese Cross of Gallantry with Palm, Streamer embroidered **VIETNAM 1966–1967** (2d Battalion, 22d Infantry cited)

Vietnamese Cross of Gallantry with Palm, Streamer embroidered **VIETNAM 1966–1968** (2d Battalion, 22d Infantry cited)

3D BATTALION, 22D INFANTRY

LINEAGE

1861   Constituted 3 May as Company C and Company F, 2d Battalion, 13th Infantry, Regular Army

1865   Organized in July at Camp Dennison, OH

1866   Reorganized and redesignated 21 September as Company C and Company F, 22d Infantry

1869   Companies C and F, 22d Infantry consolidated 1 May; consolidated unit designated Company C, 22d Infantry

1923   Assigned 24 March to 4th Division

1927   Inactivated 30 June at Fort McPherson, GA

1940   Activated 1 June at Fort McClellan, AL

1946   Inactivated 1 March at Camp Butner, NC

1947	Activated 15 July at Fort Ord, CA
1957	Inactivated 1 April at Fort Lewis, WA, relieved from assignment to 4th Infantry Division; reorganized and redesignated Headquarters and Headquarters Company, 3d Battle Group, 22d Infantry
1959	Withdrawn 29 April from Regular Army, allotted to Army Reserve and assigned to 96th Infantry Division; Battle Group activated 1 June at Boise, ID
1963	Inactivated 15 March and relieved from assignment to 96th Infantry Division
1965	Redesignated 16 September as 3d Battalion, 22d Infantry, withdrawn from Army Reserve, allotted to Regular Army, and assigned to 4th Infantry Division; activated 1 November at Fort Lewis, WA
1967	Relieved 1 August from assignment to 4th Infantry Division and assigned to 25th Infantry Division

CAMPAIGN PARTICIPATION

Indian Wars

Little Big Horn
Pine Ridge
North Dakota 1867
North Dakota 1868
North Dakota 1869
Montana 1872

San Isidro
Mindanao
Jolo
Luzon 1900

War With Spain

Santiago

Philippine Insurrection

Manila
Malolos

World War II

Normandy (with arrowhead)
Northern France
Rhineland
Ardennes-Alsace
Central Europe

Vietnam

Counteroffensive, Phase II
Counteroffensive, Phase III
Tet Counteroffensive
Counteroffensive, Phase IV
Counteroffensive, Phase V
Counteroffensive, Phase VI
Tet 69 Counteroffensive
Summer–Fall 1969
Winter–Spring 1970
Sanctuary Counteroffensive
Counteroffensive, Phase VII

DECORATIONS

Presidential Unit Citation (Army), Streamer embroidered **HURTGEN FOREST** (22d Infantry cited)

Presidential Unit Citation (Army), Streamer embroidered **ST. GILLIS-MARIGNY** (22d Infantry cited)

Presidential Unit Citation (Army), Streamer embroidered **CARENTAN**

Presidential Unit Citation (Army), Streamer embroidered **SUOI TRE, VIETNAM** (3d Battalion [less Company C], 22d Infantry cited)

Valorous Unit Award, Streamer embroidered **TAY NINH PROVINCE** (3d Battalion, 22d Infantry cited)

Belgian Fourragere 1940 (22d Infantry cited)

Cited in the Order of the Day of the Belgian Army for action in **BELGIUM** (22d Infantry cited)

Cited in the Order of the Day of the Belgian Army for action in the **ARDENNES** (22d Infantry cited)

Vietnamese Cross of Gallantry with Palm, Streamer embroidered **VIETNAM 1966-1967** (3d Battalion, 22d Infantry cited)

Vietnamese Cross of Gallantry with Palm, Streamer embroidered **VIETNAM 1967-1968** (3d Battalion, 22d Infantry cited)

23D INFANTRY

COAT OF ARMS

Motto: We Serve

Symbolism: The shield is blue and white, the present and old infantry colors. Civil War service is indicated by the white cross of the V Corps, and Philippine Insurrection service by the sea lion taken from the seal of Manila. The Mont Blanc operation of October 1918 in World War I is commemorated by the outline of the lower half of the shield. The 23d Infantry has the unique distinction of being the first American regiment to circumnavigate the globe and this is indicated in the base of the shield.

The 23d Infantry went to Alaska in 1867 to take over possession of the territory from the Russians. This is shown in the crest in true Alaskan Indian symbolism. The totem pole is composed of the bear, the old owner, and the eagle, the new owner, and between them is a plate. The bear gave a feast to the eagle when the new owner moved in. The French Fourragere authorized for informal use was awarded to the regiment for service in World War I.

DISTINCTIVE INSIGNIA

The distinctive insignia is the shield and motto of the coat of arms.

LINEAGE

1861   Constituted 3 May as 1st Battalion, 14th Infantry, Regular Army; organized 8 July at Fort Trumbull, CT

1962   Redesignated 30 April as 2d Battalion, 14th Infantry

1866   Reorganized and redesignated 21 September as 23d Infantry

1917   Assigned 22 September to 2d Division

1957   Relieved 20 June from assignment to 2d Infantry Division and reorganized as a parent regiment under CARS

CAMPAIGN PARTICIPATION

Civil War

Peninsula
Manassas
Antietam
Fredericksburg
Chancellorsville
Gettysburg
Wilderness
Spotsylvania
Cold Harbor
Petersburg
Virginia 1862
Virginia 1863

Indian Wars

Little Big Horn
Arizona 1866
Idaho 1868

War With Spain

Manila

Philippine Insurrection

Manila
Malolos
Mindanao
Jolo
Jolo 1903

World War I

Aisne
Aisne-Marne
St. Mihiel
Meuse-Argonne
Lorraine 1918
Ile de France 1918

World War II

Normandy
Northern France
Rhineland
Ardennes-Alsace
Central Europe

Korean War

UN defensive
UN offensive
CCF intervention
First UN counteroffensive
CCF spring offensive
UN summer-fall offensive
Second Korean winter
Korea, summer-fall 1952
Third Korean winter
Korea, summer 1953

Vietnam

Counteroffensive
Counteroffensive, Phase II
Counteroffensive, Phase III
Tet Counteroffensive
Counteroffensive, Phase IV
Counteroffensive, Phase V
Counteroffensive, Phase VI
Tet 69 Counteroffensive
Summer-Fall 1969
Winter-Spring 1970

DECORATIONS

Presidential Unit Citation (Army), Streamer embroidered **WIRTZFELD, BELGIUM** (1st Battalion, 23d Infantry cited)

Presidential Unit Citation (Army), Streamer embroidered **ST. VITH** (2d Battalion, 23d Infantry cited)

Presidential Unit Citation (Army), Streamer embroidered **KRINKELTER WALD, BELGIUM** (3d Battalion, 23d Infantry cited)

Presidential Unit Citation (Army), Streamer embroidered **BREST, FRANCE** (3d Battalion, 23d Infantry cited)

Presidential Unit Citation (Army), Streamer embroidered **TWIN TUNNELS** (3d Battalion, 23d Infantry cited)

Presidential Unit Citation (Army), Streamer embroidered **CHIPYONG-NI** (23d Infantry cited)

Presidential Unit Citation (Army), Streamer embroidered **HONGCHON** (2d Infantry Division cited)

Valorous Unit Award, Streamer embroidered **TAY NINH PROVINCE** (4th Battalion, 23d Infantry cited)

Valorous Unit Award, Streamer embroidered **SAIGON** (4th Battalion, 23d Infantry cited)

French Croix de Guerre with Palm, World War I, Streamer embroidered **AISNE-MARNE** (23d Infantry cited)

French Croix de Guerre with Palm, World War I, Streamer embroidered **MEUSE-ARGONNE** (23d Infantry cited)

French Croix de Guerre with Palm, World War I, Streamer embroidered **CHATEAU THIERRY** (23d Infantry cited)

French Croix de Guerre, World War I, Fourragere (23d Infantry cited)

Republic of Korea Presidential Unit Citation, Streamer embroidered **NAKTONG RIVER LINE** (23d Infantry cited)

Republic of Korea Presidential Unit Citation, Streamer embroidered **KOREA 1950-1953** (1st Battalion, 23d Infantry cited)

Republic of Korea Presidential Unit Citation, Streamer embroidered **KOREA 1952-1953** (23d Infantry cited)

Belgian Fourragere 1940 (23d Infantry cited)

Cited in the Order of the Day of the Belgian Army for action in the **ARDENNES** (23d Infantry cited)

Cited in the Order of the Day of the Belgian Army for action at **ELSENBORN CREST** (23d Infantry cited)

1st Battalion, 23d Infantry

LINEAGE

1861   Constituted 3 May as Company A, 1st Battalion, 14th Infantry, Regular Army; organized 8 July at Fort Trumbull, CT

1962   Redesignated 30 April as Company A, 2d Battalion, 14th Infantry

1866   Reorganized and redesignated 21 September as Company A, 23d Infantry

1917   Assigned 22 September to 2d Division

1957   Reorganized and redesignated 20 June as Headquarters and Headquarters Company, 1st Battle Group, 23d Infantry; assigned to 2d Infantry Division, and relieved 16 December from assignment to 2d Infantry Division

1963   Reorganized and redesignated 25 January as 1st Battalion, 23d Infantry and assigned to 2d Infantry Division

CAMPAIGN PARTICIPATION

Civil War

Peninsula
Manassas
Antietam
Fredericksburg
Chancellorsville
Gettysburg
Wilderness
Spotsylvania
Cold Harbor
Petersburg
Virginia 1862
Virginia 1863

Indian Wars

Little Big Horn
Arizona 1866
Idaho 1868

War With Spain

Manila

Philippine Insurrection

Manila
Malolos
Mindanao
Jolo
Jolo 1903

World War I

Aisne
Aisne–Marne
St. Mihiel
Meuse–Argonne
Lorraine 1918
Ile de France 1918

World War II

Normandy
Northern France
Rhineland
Ardennes–Alsace
Central Europe

Korean War

UN defensive
UN offensive
CCF intervention
First UN counteroffensive
CCF spring offensive
UN summer–fall offensive
Second Korean winter
Korea, summer–fall 1952
Third Korean winter
Korea, summer 1953

DECORATIONS

Presidential Unit Citation (Army), Streamer embroidered **WIRTZFELD, BELGIUM** (1st Battalion, 23d Infantry cited)

Presidential Unit Citation (Army), Streamer embroidered **ST. VITH**

Presidential Unit Citation (Army), Streamer embroidered **KRINKELTER WALD, BELGIUM**

Presidential Unit Citation (Army), Streamer embroidered **BREST, FRANCE**

Presidential Unit Citation (Army), Streamer embroidered **TWIN TUNNELS**

Presidential Unit Citation (Army), Streamer embroidered **CHIPYONG-NI** (23d Infantry cited)

Presidential Unit Citation (Army), Streamer embroidered **HONGCHON** (2d Infantry Division cited)

French Croix de Guerre with Palm, World War I, Streamer embroidered **AISNE–MARNE** (23d Infantry cited)

French Croix de Guerre with Palm, World War I, Streamer embroidered **MEUSE–ARGONNE** (23d Infantry cited)

French Croix de Guerre with Palm, World War I, Streamer embroidered **CHATEAU THIERRY** (23d Infantry cited)

French Croix de Guerre, World War I, Fourragere (23d Infantry cited)

Republic of Korea Presidential Unit Citation, Streamer embroidered **NAKTONG RIVER LINE** (23d Infantry cited)

Republic of Korea Presidential Unit Citation, Streamer embroidered **KOREA 1950–1952** (1st Battalion, 23d Infantry cited)

Republic of Korea Presidential Unit Citation, Streamer embroidered **KOREA 1950–1953** (23d Infantry cited)

Republic of Korea Presidential Unit Citation, Streamer embroidered **KOREA 1952–1953** (23d Infantry cited)

Belgian Fourragere 1940 (23d Infantry cited)

Cited in the Order of the Day of the Belgian Army for action in the **ARDENNES** (23d Infantry cited)

Cited in the Order of the Day of the Belgian Army for action at **ELSENBORN CREST** (23d Infantry cited)

2D BATTALION, 23D INFANTRY

LINEAGE

1861   Constituted 3 May as Company A, 1st Battalion, 14th Infantry, Regular Army; organized 8 July at Fort Trumbull, CT

1962   Redesignated 30 April as Company B, 2d Battalion, 14th Infantry

1866   Reorganized and redesignated 21 September as Company B, 23d Infantry

1917   Assigned 22 September to 2d Division

1957   Inactivated 20 June in Alaska, relieved from assignment to 2d Infantry Division, and redesignated Headquarters and Headquarters Company, 2d Battle Group, 23d Infantry

1958   Assigned 17 March to 2d Infantry Division; Battle Group activated 14 June at Fort Benning, GA

1963   Reorganized and redesignated 1 February as 2d Battalion, 23d Infantry

CAMPAIGN PARTICIPATION

Civil War
Peninsula
Manassas
Antietam
Fredericksburg
Chancellorsville
Gettysburg
Wilderness
Spotsylvania
Cold Harbor
Petersburg
Virginia 1862
Virginia 1863

Indian Wars
Little Big Horn
Arizona 1866
Idaho 1868

War With Spain
Manila

Philippine Insurrection
Manila
Malolos
Mindanao
Jolo
Jolo 1903

World War I
Aisne
Aisne-Marne
St. Mihiel
Meuse-Argonne
Lorraine 1918
Ile de France 1918

World War II
Normandy
Northern France
Rhineland
Ardennes-Alsace
Central Europe

Korean War
UN defensive
UN offensive
CCF intervention
First UN counteroffensive
CCF spring offensive
UN summer-fall offensive
Second Korean winter
Korea, summer-fall 1952
Third Korean winter
Korea, summer 1953

DECORATIONS

Presidential Unit Citation (Army), Streamer embroidered **WIRTZFELD, BELGIUM** (1st Battalion, 23d Infantry cited)

Presidential Unit Citation (Army), Streamer embroidered **ST. VITH**

Presidential Unit Citation (Army), Streamer embroidered **KRINKELTER WALD, BELGIUM**

Presidential Unit Citation (Army), Streamer embroidered **BREST, FRANCE**

Presidential Unit Citation (Army), Streamer embroidered **TWIN TUNNELS**

Presidential Unit Citation (Army), Streamer embroidered **CHIPYONG-NI** (23d Infantry cited)

Presidential Unit Citation (Army), Streamer embroidered **HONGCHON** (2d Infantry Division cited)

French Croix de Guerre with Palm, World War I, Streamer embroidered **AISNE-MARNE** (23d Infantry cited)

French Croix de Guerre with Palm, World War I, Streamer embroidered **MEUSE-ARGONNE** (23d Infantry cited)

French Croix de Guerre with Palm, World War I, Streamer embroidered **CHATEAU THIERRY** (23d Infantry cited)

French Croix de Guerre, World War I, Fourragere (23d Infantry cited)

Republic of Korea Presidential Unit Citation, Streamer embroidered **NAKTONG RIVER LINE** (23d Infantry cited)

Republic of Korea Presidential Unit Citation, Streamer embroidered **KOREA 1950-1952** (1st Battalion, 23d Infantry cited)

Republic of Korea Presidential Unit Citation, Streamer embroidered **KOREA 1950-1953** (23d Infantry cited)

Republic of Korea Presidential Unit Citation, Streamer embroidered **KOREA 1952-1953** (23d Infantry cited)

Belgian Fourragere 1940 (23d Infantry cited)

Cited in the Order of the Day of the Belgian Army for action in the **ARDENNES** (23d Infantry cited)

Cited in the Order of the Day of the Belgian Army for action at **ELSENBORN CREST** (23d Infantry cited)

3D BATTALION, 23D INFANTRY

LINEAGE

1861   Constituted 3 May as Company C, 1st Battalion, 14th Infantry, Regular Army; organized 8 July at Fort Trumbull, CT

1962   Redesignated 30 April as Company C, 2d Battalion, 14th Infantry

1866   Reorganized and redesignated 21 September as Company C, 23d Infantry

1917   Assigned 22 September to 2d Division

1957   Inactivated 20 June in Alaska, relieved from assignment to 2d Infantry Division, and redesignated Headquarters and Headquarters Company, 3d Battle Group, 23d Infantry

1959   Withdrawn 19 March from Regular Army, allotted to Army Reserve, and assigned to 90th Infantry Division; Battle Group activated 1 April at Harlingen, TX

1963   Inactivated 27 March and relieved from assignment to 90th Infantry Division

1965   Redesignated 1 July as 3d Battalion, 23d Infantry, withdrawn from Army Reserve, and allotted to Regular Army; assigned to 2d Infantry Division and activated in Korea

CAMPAIGN PARTICIPATION

Civil War

Peninsula
Manassas
Antietam
Fredericksburg
Chancellorsville
Gettysburg
Wilderness
Spotsylvania
Cold Harbor
Petersburg
Virginia 1862
Virginia 1863

Indian Wars

Little Big Horn
Arizona 1866
Oregon 1866
Idaho 1868

War With Spain

Manila

Philippine Insurrection

Manila
Malolos
Mindanao
Jolo
Jolo 1903

World War I

Aisne
Aisne–Marne
St. Mihiel
Meuse–Argonne
Lorraine 1918
Ile de France 1918

World War II

Normandy
Northern France
Rhineland
Ardennes–Alsace
Central Europe

Korean War

UN defensive
UN offensive
CCF intervention
First UN counteroffensive
CCF spring offensive
UN summer–fall offensive
Second Korean winter
Korea, summer–fall 1952
Third Korean winter
Korea, summer 1953

DECORATIONS

Presidential Unit Citation (Army), Streamer embroidered **WIRTZFELD, BELGIUM** (1st Battalion, 23d Infantry cited)

Presidential Unit Citation (Army), Streamer embroidered **ST. VITH**

Presidential Unit Citation (Army), Streamer embroidered **KRINKELTER WALD, BELGIUM**

Presidential Unit Citation (Army), Streamer embroidered **BREST, FRANCE**

Presidential Unit Citation (Army), Streamer embroidered **TWIN TUNNELS**

Presidential Unit Citation (Army), Streamer embroidered **CHIPYONG-NI** (23d Infantry cited)

Presidential Unit Citation (Army), Streamer embroidered **HONGCHON** (2d Infantry Division cited)

French Croix de Guerre with Palm, World War I, Streamer embroidered **AISNE-MARNE** (23d Infantry cited)

French Croix de Guerre with Palm, World War I, Streamer embroidered **MEUSE-ARGONNE** (23d Infantry cited)

French Croix de Guerre with Palm, World War I, Streamer embroidered **CHATEAU THIERRY** (23d Infantry cited)

French Croix de Guerre, World War I, Fourragere (23d Infantry cited)

Republic of Korea Presidential Unit Citation, Streamer embroidered **NAKTONG RIVER LINE** (23d Infantry cited)

Republic of Korea Presidential Unit Citation, Streamer embroidered **KOREA 1950–1952** (1st Battalion, 23d Infantry cited)

Republic of Korea Presidential Unit Citation, Streamer embroidered **KOREA 1950–1953** (23d Infantry cited)

Republic of Korea Presidential Unit Citation, Streamer embroidered **KOREA 1952–1953** (23d Infantry cited)

Belgian Fourragere 1940 (23d Infantry cited)

Cited in the Order of the Day of the Belgian Army for action in the **ARDENNES** (23d Infantry cited)

Cited in the Order of the Day of the Belgian Army for action at **ELSENBORN CREST** (23d Infantry cited)

4TH BATTALION, 23D INFANTRY

LINEAGE

1861   Constituted 3 May as Company D, 1st Battalion, 14th Infantry, Regular Army; organized 8 July at Fort Trumbull, CT

1962   Redesignated 30 April as Company D, 2d Battalion, 14th Infantry

1866   Reorganized and redesignated 21 September as Company A, 23d Infantry

1917   Assigned 22 September to 2d Division

1957   Inactivated 20 June in Alaska, relieved from assignment to 2d Infantry Division, and redesignated as Headquarters and Headquarters Company, 4th Battle Group, 23d Infantry

1963   Activated 25 January in Alaska, assigned 20 May to 172d Infantry Brigade, reorganized and redesignated 1 July as 4th Battalion, 23d Infantry

1966   Relieved 14 January from assignment to 172d Infantry Brigade and assigned to 25th Infantry Division

CAMPAIGN PARTICIPATION

Civil War

Peninsula
Manassas
Antietam
Fredericksburg
Chancellorsville
Gettysburg
Wilderness
Spotsylvania
Cold Harbor
Petersburg
Virginia 1862
Virginia 1863

Indian Wars

Little Big Horn
Arizona 1866
Idaho 1868

War With Spain

Manila

Philippine Insurrection

Manila
Malolos
Mindanao
Jolo
Jolo 1903

World War I

Aisne
Aisne–Marne
St. Mihiel
Meuse–Argonne
Lorraine 1918
Ile de France 1918

World War II

Normandy
Northern France
Rhineland
Ardennes–Alsace
Central Europe

Korean War

UN defensive
UN offensive
CCF intervention
First UN counteroffensive
CCF spring offensive
UN summer–fall offensive
Second Korean winter
Korea, summer–fall 1952
Third Korean winter
Korea, summer 1953

Vietnam

Counteroffensive
Counteroffensive, Phase II
Counteroffensive, Phase III
Tet Counteroffensive
Counteroffensive, Phase IV
Counteroffensive, Phase V
Counteroffensive, Phase VI
Tet 69 Counteroffensive
Summer–Fall 1969
Winter–Spring 1970

DECORATIONS

Presidential Unit Citation (Army), Streamer embroidered **WIRTZFELD, BELGIUM** (1st Battalion, 23d Infantry cited)

Presidential Unit Citation (Army), Streamer embroidered **ST. VITH**

Presidential Unit Citation (Army), Streamer embroidered **KRINKELTER WALD, BELGIUM**

Presidential Unit Citation (Army), Streamer embroidered **BREST, FRANCE**

Presidential Unit Citation (Army), Streamer embroidered **TWIN TUNNELS**

Presidential Unit Citation (Army), Streamer embroidered **CHIPYONG-NI** (23d Infantry cited)

Presidential Unit Citation (Army), Streamer embroidered **HONGCHON** (2d Infantry Division cited)

Valorous Unit Award, Streamer embroidered **TAY NINH PROVINCE** (4th Battalion, 23d Infantry cited)

Valorous Unit Award, Streamer embroidered **SAIGON** (4th Battalion, 23d Infantry cited)

French Croix de Guerre with Palm, World War I, Streamer embroidered **AISNE–MARNE** (23d Infantry cited)

French Croix de Guerre with Palm, World War I, Streamer embroidered **MEUSE-ARGONNE** (23d Infantry cited)

French Croix de Guerre with Palm, World War I, Streamer embroidered **CHATEAU THIERRY** (23d Infantry cited)

French Croix de Guerre, World War I, Fourragere (23d Infantry cited)

Republic of Korea Presidential Unit Citation, Streamer embroidered **NAKTONG RIVER LINE** (23d Infantry cited)

Republic of Korea Presidential Unit Citation, Streamer embroidered **KOREA 1950-1952** (1st Battalion, 23d Infantry cited)

Republic of Korea Presidential Unit Citation, Streamer embroidered **KOREA 1950-1953** (23d Infantry cited)

Republic of Korea Presidential Unit Citation, Streamer embroidered **KOREA 1952-1953** (23d Infantry cited)

Belgian Fourragere 1940 (23d Infantry cited)

Cited in the Order of the Day of the Belgian Army for action in the **ARDENNES** (23d Infantry cited)

Cited in the Order of the Day of the Belgian Army for action at **ELSENBORN CREST** (23d Infantry cited)

Vietnamese Cross of Gallantry with Palm, Streamer embroidered **VIETNAM 1966-1968** (4th Battalion, 23d Infantry cited)

5TH BATTALION, 23D INFANTRY

LINEAGE

1861   Constituted 3 May as Company E, 1st Battalion, 14th Infantry, Regular Army; organized 8 July at Fort Trumbull, CT

1962   Redesignated 30 April as Company E, 2d Battalion, 14th Infantry

1866   Reorganized and redesignated 21 September as Company E, 23d Infantry

1917   Assigned 22 September to 2d Division

1957   Inactivated 20 June in Alaska, relieved from assignment to 2d Infantry Division, and redesignated as Headquarters and Headquarters Company, 5th Battle Group, 23d Infantry

1965   Redesignated 17 December as Headquarters and Headquarters Company, 5th Battalion, 23d Infantry, and assigned to 172d Infantry Brigade; activated 20 December in Alaska

CAMPAIGN PARTICIPATION

Civil War

Peninsula
Manassas
Antietam
Fredericksburg
Chancellorsville
Gettysburg
Wilderness
Spotsylvania
Cold Harbor
Petersburg
Virginia 1862
Virginia 1863

Indian Wars

Little Big Horn
Arizona 1866
Idaho 1868

War With Spain

Manila

Philippine Insurrection

Manila
Malolos
Mindanao
Jolo
Jolo 1903

World War I

Aisne
Aisne-Marne
St. Mihiel
Meuse-Argonne
Lorraine 1918
Ile de France 1918

World War II

Normandy
Northern France
Rhineland
Ardennes-Alsace
Central Europe

Korean War

UN defensve
UN offensive
CCF intervention
First UN counteroffensive
CCF spring offensive
UN summer-fall offensive
Second Korean winter
Korea, summer-fall 1952
Third Korean winter
Korea, summer 1953

DECORATIONS

Presidential Unit Citation (Army), Streamer embroidered **WIRTZFELD, BELGIUM**

Presidential Unit Citation (Army), Streamer embroidered **ST. VITH** (2d Battalion, 23d Infantry cited)

Presidential Unit Citation (Army), Streamer embroidered **KRINKELTER WALD, BELGIUM**

Presidential Unit Citation (Army), Streamer embroidered **BREST, FRANCE**

Presidential Unit Citation (Army), Streamer embroidered **TWIN TUNNELS**

Presidential Unit Citation (Army), Streamer embroidered **CHIPYONG-NI** (23d Infantry cited)

Presidential Unit Citation (Army), Streamer embroidered **HONGCHON** (2d Infantry Division cited)

French Croix de Guerre with Palm, World War I, Streamer embroidered **AISNE–MARNE** (23d Infantry cited)

French Croix de Guerre with Palm, World War I, Streamer embroidered **MEUSE–ARGONNE** (23d Infantry cited)

French Croix de Guerre with Palm, World War I, Streamer embroidered **CHATEAU THIERRY** (23d Infantry cited)

French Croix de Guerre, World War I, Fourragere (23d Infantry cited)

Republic of Korea Presidential Unit Citation, Streamer embroidered **NAKTONG RIVER LINE** (23d Infantry cited)

Republic of Korea Presidential Unit Citation, Streamer embroidered **KOREA 1950–1953** (23d Infantry cited)

Republic of Korea Presidential Unit Citation, Streamer embroidered **KOREA 1952–1953** (23d Infantry cited)

Belgian Fourragere 1940 (23d Infantry cited)

Cited in the Order of the Day of the Belgian Army for action in the **ARDENNES** (23d Infantry cited)

Cited in the Order of the Day of the Belgian Army for action at **ELSENBORN CREST** (23d Infantry cited)

COMPANY F, 23D INFANTRY

LINEAGE

1861	Constituted 3 May as Company F, 1st Battalion, 14th Infantry, Regular Army; organized 8 July at Fort Trumbull, CT
1962	Redesignated 30 April as Company F, 2d Battalion, 14th Infantry
1866	Reorganized and redesignated 21 September as Company F, 23d Infantry
1917	Assigned 22 September to 2d Division
1957	Inactivated 20 June in Alaska, relieved from assignment to 2d Infantry Division, and redesignated as Headquarters and Headquarters Company, 6th Battle Group, 23d Infantry
1963	Redesignated 23 September as Company F, 23d Infantry and activated 24 September in Korea
1966	Inactivated 1 January in Korea

CAMPAIGN PARTICIPATION

Civil War

Peninsula
Manassas
Antietam
Fredericksburg
Chancellorsville
Gettysburg
Virginia 1862

War With Spain

Manila

Philippine Insurrection

Malolos

World War I

Aisne
Aisne–Marne
St. Mihiel
Meuse–Argonne
Lorraine 1918
Ile de France 1918

World War II-EAME

Normandy
Northern France
Rhineland
Ardennes–Alsace
Central Europe

Korean War

UN defensve
UN offensive

CCF intervention
First UN counteroffensive
CCF spring offensive
UN summer–fall offensive
Second Korean winter
Korea, summer–fall 1952
Third Korean winter
Korea, summer 1953

DECORATIONS

Presidential Unit Citation (Army), Streamer embroidered **ST. VITH** (2d Battalion, 23d Infantry cited)

Presidential Unit Citation (Army), Streamer embroidered **CHIPYONG-NI** (23d Infantry cited)

Presidential Unit Citation (Army), Streamer embroidered **HONGCHON** (2d Infantry Division cited)

French Croix de Guerre with Palm, World War I, Streamer embroidered **AISNE–MARNE** (23d Infantry cited)

French Croix de Guerre with Palm, World War I, Streamer embroidered **MEUSE–ARGONNE** (23d Infantry cited)

French Croix de Guerre with Palm, World War I, Streamer embroidered **CHATEAU THIERRY** (23d Infantry cited)

French Croix de Guerre, World War I, Fourragere (23d Infantry cited)

Republic of Korea Presidential Unit Citation, Streamer embroidered **NAKTONG RIVER LINE** (23d Infantry cited)

Republic of Korea Presidential Unit Citation, Streamer embroidered **KOREA 1950–1953** (23d Infantry cited)

Republic of Korea Presidential Unit Citation, Streamer embroidered **KOREA 1952–1953** (23d Infantry cited)

Belgian Fourragere 1940 (23d Infantry cited)

Cited in the Order of the Day of the Belgian Army for action in the **ARDENNES** (23d Infantry cited)

Cited in the Order of the Day of the Belgian Army for action at **ELSENBORN CREST** (23d Infantry cited)

26TH INFANTRY

COAT OF ARMS

Motto: *Palman Qui Meruit Ferat* (Let Him Bear the Palm Who Has Won It)

Symbolism: The shield is white with a blue chief, the old and the present infantry colors. The dividing line embattled stands for the entrenchments which the regiment has so many times assaulted. The Mohawk arrowhead was the regimental insignia during World War I. It was selected by Colonel Hamilton A. Smith as indicating the American virtues and the regimental spirit of courage, resourceful daring, and relentless pursuit of an enemy. Colonel Smith was killed while leading the regiment in the first great offensive in which it took part. The arrow is repeated five times because in five major offensives the regiment exhibited these qualities indicated by the badge which it had adopted and by which it was designated during these engagements. The palm of victory displayed on the shield and the motto refer to the only award the regiment seeks.

The arrowhead is repeated in the crest to indicate the same regimental spirit under all conditions. The sun, taken from the Katupunan flag, symbolizes service in the Philippine Insurrection.

DISTINCTIVE INSIGNIA

The distinctive insignia is the characteristic device of the regiment, an Indian arrowhead, in blue, displayed on a white shield.

LINEAGE

1901	Constituted 2 February as 26th Infantry Regular Army; organized 22 February with Headquarters at Fort McPherson, GA
1917	Assigned 8 June to 1st Expeditionary Division (later designated 1st Infantry Division)
1957	Relieved 15 February from assignment to 1st Infantry Division and reorganized as a parent regiment under CARS

CAMPAIGN PARTICIPATION

Philippine Insurrection

Without inscription

World War I

Montdidier-Noyon
Aisne-Marne
St. Mihiel
Meuse-Argonne
Lorraine 1917
Lorraine 1918
Picardy 1918

World War II

Algeria-French Morocco
  (with arrowhead)
Tunisia
Sicily (with arrowhead)

Normandy (with
  arrowhead)
Northern France
Rhineland
Ardennes-Alsace
Central Europe

Vietnam

Defense
Counteroffensive
Counteroffensive,
  Phase II
Counteroffensive,
  Phase III
Tet Counteroffensive
Counteroffensive,
  Phase IV
Counteroffensive,
  Phase V
Counteroffensive,
  Phase VI
Tet 69 Counteroffensive
Summer-Fall 1969
Winter-Spring 1970

DECORATIONS

Presidential Unit Citation (Army), Streamer embroidered **STOLBERG** (1st Battalion, 26th Infantry cited)

Valorous Unit Award, Streamer embroidered **AP GU** (1st Battalion, 26th infantry cited)

French Croix de Guerre with Palm, World War I, Streamer embroidered **AISNE-MARNE** (26th Infantry cited)

French Croix de Guerre with Palm, World War I, Streamer embroidered **MEUSE-ARGONNE** (26th Infantry cited)

French Croix de Guerre with Palm, World War II, Streamer embroidered **KASSERINE** (26th Infantry cited)

French Croix de Guerre with Palm, World War II, Streamer embroidered **NORMANDY** (26th Infantry cited)

French Medaille Militaire, Streamer embroidered **FRANCE** (26th Infantry cited)

French Medaille Militaire, Fourragere (26th Infantry cited)

Belgian Fourragere 1940 (26th Infantry cited)

Cited in the Order of the Day of the Belgian Army for action at **MONS** (26th Infantry cited)

Cited in the Order of the Day of the Belgian Army for action at **EUPEN-MALMEDY** (26th Infantry cited)

1ST BATTALION, 26TH INFANTRY

LINEAGE

1900	Organized 25 December as Company A, 1st Provisional Battalion of Infantry, Regular Army at Model Camp Presidio, San Francisco, CA
1901	Redesignated 7 February as Company A, 26th Infantry
1957	Reorganized and redesignated 15 February as Headquarters and Headquarters Company, 1st Battle Group, 26th Infantry and assigned to 1st Infantry Division
1959	Relieved 14 April from assignment to 1st Infantry Division and assigned to 8th Infantry Division
1962	Relieved 24 October from assignment to 8th Infantry Division and assigned to 2d Infantry Division
1963	Relieved 15 February from assignment to 2d Infantry Division and assigned to 1st Infantry Division
1964	Reorganized and redesignated 13 January as 1st Battalion, 26th Infantry

CAMPAIGN PARTICIPATION

Philippine Insurrection

Without inscription

World War I

Montdidier–Noyon
Aisne–Marne
St. Mihiel
Meuse–Argonne
Lorraine 1917
Lorraine 1918
Picardy 1918

World War II

Algeria–French Morocco
(with arrowhead)
Tunisia
Sicily (with arrowhead)
Normandy (with
arrowhead)
Northern France

Rhineland
Ardennes–Alsace
Central Europe

Vietnam

Defense
Counteroffensive
Counteroffensive,
Phase II
Counteroffensive,
Phase III
Tet Counteroffensive
Counteroffensive,
Phase IV
Counteroffensive,
Phase V
Counteroffensive,
Phase VI
Tet 69 Counteroffensive
Summer–Fall 1969
Winter–Spring 1970

Valorous Unit Award, Streamer embroidered **AP GU** (1st Battalion, 26th infantry cited)

French Croix de Guerre with Palm, World War I, Streamer embroidered **AISNE–MARNE** (26th Infantry cited)

French Croix de Guerre with Palm, World War I, Streamer embroidered **MEUSE–ARGONNE** (26th Infantry cited)

French Croix de Guerre with Palm, World War II, Streamer embroidered **KASSERINE** (26th Infantry cited)

French Croix de Guerre with Palm, World War II, Streamer embroidered **NORMANDY** (26th Infantry cited)

French Medaille Militaire, Streamer embroidered **FRANCE** (26th Infantry cited)

French Medaille Militaire, Fourragere (26th Infantry cited)

Belgian Fourragere 1940 (26th Infantry cited)

Cited in the Order of the Day of the Belgian Army for action at **MONS** (26th Infantry cited)

Cited in the Order of the Day of the Belgian Army for action at **EUPEN–MALMEDY** (26th Infantry cited)

Vietnamese Cross of Gallantry with Palm, Streamer embroidered **VIETNAM 1965–1968** (1st Battalion, 26th Infantry cited)

Vietnamese Civil Action Honor Medal, First Class, Streamer embroidered **VIETNAM 1965–1970** (1st Battalion, 26th infantry cited)

DECORATIONS

Presidential Unit Citation (Army), Streamer embroidered **STOLBERG** (1st Battalion, 26th Infantry cited)

2D BATTLE GROUP, 26TH INFANTRY

LINEAGE

1900	Organized 28 December as Company B, 1st Provisional Battalion of Infantry, Regular Army at Model Camp Presidio, San Francisco, CA
1901	Redesignated 7 February as Company B, 26th Infantry
1957	Inactivated 15 February at Fort Riley, KS, relieved from assignment to 1st Infantry Division, and redesignated as Headquarters and Headquarters Company, 2d Battle Group, 26th Infantry
1963	Activated 1 February at Fort Riley, KS, and assigned to 1st Infantry Division
1964	Inactivated 13 January at Fort Riley, KS, and relieved from assignment to 1st Infantry Division

CAMPAIGN PARTICIPATION

Philippine Insurrection

Without inscription

World War I

Montdidier–Noyon
Aisne–Marne
St. Mihiel
Meuse–Argonne
Lorraine 1917
Lorraine 1918
Picardy 1918

World War II

Algeria–French Morocco
(with arrowhead)
Tunisia
Sicily (with arrowhead)
Normandy (with
arrowhead)
Northern France
Rhineland
Ardennes–Alsace
Central Europe

DECORATIONS

Presidential Unit Citation (Army), Streamer embroidered **STOLBERG** (1st Battalion, 26th Infantry cited)

French Croix de Guerre with Palm, World War I, Streamer embroidered **AISNE–MARNE** (26th Infantry cited)

French Croix de Guerre with Palm, World War I, Streamer embroidered **MEUSE–ARGONNE** (26th Infantry cited)

French Croix de Guerre with Palm, World War II, Streamer embroidered **KASSERINE** (26th Infantry cited)

French Croix de Guerre with Palm, World War II, Streamer embroidered **NORMANDY** (26th Infantry cited)

French Medaille Militaire, Streamer embroidered **FRANCE** (26th Infantry cited)

French Medaille Militaire, Fourragere (26th Infantry cited)

Belgian Fourragere 1940 (26th Infantry cited)

Cited in the Order of the Day of the Belgian Army for action at **MONS** (26th Infantry cited)

Cited in the Order of the Day of the Belgian Army for action at **EUPEN–MALMEDY** (26th Infantry cited)

3D BATTALION, 26TH INFANTRY

LINEAGE

1900	Organized 25 December as Company C, 1st Provisional Battalion of Infantry, Regular Army at Model Camp Presidio, San Francisco, CA
1901	Redesignated 7 February as Company C, 26th Infantry
1957	Inactivated 15 February at Fort Riley, KS, relieved from assignment to 1st Infantry Division, and redesignated as Headquarters and Headquarters Company, 3d Battle Group, 26th Infantry
1959	Withdrawn 7 April from Regular Army, allotted to the Army Reserve, and assigned to 77th Infantry Division; Battle Group activated 1 May at New York, NY
1963	Inactivated 26 March and relieved from assignment to 77th Infantry Division
1967	Redesignated 10 May as 3d Battalion, 26th Infantry, withdrawn from Army Reserve, allotted to Regular Army, and assigned to 198th Infantry Brigade; activated at Fort Hood, TX, inactivated 12 May, and relieved from assignment to 198th Infantry Brigade

CAMPAIGN PARTICIPATION

Philippine Insurrection

Without inscription

World War I

Montdidier–Noyon
Aisne–Marne
St. Mihiel
Meuse–Argonne
Lorraine 1917
Lorraine 1918
Picardy 1918

World War II

Algeria–French Morocco (with arrowhead)
Tunisia
Sicily (with arrowhead)
Normandy (with arrowhead)
Northern France
Rhineland
Ardennes–Alsace
Central Europe

DECORATIONS

Presidential Unit Citation (Army), Streamer embroidered **STOLBERG** (1st Battalion, 26th Infantry cited)

French Croix de Guerre with Palm, World War I, Streamer embroidered **AISNE–MARNE** (26th Infantry cited)

French Croix de Guerre with Palm, World War I, Streamer embroidered **MEUSE–ARGONNE** (26th Infantry cited)

French Croix de Guerre with Palm, World War II, Streamer embroidered **KASSERINE** (26th Infantry cited)

French Croix de Guerre with Palm, World War II, Streamer embroidered **NORMANDY** (26th Infantry cited)

French Medaille Militaire, Streamer embroidered **FRANCE** (26th Infantry cited)

French Medaille Militaire, Fourragere (26th Infantry cited)

Belgian Fourragere 1940 (26th Infantry cited)

Cited in the Order of the Day of the Belgian Army for action at **MONS** (26th Infantry cited)

Cited in the Order of the Day of the Belgian Army for action at **EUPEN–MALMEDY** (26th Infantry cited)

INFANTRY REGIMENTS

Regimental Coat of Arms
and
Distinctive Insignia

1st Infantry

2d Infantry

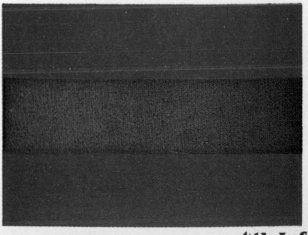

3d Infantry

4th Infantry

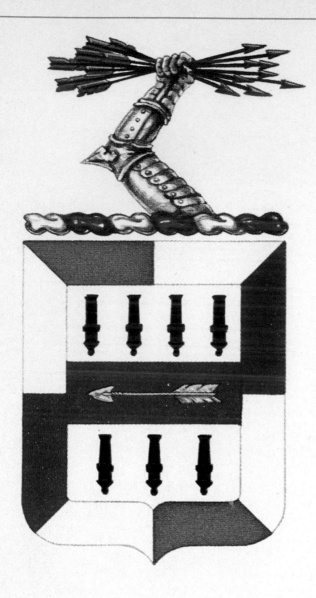

5th Infantry

6th Infantry

7th Infantry

8th Infantry

9th Infantry

10th Infantry

11th Infantry

12th Infantry

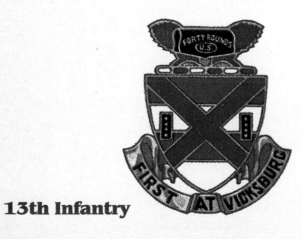

13th Infantry

14th Infantry

15th Infantry

16th Infantry

17th Infantry

18th Infantry

IN OMNIA PARATUS

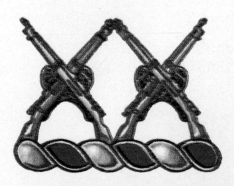

19th Infantry

20th Infantry

21st Infantry

22d Infantry

23rd Infantry

WE SERVE

26th Infantry

27th Infantry

28th Infantry

29th Infantry

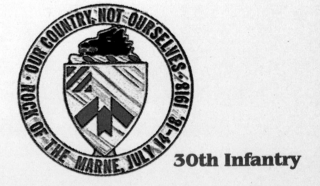

30th Infantry

31st Infantry

32d Infantry

39th Infantry

41st Infantry

46th Infantry

47th Infantry

48th Infantry

50th Infantry

51st Infantry

52d Infantry

54th Infantry

LOVE OF COUNTRY

58th Infantry

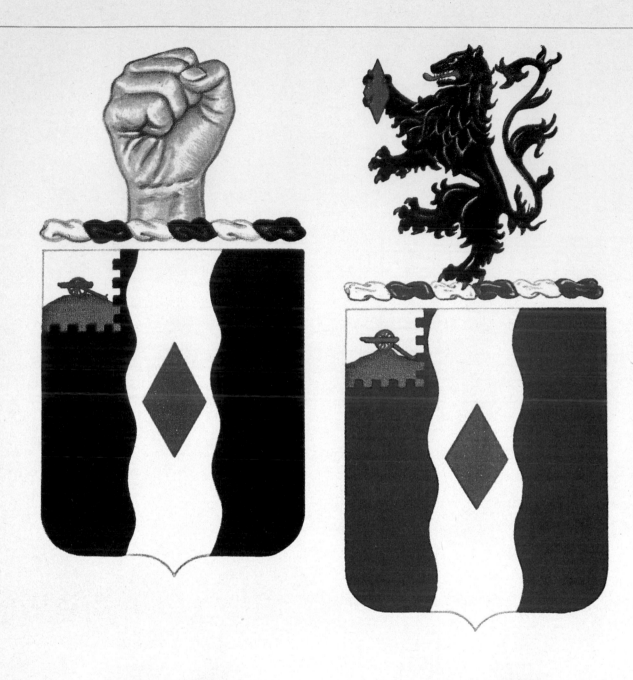

60th Infantry

61st Infantry

75th Infantry

VIRES MONTESQUE VINCIMUS **87th Infantry**

187th Infantry

NE DESIT VIRTUS

WINGED ATTACK

188th Infantry

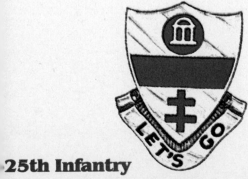

25th Infantry

327th Infantry

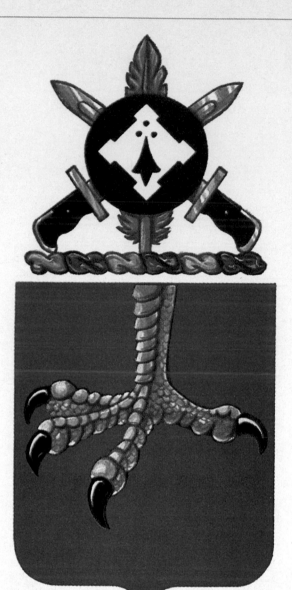

501st Infantry

502d Infantry

03rd Infantry

504th Infantry

505th Infantry

506th Infantr

508th Infantry

509th Infantry

511th Infantry

1st Special Forces

27TH INFANTRY
(The Wolfhounds)

COAT OF ARMS

Motto: *Nec Aspera Terrent* (Frightened by No Difficulties)

Symbolism: Service with the Siberian American Expeditionary Force is indicated by the charge on the shield, the shrapnel case in blue outline with the blue polar bear seated. Fighting in the Philippine Insurrection, particularly in the Lake Lanao Expedition, is represented by the crest. The motto, "Frightened by No Difficulties," has been used by the regiment for many years.

DISTINCTIVE INSIGNIA

Badge: On a black oblong a wolf's head erased in gold above the motto, *Nec Aspera Terrent*, in gold letters. The wolf's head is a design developed as a result of the regiment's traditional designation, "The Wolfhounds." This designation was adopted by the 27th Infantry in commemoration of its service in Siberia.

LINEAGE

1901   Constituted 2 February as 27th Infantry, Regular Army; organized 19 February at Plattsburg Barracks, NY

       (1st Battalion organized in January at Presidio, San Francisco, CA, as 2d Provisional Battalion of Infantry; redesignated 8 February as 1st Battalion, 27th Infantry; redesignated 29 May as 3d Battalion, 26th Infantry—hereafter separate lineage; concurrently 2d Battalion, 26th Infantry (organized March–April at Fort McPherson, GA); redesignated as new 1st Battalion, 27th Infantry)

1921   Assigned 1 March to Hawaiian Division

1941   Relieved 26 August from assignment to Hawaiian Division and assigned to 25th Infantry Division

1957   Relieved 1 February from assignment to 25th Infantry Division and reorganized as a parent regiment under CARS

CAMPAIGN PARTICIPATION

Philippine Insurrection

Mindanao

World War I

Siberia 1918
Siberia 1919

World War II

Central Pacific
Guadalcanal
Northern Solomons (with arrowhead)
Luzon

Korean War

UN defensive
UN offensive
CCF intervention
First UN counteroffensive
CCF spring offensive
UN summer-fall offensive
Second Korean winter
Korea, summer-fall 1952
Third Korean winter
Korea, summer 1953

Vietnam

Counteroffensive
Counteroffensive, Phase II
Counteroffensive, Phase III
Tet Counteroffensive
Counteroffensive, Phase IV
Counteroffensive, Phase V
Counteroffensive, Phase VI
Tet 69 Counteroffensive
Summer-Fall 1969
Winter-Spring 1970
Sanctuary Counteroffensive
Counteroffensive, Phase VII

DECORATIONS

Presidential Unit Citation (Army), Streamer embroidered **TAEGU** (27th Infantry [less Heavy Tank Company] cited)

Presidential Unit Citation (Army), Streamer embroidered **SANGNYONG-NI** (27th Infantry [less Heavy Tank Company and 3d Battalion] cited)

Presidential Unit Citation (Army), Streamer embroidered **HAN RIVER** (3d Battalion, 27th Infantry cited)

Valorous Unit Award, Streamer embroidered **CU CHI DISTRICT** (1st and 2d Battalions, 27th Infantry cited)

Valorous Unit Award, Streamer embroidered **SAIGON** (2d Battalion, 27th Infantry cited)

Philippine Presidential Unit Citation, Streamer embroidered **17 OCTOBER 1944 TO 4 JULY 1945** (25th Infantry Division cited)

Republic of Korea Presidential Unit Citation, Streamer embroidered **MASAN-CHIN JU** (27th Infantry cited)

Republic of Korea Presidential Unit Citation, Streamer embroidered **MUNSAN-NI** (27th Infantry cited)

Republic of Korea Presidential Unit Citation, Streamer embroidered **KOREA** (27th Infantry cited)

1ST BATTALION, 27TH INFANTRY
(The Wolfhounds)

LINEAGE

1901   Constituted 2 February as Company E, 26th Infantry, Regular Army; organized 6 March at Fort McPherson, GA, and redesignated 29 May as Company A, 27th Infantry

1921   Assigned 1 March to Hawaiian Division

1941   Relieved 26 August from assignment to Hawaiian Division and assigned to the 25th Infantry Division

1957   Reorganized and redesignated 1 February as Headquarters and Headquarters Company, 1st Battle Group, 27th Infantry; assigned to 25th Infantry Division

1963   Reorganized and redesignated 26 August as 1st Battalion, 27th Infantry

CAMPAIGN PARTICIPATION

Philippine Insurrection

Mindanao

World War I

Siberia 1918
Siberia 1919

World War II

Central Pacific
Guadalcanal
Northern Solomons (with
arrowhead)
Luzon

Korean War

UN defensive
UN offensive
CCF intervention
First UN counteroffensive
CCF spring offensive
UN summer-fall offensive
Second Korean winter

Korea, summer-fall 1952
Third Korean winter
Korea, summer 1953

Vietnam

Counteroffensive
Counteroffensive,
Phase II
Counteroffensive,
Phase III
Tet Counteroffensive
Counteroffensive,
Phase IV
Counteroffensive,
Phase V
Counteroffensive,
Phase VI
Tet 69 Counteroffensive
Summer-Fall 1969
Winter-Spring 1970
Sanctuary
Counteroffensive
Counteroffensive,
Phase VII

DECORATIONS

Presidential Unit Citation (Army), Streamer embroidered
TAEGU (27th Infantry [less Heavy Tank Company] cited)

Presidential Unit Citation (Army), Streamer embroidered
SANGNYONG-NI (27th Infantry [less Heavy Tank Company and 3d Battalion] cited)

Presidential Unit Citation (Army), Streamer embroidered
HAN RIVER

Valorous Unit Award, Streamer embroidered **CU CHI DISTRICT** (1st Battalion, 27th Infantry cited)

Philippine Presidential Unit Citation, Streamer embroidered
17 OCTOBER 1944 TO 4 JULY 1945 (25th Infantry Division cited)

Republic of Korea Presidential Unit Citation, Streamer embroidered **MASAN-CHIN JU** (27th Infantry cited)

Republic of Korea Presidential Unit Citation, Streamer embroidered **MUNSAN-NI** (27th Infantry cited)

Republic of Korea Presidential Unit Citation, Streamer embroidered **KOREA** (27th Infantry cited)

Vietnamese Cross of Gallantry with Palm, Streamer embroidered **VIETNAM 1966-1968** (1st Battalion, 27th Infantry cited)

2D BATTALION, 27TH INFANTRY
(The Wolfhounds)

LINEAGE

1901 Constituted 2 February as Company F, 26th Infantry, Regular Army; organized 18 March at Fort McPherson, GA, and redesignated 29 May as Company B, 27th Infantry

1921 Assigned 1 March to Hawaiian Division

1941 Relieved 26 August from assignment to Hawaiian Division and assigned to the 25th Infantry Division

1957 Inactivated 1 February in Hawaii, relieved from assignment to 25th Infantry Division, and redesignated as Headquarters and Headquarters Company, 2d Battle Group, 27th Infantry

1960 Redesignated 22 June as Company B, 27th Infantry, and activated 26 March in Korea

1962 Inactivated 26 March in Korea

1963 Redesignated 21 June as Headquarters and Headquarters Company, 2d Battalion, 27th Infantry, and assigned to 25th Infantry Division; Battalion activated 26 August in Hawaii

CAMPAIGN PARTICIPATION

Philippine Insurrection

Mindanao

World War I

Siberia 1918
Siberia 1919

World War II

Central Pacific
Guadalcanal

Northern Solomons (with
arrowhead)
Luzon

Korean War

UN defensive
UN offensive
CCF intervention
First UN counteroffensive
CCF spring offensive
UN summer-fall offensive

Second Korean winter	Counteroffensive,
Korea, summer-fall 1952	Phase III
Third Korean winter	Tet Counteroffensive
Korea, summer 1953	Summer-Fall 1969
	Winter-Spring 1970
Vietnam	Sanctuary
Counteroffensive	Counteroffensive
Counteroffensive,	Counteroffensive,
Phase II	Phase VII

DECORATIONS

Presidential Unit Citation (Army), Streamer embroidered **TAEGU** (27th Infantry [less Heavy Tank Company] cited)

Presidential Unit Citation (Army), Streamer embroidered **SANGNYONG-NI** (27th Infantry [less Heavy Tank Company and 3d Battalion] cited)

Presidential Unit Citation (Army), Streamer embroidered **HAN RIVER**

Valorous Unit Award, Streamer embroidered **CU CHI DISTRICT** (1st Battalion, 27th Infantry cited)

Valorous Unit Award, Streamer embroidered **SAIGON** (2d Battalion, 27th Infantry cited)

Philippine Presidential Unit Citation, Streamer embroidered **17 OCTOBER 1944 TO 4 JULY 1945** (25th Infantry Division cited)

Republic of Korea Presidential Unit Citation, Streamer embroidered **MASAN-CHIN JU** (27th Infantry cited)

Republic of Korea Presidential Unit Citation Streamer embroidered **MUNSAN-NI** (27th Infantry cited)

Republic of Korea Presidential Unit Citation, Streamer embroidered **KOREA** (27th Infantry cited)

Vietnamese Cross of Gallantry with Palm, Streamer embroidered **VIETNAM 1966–1968** (2d Battalion, 27th Infantry cited)

3D BATTALION, 27TH INFANTRY
(The Wolfhounds)

LINEAGE

1901	Constituted 2 February as Company G, 26th Infantry, Regular Army; organized 26 March at Fort McPherson, GA, and redesignated 29 May as Company C, 27th Infantry

Company lineage follows that of 27th Infantry from 1901 through 31 March 1959 assignment to 63d Infantry Division

1943	Another Company constituted 18 January as Headquarters and Headquarters Company, 255th Infantry, an element of 63d Infantry Division, Army of the United States; activated 15 June at Camp Blanding, FL

255th Company lineage differs from that of 27th Infantry from its constitution through 1959 consolidation as follows:

1945	*Inactivated 29 September at Camp Kilmer, NJ*
1952	*63d Infantry Division allotted 22 February to Organized Reserve Corps; activated 1 March*
1959	Company C, 27th Infantry withdrawn 31 March from Regular Army, allotted to Army Reserve, and assigned to 63d Infantry Division; Battle Group activated 1 May at Los Angeles, CA, and consolidated with Headquarters and Headquarters Company, 255th Infantry to form Headquarters and Headquarters Company, 3d Battle Group, 27th Infantry
1963	Reorganized and redesignated 1 April as 3d Battalion, 27th Infantry
1965	Inactivated 31 December at Los Angeles, CA and relieved from assignment to 63d Infantry Division
1969	Withdrawn 6 December from Army Reserve, allotted to Regular Army, and activated in Hawaii as an element of the 25th Infantry Division
1970	Inactivated 15 December in Hawaii

CAMPAIGN PARTICIPATION

Philippine Insurrection	*World War I*
Mindanao	Siberia 1918
	Siberia 1919

World War II

Central Pacific
Guadalcanal
Northern Solomons (with
  arrowhead)
Luzon
Rhineland
Ardennes-Alsace
Central Europe

Korean War

UN defensive
UN offensive
CCF intervention
First UN counteroffensive
CCF spring offensive
UN summer-fall offensive
Second Korean winter
Korea, summer-fall 1952
Third Korean winter
Korea, summer 1953

DECORATIONS

Presidential Unit Citation (Army), Streamer embroidered **TAEGU** (27th Infantry [less Heavy Tank Company] cited)

Presidential Unit Citation (Army), Streamer embroidered

SANGNYONG-NI (27th Infantry [less Heavy Tank Company and 3d Battalion] cited)

Presidential Unit Citation (Army), Streamer embroidered **HAN RIVER**

Philippine Presidential Unit Citation, Streamer embroidered **17 OCTOBER 1944 TO 4 JULY 1945** (25th Infantry Division cited)

Republic of Korea Presidential Unit Citation, Streamer embroidered **MASAN-CHIN JU** (27th Infantry cited)

Republic of Korea Presidential Unit Citation, Streamer embroidered **MUNSAN-NI** (27th Infantry cited)

Republic of Korea Presidential Unit Citation, Streamer embroidered **KOREA** (27th Infantry cited)

Headquarters Company additionally entitled to: Meritorious Unit Commendation, Streamer embroidered **EUROPEAN THEATER** (Headquarters Company, 255th Infantry cited)

4TH BATTALION, 27TH INFANTRY
(The Wolfhounds)

LINEAGE

1901	Constituted 2 February as Company H, 26th Infantry, Regular Army; organized 16 April at Fort McPherson, GA, and redesignated 29 May as Company D, 27th Infantry
1921	Assigned 1 March to Hawaiian Division
1941	Relieved 26 August from assignment to Hawaiian Division and assigned to 25th Infantry Division
1957	Inactivated 1 February in Hawaii, relieved from assignment to 25th Infantry Division, and redesignated as Headquarters and Headquarters Company, 4th Battle Group, 27th Infantry
1963	Redesignated 27 March as Headquarters and Headquarters Company, 4th Battalion, 27th Infantry; withdrawn from Regular Army, allotted to Army Reserve, and assigned to 63d Infantry Division; Battalion activated 1 April at Long Beach, CA
1965	Inactivated 31 December at Long Beach, California

CAMPAIGN PARTICIPATION

Philippine Insurrection

Mindanao

World War I

Siberia 1918
Siberia 1919

World War II

Central Pacific
Guadalcanal
Northern Solomons (with
  arrowhead)
Luzon

Korean War

UN defensive
UN offensive
CCF intervention
First UN counteroffensive
CCF spring offensive
UN summer-fall offensive
Second Korean winter
Korea, summer-fall 1952
Third Korean winter
Korea, summer 1953

DECORATIONS

Presidential Unit Citation (Army), Streamer embroidered **TAEGU** (27th Infantry [less Heavy Tank Company] cited)

Presidential Unit Citation (Army), Streamer embroidered **SANGNYONG-NI** (27th Infantry [less Heavy Tank Company and 3d Battalion] cited)

Presidential Unit Citation (Army), Streamer embroidered **HAN RIVER**

Philippine Presidential Unit Citation, Streamer embroidered **17 OCTOBER 1944 TO 4 JULY 1945** (25th Infantry Division cited)

Republic of Korea Presidential Unit Citation, Streamer embroidered **MASAN-CHIN JU** (27th Infantry cited)

Republic of Korea Presidential Unit Citation, Streamer embroidered **MUNSAN-NI** (27th Infantry cited)

Republic of Korea Presidential Unit Citation, Streamer embroidered **KOREA** (27th Infantry cited)

28TH INFANTRY
(Lions of Cantigny)

COAT OF ARMS

Motto: *Vincit Amor Patriae* (Love of Country Conquers).

Symbolism: When this regiment was organized in 1901, the color of infantry facings was white, which has been taken for the color of the shield. As soon as organized, the regiment went to the Philippines, seeing active service against the Moros in Mindanao. The kris and kampilan, the Moro weapons, commemorate such service. During World War I the 28th Infantry was in the 1st Division and was the attacking regiment at Cantigny. Cantigny is in the ancient province of Picardy, whose arms carried three black rampant lions. The regiment received two French Croix de Guerre with Palm for distinguished services rendered during World War I and was also awarded the French Fourragere, which is incorporated in the crest.

DISTINCTIVE INSIGNIA

The distinctive insignia is the shield of the coat of arms.

LINEAGE

1901	Constituted 2 February as the 28th Infantry, Regular Army; organized March–June at Vancouver Barracks, WA
1917	Assigned 8 June to 1st Expeditionary Division (later designated the 1st Division)
1933	Inactivated 30 September at Fort Hayes, OH
1939	Relieved 16 October from assignment to 1st Division
1940	Assigned 22 June to the 8th Division and activated 10 October at Fort Niagara, NY
1945	Inactivated 1 November at Fort Leonard Wood, MO
1950	Activated 17 August at Fort Jackson, SC
1957	Relieved 1 August from assignment to 8th Infantry Division and reorganized as a parent regiment under CARS

CAMPAIGN PARTICIPATION

Philippine Insurrection

Mindanao

World War I

Montdidier-Noyon
Aisne-Marne
St. Mihiel
Meuse-Argonne

Lorraine 1917
Lorraine 1918
Picardy 1918

World War II

Normandy
Northern France
Rhineland
Central Europe

Vietnam

Defense
Counteroffensive
Counteroffensive, Phase II
Counteroffensive, Phase III
Tet Counteroffensive
Counteroffensive, Phase IV
Counteroffensive, Phase V
Counteroffensive, Phase VI
Tet 69 Counteroffensive
Summer-Fall 1969
Winter-Spring 1970

DECORATIONS

Presidential Unit Citation (Army), Streamer embroidered **STOCKHEIM** (3d Battalion, 28th Infantry cited)

Presidential Unit Citation (Army), Streamer embroidered **NORMANDY** (1st Battalion, 28th Infantry cited)

Presidential Unit Citation (Army), Streamer embroidered **BERGSTEIN** (3d Battalion, 28th Infantry cited)

Presidential Unit Citation (Army), Streamer embroidered **TAY NINH PROVINCE** (1st Battalion, 28th Infantry cited)

Valorous Unit Award, Streamer embroidered **LO KE RUBBER PLANTATION** (2d Battalion, 28th Infantry cited)

French Croix de Guerre with Palm, World War I, Streamer embroidered **PICARDY** (28th Infantry cited)

French Croix de Guerre with Palm, World War I, Streamer embroidered **AISNE-MARIE** (28th Infantry cited)

French Croix de Guerre with Palm, World War I, Fourragere (28th Infantry cited)

Luxembourg Croix de Guerre, Streamer embroidered **LUXEMBOURG** (8th Infantry Division cited)

1ST BATTALION, 28TH INFANTRY
(Lions of Cantigny)

LINEAGE

1901	Constituted 2 February as Company A, 28th Infantry, Regular Army; organized 10 June at Vancouver Barracks, WA
1933	Inactivated 30 September at Fort Hayes, OH
1940	Activated 10 October at Fort Niagara, NY
1945	Inactivated 1 November at Fort Leonard Wood, MO
1950	Activated 17 August at Fort Jackson, SC
1957	Reorganized and redesignated 1 August as Headquarters and Headquarters Company, 1st Battle Group, 28th Infantry; assigned to 8th Infantry Division
1959	Relieved 1 May from assignment to 8th Infantry Division and assigned to 1st Infantry Division
1964	Reorganized and redesignated 13 January as 1st Battalion, 28th Infantry

CAMPAIGN PARTICIPATION

Philippine Insurrection

Mindanao

World War I

Montdidier-Noyon
Aisne-Marne
St. Mihiel
Meuse-Argonne
Lorraine 1917
Lorraine 1918
Picardy 1918

World War II

Normandy
Northern France
Rhineland
Central Europe

Vietnam

Defense
Counteroffensive
Counteroffensive,
    Phase II
Counteroffensive,
    Phase III
Tet Counteroffensive
Counteroffensive,
    Phase IV
Counteroffensive,
    Phase V
Counteroffensive,
    Phase VI
Tet 69 Counteroffensive
Summer-Fall 1969
Winter-Spring 1970

DECORATIONS

Presidential Unit Citation (Army), Streamer embroidered **STOCKHEIM**

Presidential Unit Citation (Army), Streamer embroidered **NORMANDY** (1st Battalion, 28th Infantry cited)

Presidential Unit Citation (Army), Streamer embroidered **BERGSTEIN**

Presidential Unit Citation (Army), Streamer embroidered **TAY NINH PROVINCE** (1st Battalion, 28th Infantry cited)

French Croix de Guerre with Palm, World War I, Streamer embroidered **PICARDY** (28th Infantry cited)

French Croix de Guerre with Palm, World War I, Streamer embroidered **AISNE-MARNE** (28th Infantry cited)

French Croix de Guerre with Palm, World War I, Fourragere (28th Infantry cited)

Luxembourg Croix de Guerre, Streamer embroidered **LUXEMBOURG** (8th Infantry Division cited)

Vietnamese Cross of Gallantry with Palm, Streamer embroidered **VIETNAM 1965–1968** (1st Battalion, 28th Infantry cited)

Vietnamese Cross of Gallantry with Palm, Streamer embroidered **VIETNAM 1969–1970** (1st Battalion, 28th Infantry cited)

Vietnamese Civil Action Honor Medal, First Class, Streamer embroidered **VIETNAM 1965–1970** (1st Battalion, 28th Infantry cited)

2D BATTALION, 28TH INFANTRY
(Lions of Cantigny)

LINEAGE

1901	Constituted 2 February as Company B, 28th Infantry, Regular Army; organized 17 June at Vancouver Barracks, WA
1933	Inactivated 30 September at Fort Hayes, OH
1940	Activated 10 October at Fort Niagara, NY
1945	Inactivated 1 November at Fort Leonard Wood, MO
1950	Activated 17 August at Fort Jackson, SC
1957	Reorganized and redesignated 15 February as Headquarters and Headquarters Company, 2d Battle Group, 28th Infantry; relieved from assignment to 8th Infantry Division and assigned to 1st Infantry Division
1958	Relieved 26 December from assignment to 1st Infantry Division and assigned to 24th Infantry Division
1963	Inactivated 1 February in Germany, relieved from assignment to 24th Infantry Division, redesignated 23 October as 2d Battalion, 28th Infantry, and assigned to 1st Infantry Division
1964	Activated 13 January at Fort Riley, KS
1970	Inactivated 15 April at Fort Riley, KS

CAMPAIGN PARTICIPATION

Philippine Insurrection

Mindanao

World War I

Montdidier-Noyon

Aisne-Marne
St. Mihiel
Meuse-Argonne
Lorraine 1917
Lorraine 1918
Picardy 1918

World War II
Normandy
Northern France
Rhineland
Central Europe

Vietnam
Defense

Counteroffensive
Counteroffensive, Phase II
Counteroffensive, Phase III
Tet Counteroffensive
Summer-Fall 1969
Winter-Spring 1970

DECORATIONS

Presidential Unit Citation (Army), Streamer embroidered **STOCKHEIM**

Presidential Unit Citation (Army), Streamer embroidered **NORMANDY** (1st Battalion, 28th Infantry cited)

Presidential Unit Citation (Army), Streamer embroidered **BERGSTEIN**

Valorous Unit Award, Streamer embroidered **LO KE RUB-BER PLANTATION** (2d Battalion, 28th Infantry cited)

French Croix de Guerre with Palm, World War I, Streamer embroidered **PICARDY** (28th Infantry cited)

French Croix de Guerre with Palm, World War I, Streamer embroidered **AISNE-MARNE** (28th Infantry cited)

French Croix de Guerre with Palm, World War I, Fourragere (28th Infantry cited)

Luxembourg Croix de Guerre, Streamer embroidered **LUX-EMBOURG** (8th Infantry Division cited)

Vietnamese Cross of Gallantry with Palm, Streamer embroidered **VIETNAM 1965-1968** (2d Battalion, 28th Infantry cited)

Vietnamese Cross of Gallantry with Palm, Streamer embroidered **VIETNAM 1969-1970** (2d Battalion, 28th Infantry cited)

Vietnamese Civil Action Honor Medal, First Class, Streamer embroidered **VIETNAM 1965-1970** (2d Battalion, 28th Infantry cited)

3D BATTALION, 28TH INFANTRY
(Lions of Cantigny)

LINEAGE

1901   Constituted 2 February as Company C, 28th Infantry, Regular Army; organized 20 June at Vancouver Barracks, WA

Company lineage follows that of 28th Infantry from 1901 through 1957 relief from assignment to 8th Infantry Division

1917   Another company constituted 5 August as Headquarters and Headquarters Company, 331st Infantry, National Army, an element of the 83d Division; organized 30 August at Camp Sherman, OH

331st Infantry lineage differs from that of 28th Infantry from its constitution through 20 March 1959 consolidation as follows:

1919   *Demobilized 9 February at Camp Sherman, OH*

1921   *Reconstituted 24 June in Organized Reserves as an element of the 83d Division; organized in November at Cleveland, OH*

1942   *Ordered into active military service 15 August and reorganized at Camp Atterbury, IN*

1946   *Inactivated 30 March at Camp Kilmer, NJ, and activated 1 October in the Organized Reserves at Cleveland, OH*

1957   Company C, 28th Infantry inactivated 1 August in Germany, relieved from assignment to the 8th Infantry Division, and redesignated Headquarters and Headquarters Company, 3d Battle Group, 28th Infantry

1959   Withdrawn 19 March from Regular Army, allotted to Army Reserve, assigned to 83d Infantry Division; Battle Group activated 20 March at Akron, OH; consolidated with Headquarters and Headquarters Company, 331st Infantry to form Headquarters and Headquarters Company, 3d Battle Group, 28th Infantry

1963   Reorganized and redesignated 15 April as 3d Battalion, 28th Infantry

1965   Inactivated 31 December at Akron, OH

CAMPAIGN PARTICIPATION

Philippine Insurrection

Mindanao

World War I

Montdidier-Noyon
Aisne-Marne
St. Mihiel
Meuse-Argonne
Lorraine 1917

Lorraine 1918
Picardy 1918

World War II

Normandy
Northern France
Rhineland
Ardennes-Alsace
Central Europe

DECORATIONS

Presidential Unit Citation (Army), Streamer embroidered **STOCKHEIM**

Presidential Unit Citation (Army), Streamer embroidered **NORMANDY** (1st Battalion, 28th Infantry cited)

Presidential Unit Citation (Army), Streamer embroidered **BERGSTEIN**

French Croix de Guerre with Palm, World War I, Streamer embroidered **PICARDY** (28th Infantry cited)

French Croix de Guerre with Palm, World War I, Streamer embroidered **AISNE-MARNE** (28th Infantry cited)

French Croix de Guerre with Palm, World War I, Fourragere (28th Infantry cited)

Luxembourg Croix de Guerre, Streamer embroidered **LUX-EMBOURG** (8th Infantry Division cited)

29TH INFANTRY

COAT OF ARMS

Motto: We Lead the Way

Symbolism: White and blue are the old and present infantry colors. The mango tree, the crossed bolo of the Filipino, and the bayonet of the regiment represent service in the Philippine Insurrection. The regiment's long association with the Infantry School at Fort Benning, GA, is indicated by the classic lamp of knowledge in the crest.

DISTINCTIVE INSIGNIA

The distinctive insignia is the shield, crest, and motto of the coat of arms.

LINEAGE

1901   Constituted 2 February as 29th Infantry, Regular Army; organized 5 March at Fort Sheridan, IL

1918   Assigned 29 July to the 17th Division

1919   Relieved 10 February from assignment to 17th Division

1933   Assigned 1 October to the 4th Division

1939   Relieved 16 October from assignment to 4th Division

1946   Inactivated 31 October in Germany

1949   Activated 1 May on Okinawa

1954   Assigned 2 December to the 23d Infantry Division

1956   Relieved 1 March from assignment to 23d Infantry Division

1957   Reorganized 25 May as a parent regiment under CARS

CAMPAIGN PARTICIPATION

Philippine Insurrection
Without inscription

World War II
Northern France
Rhineland

Ardennes-Alsace
Central Europe

Korean War
UN Defense

DECORATIONS

Presidential Unit Citation (Army), Streamer embroidered **NAM RIVER** (1st Battalion, 29th Infantry cited)

1st Battalion, 29th Infantry

LINEAGE

1901   Constituted 2 February as Company A, 29th Infantry, Regular Army; organized 5 March at Fort Sheridan, IL

          Company lineage follows that of 29th Infantry from 1901 through 1956 relief from assignment to 23d Infantry Division

1957   Reorganized and redesignated 25 May as Headquarters and Headquarters Company, 1st Battle Group, 29th Infantry

1958   Assigned 25 July to 1st Infantry Brigade

1962   Relieved 20 September from assignment to 1st Infantry Brigade and inactivated 24 September at Fort Benning, GA

1963   Redesignated 4 January as 1st Battalion, 29th Infantry, assigned to 197th Infantry Brigade, and activated 1 February at Fort Benning, GA

CAMPAIGN PARTICIPATION

Philippine Insurrection
Without inscription

World War II
Northern France
Rhineland

Ardennes-Alsace
Central Europe

Korean War
UN Defense

DECORATIONS

Presidential Unit Citation (Army), Streamer embroidered **NAM RIVER** (1st Battalion, 29th Infantry cited)

2D BATTALION, 29TH INFANTRY

LINEAGE

1901 Constituted 2 February as Company B, 29th Infantry, Regular Army; organized 5 March at Fort Sheridan, IL

Company lineage follows that of 29th Infantry from 1901 through 1956 relief from assignment to 23d Infantry Division

1957 Inactivated 1 July at Fort Benning, GA, redesignated as Headquarters and Headquarters Company, 2d Battle Group, 29th Infantry; assigned to the 10th Infantry Division and activated in Germany

1958 Inactivated 14 June in Germany and relieved from assignment to 10th Infantry Division

1963 Redesignated 4 January as 2d Battalion, 29th Infantry, assigned to 197th Infantry Brigade, and activated 1 February at Fort Benning, GA

1965 Inactivated 14 November at Fort Benning, GA

CAMPAIGN PARTICIPATION

Philippine Insurrection
Without inscription

World War II
Northern France

Rhineland
Ardennes-Alsace
Central Europe

Korean War
UN Defense

DECORATIONS

Presidential Unit Citation (Army), Streamer embroidered **NAM RIVER** (1st Battalion, 29th Infantry cited)

3D BATTALION, 29TH INFANTRY

LINEAGE

1901 Constituted 2 February as Company C, 29th Infantry, Regular Army; organized 5 March at Fort Sheridan, IL

Company lineage follows that of 29th Infantry from 1901 through 1956 relief from assignment to 23d Infantry Division

1946 Another company constituted 15 July as Headquarters and Headquarters Company, 519th Parachute Infantry, Organized Reserves, an element of the 108th Airborne Division; activated 6 August at Atlanta, GA

The 519th Parachute Infantry lineage differs from that of 29th Infantry from its constitution to 1 May 1959 consolidation as follows:

1951 *Reorganized and redesignated 1 February as Headquarters and Headquarters Company, 519th Airborne Infantry*

1952 *Reorganized and redesignated 1 March as Headquarters and Headquarters Company, 519th Infantry; relieved from assignment to 108th Airborne Division and assigned to the 81st Infantry Division*

1957 *Company C, 29th Infantry inactivated 25 May at Fort Benning, GA, redesignated as Headquarters and Headquarters Company, 3d Battle Group, 29th Infantry; withdrawn 10 April from Regular Army, allotted to Army Reserve, and assigned to the 81st Infantry Division*

1959 Battle Group activated 1 May at Atlanta, Georgia; consolidated with Headquarters and Headquarters Company, 519th Infantry to form Headquarters and Headquarters Company, 3d Battle Group, 29th Infantry

1963 Reorganized and redesignated 1 April as 3d Battalion, 29th Infantry and location changed 1 October to Columbus, GA

1965 Inactivated 31 December at Columbus, GA

CAMPAIGN PARTICIPATION

Philippine Insurrection
Without inscription

World War II
Northern France
Rhineland

Ardennes-Alsace
Central Europe

Korean War
UN Defense

DECORATIONS

Presidential Unit Citation (Army), Streamer embroidered
NAM RIVER (1st Battalion, 29th Infantry cited)

4TH BATTALION, 29TH INFANTRY

LINEAGE

1901   Constituted 2 February as Company D, 29th Infantry, Regular Army; organized 5 March at Fort Sheridan, IL

Company lineage follows that of 29th Infantry from 1901 through 1956 relief from assignment to 23d Infantry Division

1957   Inactivated 25 May at Fort Benning, GA, redesignated as Headquarters and Headquarters Company, 4th Battle Group, 29th Infantry

1962   Redesignated 20 September as Headquarters and Headquarters Company, 4th Battalion, 29th Infantry, and assigned to the 197th Infantry Brigade; activated 24 September at Fort Benning, GA

1963   Relieved 4 January from assignment to 197th Infantry Brigade, inactivated 1 February at Fort Benning, GA; withdrawn 26 March from the Regular Army, allotted to the Army Reserve and assigned to the 81st Infantry Division; activated 1 April at Tifton, GA

1965   Inactivated 31 December at Tifton, GA

CAMPAIGN PARTICIPATION

Philippine Insurrection
Without inscription

World War II
Northern France
Rhineland

Ardennes-Alsace
Central Europe

Korean War
UN Defense

DECORATIONS

Presidential Unit Citation (Army), Streamer embroidered
NAM RIVER (1st Battalion, 29th Infantry cited)

30TH INFANTRY

COAT OF ARMS

Motto: Our Country, Not Ourselves

Symbolism: This regiment's assignment to the 3d Division during World War I is shown by the simulation of the divisional shoulder sleeve insignia on the canton. The broken chevron represents the part taken by the 30th Infantry in pushing back the point of the German drive at the Marne in July 1918, for which services the regiment was awarded the French Croix de Guerre with Palm. The boar's head represents the subsequent passage through the German lines and occupation of German territory by this regiment.

DISTINCTIVE INSIGNIA

The distinctive insignia is the shield and crest of the coat of arms within a circlet bearing the motto of the coat of arms and "Rock of the Marne, July 14–18, 1918."

LINEAGE

1901   Constituted 2 February as the 30th Infantry, Regular Army; organized 12 February–19 August at Fort Logan, CO, at the Presidio of San Francisco, CA, and the Philippine Islands

1917   Assigned 21 November to the 3d Division

1940   Relieved 12 January from assignment to 3d Division and assigned 15 May to the 3d Division

1951   Relieved 6 April from assignment to 3d Infantry Division

1954   Assigned 2 December to the 3d Infantry Division

1957   Relieved 1 July from assignment to 3d Infantry Division and reorganized as a parent regiment under CARS

CAMPAIGN PARTICIPATION

Philippine Insurrection
Mindoro 1901

World War I
Aisne
Champagne–Marne
Aisne–Marne
St. Mihiel
Meuse–Argonne
Champagne 1918

World War II
Algeria–French Morocco (with arrowhead)
Tunisia
Sicily (with arrowhead)
Naples–Foggia
Anzio (with arrowhead)
Rome–Arno
Southern France (with arrowhead)
Rhineland
Ardennes–Alsace
Central Europe

DECORATIONS

Presidential Unit Citation (Army), Streamer embroidered **COLMAR** (3d Infantry Division cited)

Presidential Unit Citation (Army), Streamer embroidered **BESANCON, FRANCE** (1st Battalion, 30th Infantry cited)

Presidential Unit Citation (Army), Streamer embroidered **SICILY** (2d Battalion, 30th Infantry cited)

Presidential Unit Citation (Army), Streamer embroidered **MOUNT ROTUNDO** (3d Battalion, 30th Infantry cited)

French Croix de Guerre with Palm, World War I, Streamer embroidered **CHAMPAGNE–MARNE** (30th Infantry cited)

French Croix de Guerre with Palm, World War II, Streamer embroidered **COLMAR** (30th Infantry cited)

French Croix de Guerre, World War II, Fourragere (30th Infantry cited)

1ST BATTALION, 30TH INFANTRY

LINEAGE

1901   Constituted 2 February as Company A, 30th Infantry, Regular Army; organized 16 March at the Presidio, San Francisco, CA

Company lineage follows that of 30th Infantry from 1901 through 1954 and assignment to 3d Infantry Division

1957   Reorganized and redesignated 1 July as Headquarters and Headquarters Company, 1st Battle Group, 30th Infantry; remained assigned to the 3d Infantry Division

1963   Reorganized and redesignated 10 July as the 1st Battalion, 30th Infantry

CAMPAIGN PARTICIPATION

Philippine Insurrection
Mindoro 1901

World War I
Aisne
Champagne–Marne
Aisne–Marne
St. Mihiel
Meuse–Argonne
Champagne 1918

World War II
Algeria–French Morocco (with arrowhead)
Tunisia
Sicily (with arrowhead)
Naples–Foggia
Anzio (with arrowhead)
Rome–Arno
Southern France (with arrowhead)
Rhineland
Ardennes–Alsace
Central Europe

DECORATIONS

Presidential Unit Citation (Army), Streamer embroidered **COLMAR** (3d Infantry Division cited)

Presidential Unit Citation (Army), Streamer embroidered **BESANCON, FRANCE** (1st Battalion, 30th Infantry cited)

Presidential Unit Citation (Army), Streamer embroidered **SICILY**

Presidential Unit Citation (Army), Streamer embroidered **MOUNT ROTUNDO**

French Croix de Guerre with Palm, World War I, Streamer embroidered **CHAMPAGNE–MARNE** (30th Infantry cited)

French Croix de Guerre with Palm, World War II, Streamer embroidered **COLMAR** (30th Infantry cited)

French Croix de Guerre, World War II, Fourragere (30th Infantry cited)

2D BATTALION, 30TH INFANTRY

LINEAGE

1901   Constituted 2 February as Company B, 30th Infantry, Regular Army; organized 16 March at the Presidio, San Francisco, CA

Company lineage follows that of 30th Infantry from 1901 through 1956 assignment to 3d Infantry Division

1957   Inactivated 1 July at Fort Benning, GA, and relieved from assignment to 3d Infantry Division

1958   Redesignated 3 January as Headquarters and Headquarters Company, 2d Battle Group, 30th Infantry; Battle Group activated 22 January at Fort Sill, IL

1963   Reorganized and redesignated 1 April as 2d Battalion, 30th Infantry; assigned to the 3d Infantry Division

DECORATIONS

Presidential Unit Citation (Army), Streamer embroidered **COLMAR** (3d Infantry Division cited)

Presidential Unit Citation (Army), Streamer embroidered **BESANCON, FRANCE** (1st Battalion, 30th Infantry cited)

Presidential Unit Citation (Army), Streamer embroidered **SICILY**

Presidential Unit Citation (Army), Streamer embroidered **MOUNT ROTUNDO**

French Croix de Guerre with Palm, World War I, Streamer embroidered **CHAMPAGNE–MARNE** (30th Infantry cited)

French Croix de Guerre with Palm, World War II, Streamer embroidered **COLMAR** (30th Infantry cited)

French Croix de Guerre, World War II, Fourragere (30th Infantry cited)

CAMPAIGN PARTICIPATION

Philippine Insurrection

Mindoro 1901

World War I

Aisne
Champagne-Marne
Aisne-Marne
St. Mihiel
Meuse-Argonne
Champagne 1918

World War II

Algeria–French Morocco (with arrowhead)
Tunisia
Sicily (with arrowhead)
Naples–Foggia
Anzio (with arrowhead)
Rome–Arno
Southern France (with arrowhead)
Rhineland
Ardennes–Alsace
Central Europe

3D BATTALION, 30TH INFANTRY

LINEAGE

1901   Constituted 2 February as Company C, 30th Infantry, Regular Army; organized 16 March at the Presidio, San Francisco, CA

Company lineage follows that of 30th Infantry from 1901 through 1956 assignment to 3d Infantry Division

1943   Another company constituted 18 January as Headquarters and Headquarters Company, 254th Infantry, Army of the United States, an element of the 63d Infantry Division, activated 15 June at Fort Blanding, FL

The 254th Infantry lineage differs from that of the 30th Infantry from its constitition to 1959 consolidation as follows:

1945   *Inactivated 29 September at Camp Kilmer, NJ*

1952   *Allotted 22 February to Organized Reserve Corps and activated 1 March at Pasadena, CA*

1957   *Company C, 30th Infantry inactivated 1 July at Fort Benning, GA, relieved from assignment to 3d Infantry Division, and redesignated as Headquarters and Headquarters Company, 3d Battle Group, 30th Infantry*

1959   Withdrawn 31 March from the Regular Army, allotted to the Army Reserve, and assigned to the 63d Infantry Division, Battle Group activated 1 May at Pasadena, CA, and consolidated with Headquarters and Headquarters Company, 254th Infantry to form Headquarters and Headquarters Company, 3d Battle Group, 30th Infantry

1963   Reorganized and redesignated 1 April as the 3d Battalion, 30th Infantry

1965   Inactivated 31 December at Pasadena, CA

CAMPAIGN PARTICIPATION

Philippine Insurrection
   Mindoro 1901

World War I
   Aisne
   Champagne–Marne
   Aisne–Marne
   St. Mihiel
   Meuse–Argonne
   Champagne 1918

World War II
   Algeria–French Morocco
   (with arrowhead)

   Tunisia
   Sicily (with arrowhead)
   Naples–Foggia
   Anzio (with arrowhead)
   Rome–Arno
   Southern France (with
     arrowhead)
   Rhineland
   Ardennes–Alsace
   Central Europe

DECORATIONS

Presidential Unit Citation (Army), Streamer embroidered **COLMAR** (3d Infantry Division and 254th Infantry cited)

Presidential Unit Citation (Army), Streamer embroidered **BESANCON, FRANCE** (1st Battalion, 30th Infantry cited)

Presidential Unit Citation (Army), Streamer embroidered **SICILY**

Presidential Unit Citation (Army), Streamer embroidered **MOUNT ROTUNDO**

French Croix de Guerre with Palm, World War I, Streamer embroidered **CHAMPAGNE–MARNE** (30th Infantry cited)

French Croix de Guerre with Palm, World War II, Streamer embroidered **COLMAR** (30th Infantry cited)

French Croix de Guerre, World War II, Fourragere (30th Infantry cited)

4TH BATTALION, 30TH INFANTRY

LINEAGE

1901   Constituted 2 February as Company D, 30th Infantry, Regular Army; organized 16 March at the Presidio, San Francisco, CA

Company lineage follows that of 30th Infantry from 1901 through 1954 assignment to 3d Infantry Division

1957   Inactivated 1 July at Fort Benning, GA; relieved from assignment to 3d Infantry Division, and redesignated as Headquarters and Headquarters Company, 4th Battle Group, 30th Infantry

1963   Battle Group activated 1 April at Fort Sill, OK, and reorganized and redesignated 24 October as 4th Battalion, 30th Infantry

CAMPAIGN PARTICIPATION

Philippine Insurrection
  Mindoro 1901

World War I
  Aisne

  Champagne–Marne
  Aisne–Marne
  St. Mihiel
  Meuse–Argonne
  Champagne 1918

World War II
  Algeria–French Morocco (with arrowhead)
  Tunisia
  Sicily (with arrowhead)
  Naples–Foggia
  Anzio (with arrowhead)

  Rome–Arno
  Southern France (with arrowhead)
  Rhineland
  Ardennes–Alsace
  Central Europe

DECORATIONS

Presidential Unit Citation (Army), Streamer embroidered **COLMAR** (3d Infantry Division cited)

Presidential Unit Citation (Army), Streamer embroidered **BESANCON, FRANCE** (1st Battalion, 30th Infantry cited)

Presidential Unit Citation (Army), Streamer embroidered **SICILY**

Presidential Unit Citation (Army), Streamer embroidered **MOUNT ROTUNDO**

French Croix de Guerre with Palm, World War I, Streamer embroidered **CHAMPAGNE–MARNE** (30th Infantry cited)

French Croix de Guerre with Palm, World War II, Streamer embroidered **COLMAR** (30th Infantry cited)

French Croix de Guerre, World War II, Fourragere (30th Infantry cited)

COMPANY E, 30TH INFANTRY

LINEAGE

1901   Constituted 2 February as Company E, 30th Infantry, Regular Army; organized 29 May at Palte, Laguna, Philippine Islands

Company lineage follows that of 30th Infantry from 1901 through 1954 assignment to 3d Infantry Division

1957   Inactivated 1 July at Fort Benning, GA; relieved from assignment to 3d Infantry Division, and redesignated as Headquarters and Headquarters Company, 5th Battle Group, 30th Infantry

1966   Redesignated 25 August as Company E, 30th Infantry and activated at Fort Ruckler, AL

CAMPAIGN PARTICIPATION

Philippine Insurrection
  Mindoro 1901

World War I
  Aisne

  Champagne–Marne
  Aisne–Marne
  St. Mihiel
  Meuse–Argonne
  Champagne 1918

World War II-EAME

Algeria–French Morocco (with arrowhead)
Tunisia
Sicily (with arrowhead)
Naples–Foggia
Anzio (with arrowhead)

Rome–Arno
Southern France (with arrowhead)
Rhineland
Ardennes–Alsace
Central Europe

Presidential Unit Citation (Army), Streamer embroidered **SICILY** (2d Battalion, 30th Infantry cited)

French Croix de Guerre with Palm, World War I, Streamer embroidered **CHAMPAGNE-MARNE** (30th Infantry cited)

French Croix de Guerre with Palm, World War II, Streamer embroidered **COLMAR** (30th Infantry cited)

French Croix de Guerre, World War II, Fourragere (30th Infantry cited)

DECORATIONS

Presidential Unit Citation (Army), Streamer embroidered **COLMAR** (3d Infantry Division cited)

COMPANY F, 30TH INFANTRY

LINEAGE

1901   Constituted 2 February as Company F, 30th Infantry, Regular Army; organized 29 May at Palte, Laguna, Philippine Islands

Company lineage follows that of 30th Infantry from 1901 through 1954 assignment to 3d Infantry Division

1957   Inactivated 1 July at Fort Benning, GA; relieved from assignment to 3d Infantry Division, redesignated as Headquarters and Headquarters Company, 6th Battle Group, 30th Infantry

1967   Redesignated 1 February as Company F, 30th Infantry; activated at Fort Riley, KS, and inactivated 25 March

CAMPAIGN PARTICIPATION

Philippine Insurrection

Mindoro 1901

World War I

Aisne
Champagne-Marne
Aisne-Marne
St. Mihiel
Meuse-Argonne
Champagne 1918

World War II-EAME

Algeria–French Morocco (with arrowhead)
Tunisia
Sicily (with arrowhead)

Naples–Foggia
Anzio (with arrowhead)
Rome–Arno
Southern France (with arrowhead)

Rhineland
Ardennes–Alsace
Central Europe

DECORATIONS

Presidential Unit Citation (Army), Streamer embroidered **COLMAR** (3d Infantry Division cited)

Presidential Unit Citation (Army), Streamer embroidered **SICILY** (2d Battalion, 30th Infantry cited)

French Croix de Guerre with Palm, World War I, Streamer embroidered **CHAMPAGNE MARNE** (30th Infantry cited)

French Croix de Guerre with Palm, World War II, Streamer embroidered **COLMAR** (30th Infantry cited)

French Croix de Guerre, World War II, Fourragere (30th Infantry cited)

31ST INFANTRY
(The Polar Bears)

COAT OF ARMS

Motto: *Pro Patria* (For Country)

Symbolism: The shield is blue for infantry. The unit's original organization in the Philippine Islands is indicated by the sea lion taken from the coat of arms of the Philippines. The regiment's service in Siberia in 1918–19 is symbolized by the polar bear crest. The motto is indicative of the spirit of the regiment, although for many years it did not set foot in the United States.

DISTINCTIVE INSIGNIA

The distinctive insignia is the crest and motto of the coat of arms.

LINEAGE

1916	Constituted 1 July as 31st Infantry, Regular Army; organized 1 August at Fort William McKinley, Philippine Islands
1921	Assigned 22 October to the Philippine Division
1931	Relieved 26 June from assignment to the Philippine Division
1941	Assigned to the Philippine Division
1942	Surrendered 9 April to the Japanese 14th Army
1946	Reorganized 19 January in Korea as an element of the 7th Infantry Division
1957	Relieved 1 July from assignment to 7th Infantry Division and reorganized as a parent regiment under CARS

CAMPAIGN PARTICIPATION

World War I

Siberia 1918
Siberia 1919

World War II

Philippine Islands

Korean War

UN defensive
UN offensive
CCF intervention
First UN counteroffensive
CCF spring offensive
UN summer–fall
  offensive

Second Korean winter
Korea, summer–fall 1952
Third Korean winter
Korea, summer 1953

Vietnam

Counteroffensive,
  Phase II
Counteroffensive,
  Phase III
Tet Counteroffensive
Counteroffensive,
  Phase IV
Counteroffensive,
  Phase V
Counteroffensive,
  Phase VI
Tet 69 Counteroffensive
Summer–Fall 1969
Winter–Spring 1970
Sanctuary
  Counteroffensive
Counteroffensive,
  Phase VII
Consolidation I

DECORATIONS

Presidential Unit Citation (Army), Streamer embroidered **LUZON 1941–1942** (31st Infantry cited)

Presidential Unit Citation (Army), Streamer embroidered **BATAAN** (31st Infantry cited)

Presidential Unit Citation (Army), Streamer embroidered **DEFENSE OF THE PHILIPPINES** (31st Infantry cited)

Presidential Unit Citation (Navy), Streamer embroidered **CHOSIN RESERVOIR** (2d Battalion [less Company E], 31st Infantry and attached units cited)

Presidential Unit Citation (Navy), Streamer embroidered **HWACHON RESERVOIR** (31st Infantry cited)

Valorous Unit Award, Streamer embroidered **QUE SON-HIEP DUC** (4th Battalion, 31st Infantry cited)

Valorous Unit Award, Streamer embroidered **SAIGON** (6th Battalion, 31st Infantry cited)

Valorous Unit Award, Streamer embroidered **PARROT'S BEAK** (6th Battalion, 31st Infantry cited)

Navy Unit Commendation, Streamer embroidered **PANMUNJOM** (31st Infantry cited)

Philippine Presidential Unit Citation, Streamer embroidered **7 DECEMBER 1941 TO 10 MAY 1942** (31st Infantry cited)

Republic of Korea Presidential Unit Citation, Streamer embroidered **INCHON** (31st Infantry cited)

Republic of Korea Presidential Unit Citation, Streamer embroidered **KOREA** (31st Infantry cited)

1ST BATTALION, 31ST INFANTRY
(The Polar Bears)

LINEAGE

1916	Constituted 1 July as Company A, 31st Infantry, Regular Army; organized 1 August at Regan Barracks, Philippine Islands

Company lineage follows that of 31st Infantry from 1916 through 1946 reorganization in Korea

1957	Reorganized and redesignated 1 July as Headquarters and Headquarters Company, 1st Battle Group, 31st Infantry; remained assigned to the 7th Infantry Division
1963	Reorganized and redesignated 1 July as 1st Battalion, 31st Infantry

CAMPAIGN PARTICIPATION

World War I

Siberia 1918
Siberia 1919

World War II

Philippine Islands

Korean War

UN defensive

UN offensive
CCF intervention
First UN counteroffensive
CCF spring offensive
UN summer–fall offensive
Second Korean winter
Korea, summer–fall 1952
Third Korean winter
Korea, summer 1953

DECORATIONS

Presidential Unit Citation (Army), Streamer embroidered **LUZON 1941–1942** (31st Infantry cited)

Presidential Unit Citation (Army), Streamer embroidered **BATAAN** (31st Infantry cited)

Presidential Unit Citation (Army), Streamer embroidered **DEFENSE OF THE PHILIPPINES** (31st Infantry cited)

Presidential Unit Citation (Navy), Streamer embroidered **CHOSIN RESERVOIR**

Presidential Unit Citation (Navy), Streamer embroidered **HWACHON RESERVOIR** (31st Infantry cited)

Navy Unit Commendation, Streamer embroidered **PAN-MUNJOM** (31st Infantry cited)

Philippine Presidential Unit Citation, Streamer embroidered **7 DECEMBER 1941 TO 10 MAY 1942** (31st Infantry cited)

Republic of Korea Presidential Unit Citation, Streamer embroidered **INCHON** (31st Infantry cited)

Republic of Korea Presidential Unit Citation, Streamer embroidered **KOREA** (31st Infantry cited)

2D BATTALION, 31ST INFANTRY
(The Polar Bears)

LINEAGE

1916   Constituted 1 July as Company B, 31st Infantry, Regular Army; organized 1 August at Regan Barracks, Philippine Islands

Company lineage follows that of 31st Infantry from 1916 through 1946 reorganization in Korea

1957   Inactivated 1 July in Korea, relieved from assignment to 7th Infantry Division; redesignated as Headquarters and Headquarters Company, 2d Battle Group, 31st Infantry

1958   Battle Group activated 24 March at Fort Rucker, AL

1963   Reorganized and redesignated 1 July as 2d Battalion, 31st Infantry and assigned to the 7th Infantry Division

CAMPAIGN PARTICIPATION

World War I

Siberia 1918
Siberia 1919

World War II

Philippine Islands

Korean War

UN defensive
UN offensive
CCF intervention
First UN counteroffensive
CCF spring offensive
UN summer–fall offensive
Second Korean winter
Korea, summer–fall 1952
Third Korean winter
Korea, summer 1953

DECORATIONS

Presidential Unit Citation (Army), Streamer embroidered **LUZON 1941–1942** (31st Infantry cited)

Presidential Unit Citation (Army), Streamer embroidered **BATAAN** (31st Infantry cited)

Presidential Unit Citation (Army), Streamer embroidered **DEFENSE OF THE PHILIPPINES** (31st Infantry cited)

Presidential Unit Citation (Navy), Streamer embroidered **CHOSIN RESERVOIR** (Company B, 31st Infantry cited)

Presidential Unit Citation (Navy), Streamer embroidered **HWACHON RESERVOIR** (31st Infantry cited)

Navy Unit Commendation, Streamer embroidered **PAN-MUNJOM** (31st Infantry cited)

Philippine Presidential Unit Citation, Streamer embroidered **7 DECEMBER 1941 TO 10 MAY 1942** (31st Infantry cited)

Republic of Korea Presidential Unit Citation, Streamer em-broidered **INCHON** (31st Infantry cited)

Republic of Korea Presidential Unit Citation, Streamer em-broidered **KOREA** (31st Infantry cited)

3D BATTALION, 31ST INFANTRY
(The Polar Bears)

LINEAGE

1916   Constituted 1 July as Company C, 31st Infantry, Regular Army; organized 1 August at Regan Barracks, Philippine Islands

Company lineage follows that of 31st Infantry from 1916 through 1946 reorganization in Korea

1943   Another company constituted 18 January as Headquarters and Headquarters Company, 253d Infantry, Army of the United States, an element of the 63d Infantry Division; activated 15 June at Camp Blanding, FL

253d Infantry lineage differs from that of 31st Infantry from its constitution to 1959 consolidation as follows.

1945   *Inactivated 28 September at Camp Miles Standish, MA*

1952   *Allotted 22 February to Organized Reserve Corps, activated 1 March at Los Angeles, CA*

1957   *Company C, 31st Infantry inactivated 1 July in Korea; relieved from assignment to 7th Infantry Division, and redesignated Headquarters and Headquarters Company, 3d Battle Group, 31st Infantry*

1959   Withdrawn 31 March from Regular Army, allotted to Army Reserve, assigned to 53d Infantry Division; Battle Group activated 1 May at Los Angeles, CA; consolidated with Headquarters and Headquarters Company, 253d Infantry to form Headquarters and Headquarters Company, 3d Battle Group, 31st Infantry

1963   Reorganized and redesignated 1 October as 3d Battalion, 31st Infantry

1964   Location of Headquarters changed 16 March to Playa del Rey, CA

1965   Inactivated 31 December at Playa del Rey, CA

CAMPAIGN PARTICIPATION

World War I
Siberia 1918
Siberia 1919

World War II
Philippine Islands
Rhineland
Ardennes–Alsace
Central Europe

Korean War
UN defensive
UN offensive
CCF intervention
First UN counteroffensive
CCF spring offensive
UN summer–fall offensive
Second Korean winter
Korea, summer–fall 1952
Third Korean winter
Korea, summer 1953

DECORATIONS

Presidential Unit Citation (Army), Streamer embroidered **LUZON 1941–1942** (31st Infantry cited)

Presidential Unit Citation (Army), Streamer embroidered **BATAAN** (31st Infantry cited)

Presidential Unit Citation (Army), Streamer embroidered **DEFENSE OF THE PHILIPPINES** (31st Infantry cited)

Presidential Unit Citation (Navy), Streamer embroidered **CHOSIN RESERVOIR**

Presidential Unit Citation (Navy), Streamer embroidered **HWACHON RESERVOIR** (31st Infantry cited)

Navy Unit Commendation, Streamer embroidered **PANMUNJOM** (31st Infantry cited)

Philippine Presidential Unit Citation, Streamer embroidered **7 DECEMBER 1941 TO 10 MAY 1942** (31st Infantry cited)

Republic of Korea Presidential Unit Citation, Streamer embroidered **INCHON** (31st Infantry cited)

Republic of Korea Presidential Unit Citation, Streamer embroidered **KOREA** (31st Infantry cited)

4TH BATTALION, 31ST INFANTRY
(The Polar Bears)

LINEAGE

1916   Constituted 1 July as Company D, 31st Infantry, Regular Army; organized 1 August at Regan Barracks, Philippine Islands

Company lineage follows that of 31st Infantry from 1916 through 1946 reorganization in Korea

1957   Inactivated 1 July in Korea, relieved from assignment to 7th Infantry Division, and redesignated as Headquarters and Headquarters Company, 4th Battle Group, 31st Infantry

1965   Redesignated 10 September as Headquarters and Headquarters Company, 4th Battalion, 31st Infantry, assigned to the 196th Infantry Brigade, and activated at Fort Devens, MA

1969   Relieved 15 February from assignment to 196th Infantry Brigade, and assigned to 23d Infantry Division

CAMPAIGN PARTICIPATION

World War I
  Siberia 1918
  Siberia 1919

World War II
  Philippine Islands

Korean War
  UN defensive
  UN offensive
  CCF intervention
  First UN counteroffensive
  CCF spring offensive
  UN summer–fall offensive
  Second Korean winter
  Korea, summer–fall 1952
  Third Korean winter
  Korea, summer 1953

Vietnam
  Counteroffensive, Phase II
  Counteroffensive, Phase III
  Tet Counteroffensive
  Counteroffensive, Phase IV
  Counteroffensive, Phase V
  Counteroffensive, Phase VI
  Tet 69 Counteroffensive
  Summer–Fall 1969
  Winter–Spring 1970
  Sanctuary Counteroffensive
  Counteroffensive, Phase VII
  Consolidation I

DECORATIONS

Presidential Unit Citation (Army), Streamer embroidered **LUZON 1941–1942** (31st Infantry cited)

Presidential Unit Citation (Army), Streamer embroidered **BATAAN** (31st Infantry cited)

Presidential Unit Citation (Army), Streamer embroidered **DEFENSE OF THE PHILIPPINES** (31st Infantry cited)

Presidential Unit Citation (Navy), Streamer embroidered **CHOSIN RESERVOIR**

Presidential Unit Citation (Navy), Streamer embroidered **HWACHON RESERVOIR** (31st Infantry cited)

Valorous Unit Award, Streamer embroidered **QUE SON-HIEP DUC** (4th Battalion, 31st Infantry cited)

Navy Unit Commendation, Streamer embroidered **PAN-MUNJOM** (31st Infantry cited)

Philippine Presidential Unit Citation, Streamer embroidered **7 DECEMBER 1941 TO 10 MAY 1942** (31st Infantry cited)

Republic of Korea Presidential Unit Citation, Streamer embroidered **INCHON** (31st Infantry cited)

Republic of Korea Presidential Unit Citation, Streamer embroidered **KOREA** (31st Infantry cited)

5TH BATTALION, 31ST INFANTRY
(The Polar Bears)

LINEAGE

1916   Constituted 1 July as Company E, 31st Infantry, Regular Army; organized 1 August at Fort William McKinley, Philippine Islands

Company lineage follows that of 31st Infantry from 1916 through 1946 reorganization in Korea

1957   Inactivated 1 July in Korea, relieved from assignment to 7th Infantry Division, and redesignated as Headquarters and Headquarters Company, 5th Battle Group, 31st Infantry

1963   Battle Group activated 1 July at Fort Rucker, AL

1964   Reorganized and redesignated 25 May a 5th Battalion, 31st Infantry

1967   Assigned 23 June to 197th Infantry Brigade

CAMPAIGN PARTICIPATION

World War I
- Siberia 1918
- Siberia 1919

World War II
- Philippine Islands

Korean War
- UN defensive
- UN offensive
- CCF intervention
- First UN counteroffensive
- CCF spring offensive
- UN summer–fall offensive
- Second Korean winter
- Korea, summer–fall 1952
- Third Korean winter
- Korea, summer 1953

DECORATIONS

Presidential Unit Citation (Army), Streamer embroidered **LUZON 1941–1942** (31st Infantry cited)

Presidential Unit Citation (Army), Streamer embroidered **BATAAN** (31st Infantry cited)

Presidential Unit Citation (Army), Streamer embroidered **DEFENSE OF THE PHILIPPINES** (31st Infantry cited)

Presidential Unit Citation (Navy), Streamer embroidered **CHOSIN RESERVOIR**

Presidential Unit Citation (Navy), Streamer embroidered **HWACHON RESERVOIR** (31st Infantry cited)

Navy Unit Commendation, Streamer embroidered **PANMUNJOM** (31st Infantry cited)

Philippine Presidential Unit Citation, Streamer embroidered **7 DECEMBER 1941 TO 10 MAY 1942** (31st Infantry cited)

Republic of Korea Presidential Unit Citation, Streamer embroidered **INCHON** (31st Infantry cited)

Republic of Korea Presidential Unit Citation, Streamer embroidered **KOREA** (31st Infantry cited)

6TH BATTALION, 31ST INFANTRY
(The Polar Bears)

LINEAGE

1916   Constituted 1 July as Company F, 31st Infantry, Regular Army; organized 1 August at Camp McGrath, Philippine Islands

Company lineage follows that of 31st Infantry from 1916 through 1946 reorganization in Korea

1957   Inactivated 1 July in Korea, relieved from assignment to 7th Infantry Division, and redesignated as Headquarters and Headquarters Company, 6th Battle Group, 31st Infantry

1967   Redesignated 1 November as Headquarters and Headquarters Company, 6th Battalion, 31st Infantry; activated at Fort Lewis, WA

1969   Assigned 15 February to 9th Infantry Division

1970   Inactivated 13 October at Fort Lewis, WA

CAMPAIGN PARTICIPATION

World War I

Siberia 1918
Siberia 1919

World War II

Philippine Islands

Korean War

UN defensive
UN offensive
CCF intervention
First UN counteroffensive
CCF spring offensive
UN summer-fall
    offensive
Second Korean winter

Korea, summer-fall 1952
Third Korean winter
Korea, summer 1953

Vietnam

Counteroffensive,
    Phase IV
Counteroffensive,
    Phase V
Counteroffensive,
    Phase VI
Tet 69 Counteroffensive
Summer-Fall 1969
Winter-Spring 1970
Sanctuary
    Counteroffensive
Counteroffensive,
    Phase VII

DECORATIONS

Presidential Unit Citation (Army), Streamer embroidered **LUZON 1941-1942** (31st Infantry cited)

Presidential Unit Citation (Army), Streamer embroidered **BATAAN** (31st Infantry cited)

Presidential Unit Citation (Army), Streamer embroidered **DEFENSE OF THE PHILIPPINES** (31st Infantry cited)

Presidential Unit Citation (Navy), Streamer embroidered **CHOSIN RESERVOIR** (2d Battalion [less Company E], 31st Infantry and attached units cited)

Presidential Unit Citation (Navy), Streamer embroidered **HWACHON RESERVOIR** (31st Infantry cited)

Valorous Unit Award, Streamer embroidered **SAIGON** (6th Battalion, 31st Infantry cited)

Valorous Unit Award, Streamer embroidered **PARROT'S BEAK** (6th Battalion, 31st Infantry cited)

Navy Unit Commendation, Streamer embroidered **PANMUNJOM** (31st Infantry cited)

Philippine Presidential Unit Citation, Streamer embroidered **7 DECEMBER 1941 TO 10 MAY 1942** (31st Infantry cited)

Republic of Korea Presidential Unit Citation, Streamer embroidered **INCHON** (31st Infantry cited)

Republic of Korea Presidential Unit Citation, Streamer embroidered **KOREA** (31st Infantry cited)

Vietnamese Cross of Gallantry with Palm, Streamer embroidered **VIETNAM, APRIL-JUNE 1968** (6th Battalion, 31st Infantry cited)

Vietnamese Cross of Gallantry with Palm, Streamer embroidered **VIETNAM, JULY-NOVEMBER 1968** (6th Battalion, 31st Infantry cited)

Vietnamese Cross of Gallantry with Palm, Streamer embroidered **VIETNAM 1969** (6th Battalion, 31st Infantry cited)

Vietnamese Civil Action Honor Medal, First Class, Streamer embroidered **VIETNAM 1968-1969** (6th Battalion, 31st Infantry cited)

32D INFANTRY

COAT OF ARMS

Motto: None

Symbolism: This regiment was originally organized on the island of Oahu in Hawaii, with personnel from the 1st and 2d Infantry. These organizations are shown on the canton, the lion indicating that both regiments took part in the War of 1812. The central device is taken from the royal Hawaiian arms to symbolize the regiment's birthplace. The puela was an ancient Hawaiian banner with many uses, one of which was in front of the king's tent leaning against two crossed spears (called alia) to indicate both tabu and protection; a saltire cross replaced the spears on the Hawaiian arms.

The colors of the crest are the royal Hawaiian colors. The crest is an ancient Hawaiian war bonnet known as a mahiole.

DISTINCTIVE INSIGNIA

The distinctive insignia is the shield and crest of the coat of arms.

LINEAGE

1916   Constituted 1 July as 32d Infantry, Regular Army; organized 7 August at Schofield Barracks, Hawaii

1918   Assigned 31 July to the 16th Division

1919   Relieved 8 March from assignment to 16th Division

1921   Inactivated 1 November at the Presidio, San Francisco, CA

1940   Activated 1 July at Camp Ord, CA, and assigned to the 7th Division

1957   Relieved 1 July from assignment to 7th Infantry Division and reorganized as a parent regiment under CARS

CAMPAIGN PARTICIPATION

World War II

Aleutian Islands (with arrowhead)
Eastern Mandates
Leyte (with arrowhead)
Ryukyus (with arrowhead)

Korean War

UN defensive
UN offensive
CCF intervention
First UN counteroffensive
CCF spring offensive
UN summer–fall offensive
Second Korean winter
Korea, summer–fall 1952
Third Korean winter
Korea, summer 1953

DECORATIONS

Presidential Unit Citation (Army), Streamer embroidered **KUMHWA** (1st Battalion, 32d Infantry cited)

Presidential Unit Citation (Army), Streamer embroidered **CENTRAL KOREA** (3d Battalion, 32d Infantry and attached units cited)

Presidential Unit Citation (Navy), Streamer embroidered **INCHON** (32d Regimental Combat Team cited)

Presidential Unit Citation (Navy), Streamer embroidered **HWACHON RESERVOIR** (32d Infantry cited)

Navy Unit Commendation, Streamer embroidered **PANMUNJOM** (32d Infantry cited)

Philippine Presidential Unit Citation, Streamer embroidered **17 OCTOBER 1944 TO 4 JULY 1945** (32d Infantry cited)

Republic of Korea Presidential Unit Citation, Streamer embroidered **INCHON** (32d Infantry cited)

Republic of Korea Presidential Unit Citation, Streamer embroidered **KOREA** (32d Infantry cited)

1st Battalion, 32d Infantry

LINEAGE

1916   Constituted 1 July as Company A, 32d Infantry, Regular Army; organized 7 August at Schofield Barracks, Hawaii

1918   Assigned 31 July to the 16th Division

1919   Relieved 8 March from assignment to 16th Division

1921   Inactivated 13 September at Vancouver Barracks, WA

1940   Activated 1 July at Camp Ord, CA, and assigned to the 7th Division

1957   Reorganized and redesignated 1 July as Headquarters and Headquarters Company, 1st Battle Group, 32d Infantry; remained assigned to the 7th Infantry Division

1963   Reorganized and redesignated 1 July as 1st Battalion, 32d Infantry

CAMPAIGN PARTICIPATION

World War II

Aleutian Islands (with arrowhead)
Eastern Mandates
Leyte (with arrowhead)
Ryukyus (with arrowhead)

Korean War

UN defensive
UN offensive
CCF intervention
First UN counteroffensive
CCF spring offensive

UN summer–fall
offebnsive
Second Korean winter

Korea, summer–fall 1952
Third Korean winter
Korea, summer 1953

DECORATIONS

Presidential Unit Citation (Army), Streamer embroidered **KUMHWA** (1st Battalion, 32d Infantry cited)

Presidential Unit Citation (Army), Streamer embroidered **CENTRAL KOREA**

Presidential Unit Citation (Navy), Streamer embroidered **INCHON** (32d Regimental Combat Team cited)

Presidential Unit Citation (Navy), Streamer embroidered **HWACHON RESERVOIR** (32d Infantry cited)

Navy Unit Commendation, Streamer embroidered **PAN-MUNJOM** (32d Infantry cited)

Philippine Presidential Unit Citation, Streamer embroidered **17 OCTOBER 1944 TO 4 JULY 1945** (32d Infantry cited)

Republic of Korea Presidential Unit Citation, Streamer embroidered **INCHON** (32d Infantry cited)

Republic of Korea Presidential Unit Citation, Streamer embroidered **KOREA** (32d Infantry cited)

2D BATTALION, 32D INFANTRY

LINEAGE

1916   Constituted 1 July as Company B, 32d Infantry, Regular Army; organized 7 August at Schofield Barracks, Hawaii

1918   Assigned 31 July to the 16th Division

1919   Relieved 8 March from assignment to 16th Division

1921   Inactivated 2 September at Fort Lawton, WA

1940   Activated 1 July at Camp Ord, CA, and assigned to the 7th Division

1957   Inactivated 1 July in Korea, relieved from assignment to 7th Infantry Division, and redesignated as Headquarters and Headquarters Company, 2d Battle Group, 32d Infantry

1963   Redesignated 7 June as Headquarters and Headquarters Company, 2d Battalion, 32d Infantry; activated 1 July in Korea and assigned to the 7th Infantry Division

CAMPAIGN PARTICIPATION

World War II

Aleutian Islands (with arrowhead)
Eastern Mandates
Leyte (with arrowhead)
Ryukyus (with arrowhead)

Korean War

UN defensive
UN offensive
CCF intervention
First UN counteroffensive
CCF spring offensive

UN summer–fall
offensive
Second Korean winter

Korea, summer–fall 1952
Third Korean winter
Korea, summer 1953

DECORATIONS

Presidential Unit Citation (Army), Streamer embroidered **KUMHWA** (1st Battalion, 32d Infantry cited)

Presidential Unit Citation (Army), Streamer embroidered **CENTRAL KOREA**

Presidential Unit Citation (Navy), Streamer embroidered **INCHON** (32d Regimental Combat Team cited)

Presidential Unit Citation (Navy), Streamer embroidered **HWACHON RESERVOIR** (32d Infantry cited)

Navy Unit Commendation, Streamer embroidered **PAN-MUNJOM** (32d Infantry cited)

Philippine Presidential Unit Citation, Streamer embroidered **17 OCTOBER 1944 TO 4 JULY 1945** (32d Infantry cited)

Republic of Korea Presidential Unit Citation, Streamer embroidered **INCHON** (32d Infantry cited)

Republic of Korea Presidential Unit Citation, Streamer embroidered **KOREA** (32d Infantry cited)

3D BATTALION, 32D INFANTRY

LINEAGE

1916 — Constituted 1 July as Company C, 32d Infantry, Regular Army; organized 7 August at Schofield Barracks, Hawaii

1918 — Assigned 31 July to the 16th Division

1919 — Relieved 8 March from assignment to 16th Division

1921 — Inactivated 2 September at Fort Lawton, WA

1940 — Activated 1 July at Camp Ord, CA, and assigned to the 7th Division

1957 — Inactivated 1 July in Korea, relieved from assignment to 7th Infantry; redesignated as Headquarters and Headquarters Company, 3d Battle Group, 32d Infantry

1958 — Redesignated 8 May as Company C, 32d Infantry, and activated at Fort Bragg, NC

1963 — Inactivated 7 February at Fort Bragg, NC, reorganized and redesignated 7 June as Headquarters and Headquarters Company, 3d Battalion, 32d Infantry; Battalion activated 1 July in Korea and assigned to the 7th Infantry Division

CAMPAIGN PARTICIPATION

World War II

Aleutian Islands (with arrowhead)
Eastern Mandates
Leyte (with arrowhead)
Ryukyus (with arrowhead)

Korean War

UN defensive
UN offensive
CCF intervention
First UN counteroffensive
CCF spring offensive
UN summer–fall offensive
Second Korean winter
Korea, summer–fall 1952
Third Korean winter
Korea, summer 1953

DECORATIONS

Presidential Unit Citation (Army), Streamer embroidered **KUMHWA** (1st Battalion, 32d Infantry cited)

Presidential Unit Citation (Army), Streamer embroidered **CENTRAL KOREA**

Presidential Unit Citation (Navy), Streamer embroidered **INCHON** (32d Regimental Combat Team cited)

Presidential Unit Citation (Navy), Streamer embroidered **HWACHON RESERVOIR** (32d Infantry cited)

Navy Unit Commendation, Streamer embroidered **PANMUNJOM** (32d Infantry cited)

Philippine Presidential Unit Citation, Streamer embroidered **17 OCTOBER 1944 TO 4 JULY 1945** (32d Infantry cited)

Republic of Korea Presidential Unit Citation, Streamer embroidered **INCHON** (32d Infantry cited)

Republic of Korea Presidential Unit Citation, Streamer embroidered **KOREA** (32d Infantry cited)

4TH BATTLE GROUP, 32D INFANTRY

LINEAGE

1916 — Constituted 1 July as Company D, 32d Infantry, Regular Army; organized 7 August at Schofield Barracks, Hawaii

1918 — Assigned 31 July to the 16th Division

1919 — Relieved 8 March from assignment to 16th Division

1921 — Inactivated 3 September at Fort Lawton, WA

1940 — Activated 1 July at Camp Ord, CA, and assigned to the 7th Division

1957	Inactivated in July in Korea, relieved from assignment to 7th Infantry Division; redesignated as Headquarters and Headquarters Company, 4th Battle Group, 32d Infantry
1959	Withdrawn 10 April from Regular Army, allotted to Army Reserve, assigned to 81st Infantry Division; Battle Group activated 1 May at Knoxville, TN
1963	Inactivated 1 April and relieved from assignment to 81st Infantry Division

CAMPAIGN PARTICIPATION

World War II

Aleutian Islands (with arrowhead)
Eastern Mandates
Leyte (with arrowhead)
Ryukyus (with arrowhead)

Korean War

UN defensive
UN offensive
CCF intervention
First UN counteroffensive
CCF spring offensive
UN summer–fall offensive
Second Korean winter
Korea, summer–fall 1952
Third Korean winter
Korea, summer 1953

DECORATIONS

Presidential Unit Citation (Army), Streamer embroidered **KUMHWA** (1st Battalion, 32d Infantry cited)

Presidential Unit Citation (Army), Streamer embroidered **CENTRAL KOREA**

Presidential Unit Citation (Navy), Streamer embroidered **INCHON** (32d Regimental Combat Team cited)

Presidential Unit Citation (Navy), Streamer embroidered **HWACHON RESERVOIR** (32d Infantry cited)

Navy Unit Commendation, Streamer embroidered **PAN-MUNJOM** (32d Infantry cited)

Philippine Presidential Unit Citation, Streamer embroidered **17 OCTOBER 1944 TO 4 JULY 1945** (32d Infantry cited)

Republic of Korea Presidential Unit Citation, Streamer embroidered **INCHON** (32d Infantry cited)

Republic of Korea Presidential Unit Citation, Streamer embroidered **KOREA** (32d Infantry cited)

34TH INFANTRY

COAT OF ARMS

Motto: *Toujours en Avant* (Always Forward).

Symbolism: The regiment was originally organized at El Paso, Texas, by transfer of personnel from the 7th, 20th, and 23d Infantry. These units are symbolized on the canton; the masoned wall is from the arms of the 7th Infantry and the white Maltese cross is from the arms of the 20th and 23d Infantry. The blue background with gold cross crosslets sharpened at the foot reflects World War I service. The 34th Infantry served in that part of the province of Lorraine which was anciently the Barony of Commercy. The arms of those Barons were blue, scattered with gold cross crosslets sharpened at the foot.

The crest commemorates Texas, the birthplace of the regiment.

DISTINCTIVE INSIGNIA

The distinctive insignia is the shield of the coat of arms.

LINEAGE

1916	Constituted 1 July as 34th Infantry, Regular Army; organized 15 July at El Paso, TX
1917	Assigned 6 December to 7th Division
1923	Relieved 24 March from assignment to 7th Division and assigned to the 8th Division
1927	Relieved 15 August from assignment to 8th Division and assigned to the 4th Division
1933	Relieved 1 October from assignment to 4th Division and assigned to 8th Division
1940	Inactivated 5 June at Fort Benning, GA, and activated 1 July at Camp Jackson, SC
1943	Relieved 12 June from assignment to 8th Infantry Division and assigned to the 24th Infantry Division
1958	Relieved 5 June from assignment to 24th Infantry Division and reorganized as a parent regiment under CARS

CAMPAIGN PARTICIPATION

World War I

Lorraine 1918

World War II

New Guinea
Leyte (with arrowhead)

Luzon
Southern Philippines

Korean War

UN defensive
UN summer-fall offensive
Korea, summer 1953

DECORATIONS

Presidential Unit Citation (Army), Streamer embroidered **KILAY RIDGE** (1st Battalion, 34th Infantry cited)

Presidential Unit Citation (Army), Streamer embroidered **CORREGIDOR** (Company A and 3d Battalion, 34th Infantry cited)

Presidential Unit Citation (Army), Streamer embroidered **DEFENSE OF KOREA** (24th Infantry Division cited)

Philippine Presidential Unit Citation, Streamer embroidered **17 OCTOBER 1944 TO 4 JULY 1945** (34th Infantry cited)

Republic of Korea Presidential Unit Citation, Streamer embroidered **PYONGTAEK** (34th Infantry cited)

Republic of Korea Presidential Unit Citation, Streamer embroidered **KOREA** (34th Infantry cited)

1ST BATTALION, 34TH INFANTRY

LINEAGE

1916	Constituted 1 July as Company A, 34th Infantry, Regular Army; organized 15 July at El Paso, TX
	Company lineage follows that of 34th Infantry from 1916 through 1943 assignment to 24th Infantry Division
1958	Redesignated 5 June as Headquarters and Headquarters Company, 1st Battle Group, 34th Infantry; remained assigned to 24th Infantry Division
1963	Reorganized and redesignated 1 February as 1st Battalion, 34th Infantry
1970	Inactivated 15 April at Fort Riley, KS

CAMPAIGN PARTICIPATION

World War I

Lorraine 1918

World War II

New Guinea
Leyte (with arrowhead)

Luzon
Southern Philippines

Korean War

UN defensive
UN summer-fall offensive
Korea, summer 1953

DECORATIONS

Presidential Unit Citation (Army), Streamer embroidered **KILAY RIDGE** (1st Battalion, 34th Infantry cited)

Presidential Unit Citation (Army), Streamer embroidered **CORREGIDOR** (Company A, 34th Infantry cited)

Presidential Unit Citation (Army), Streamer embroidered **DEFENSE OF KOREA** (24th Infantry Division cited)

Philippine Presidential Unit Citation, Streamer embroidered **17 OCTOBER 1944 TO 4 JULY 1945** (34th Infantry cited)

Republic of Korea Presidential Unit Citation, Streamer embroidered **PYONGTAEK** (34th Infantry cited)

Republic of Korea Presidential Unit Citation, Streamer embroidered **KOREA** (34th Infantry cited)

2D BATTALION, 34TH INFANTRY

LINEAGE

1916   Constituted 1 July as Company B, 34th Infantry, Regular Army; organized 15 July at El Paso, TX

Company lineage follows that of 34th Infantry from 1916 through 1943 assignment to 24th Infantry Division

1957   Reorganized and redesignated 1 July as Headquarters and Headquarters Company, 2d Battle Group, 34th Infantry; relieved from assignment to 24th Infantry Division and assigned to the 7th Infantry Division

1963   Redesignated 1 February as 2d Battalion, 34th Infantry; relieved from assignment to 7th Infantry Division and assigned to the 24th Infantry Division

1970   Inactivated 15 April at Fort Riley, KS

CAMPAIGN PARTICIPATION

World War I

Lorraine 1918

World War II

New Guinea

Leyte (with arrowhead)
Luzon
Southern Philippines

Korean War

UN defensive
UN summer-fall offensive
Korea, summer 1953

DECORATIONS

Presidential Unit Citation (Army), Streamer embroidered **KILAY RIDGE** (1st Battalion, 34th Infantry cited)

Presidential Unit Citation (Army), Streamer embroidered **CORREGIDOR**

Presidential Unit Citation (Army), Streamer embroidered **DEFENSE OF KOREA** (24th Infantry Division cited)

Philippine Presidential Unit Citation, Streamer embroidered **17 OCTOBER 1944 TO 4 JULY 1945** (34th Infantry cited)

Republic of Korea Presidential Unit Citation, Streamer embroidered **PYONGTAEK** (34th Infantry cited)

Republic of Korea Presidential Unit Citation, Streamer embroidered **KOREA** (34th Infantry cited)

3D BATTALION, 34TH INFANTRY

LINEAGE

1916   Constituted 1 July as Company C, 34th Infantry, Regular Army; organized 15 July at El Paso, TX

Company lineage follows that of 34th Infantry from 1916 through 1943 assignment to 24th Infantry Division

1958   Inactivated 5 June, relieved from assignment to 24th Infantry Division, and redesignated as Headquarters and Headquarters Company, 3d Battle Group, 34th Infantry

1959   Withdrawn 17 March from Regular Army, allotted to Army Reserve, assigned to 79th Infantry Division; Battle Group activated 23 March at Uniontown, PA

1963   Inactivated 28 March and relieved from assignment to 79th Infantry Division

CAMPAIGN PARTICIPATION

World War I

Lorraine 1918

World War II

New Guinea
Leyte (with arrowhead)
Luzon
Southern Philippines

Korean War

UN defensive
UN summer fall offensive
Korea, summer 1953

DECORATIONS

Presidential Unit Citation (Army), Streamer embroidered **KILAY RIDGE** (1st Battalion, 34th Infantry cited)

Presidential Unit Citation (Army), Streamer embroidered **CORREGIDOR**

Presidential Unit Citation (Army), Streamer embroidered **DEFENSE OF KOREA** (24th Infantry Division cited)

Philippine Presidential Unit Citation, Streamer embroidered **17 OCTOBER 1944 TO 4 JULY 1945** (34th Infantry cited)

Republic of Korea Presidential Unit Citation, Streamer embroidered **PYONGTAEK** (34th Infantry cited)

Republic of Korea Presidential Unit Citation, Streamer embroidered **KOREA** (34th Infantry cited)

35TH INFANTRY
(The Cacti)

COAT OF ARMS

Motto: Take Arms

Symbolism: The regiment was originally organized in Arizona with personnel from the 11th, 18th, and 22d Infantry. These organizations are shown on the canton. During the Civil War the predecessor of the 11th Infantry was in the 2d Division, V Corps, the badge of which was a white Maltese cross; the 18th Infantry was in the 1st Division, XIV Corps, with a red acorn as the badge. The 22d Infantry is represented by the embattled partition line of the canton. The cactus represents the original service of the 35th Infantry on the Mexican border.

The crest commemorates the regiment's baptism of fire at Nogales, the Spanish for walnut trees.

DISTINCTIVE INSIGNIA

The distinctive insignia is the shield of the coat of arms.

LINEAGE

1916	Constituted 1 July as 35th Infantry, Regular Army; organized 8–19 July at Douglas, AZ
1918	Assigned 7 August to 18th Division
1919	Relieved 14 February from assignment to 18th Division
1922	Assigned 17 October to Hawaiian Division
1941	Relieved 26 August from assignment to Hawaiian Division and assigned to 25th Infantry Division
1957	Relieved 1 February from assignment to 25th Infantry Division and reorganized as a parent regiment under CARS

CAMPAIGN PARTICIPATION

World War II

Central Pacific
Guadalcanal
Northern Solomons (with arrowhead)
Luzon

Korean War

UN defensive
UN offensive
CCF intervention
First UN counteroffensive
CCF spring offensive
UN summer-fall offensive
Second Korean winter
Korea, summer-fall 1952
Third Korean winter
Korea, summer 1953

Vietnam

Counteroffensive
Counteroffensive, Phase II
Counteroffensive, Phase III
Tet Counteroffensive
Counteroffensive, Phase IV
Counteroffensive, Phase V
Counteroffensive, Phase VI
Tet 69 Counteroffensive
Summer-Fall 1969
Winter-Spring 1970
Sanctuary Counteroffensive
Counteroffensive, Phase VII

DECORATIONS

Presidential Unit Citation (Army), Streamer embroidered **GUADALCANAL** (35th Infantry cited)

Presidential Unit Citation (Army), Streamer embroidered **NAM RIVER** (35th Infantry [less 3d Battalion and Heavy Tank Company] cited)

Meritorious Unit Commendation, Streamer embroidered **VIETNAM 1967–1968** (2d Battalion, 35th Infantry cited)

Philippine Presidential Unit Citation, Streamer embroidered **17 OCTOBER 1944 TO 4 JULY 1945** (25th Infantry Division cited)

Republic of Korea Presidential Unit Citation, Streamer embroidered **MASAN-CHINJU** (35th Infantry cited)

Republic of Korea Presidential Unit Citation, Streamer embroidered **MUNSAN-NI** (35th Infantry cited)

Republic of Korea Presidential Unit Citation, Streamer embroidered **KOREA** (35th Infantry cited)

1ST BATTALION, 35TH INFANTRY
(The Cacti)

LINEAGE

1916	Constituted 1 July as Company A, 35th Infantry, Regular Army; organized 13 July at Douglas, AZ
	Company lineage follows that of 35th Infantry from 1916 through assignment to 25th Infantry Division
1957	Reorganized and redesignated 1 February as Headquarters and Headquarters Company, 1st Battle Group, 35th Infantry; assigned to 25th Infantry Division
1963	Reorganized and redesignated 12 August as 1st Battalion, 35th Infantry
1967	Relieved 1 August from assignment to 25th Infantry Division and assigned to 4th Infantry Division
1970	Inactivated 10 April at Fort Lewis, WA

CAMPAIGN PARTICIPATION

World War II

Central Pacific
Guadalcanal
Northern Solomons (with arrowhead)
Luzon

Korean War

UN defensive
UN offensive
CCF intervention
First UN counteroffensive
CCF spring offensive
UN summer-fall offensive
Second Korean winter
Korea, summer-fall 1952
Third Korean winter
Korea, summer 1953

Vietnam

Counteroffensive
Counteroffensive, Phase II
Counteroffensive, Phase III
Tet Counteroffensive
Counteroffensive, Phase IV
Counteroffensive, Phase V
Counteroffensive, Phase VI
Tet 69 Counteroffensive
Summer-Fall 1969
Winter-Spring 1970

DECORATIONS

Presidential Unit Citation (Army), Streamer embroidered **GUADALCANAL** (35th Infantry cited)

Presidential Unit Citation (Army), Streamer embroidered **NAM RIVER** (35th Infantry [less 3d Battalion and Heavy Tank Company] cited)

Philippine Presidential Unit Citation, Streamer embroidered **17 OCTOBER 1944 TO 4 JULY 1945** (25th Infantry Division cited)

Republic of Korea Presidential Unit Citation, Streamer embroidered **MASAN-CHINJU** (35th Infantry cited)

Republic of Korea Presidential Unit Citation, Streamer embroidered **MUNSAN-NI** (35th Infantry cited)

Republic of Korea Presidential Unit Citation, Streamer embroidered **KOREA** (35th Infantry cited)

Vietnamese Cross of Gallantry with Palm, Streamer embroidered **VIETNAM 1966–1967** (1st Battalion, 35th Infantry cited)

Vietnamese Cross of Gallantry with Palm, Streamer embroidered **VIETNAM 1967–1969** (1st Battalion, 35th Infantry cited)

Vietnamese Civil Action Honor Medal, First Class, Streamer embroidered **VIETNAM 1967–1969** (1st Battalion, 35th Infantry cited)

Company A additionally entitled to: Presidential Unit Citation (Army), Streamer embroidered **PLEIKU PROVINCE** (Company A, 1st Battalion, 35th Infantry cited); Valorous Unit Award, Streamer embroidered **DARLAC PROVINCE** (Company A, 1st Battalion, 35th Infantry cited)

2D BATTALION, 35TH INFANTRY
(The Cacti)

LINEAGE

1916   Constituted 1 July as Company B, 35th Infantry, Regular Army; organized 13 July at Douglas, AZ

Company lineage follows that of 35th Infantry from 1916 through assignment to 25th Infantry Division

1957   Inactivated 1 February in Hawaii, relieved from assignment to 25th Infantry Division; redesignated Headquarters and Headquarters Company, 2d Battle Group, 35th Infantry

1962   Activated 19 February in Hawaii and assigned to 25th Infantry Division

1963   Reorganized and redesignated 12 August as 2d Battalion, 35th Infantry

1967   Relieved 1 August from assignment to 25th Infantry Division and assigned to 4th Infantry Division

1970   Relieved 15 December from assignment to 4th Infantry and assigned to 25th Infantry Division

CAMPAIGN PARTICIPATION

World War II

Central Pacific
Guadalcanal
Northern Solomons (with arrowhead)
Luzon

Korean War

UN defensive
UN offensive
CCF intervention
First UN counteroffensive
CCF spring offensive

UN summer-fall offensive
Second Korean winter
Korea, summer-fall 1952
Third Korean winter
Korea, summer 1953

Vietnam

Counteroffensive
Counteroffensive,
    Phase II
Counteroffensive,
    Phase III
Tet Counteroffensive

Counteroffensive,
    Phase IV
Counteroffensive,
    Phase V
Counteroffensive,
    Phase VI
Tet 69 Counteroffensive
Summer-Fall 1969
Winter-Spring 1970
Sanctuary
    Counteroffensive
Counteroffensive,
    Phase VII

DECORATIONS

Presidential Unit Citation (Army), Streamer embroidered **GUADALCANAL** (35th Infantry cited)

Presidential Unit Citation (Army), Streamer embroidered **NAM RIVER** (35th Infantry [less 3d Battalion and Heavy Tank Company] cited)

Meritorious Unit Commendation, Streamer embroidered **VIETNAM 1967–1968** (2d Battalion, 35th Infantry cited)

Philippine Presidential Unit Citation, Streamer embroidered **17 OCTOBER 1944 TO 4 JULY 1945** (25th Infantry Division cited)

Republic of Korea Presidential Unit Citation, Streamer embroidered **MASAN-CHINJU** (35th Infantry cited)

Republic of Korea Presidential Unit Citation, Streamer embroidered **MUNSAN-NI** (35th Infantry cited)

Republic of Korea Presidential Unit Citation, Streamer embroidered **KOREA** (35th Infantry cited)

Vietnamese Cross of Gallantry with Palm, Streamer embroidered **VIETNAM 1966–1967** (2d Battalion, 35th Infantry cited)

Vietnamese Cross of Gallantry with Palm, Streamer embroidered **VIETNAM 1967–1969** (2d Battalion, 35th Infantry cited)

Vietnamese Civil Action Honor Medal, First Class, Streamer embroidered **VIETNAM 1967–1969** (2d Battalion, 35th Infantry cited)

Company A additionally entitled to: Valorous Unit Award, Streamer embroidered **PLEIKU PROVINCE** (Company A, 2d Battalion, 35th Infantry cited)

Company B additionally entitled to: Presidential Unit Citation (Army), Streamer embroidered **PLEIKU PROVINCE** (Company B, 2d Battalion, 35th Infantry cited)

3D BATTALION, 35TH INFANTRY
(The Cacti)

LINEAGE

1916   Constituted 1 July as Company C, 35th Infantry, Regular Army; organized 13 July at Douglas, AZ

Company lineage follows that of 35th Infantry from 1916 through assignment to 25th Infantry Division

1921   Another Company constituted 24 June as Headquarters and Headquarters Company, 2d Battalion, 376th Infantry, Organized Reserves, an element of the 94th Division; organized in November at Winchester, MA

376th Infantry lineage differs from that of 35th Infantry from its constitution to 1959 consolidation as follows:

1942   *Ordered into active military service 15 September and reorganized at Fort Custer, MI*

1946   *Inactivated 1 February at Camp Kilmer, NJ*

1947   *Activated 13 February in Organized Reserves at Springfield, MA*

1957   Company C, 35th Infantry inactivated 1 February in Hawaii, relieved from assignment to 25th Infantry Division, and redesignated as Headquarters and Headquarters Company, 3d Battle Group, 35th Infantry

1959   Withdrawn 6 April from Regular Army, allotted to Army Reserve, and assigned to 94th Infantry Division; Battle Group activated 1 May at Springfield, MA, and consolidated 1 May with Headquarters and Headquarters Company, 2d Battalion, 376th Infantry to form Headquarters and Headquarters Company, 3d Battle Group, 35th Infantry

1962　Reorganized and redesignated 5 November as 3d Battalion, 35th Infantry

1963　Relieved 7 January from assignment to 94th Infantry Division, and assigned to 187th Infantry Brigade

CAMPAIGN PARTICIPATION

World War II
Central Pacific
Guadalcanal
Northern Solomons (with arrowhead)
Luzon
Northern France
Rhineland
Ardennes-Alsace
Central Europe

Korean War
UN defensive
UN offensive
CCF intervention
First UN counteroffensive
CCF spring offensive
UN summer-fall offensive
Second Korean winter
Korea, summer-fall 1952
Third Korean winter
Korea, summer 1953

DECORATIONS

Presidential Unit Citation (Army), Streamer embroidered **GUADALCANAL** (35th Infantry cited)

Presidential Unit Citation (Army), Streamer embroidered **NAM RIVER** (35th Infantry [less 3d Battalion and Heavy Tank Company] cited)

Philippine Presidential Unit Citation, Streamer embroidered **17 OCTOBER 1944 TO 4 JULY 1945** (25th Infantry Division cited)

Republic of Korea Presidential Unit Citation, Streamer embroidered **MASAN-CHINJU** (35th Infantry cited)

Republic of Korea Presidential Unit Citation, Streamer embroidered **MUNSAN-NI** (35th Infantry cited)

Republic of Korea Presidential Unit Citation, Streamer embroidered **KOREA** (35th Infantry cited)

36TH INFANTRY

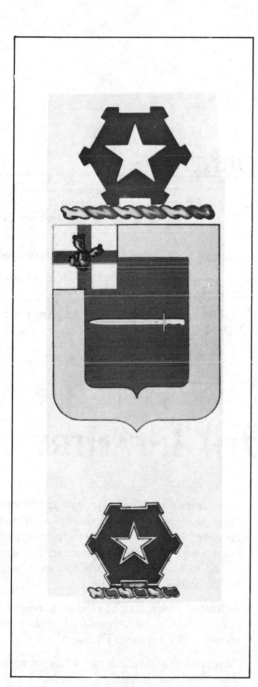

COAT OF ARMS

Motto: Deeds Not Words

Symbolism: The field of the shield is blue, the infantry color. The sword bayonet and bordure are taken from the unofficial insignia adopted by the 12th Division to which the 36th Infantry was assigned in 1918–1919. The regiment was originally organized at Brownsville, Texas, with personnel from the 4th, 26th, and 28th Infantry. These units are symbolized on the canton. The 4th and 28th Infantry both took part in the Vera Cruz expedition of 1914, the name suggesting the cross in blue for infantry. The cactus represents the Mexican border service of all three regiments.

The crest symbolizes the birthplace of the 36th Infantry. The origin of Brownsville was the fort built by General Zachary Taylor in 1846, known as Fort Texas. During the Mexican War the 4th Infantry participated in the battles of Palo Alto and Resaca de la Palma, which were fought for the defense of Fort Texas. This is shown by the six-bastioned fort in green, an allusion to the Mexican color, charged with the silver lone star of Texas.

DISTINCTIVE INSIGNIA

The distinctive insignia is the crest of the coat of arms.

LINEAGE

1916   Constituted 1 July as 36th Infantry, Regular Army; organized 27 July at Brownsville, TX

1918   Assigned 5 July to 12th Division

1919   Relieved 31 January from assignment to 12th Division

1921   Inactivated 12 October at Fort Jay, NY

1923   Assigned 24 March to 9th Division

1940   Relieved 1 August from assignment to 9th Division

1941   Activated 15 April at Camp Beauregard, LA, as 36th Infantry (Armored), an element of 3d Armored Division

1942   Redesignated 1 Janaury as 36th Armored Infantry

1945   Inactivated 10 November in Germany

1947   Broken up 7 July and redesignated as elements of the 3d Armored Division as follows: 1st Battalion formed 36th Armored Infantry Battalion; 2d Battalion formed 37th Armored Infantry Battalion; 3d Battalion formed 13th Armored Infantry Battalion; and Battalions activated 15 July at Fort Knox, KY

1957   The 36th, 37th, and 13th Armored Infantry Battalions relieved 1 October from assignment to 3d Armored Divisions, consolidated to form 36th Infantry, a parent regiment under CARS

Concurrently former Headquarters, Reserve Command, 3d Armored Division expanded and redesignated as Headquarters, 36th Infantry, and Headquarters and Headquarters Company, Combat Command C, 3d Armored Division, which follows a separate lineage

CAMPAIGN PARTICIPATION

World War II
   Normandy
   Northern France
   Rhineland
   Ardennes-Alsace
   Central Europe

DECORATIONS

Presidential Unit Citation (Army), Streamer embroidered **SIEGFRIED LINE** (1st Battalion, 36th Armored Infantry cited)

Belgian Fourragere 1940 (36th Armored Infantry cited)

Cited in the Order of the Day of the Belgian Army for action in **BELGIUM** (36th Armored Infantry cited)

Cited in the Order of the Day of the Belgian Army for action in the **ARDENNES** (36th Armored Infantry cited)

1ST BATTALION, 36TH INFANTRY

LINEAGE

1916   Constituted 1 July as Company A, 36th Infantry, Regular Army; organized 27 July at Brownsville, TX

Company lineage follows that of 36th Infantry from 1916 through 1945 inactivation in Germany

1947   Redesignated 7 July as Company A, 36th Armored Infantry Battalion, an element of the 3d Armored Division; activated 15 July at Fort Knox, KY

1957   Reorganized and redesignated 15 February as Headquarters and Headquarters Company, 1st Armored Rifle Battalion, 36th Infantry; relieved from assignment to 3d Armored Division, assigned to 1st Armored Division and inactivated 23 December at Fort Polk, LA

1962   Activated 3 February in Germany, relieved from assignment to 1st Armored Division and assigned to 3d Armored Division

1963   Reorganized and redesignated 1 September as 1st Battalion, 36th Infantry

CAMPAIGN PARTICIPATION

World War II

Normandy
Northern France
Rhineland
Ardennes-Alsace
Central Europe

DECORATIONS

Presidential Unit Citation (Army), Streamer embroidered **SIEGFRIED LINE** (1st Battalion, 36th Armored Infantry cited)

Presidential Unit Citation (Army), Streamer embroidered **ECHTZ** (Company A, 36th Armored Infantry cited)

Belgian Fourragere 1940 (36th Armored Infantry cited)

Cited in the Order of the Day of the Belgian Army for action in **BELGIUM** (36th Armored Infantry cited)

Cited in the Order of the Day of the Belgian Army for action in the **ARDENNES** (36th Armored Infantry cited)

2D BATTALION, 36TH INFANTRY

LINEAGE

1916   Constituted 1 July as Company B, 36th Infantry, Regular Army; organized 27 July at Brownsville, TX

Company lineage follows that of 36th Infantry from 1916 through 1945 inactivation in Germany

1947   Redesignated 7 July as Company B, 36th Armored Infantry Battalion, an element of the 3d Armored Division; activated 15 July at Fort Knox, KY

1957   Reorganized and redesignated 1 October as Headquarters and Headquarters Company, 2d Armored Rifle Battalion, 36th Infantry; assigned to the 3d Armored Division

1963   Reorganized and redesignated 1 September as 2d Battalion, 36th Infantry

CAMPAIGN PARTICIPATION

World War II

Normandy
Northern France
Rhineland
Ardennes-Alsace
Central Europe

DECORATIONS

Presidential Unit Citation (Army), Streamer embroidered **SIEGFRIED LINE** (1st Battalion, 36th Armored Infantry cited)

Belgian Fourragere 1940 (36th Armored Infantry cited)

Cited in the Order of the Day of the Belgian Army for action in **BELGIUM** (36th Armored Infantry cited)

Cited in the Order of the Day of the Belgian Army for action in the **ARDENNES** (36th Armored Infantry cited)

3D BATTALION, 36TH INFANTRY

LINEAGE

1916   Constituted 1 July as Company C, 36th Infantry, Regular Army; organized 27 July at Brownsville, TX

Company lineage follows that of 36th Infantry from 1916 through 1945 inactivation in Germany

1947   Redesignated 7 July as Company C, 36th Armored Infantry Battalion, an element of the 3d Armored Division; activated 15 July at Fort Knox, KY

1957	Inactivated 1 October in Germany, relieved from assignment to 3d Armored Division, and redesignated as Headquarters and Headquarters Company, 3d Battle Group, 36th Infantry
1962	Redesignated 3 February as Headquarters and Headquarters Company, 3d Armored Rifle Battalion, 36th Infantry; assigned to 3d Armored Division and activated in Germany
1963	Reorganized and redesignated 1 September as 3d Battalion, 36th Infantry

CAMPAIGN PARTICIPATION

World War II

Normandy
Northern France

Rhineland
Ardennes-Alsace
Central Europe

DECORATIONS

Presidential Unit Citation (Army), Streamer embroidered **SIEGFRIED LINE** (1st Battalion, 36th Armored Infantry cited)

Presidential Unit Citation (Army), Streamer embroidered **OBERGEICH-HOVEN** (Company C, 36th Armored Infantry cited)

Belgian Fourragere 1940 (36th Armored Infantry cited)

Cited in the Order of the Day of the Belgian Army for action in **BELGIUM** (36th Armored Infantry cited)

Cited in the Order of the Day of the Belgian Army for action in the **ARDENNES** (36th Armored Infantry cited)

38TH INFANTRY
(Rock of the Marne)

COAT OF ARMS

Motto: The Rock of the Marne

Symbolism: This regiment served in World War I as an element of the 3d division. Its most remarkable feat was near Chateau Thierry on the Marne on 15 July 1918, where it broke the point of the German attack. This achievement is shown by the broken chevron, the rock, and the motto. The divisional insignia is suggested by the base of the shield.

DISTINCTIVE INSIGNIA

The distinctive insignia is the shield, crest, and motto of the coat of arms.

LINEAGE

1917	Constituted 15 May as 38th Infantry, Regular Army; organized 1 June at Syracuse, NY, and assigned 1 October to 3d Division
1939	Relieved 16 October from assignment to 3d Division and assigned to 2d Division
1957	Relieved 8 November from assignment to 2d Infantry Division and reorganized as a parent regiment under CARS

CAMPAIGN PARTICIPATION

World War I

Aisne
Champagne–Marne
Aisne–Marne
St. Mihiel
Meuse–Argonne
Champagne 1918

World War II

Normandy
Northern France
Rhineland
Ardennes–Alsace
Central Europe

Korean War

UN defensive
UN offensive
CCF intervention
First UN counteroffensive
CCF spring offensive
UN summer–fall offensive
Second Korean winter
Korea, summer–fall 1952
Third Korean winter
Korea, summer 1953

DECORATIONS

Presidential Unit Citation (Army), Streamer embroidered **KRINKELT** (1st, 2d, and 3d Battalions, 38th Infantry cited)

Presidential Unit Citation (Army), Streamer embroidered **HILL 154, BREST** (3d Battalion, 38th Infantry cited)

Presidential Unit Citation (Army), Streamer embroidered **HONGCHON** (2d Infantry Division cited)

French Croix de Guerre with Palm, World War I, Streamer embroidered **MARNE RIVER** (38th Infantry cited)

French Croix de Guerre with Silver-Gilt Star, World War II, Streamer embroidered **BREST** (38th Infantry cited)

Republic of Korea Presidential Unit Citation, Streamer embroidered **NAKTONG RIVER LINE** (38th Infantry cited)

Republic of Korea Presidential Unit Citation, Streamer embroidered **KOREA 1950–1952** (38th Infantry cited)

Republic of Korea Presidential Unit Citation, Streamer embroidered **KOREA 1950–1953** (38th Infantry cited)

Belgian Fourragere 1940 (38th Infantry cited)

Cited in the Order of the Day of the Belgian Army for action in the **ARDENNES** (38th Infantry cited)

Cited in the Order of the Day of the Belgian Army for action at **ELSENBORN CREST** (38th Infantry cited)

1ST BATTALION, 38TH INFANTRY
(Rock of the Marne)

LINEAGE

1917	Constituted 15 May as Company A, 38th Infantry, Regular Army; organized 1 June at Syracuse, NY, and assigned 1 October to 3d Division
1933	Inactivated 1 October at Fort Sill, OK
1939	Activated 1 May at Fort Sill, OK, relieved 16 October from assignment to 3d Division, and assigned to 2d Division
1957	Redesignated 8 November as Headquarters and Headquarters Company, 1st Battle Group, 38th Infantry
1958	Inactivated 4 March
1962	Battle Group activated 19 February at Fort Benning, GA, and reassigned to 2d Infantry Division
1963	Reorganized and redesignated 10 May as 1st Battalion, 38th Infantry

CAMPAIGN PARTICIPATION

World War I

Aisne
Champagne–Marne
Aisne–Marne
St. Mihiel
Meuse–Argonne
Champagne 1918

World War II

Normandy
Northern France
Rhineland
Ardennes–Alsace
Central Europe

Korean War

UN defensive
UN offensive
CCF intervention
First UN counteroffensive
CCF spring offensive

UN summer–fall offensive
Second Korean winter
Korea, summer–fall 1952
Third Korean winter
Korea, summer 1953

DECORATIONS

Presidential Unit Citation (Army), Streamer embroidered **KRINKELT** (1st Battalion, 38th Infantry cited) cited)

Presidential Unit Citation (Army), Streamer embroidered **HILL 154, BREST**

Presidential Unit Citation (Army), Streamer embroidered **HONGCHON** (2d Infantry Division cited)

French Croix de Guerre with Palm, World War I, Streamer embroidered **MARNE RIVER** (38th Infantry cited)

French Croix de Guerre with Silver-Gilt Star, World War II, Streamer embroidered **BREST** (38th Infantry cited)

Republic of Korea Presidential Unit Citation, Streamer embroidered **NAKTONG RIVER LINE** (38th Infantry cited)

Republic of Korea Presidential Unit Citation, Streamer embroidered **KOREA 1950–1952** (38th Infantry cited)

Republic of Korea Presidential Unit Citation, Streamer embroidered **KOREA 1950–1953** (38th Infantry cited)

Belgian Fourragere 1940 (38th Infantry cited)

Cited in the Order of the Day of the Belgian Army for action in the **ARDENNES** (38th Infantry cited)

Cited in the Order of the Day of the Belgian Army for action at **ELSENBORN CREST** (38th Infantry cited)

2D BATTALION, 38TH INFANTRY
(Rock of the Marne)

LINEAGE

1917	Constituted 15 May as Company B, 38th Infantry, Regular Army; organized 1 June at Syracuse, NY, and assigned 1 October to 3d Division
1933	Inactivated 1 October at Fort Sill, OK
1939	Activated 1 May, relieved 16 October from assignment to 3d Division, and assigned to 2d Division
1957	Reorganized and redesignated 1 July as Headquarters and Headquarters Company, 2d Battle Group, 38th Infantry; relieved from assignment to 2d Infantry Division and assigned to 3d Infantry Division
1963	Reorganized and redesignated 1 April as 2d Battalion, 38th Infantry; relieved from 3d Infantry Division and assigned to 2d Infantry Division

CAMPAIGN PARTICIPATION

World War I

Aisne
Champagne–Marne
Aisne–Marne
St. Mihiel
Meuse–Argonne
Champagne 1918

World War II

Normandy
Northern France
Rhineland
Ardennes–Alsace
Central Europe

Korean War

UN defensive
UN offensive
CCF intervention
First UN counteroffensive
CCF spring offensive
UN summer–fall offensive
Second Korean winter
Korea, summer–fall 1952
Third Korean winter
Korea, summer 1953

DECORATIONS

Presidential Unit Citation (Army), Streamer embroidered **KRINKELT** (1st Battalion, 38th Infantry cited)

Presidential Unit Citation (Army), Streamer embroidered **HILL 154, BREST**

Presidential Unit Citation (Army), Streamer embroidered **HONGCHON** (2d Infantry Division cited)

French Croix de Guerre with Palm, World War I, Streamer embroidered **MARNE RIVER** (38th Infantry cited)

French Croix de Guerre with Silver-Gilt Star, World War II, Streamer embroidered **BREST** (38th Infantry cited)

Republic of Korea Presidential Unit Citation, Streamer embroidered **NAKTONG RIVER LINE** (38th Infantry cited)

Republic of Korea Presidential Unit Citation, Streamer embroidered **KOREA 1950–1952** (38th Infantry cited)

Republic of Korea Presidential Unit Citation, Streamer embroidered **KOREA 1950–1953** (38th Infantry cited)

Belgian Fourragere 1940 (38th Infantry cited)

Cited in the Order of the Day of the Belgian Army for action in the **ARDENNES** (38th Infantry cited)

Cited in the Order of the Day of the Belgian Army for action at **ELSENBORN CREST** (38th Infantry cited)

3D BATTALION, 38TH INFANTRY
(Rock of the Marne)

LINEAGE

1917   Constituted 15 May as Company C, 38th Infantry, Regular Army; organized 1 June at Syracuse, NY, and assigned 1 October to 3d Division

1933   Inactivated 1 October at Fort Sill, OK

1939   Activated 1 May, relieved 16 October from assignment to 3d Division, and assigned to 2d Division

1957   Redesignated 8 November as Headquarters and Headquarters Company, 3d Battle Group, 38th Infantry; relieved from assignment to 2d Infantry Division

1958   Inactivated 4 March

1959   Withdrawn 29 April from Regular Army, allotted to Army Reserve, assigned to 96th Infantry Division; Battle Group activated 1 June at Provo, UT

1963   Reorganized and redesignated 15 March as 3d Battalion, 38th Infantry; relieved from assignment to 96th Infantry Division and assigned 10 August to 191st Infantry Brigade

1968   Inactivated 29 February at Provo, UT

CAMPAIGN PARTICIPATION

World War I

Aisne
Champagne-Marne
Aisne-Marne
St. Mihiel
Meuse-Argonne
Champagne 1918

World War II

Normandy
Northern France
Rhineland
Ardennes-Alsace
Central Europe

Korean War

UN defensive
UN offensive
CCF intervention
First UN counteroffensive
CCF spring offensive
UN summer-fall offensive
Second Korean winter
Korea, summer-fall 1952
Third Korean winter
Korea, summer 1953

DECORATIONS

Presidential Unit Citation (Army), Streamer embroidered **KRINKELT** (1st Battalion, 38th Infantry cited)

Presidential Unit Citation (Army), Streamer embroidered **HILL 154, BREST**

Presidential Unit Citation (Army), Streamer embroidered **HONGCHON** (2d Infantry Division cited)

French Croix de Guerre with Palm, World War I, Streamer embroidered **MARNE RIVER** (38th Infantry cited)

French Croix de Guerre with Silver-Gilt Star, World War II, Streamer embroidered **BREST** (38th Infantry cited)

Republic of Korea Presidential Unit Citation, Streamer embroidered **NAKTONG RIVER LINE** (38th Infantry cited)

Republic of Korea Presidential Unit Citation, Streamer embroidered **KOREA 1950–1952** (38th Infantry cited)

Republic of Korea Presidential Unit Citation, Streamer embroidered **KOREA 1950–1953** (38th Infantry cited)

Belgian Fourragere 1940 (38th Infantry cited)

Cited in the Order of the Day of the Belgian Army for action in the **ARDENNES** (38th Infantry cited)

Cited in the Order of the Day of the Belgian Army for action at **ELSENBORN CREST** (38th Infantry cited)

39TH INFANTRY
(AAA-O)

COAT OF ARMS

Motto: *D'une Vaillance Admirable* (With a Military Courage Worthy of Admiration)

Symbolism: The shield is blue for infantry. The fleur-de-lis from the arms of Soissons and the two trees representing the Grove of Cresnes, the capture of which was the regiment's first success, are used to show service in the Aisne-Marne campaign. The boar's head on the canton is from the crest of the 30th Infantry and indicates that this regiment was organized with personnel from the 30th.

The crest is a falcon's head for Montfaucon in the Meuse-Argonne, holding in his bill an ivy leaf from the shoulder sleeve insignia of the 4th Division, to which the 39th was assigned during World War I. The motto is a quotation from the French citation awarding the Croix de Guerre with Gilt Star to the regiment for service in World War I

DISTINCTIVE INSIGNIA

The distinctive insignia is the shield, crest, and motto of the coat of arms.

LINEAGE

1917   Constituted 15 May as 39th Infantry, Regular Army; organized 1 June at Syracuse, NY, and assigned 19 November to 4th Division

1921   Inactivated 21 September at Camp Lewis, WA

1927   Relieved 15 August from assignment to 4th Division and assigned to 7th Division

1933   Relieved 1 October from assignment to 7th Division and assigned to 4th Division

1940   Relieved 1 August from assignment to 4th Division, assigned to 9th Division, and activated 9 August at Ford Bragg, NC

1946   Inactivated 30 November in Germany

1947   Activated 15 July at Fort Dix, NJ

1957   Relieved 1 December from assignment to 9th Division and reorganized as a parent regiment under CARS

CAMPAIGN PARTICIPATION

World War I
Aisne-Marne
St. Mihiel
Meuse-Argonne
Champagne 1918
Lorraine 1918

World War II
Algeria-French Morocco (with arrowhead)
Tunisia
Sicily
Normandy
Northern France
Rhineland
Ardennes-Alsace
Central Europe

Vietnam
Counteroffensive, Phase II
Counteroffensive, Phase III
Tet Counteroffensive
Counteroffensive, Phase IV
Counteroffensive, Phase V
Counteroffensive, Phase VI
Tet 69 Counteroffensive
Summer–Fall 1969

DECORATIONS

Presidential Unit Citation (Army), Streamer embroidered **COTENTIN PENINSULA** (1st Battalion, 39th Infantry cited)

Presidential Unit Citation (Army), Streamer embroidered **CHERENCE LE ROUSSEL** (1st Battalion, 39th Infantry cited)

Presidential Unit Citation (Army), Streamer embroidered **LE DESERT** (2d Battalion, 39th Infantry cited)

Presidential Unit Citation (Army), Streamer embroidered **DINH TUONG PROVINCE** (2d Battalion, 39th Infantry cited)

Valorous Unit Award, Streamer embroidered **BEN TRE CITY** (2d Battalion and 3d Battalion [less Companies A, D, and E], 39th Infantry cited)

Valorous Unit Award, Streamer embroidered **SAIGON** (3d and 4th Battalions, 39th Infantry cited)

French Croix de Guerre with Gilt Star, World War I, Streamer embroidered **AISNE-MARNE** (39th Infantry cited)

Belgian Fourragere 1940 (39th Infantry cited)

Cited in the Order of the Day of the Belgian Army for action on the **MEUSE RIVER** (39th Infantry cited)

Cited in the Order of the Day of the Belgian Army for action in the **ARDENNES** (39th Infantry cited)

1ST BATTALION, 39TH INFANTRY
(AAA-O)

LINEAGE

1917   Constituted 15 May as Company A, 39th Infantry, Regular Army, organized 1 June at Syracuse, NY, and assigned 19 November to 4th Division

Company lineage follows that of 39th Infantry from 1917 through 1947 activation at Fort Dix, NJ

1957   Reorganized and redesignated 1 December as Headquarters and Headquarters Company, 1st Battle Group, 39th Infantry, and assigned to 9th Infantry Division

1962 Inactivated 31 January at Fort Carson, CO, redesignated 20 September as 1st Battalion, 39th Infantry, and relieved from assignment to 9th Infantry Division; assigned to 197th Infantry Brigade and activated 24 September at Fort Benning, GA

1963 Relieved 4 January from assignment to 197th Infantry Brigade, inactivated 1 February at Fort Benning, GA; assigned 27 March to 8th Infantry Division and activated 1 April in Germany

CAMPAIGN PARTICIPATION

World War I

Aisne-Marne
St. Mihiel
Meuse-Argonne
Champagne 1918
Lorraine 1918

World War II

Algeria-French Morocco
 (with arrowhead)
Tunisia
Sicily
Normandy
Northern France
Rhineland
Ardennes-Alsace
Central Europe

DECORATIONS

Presidential Unit Citation (Army), Streamer embroidered **COTENTIN PENINSULA** (1st Battalion, 39th Infantry cited)

Presidential Unit Citation (Army), Streamer embroidered **CHERENCE LE ROUSSEL** (1st Battalion, 39th Infantry cited)

Presidential Unit Citation (Army), Streamer embroidered **LE DESERT**

French Croix de Guerre with Gilt Star, World War I, Streamer embroidered **AISNE-MARNE** (39th Infantry cited)

French Croix de Guerre with Palm, World War II, Streamer embroidered **SAINT JACQUES DE NEHOU** (1st Battalion, 39th Infantry cited)

French Croix de Guerre with Palm, World War II, Streamer embroidered **CHERENCE LE ROUSSEL** (1st Battalion, 39th Infantry cited)

French Croix de Guerre, World War II, Fourragere (1st Battalion, 39th Infantry cited)

Belgian Fourragere 1940 (39th Infantry cited)

Cited in the Order of the Day of the Belgian Army for action on the **MEUSE RIVER** (39th Infantry cited)

Cited in the Order of the Day of the Belgian Army for action in the **ARDENNES** (39th Infantry cited)

2D BATTALION, 39TH INFANTRY
(AAA-O)

LINEAGE

1917 Constituted 15 May as Company B, 39th Infantry, Regular Army, organized 1 June at Syracuse, NY, and assigned 19 November to 4th Division

Company lineage follows that of 39th Infantry from 1917 through 1947 activation at Fort Dix, NJ

1957 Reorganized and redesignated 1 April as Headquarters and Headquarters Company, 2d Battle Group, 39th Infantry; relieved from assignment to 9th Infantry Division and assigned to 4th Infantry Division

1963 Inactivated 1 October at Fort Lewis, WA, and relieved from assignment to 4th Infantry Division

1966 Redesignated 1 February as 2d Battalion, 39th Infantry, assigned to 4th Infantry Division and activated at Fort Riley, KS

1969 Inactivated 25 September at Schofield Barracks, Hawaii

CAMPAIGN PARTICIPATION

World War I

Aisne-Marne
St. Mihiel
Meuse-Argonne
Champagne 1918
Lorraine 1918

World War II

Algeria-French Morocco
 (with arrowhead)
Tunisia
Sicily
Normandy

Northern France
Rhineland
Ardennes-Alsace
Central Europe

Vietnam

Counteroffensive,
  Phase II
Counteroffensive,
  Phase III
Counteroffensive,
  Phase IV
Counteroffensive,
  Phase V
Counteroffensive,
  Phase VI
Tet 69 Counteroffensive
Summer–Fall 1969

French Croix de Guerre with Gilt Star, World War I, Streamer embroidered **AISNE-MARNE** (39th Infantry cited)

French Croix de Guerre with Palm, World War II, Streamer embroidered **SAINT JACQUES DE NEHOU** (1st Battalion, 39th Infantry cited)

French Croix de Guerre with Palm, World War II, Streamer embroidered **CHERENCE LE ROUSSEL** (1st Battalion, 39th Infantry cited)

French Croix de Guerre, World War II, Fourragere (1st Battalion, 39th Infantry cited)

Belgian Fourragere 1940 (39th Infantry cited)

Cited in the Order of the Day of the Belgian Army for action on the **MEUSE RIVER** (39th Infantry cited)

Cited in the Order of the Day of the Belgian Army for action in the **ARDENNES** (39th Infantry cited)

Vietnamese Cross of Gallantry with Palm, Streamer embroidered **VIETNAM 1967–1968** (2d Battalion, 39th Infantry cited)

Vietnamese Cross of Gallantry with Palm, Streamer embroidered **VIETNAM 1968** (2d Battalion, 39th Infantry cited)

Vietnamese Cross of Gallantry with Palm, Streamer embroidered **VIETNAM 1969** (2d Battalion, 39th Infantry cited)

Vietnamese Civil Action Honor Medal, First class, Streamer embroidered **VIETNAM 1967–1969** (2d Battalion, 39th Infantry cited)

DECORATIONS

Presidential Unit Citation (Army), Streamer embroidered **COTENTIN PENINSULA** (1st Battalion, 39th Infantry cited)

Presidential Unit Citation (Army), Streamer embroidered **CHERENCE LE ROUSSEL** (1st Battalion, 39th Infantry cited)

Presidential Unit Citation (Army), Streamer embroidered **LE DESERT**

Presidential Unit Citation (Army), Streamer embroidered **DINH TUONG PROVINCE** (2d Battalion, 39th Infantry cited)

Valorous Unit Award, Streamer embroidered **BEN TRE CITY** (2d Battalion, 39th Infantry cited)

3D BATTALION, 39TH INFANTRY
(AAA-O)

LINEAGE

1917   Constituted 15 May as Company C, 39th Infantry, Regular Army, organized 1 June at Syracuse, NY, and assigned 19 November to 4th Division

Company lineage follows that of 39th Infantry from 1917 through 1947 activation at Fort Dix, NJ

1957   Inactivated 1 December at Fort Carson, CO; relieved from assignment to 9th Infantry, and redesignated as Headquarters and Headquarters Company, 3d Battle Group, 39th Infantry

1966   Redesignated 1 February as Headquarters and Headquarters Company, 3d Battalion, 39th Infantry, assigned to 9th Infantry Division, and activated at Fort Riley, KS

1969   Inactivated 25 September at Schofield Barracks, Hawaii

CAMPAIGN PARTICIPATION

World War I

Aisne-Marne
St. Mihiel
Meuse-Argonne
Champagne 1918
Lorraine 1918

World War II

Algeria-French Morocco
  (with arrowhead)
Tunisia
Sicily
Normandy
Northern France
Rhineland
Ardennes-Alsace
Central Europe

Counteroffensive,
Phase II
Counteroffensive,
Phase III
Counteroffensive,
Phase IV

Counteroffensive,
Phase V
Counteroffensive,
Phase VI
Tet 69 Counteroffensive
Summer–Fall 1969

DECORATIONS

Presidential Unit Citation (Army), Streamer embroidered **COTENTIN PENINSULA** (1st Battalion, 39th Infantry cited)

Presidential Unit Citation (Army), Streamer embroidered **CHERENCE LE ROUSSEL** (1st Battalion, 39th Infantry cited)

Presidential Unit Citation (Army), Streamer embroidered **LE DESERT**

Valorous Unit Award, Streamer embroidered **BEN TRE CITY** (3d Battalion [less Companies A, D, and E], 39th Infantry cited)

Valorous Unit Award, Streamer embroidered **SAIGON** (3d Battalion, 39th Infantry cited)

French Croix de Guerre with Gilt Star, World War I, Streamer embroidered **AISNE-MARNE** (39th Infantry cited)

French Croix de Guerre with Palm, World War II, Streamer embroidered **SAINT JACQUES DE NEHOU** (1st Battalion, 39th Infantry cited)

French Croix de Guerre with Palm, World War II, Streamer embroidered **CHERENCE LE ROUSSEL** (1st Battalion, 39th Infantry cited)

French Croix de Guerre, World War II, Fourragere (1st Battalion, 39th Infantry cited)

Belgian Fourragere 1940 (39th Infantry cited)

Cited in the Order of the Day of the Belgian Army for action on the **MEUSE RIVER** (39th Infantry cited)

Cited in the Order of the Day of the Belgian Army for action in the **ARDENNES** (39th Infantry cited)

Vietnamese Cross of Gallantry with Palm, Streamer embroidered **VIETNAM 1967–1968** (3d Battalion, 39th Infantry cited)

Vietnamese Cross of Gallantry with Palm, Streamer embroidered **VIETNAM 1968** (3d Battalion, 39th Infantry cited)

Vietnamese Cross of Gallantry with Palm, Streamer embroidered **VIETNAM 1969** (3d Battalion, 39th Infantry cited)

Vietnamese Civil Action Honor Medal, First class, Streamer embroidered **VIETNAM 1967–1969** (3d Battalion, 39th Infantry cited)

4TH BATTALION, 39TH INFANTRY
(AAA-O)

LINEAGE

1917   Constituted 15 May as Company D, 39th Infantry, Regular Army; organized 1 June at Syracuse, NY, and assigned 19 November to 4th Division

Company lineage follows that of 39th Infantry from 1917 through 1947 activation at Fort Dix, NJ

1957   Inactivated 1 December at Fort Carson, CO, relieved from assignment to 9th Infantry Division; redesignated Headquarters and Headquarters Company, 4th Battle Group, 39th Infantry

1966   Redesignated 1 February as Headquarters and Headquarters Company, 4th Battalion, 39th Infantry; assigned to 9th Infantry Division and activated at Fort Riley, KS

1969   Inactivated 25 September at Schofield Barracks, Hawaii

CAMPAIGN PARTICIPATION

World War I

Aisne-Marne
St. Mihiel
Meuse-Argonne
Champagne 1918
Lorraine 1918

World War II

Algeria-French Morocco
(with arrowhead)
Tunisia
Sicily
Normandy
Northern France
Rhineland
Ardennes-Alsace

Central Europe

Vietnam

Counteroffensive,
Phase II
Counteroffensive,
Phase III
Tet Counteroffensive
Counteroffensive,
Phase IV
Counteroffensive,
Phase V
Counteroffensive,
Phase VI
Tet 69 Counteroffensive
Summer–Fall 1969

DECORATIONS

Presidential Unit Citation (Army), Streamer embroidered **COTENTIN PENINSULA** (1st Battalion, 39th Infantry cited)

Presidential Unit Citation (Army), Streamer embroidered **CHERENCE LE ROUSSEL** (1st Battalion, 39th Infantry cited)

Presidential Unit Citation (Army), Streamer embroidered **LE DESERT**

Valorous Unit Award, Streamer embroidered **SAIGON** (4th Battalion, 39th Infantry cited)

French Croix de Guerre with Gilt Star, World War I, Streamer embroidered **AISNE-MARNE** (39th Infantry cited)

French Croix de Guerre with Palm, World War II, Streamer embroidered **SAINT JACQUES DE NEHOU** (1st Battalion, 39th Infantry cited)

French Croix de Guerre with Palm, World War II, Streamer embroidered **CHERENCE LE ROUSSEL** (1st Battalion, 39th Infantry cited)

French Croix de Guerre, World War II, Fourragere (1st Battalion, 39th Infantry cited)

Belgian Fourragere 1940 (39th Infantry cited)

Cited in the Order of the Day of the Belgian Army for action on the **MEUSE RIVER** (39th Infantry cited)

Cited in the Order of the Day of the Belgian Army for action in the **ARDENNES** (39th Infantry cited)

Vietnamese Cross of Gallantry with Palm, Streamer embroidered **VIETNAM 1967–1968** (4th Battalion, 39th Infantry cited)

Vietnamese Cross of Gallantry with Palm, Streamer embroidered **VIETNAM 1968** (4th Battalion, 39th Infantry cited)

Vietnamese Cross of Gallantry with Palm, Streamer embroidered **VIETNAM 1969** (4th Battalion, 39th Infantry cited)

Vietnamese Civil Action Honor Medal, First class, Streamer embroidered **VIETNAM 1967–1969** (4th Battalion, 39th Infantry cited)

Company B additionally entitled to: Valorous Unit Award, Streamer embroidered **LONG BINH–BIEN HOA** (Company B, 4th Battalion, 39th Infantry cited)

41ST INFANTRY

COAT OF ARMS

Motto: Straight and Stalwart

Symbolism: The field is blue for infantry. The charges on the canton show that the regiment was originally organized with personnel from the 36th Infantry at Fort Snelling, MN, represented by the tower. During World War I it was in the 10th Division; the annulet is taken from the unofficial insignia of that division.

The lion rampant is from the coat of arms of Belgium; it refers to the regiment's participation in the Battle of the Bulge in Belgium during World War II. The lion is red for valor; the upper part is white in reference to the snow-covered terrain of the battle. The broken spear refers to the breaking of the German salient or spearhead. The crescent stands for Algeria and alludes to the regiment's first combat service in World War II. The tower represents the fortress of Europe; its four battlements stand for the unit's four Presidential Unit Citations (Army). The waves refer to the regiment's assault landings in World War II.

DISTINCTIVE INSIGNIA

The distinctive insignia is the shield and motto of the coat of arms.

LINEAGE

1917	Constituted 15 May as 41st Infantry, Regular Army; organized 20 June at Fort Snelling, MN
1918	Assigned 9 July to 10th Division
1921	Inactivated 22 September at Camp Meade, MD
1940	Activated 15 July at Fort Benning, GA, as 41st Infantry (Armored), and assigned to 2d Armored Division
1942	Redesignated 1 January as 41st Armored Infantry
1946	Broken up 25 March and redesignated as elements of 2d Armored Division as follows: Headquarters formed Headquarters Reserve Command; 1st Battalion formed 41st Armored Infantry Battalion; 2d Battalion formed 42d Armored Infantry Battalion; 3d Battalion formed 12th Armored Infantry Battalion
1957	The 41st, 2d, and 12th Armored Infantry Battalions relieved 1 July from assignment to 2d Armored division and consolidated to form 41st Infantry, a parent regiment under CARS
	Headquarters, Reserve Command, 2d Armored Division expanded and redesignated as Headquarters, 41st Infantry (and as Headquarters and Headquarters Company, Combat Command C, 2d Armored Division, which follows a separate lineage)

CAMPAIGN PARTICIPATION

World War II

Algeria-French Morocco (with arrowhead)
Sicily (with arrowhead)

Normandy
Northern France
Rhineland
Ardennes-Alsace
Central Europe

DECORATIONS

Presidential Unit Citation (Army), Streamer embroidered **NORMANDY** (1st and 3rd Battalions, 41st Armored Infantry cited)

Presidential Unit Citation (Army), Streamer embroidered **CHERBOURG** (Headquarters and Headquarters Company, 41st Armored Infantry cited)

Presidential Unit Citation (Army), Streamer embroidered **ARDENNES** (1st Battalion, 41st Armored Infantry cited)

Presidential Unit Citation (Army), Streamer embroidered **PUFFENDORF-ROER** (2d Battalion, 41st Armored Infantry cited)

Belgian Fouragere 1940 (41st Armored Infantry cited)

Cited in the Order of the Day of the Belgian Army for action in **BELGIUM** (41st Armored Infantry cited)

Cited in the Order of the Day of the Belgian Army for action in the **ARDENNES** (41st Armored Infantry cited)

1st Battalion, 41st Infantry

LINEAGE

1917	Constituted 15 May as Company A, 41st Infantry, Regular Army; organized 20 June at Fort Snelling, MN
	Company lineage follows that of 41st Infantry from 1917 through 1942 redesignation
1946	Reorganized and redesignated 25 March as Company A, 41st Armored Infantry Battalion, an element of 2d Armored Division
1957	Reorganized and redesignated 1 July as Headquarters and Headquarters Company, 1st Armored Rifle Battalion, 41st Infantry; assigned to 2d Armored Division
1963	Reorganized and redesignated 1 July as 1st Battalion, 41st Infantry

CAMPAIGN PARTICIPATION

World War II

Algeria-French Morocco (with arrowhead)
Sicily (with arrowhead)
Normandy
Northern France
Rhineland
Ardennes-Alsace
Central Europe

DECORATIONS

Presidential Unit Citation (Army), Streamer embroidered **NORMANDY** (1st Battalion, 41st Armored Infantry cited)

Presidential Unit Citation (Army), Streamer embroidered **CHERBOURG**

Presidential Unit Citation (Army), Streamer embroidered **ARDENNES** (1st Battalion, 41st Armored Infantry cited)

Presidential Unit Citation (Army), Streamer embroidered **PUFFENDORF-ROER**

Belgian Fouragere 1940 (41st Armored Infantry cited)

Cited in the Order of the Day of the Belgian Army for action in **BELGIUM** (41st Armored Infantry cited)

Cited in the Order of the Day of the Belgian Army for action in the **ARDENNES** (41st Armored Infantry cited)

2D BATTALION, 41ST INFANTRY

LINEAGE

1917   Constituted 15 May as Company B, 41st Infantry, Regular Army; organized 20 June at Fort Snelling, MN

Company lineage follows that of 41st Infantry from 1917 through 1942 redesignation

1946   Reorganized and redesignated 25 March as Company B, 41st Armored Infantry Battalion, an element of 2d Armored Division

1957   Reorganized and redesignated 1 April as Headquarters and Headquarters Company, 2d Armored Rifle Battalion, 41st Infantry; relieved from assignment to 2d Armored Division and assigned to 4th Armored Division

1963   Reorganized and redesignated 1 July as 2d Battalion, 41st Infantry, relieved from assignment to 4th Armored Division and assigned to 2d Armored Division

DECORATIONS

Presidential Unit Citation (Army), Streamer embroidered **NORMANDY** (1st Battalion, 41st Armored Infantry cited)

Presidential Unit Citation (Army), Streamer embroidered **CHERBOURG**

Presidential Unit Citation (Army), Streamer embroidered **ARDENNES** (1st Battalion, 41st Armored Infantry cited)

Presidential Unit Citation (Army), Streamer embroidered **PUFFENDORF-ROER**

Belgian Fouragere 1940 (41st Armored Infantry cited)

Cited in the Order of the Day of the Belgian Army for action in **BELGIUM** (41st Armored Infantry cited)

Cited in the Order of the Day of the Belgian Army for action in the **ARDENNES** (41st Armored Infantry cited)

CAMPAIGN PARTICIPATION

World War II

Algeria-French Morocco (with arrowhead)
Sicily (with arrowhead)
Normandy
Northern France
Rhineland
Ardennes-Alsace
Central Europe

3D BATTALION, 41ST INFANTRY

LINEAGE

1917   Constituted 15 May as Company C, 41st Infantry, Regular Army; organized 20 June at Fort Snelling, MN

Company lineage follows that of 41st Infantry from 1917 through 1942 redesignation

1946   Reorganized and redesignated 25 March as Company C, 41st Armored Infantry Battalion, an element of 2d Armored Division

1957   Inactivated 1 July in Germany, relieved from assignment to 2d Armored Division, and redesignated Headquarters and Headquarters Company, 3d Armored Rifle Battalion, 41st Infantry

1961   Activated 25 April at Fort Ord, CA

1962   Inactivated 21 December

CAMPAIGN PARTICIPATION

World War II

Algeria-French Morocco (with arrowhead)
Sicily (with arrowhead)
Normandy

Northern France
Rhineland
Ardennes-Alsace
Central Europe

DECORATIONS

Presidential Unit Citation (Army), Streamer embroidered **NORMANDY** (1st Battalion, 41st Armored Infantry cited)

Presidential Unit Citation (Army), Streamer embroidered **CHERBOURG**

Presidential Unit Citation (Army), Streamer embroidered **ARDENNES** (1st Battalion, 41st Armored Infantry cited)

Presidential Unit Citation (Army), Streamer embroidered **PUFFENDORF-ROER**

Belgian Fouragere 1940 (41st Armored Infantry cited)

Cited in the Order of the Day of the Belgian Army for action in **BELGIUM** (41st Armored Infantry cited)

Cited in the Order of the Day of the Belgian Army for action in the **ARDENNES** (41st Armored Infantry cited)

COMPANY D, 41ST INFANTRY

LINEAGE

1917   Constituted 15 May as Company D, 41st Infantry, Regular Army; organized 20 June at Fort Snelling, MN

Company lineage follows that of 41st Infantry from 1917 through 1942 redesignation

1946   Reorganized and redesignated 25 March as Company A, 42d Armored Infantry Battalion, an element of 2d Armored Division

1957   Inactivated 1 July in Germany, relieved from assignment to 2d Armored Division, redesignated as Headquarters and Headquarters Company, 4th Armored Rifle Battalion, 41st Infantry

1962   Redesignated 2 October as Headquarters and Headquarters Company, 4th Battalion, 41st Infantry; assigned to the 194th Armored Brigade and activated 21 December at Fort Ord, CA

1968   Inactivated 4 January at Fort Ord, CA, and redesignated Company D, 41st Infantry; and activated at Fort Ord, CA

CAMPAIGN PARTICIPATION

World War II

Sicily (with arrowhead)
Normandy
Northern France
Rhineland
Ardennes-Alsace
Central Europe

DECORATIONS

Presidential Unit Citation (Army), Streamer embroidered **PUFFENDORF-ROER** (2d Battalion, 41st Armored Infantry cited)

French Croix de Guerre with Silver-Gilt Star, World War II, Streamer embroidered **PUFFENDORF-ROER** (2d Battalion, 41st Armored Infantry cited)

Belgian Fourragere 1940 (41st Armored Infantry cited)

Cited in the Order of the Day of the Belgian Army for action in **BELGIUM** (41st Armored Infantry cited)

Cited in the Order of the Day of the Belgian Army for action in the **ARDENNES** (41st Armored Infantry cited)

COMPANY E, 41ST INFANTRY

LINEAGE

1917	Constituted 15 May as Company E, 41st Infantry, Regular Army; organized 20 June at Fort Snelling, MN
	Company lineage follows that of 41st Infantry from 1917 through 1942 redesignation
1946	Reorganized and redesignated 25 March as Company B, 42d Armored Infantry Battalion, an element of 2d Armored Division
1957	Inactivated 1 July in Germany, relieved from assignment to 2d Armored Division, and redesignated as Headquarters and Headquarters Company, 5th Armored Rifle Battalion, 41st Infantry
1962	Activated 18 December at Fort Chaffee, AR
1963	Inactivated 25 March
1968	Redesignated 4 January as Company E, 41st Infantry and activated at Fort Ord, CA

CAMPAIGN PARTICIPATION

World War II-EAME

Sicily (with arrowhead)
Normandy
Northern France

Rhineland
Ardennes-Alsace
Central Europe

DECORATIONS

Presidential Unit Citation (Army), Streamer embroidered **PUFFENDORF-ROER** (2d Battalion, 41st Armored Infantry cited)

French Croix de Guerre with Silver-Gilt Star, World War II, Streamer embroidered **PUFFENDORF-ROER** (2d Battalion, 41st Armored Infantry cited)

Belgian Fourragere 1940 (41st Armored Infantry cited)

Cited in the Order of the Day of the Belgian Army for action in **BELGIUM** (41st Armored Infantry cited)

Cited in the Order of the Day of the Belgian Army for action in the **ARDENNES** (41st Armored Infantry cited)

COMPANY F, 41ST INFANTRY

LINEAGE

1917 Constituted 15 May as Company F, 41st Infantry, Regular Army; organized 20 June at Fort Snelling, MN

Company lineage follows that of 41st Infantry from 1917 through 1942 redesignation

1946 Reorganized and redesignated 25 March as Company C, 42d Armored Infantry Battalion, an element of 2d Armored Division

1957 Inactivated 1 July in Germany, relieved from assignment to 2d Armored Division, and redesignated as Headquarters and Headquarters Company, 6th Armored Rifle Battalion, 41st Infantry

1968 Redesignated 4 January as Company F, 41st Infantry and activated at Fort Ord, CA

CAMPAIGN PARTICIPATION

World War II-EAME

Sicily (with arrowhead)
Normandy
Northern France
Rhineland
Ardennes-Alsace
Central Europe

DECORATIONS

Presidential Unit Citation (Army), Streamer embroidered **PUFFENDORF-ROER** (2d Battalion, 41st Armored Infantry cited)

French Croix de Guerre with Silver-Gilt Star, World War II, Streamer embroidered **PUFFENDORF-ROER** (2d Battalion, 41st Armored Infantry cited)

Belgian Fourragere 1940 (41st Armored Infantry cited)

Cited in the Order of the Day of the Belgian Army for action in **BELGIUM** (41st Armored Infantry cited)

Cited in the Order of the Day of the Belgian Army for action in the **ARDENNES** (41st Armored Infantry cited)

COMPANY G, 41ST INFANTRY

LINEAGE

1917 Constituted 15 May as Company G, 41st Infantry, Regular Army; organized 20 June at Fort Snelling, MN

Company lineage follows that of 41st Infantry from 1917 through 1942 redesignation

1946 Reorganized and redesignated 25 March as Company A, 12th Armored Infantry Battalion, an element of the 2d Armored Division

1957 Inactivated 1 July in Germany, relieved from assignment to the 2d Armored Division, and redesignated as Headquarters and Headquarters Company, 7th Armored Rifle Battalion, 41st Infantry

1968 Redesignated 4 January as Company G, 41st Infantry and activated at Fort Ord, CA

1970 Inactivated 30 March

CAMPAIGN PARTICIPATION

World War II-EAME

Sicily (with arrowhead)
Normandy
Northern France
Rhineland
Ardennes-Alsace
Central Europe

DECORATIONS

Presidential Unit Citation (Army), Streamer embroidered **NORMANDY** (3d Battalion, 41st Armored Infantry cited)

Belgian Fourragere 1940 (41st Armored Infantry cited)

Cited in the Order of the Day of the Belgian Army for action in **BELGIUM** (41st Armored Infantry cited)

Cited in the Order of the Day of the Belgian Army for action in the **ARDENNES** (41st Armored Infantry cited)

COMPANY H, 41ST INFANTRY

LINEAGE

1917   Constituted 15 May as Company H, 41st Infantry, Regular Army; organized 20 June at Fort Snelling, MN

Company lineage follows that of 41st Infantry from 1917 through 1942 redesignation

1946   Reorganized and redesignated 25 March as Company B, 12th Armored Infantry Battalion, an element of 2d Armored Division

1957   Inactivated 1 July in Germany, relieved from assignment to 2d Armored Division, and redesignated as Headquarters and Headquarters Company, 8th Armored Rifle Battalion, 41st Infantry

1968   Redesignated 4 January as Company H, 41st Infantry and activated at Fort Ord, CA

1970   Inactivated 30 March

CAMPAIGN PARTICIPATION

World War II-EAME

Sicily (with arrowhead)
Normandy
Northern France

Rhineland
Ardennes-Alsace
Central Europe

DECORATIONS

Presidential Unit Citation (Army), Streamer embroidered **NORMANDY** (3d Battalion, 41st Armored Infantry cited)

Presidential Unit Citation (Army), Streamer embroidered **BARENTON** (Company H, 41st Armored Infantry cited)

French Croix de Guerre with Silver Star, World War II, Streamer embroidered **MORTAIN** (Company H, 41st Armored Infantry cited)

Belgian Fourragere 1940 (41st Armored Infantry cited)

Cited in the Order of the Day of the Belgian Army for action in **BELGIUM** (41st Armored Infantry cited)

Cited in the Order of the Day of the Belgian Army for action in the **ARDENNES** (41st Armored Infantry cited)

46TH INFANTRY
(The Professionals)

COAT OF ARMS

Motto: None

Symbolism: This regiment was originally organized at Fort Benjamin Harrison, IN, with personnel from the 10th Infantry. The field is blue, the infantry color. The charge, a gold torch and star, is taken from the flag of the state of Indiana, while the badge of the 10th Infantry is shown on the canton.

The spearhead bearing a fleur-de-lis represents the unit's participation in the drive from the Normandy Peninsula through Northern France. The black castle signifies the penetration of the Siegfried Line. The operations in Luxembourg, for which the unit received the Croix de Guerre, are noted by the white lion rampant (adopted from the arms of the town of Diekirch). The red pine trees represent the bitter, arduous fighting in the area of the Hurtgen Forest of Germany.

DISTINCTIVE INSIGNIA

The distinctive insignia is the shield of the coat of arms.

LINEAGE

1917 Constituted 15 May as 46th Infantry, Regular Army; organized 4 June at Fort Benjamin Harrison, IN

1918 Assigned 5 July to the 9th Division

1919 Relieved 15 February from assignment to 9th Division

1921 Inactivated 16 November at Camp Travis, TX

1922 Demobilized 31 July

1941 Reconstituted 28 August as 46th Infantry (Armored), Regular Army, an element of the 5th Armored Division; activated 1 October at Fort Knox, KY

1942 Redesignated 1 January as 46th Armored Infantry

1943 Regiment broken up 20 September and its element reorganized and redesignated as elements of the 5th Armored Division as follows: 46th Armored Infantry (less 1st and 2d Battalions) formed the 46th Armored Infantry Battalion; 1st Battalion formed the 47th Armored Infantry Battalion; 2d Battalion formed 15th Armored Infantry Battalion

1945 Battalions inactivated 3–13 October at Camp Myles Standish, MA

1948 Activated 6 July at Camp Chaffee, AR

1950 Inactivated 1 February and activated 1 September

1956 Inactivated 16 March

1957 Relieved 15 February from assignment to the 5th Armored Division

1959 The 46th, 47th, and 15th Armored Infantry Battalions consolidated 1 July to form the 46th Infantry, a parent regiment under CARS

CAMPAIGN PARTICIPATION

World War II

Normandy
Northern France
Rhineland
Ardennes-Alsace
Central Europe

Vietnam

Counteroffensive, Phase III
Tet Counteroffensive
Counteroffensive, Phase IV
Counteroffensive, Phase V
Counteroffensive, Phase VI
Tet 69 Counteroffensive
Summer-Fall 1969
Winter-Spring 1970
Sanctuary Counteroffensive
Counteroffensive, Phase VII
Consolidation I
Consolidation II
Cease-Fire

DECORATIONS

Presidential Unit Citation (Army), Streamer embroidered **HURTGEN FOREST** (47th Armored Infantry Battalion cited)

Luxembourg Croix de Guerre, Streamer embroidered **LUXEMBOURG** (46th, 47th, and 15th Armored Infantry Battalions cited)

1ST BATTALION, 46TH INFANTRY
(The Professionals)

LINEAGE

1917 Constituted 15 May as Company A, 46th Infantry, Regular Army; organized 4 June at Fort Benjamin Harrison, IN

Company lineage follows that of 46th Infantry from 1917 through 1942 redesignation as 46th Armored Infantry

1943 Reorganized and redesignated 20 September as Company A, 47th Armored Infantry Battalion, an element of the 5th Armored Division

1945 Inactivated 8 October at Camp Myles Standish, MA

1948 Activated 6 July at Camp Chaffee, AR

1950 Inactivated 1 February and activated 1 September

1956	Inactivated 16 March
1957	Redesignated 15 February as Headquarters and Headquarters Company, 1st Armored Rifle Battalion, 46th Infantry, and relieved from assignment to 5th Armored Division; assigned to 1st Armored Division, activated at Fort Polk, LA, and inactivated 23 December
1958	Activated 1 April in Germany
1962	Reorganized and redesignated 3 February as 1st Battalion, 46th Infantry, and assigned to the 1st Armored Division
1967	Relieved 12 May from assignment to 1st Armored Division and assigned to the 198th Infantry Brigade
1969	Relieved 25 February from assignment to 198th Infantry Brigade and assigned to 23d Infantry Division

CAMPAIGN PARTICIPATION

World War II

Normandy
Northern France
Rhineland
Ardennes-Alsace
Central Europe

Vietnam

Counteroffensive,
  Phase III
Tet Counteroffensive
Counteroffensive,
  Phase IV
Counteroffensive,
  Phase V
Counteroffensive,
  Phase VI
Tet 69 Counteroffensive
Summer-Fall 1969
Winter-Spring 1970
Sanctuary
  Counteroffensive
Counteroffensive,
  Phase VII
Consolidation I
Consolidation II
Cease-Fire

DECORATIONS

Presidential Unit Citation (Army), Streamer embroidered **HURTGEN FOREST** (47th Armored Infantry Battalion cited)

French Croix de Guerre with Silver Star, World War II, Streamer embroidered **WALLENDORF** (47th Armored Infantry Battalion cited)

Luxembourg Croix de Guerre, Streamer embroidered **LUXEMBOURG** (47th Armored Infantry Battalion cited)

Cited in the Order of the Day of the Belgian Army for action in the **ARDENNES** (Company A, 47th Armored Infantry Battalion cited)

2D BATTALION, 46TH INFANTRY
(The Professionals)

LINEAGE

1917	Constituted 15 May as Company B, 46th Infantry, Regular Army; organized 4 June at Fort Benjamin Harrison, IN
	Company lineage follows that of 46th Infantry from 1917 through 1942 redesignation as 46th Armored Infantry
1943	Reorganized and redesignated as Company B, 47th Armored Infantry Battalion, an element of the 5th Armored Infantry
1945	Inactivated 8 October at Camp Myles Standish, MA
1948	Activated 6 July at Camp Chaffee, AR
1950	Inactivated 1 February at Camp Chaffee and activated 1 September
1956	Inactivated 16 March
1957	Relieved 15 February from assignment to 5th Armored Division, redesignated 1 October as Headquarters and Headquarters Company, 2d Armored Rifle Battalion, 46th Infantry, and assigned to the 3d Armored Division and activated in Germany
1962	Reorganized and redesignated 3 February as 2d Battalion, 46th Infantry, relieved from assignment to 3d Armored Division, and assigned to 1st Armored Division

CAMPAIGN PARTICIPATION

World War II

Normandy
Northern France
Rhineland
Ardennes-Alsace
Central Europe

DECORATIONS

Presidential Unit Citation (Army), Streamer embroidered **HURTGEN FOREST** (47th Armored Infantry Battalion cited)

Presidential Unit Citation (Army), Streamer embroidered **MEUSE RIVER** (Company B, 47th Armored Infantry Battalion cited)

French Croix de Guerre with Silver Star, World War II, Streamer embroidered **WALLENDORF** (47th Armored Infantry Battalion cited)

Luxembourg Croix de Guerre, Streamer embroidered **LUXEMBOURG** (47th Armored Infantry Battalion cited)

3D ARMORED RIFLE BATTALION, 46TH INFANTRY
(The Professionals)

LINEAGE

1917   Constituted as Company C, 46th Infantry, Regular Army; organized 4 June at Fort Benjamin Harrison, IN

Company lineage follows that of 46th Infantry from 1917 through 1942 redesignation as 46th Armored Infantry

1943   Reorganized and redesignated 20 September as Company C, 47th Armored Infantry, an element of the 5th Armored Division

1945   Inactivated 8 October at Camp Myles Standish, MA

1948   Activated 6 July at Camp Chaffee, AR

1950   Inactivated 1 February and activated 1 September

1956   Inactivated 16 March

1957   Relieved from assignment to 5th Armored Division

1959   Redesignated 1 July as Headquarters and Headquarters Company, 3d Battle Group, 46th Infantry

1962   Redesignated 3 February as Headquarters and Headquarters Company, 3d Armored Rifle Battalion, 46th Infantry and activated in Germany

1963   Inactivated 1 February in Germany

CAMPAIGN PARTICIPATION

World War II

Normandy	Rhineland
Northern France	Ardennes-Alsace
	Central Europe

DECORATIONS

Presidential Unit Citation (Army), Streamer embroidered **HURTGEN FOREST** (47th Armored Infantry Battalion cited)

Presidential Unit Citation (Army), Streamer embroidered **MEUSE RIVER** (Company C, 47th Armored Infantry Battalion cited)

French Croix de Guerre with Silver Star, World War II, Streamer embroidered **WALLENDORF** (47th Armored Infantry Battalion cited)

Luxembourg Croix de Guerre, Streamer embroidered **LUXEMBOURG** (47th Armored Infantry Battalions cited)

4TH BATTALION, 46TH INFANTRY
(The Professionals)

LINEAGE

1917   Constituted 15 May as Company D, 46th Infantry, Regular Army; organized 4 June at Fort Benjamin Harrison, IN

Company lineage follows that of 46th Infantry from 1917 through 1942 redesignation as 46th Armored Infantry

1943   Reorganized and redesignated 20 September as Company A, 15th Armored Infantry Battalion, an element of the 5th Armored Division

1945   Inactivated 8 October at Camp Myles Standish, MA

1948   Activated 6 July at Camp Chaffee, AR

1950   Inactivated 1 February and activated 1 September

1956   Inactivated 16 March

1957   Relieved 15 February from assignment to 5th Armored Division

1959   Redesignated 1 July as Headquarters and Headquarters Company, 4th Battle Group, 46th Infantry

1967   Redesignated 9 May as Headquarters and Headquarters Company, 4th Battalion, 46th Infantry; assigned to the 1st Armored Division, and Battalion activated 12 May at Fort Hood, TX

CAMPAIGN PARTICIPATION

World War II
   Normandy
   Northern France
   Rhineland
   Ardennes-Alsace
   Central Europe

DECORATIONS

Presidential Unit Citation (Army), Streamer embroidered **HURTGEN FOREST**

Luxembourg Croix de Guerre, Streamer embroidered **LUXEMBOURG** (15th Armored Infantry Battalion cited)

5TH BATTALION, 46TH INFANTRY
(The Professionals)

LINEAGE

1917   Constituted 15 May as Company E, 46th Infantry, Regular Army; organized 4 June at Fort Benjamin Harrison, IN

Company lineage follows that of 46th Infantry from 1917 through 1942 redesignation as 46th Armored Infantry

1943   Reorganized and redesignated 20 September as Company B, 15th Armored Infantry Battalion, an element of the 5th Armored Division

1945   Inactivated 8 October at Camp Myles Standish, MA

1948   Activated 6 July at Camp Chaffee, AR

1950   Inactivated 1 February and activated 1 September

1956   Inactivated 16 March

1957   Relieved 15 February from assignment to 5th Armored Division

1959	Redesignated 1 July as Headquarters and Headquarters Company, 5th Battle Group, 46th Infantry
1967	Redesignated 2 October as Headquarters and Headquarters Company, 5th Battalion, 46th Infantry; activated at Fort Hood, TX
1968	Assigned 31 March to 198th Infantry Brigade
1969	Relieved 15 February from assignment to 198th Infantry and assigned to the 23d Infantry Division

CAMPAIGN PARTICIPATION

World War II

Normandy
Northern France
Rhineland
Ardennes-Alsace
Central Europe

Vietnam

Tet Counteroffensive
Counteroffensive,
    Phase IV
Counteroffensive,
    Phase V
Counteroffensive,
    Phase VI
Tet 69 Counteroffensive
Summer-Fall 1969
Winter-Spring 1970
Sanctuary
    Counteroffensive
Counteroffensive,
    Phase VII

DECORATIONS

Presidential Unit Citation (Army), Streamer embroidered **HURTGEN FOREST**

Luxembourg Croix de Guerre, Streamer embroidered **LUXEMBOURG** (15th Armored Infantry Battalion cited)

47TH INFANTRY

COAT OF ARMS

Motto: *Ex Virtute Honos* (Honor Comes From Virtue)

Symbolism: This regiment was originally organized with personnel from the 9th Infantry, as shown by the canton taken from its arms. Service of the 47th during World War I with the 4th Division is represented by the divisional insignia on the shield.

The water wheel and the fleur-de-lis symbolize engagements in France. The first important battle in which the unit participated was at Sergy on the Ourcq River. The water wheel represents the mill located at the approach to Sergy. Later the 47th also fought at Bazoches on the Vesle. Both Sergy and Bazoches were formerly included in the province of Ile de France, which bore the royal arms, three gold fleurs-de-lis on a blue field.

DISTINCTIVE INSIGNIA

The distinctive insignia is the shield of the coat of arms.

LINEAGE

1917	Constituted 15 May as 47th Infantry, Regular Army; organized 1 June at Syracuse, NY, and assigned 19 November to the 4th Division
1921	Inactivated 22 September at Camp Lewis, WA
1927	Relieved 15 August from assignment to 4th Division and assigned to 7th Division
1933	Relieved 1 October from assignment to 7th Division
1940	Assigned 1 August to the 9th Division and activated 10 August at Fort Bragg, NC
1946	Inactivated 31 December in Germany
1947	Activated 15 July at Fort Dix, NJ
1957	Relieved from assignment to 9th Infantry Division and reorganized as a parent regiment under CARS

CAMPAIGN PARTICIPATION

World War I

Aisne-Marne
St. Mihiel
Meuse-Argonne
Lorraine 1918
Champagne 1918

World War II

Algeria-French Morocco
 (with arrowhead)
Tunisia
Sicily
Normandy
Northern France
Rhineland
Ardennes-Alsace
Central Europe

Vietnam

Counteroffensive,
 Phase II
Counteroffensive,
 Phase III
Tet Counteroffensive
Counteroffensive,
 Phase IV
Counteroffensive,
 Phase V
Counteroffensive,
 Phase VI
Tet 69 Counteroffensive
Summer-Fall 1969
Winter-Spring 1970
Sanctuary
 Counteroffensive
Counteroffensive,
 Phase VII

DECORATIONS

Presidential Unit Citation (Army), Streamer embroidered **CHERBOURG** (2d Battalion, 47th Infantry cited)

Presidential Unit Citation (Army), Streamer embroidered **HAGUE PENINSULA** (3d Battalion, 47th Infantry cited)

Presidential Unit Citation (Army), Streamer embroidered **ROETGEN, GERMANY** (3d Battalion, 47th Infantry cited)

Presidential Unit Citation (Army), Streamer embroidered **NOTHBERG, GERMANY** (1st Battalion, 47th Infantry cited)

Presidential Unit Citation (Army), Streamer embroidered **FREUZENBERG CASTLE** (2d Battalion, 47th Infantry cited)

Presidential Unit Citation (Army), Streamer embroidered **REMAGEN, GERMANY** (47th Infantry cited)

Presidential Unit Citation (Army), Streamer embroidered **OBERKIRCHEN, GERMANY** (2d Battalion, 47th Infantry cited)

Presidential Unit Citation (Army), Streamer embroidered **MEKONG DELTA** (3d Battalion, 47th Infantry cited)

Valorous Unit Award, Streamer embroidered **LONG BINH–BIEN HOA** (2d Battalion, 47th Infantry cited)

Valorous Unit Award, Streamer embroidered **SAIGON** (2d Battalion, 47th Infantry cited)

Meritorious Unit Commendation, Streamer embroidered **VIETNAM 1968** (3d Battalion, 47th Infantry cited)

French Croix de Guerre with Palm, World War II, Streamer embroidered **CHERBOURG** (47th Infantry cited)

Belgian Fourragere 1940 (47th Infantry cited)

Cited in the Order of the Day of the Belgian Army for action at the **MEUSE RIVER** (47th Infantry cited)

Cited in the Order of the Day of the Belgian Army for action in the **ARDENNES** (47th Infantry cited)

1st Battalion, 47th Infantry

LINEAGE

1917   Constituted 15 May as Company A, 47th Infantry, Regular Army; organized 1 June at Syracuse, NY, and assigned 19 November to the 4th Division

Company lineage follows that of 47th Infantry from 1917 through 1947 activation at Fort Dix, NJ

1957   Reorganized and redesignated 1 December as Headquarters and Headquarters Company, 1st Battle Group, 47th Infantry, and remained assigned to 9th Infantry Division

1962   Inactivated 31 January at Fort Carson, CO

1963   Redesignated 20 May as 1st Battalion, 47th Infantry, and relieved from assignment to the 9th Infantry Division; assigned to the 171st Infantry Brigade and activated 1 July in Alaska

CAMPAIGN PARTICIPATION

World War I

Aisne-Marne
St. Mihiel
Meuse-Argonne
Lorraine 1918
Champagne 1918

World War II

Algeria-French Morocco (with arrowhead)
Tunisia
Sicily
Normandy
Northern France
Rhineland
Ardennes-Alsace
Central Europe

DECORATIONS

Presidential Unit Citation (Army), Streamer embroidered **CHERBOURG**

Presidential Unit Citation (Army), Streamer embroidered **HAGUE PENINSULA**

Presidential Unit Citation (Army), Streamer embroidered **ROETGEN, GERMANY**

Presidential Unit Citation (Army), Streamer embroidered **NOTHBERG, GERMANY** (1st Battalion, 47th Infantry cited)

Presidential Unit Citation (Army), Streamer embroidered **FREUZENBERG CASTLE**

Presidential Unit Citation (Army), Streamer embroidered **REMAGEN, GERMANY** (47th Infantry cited)

Presidential Unit Citation (Army), Streamer embroidered **OBERKIRCHEN, GERMANY**

French Croix de Guerre with Palm, World War II, Streamer embroidered **CHERBOURG** (47th Infantry cited)

Belgian Fourragere 1940 (47th Infantry cited)

Cited in the Order of the Day of the Belgian Army for action at the **MEUSE RIVER** (47th Infantry cited)

Cited in the Order of the Day of the Belgian Army for action in the **ARDENNES** (47th Infantry cited)

2d Battalion, 47th Infantry

LINEAGE

1917   Constituted 15 May as Company B, 47th Infantry, Regular Army; organized 1 June at Syracuse, NY, and assigned 19 November to 4th Division

Company lineage follows that of 47th Infantry from 1917 through 1947 activation at Fort Dix, NJ

1957   Reorganized and redesignated 1 April as Headquarters and Headquarters Company, 2d Battle Group, 47th Infantry; relieved from assignment to the 9th Infantry Division and assigned to the 4th Infantry Division

1963   Inactivated 1 October at Fort Lewis, WA, and relieved from assignment to 4th Infantry Division

| 1966 | Redesignated 1 February as 2d Battalion, 47th Infantry, assigned to the 9th Infantry Division, and activated at Fort Riley, KS |
| 1970 | Inactivated 13 October at Fort Lewis, WA |

CAMPAIGN PARTICIPATION

World War I

Aisne-Marne
St. Mihiel
Meuse-Argonne
Lorraine 1918
Champagne 1918

World War II

Algeria-French Morocco
  (with arrowhead)
Tunisia
Sicily
Normandy
Northern France
Rhineland
Ardennes-Alsace
Central Europe

Vietnam

Counteroffensive,
  Phase II
Counteroffensive,
  Phase III
Tet Counteroffensive
Counteroffensive,
  Phase IV
Counteroffensive,
  Phase V
Counteroffensive,
  Phase VI
Tet 69 Counteroffensive
Summer-Fall 1969
Winter-Spring 1970
Sanctuary
  Counteroffensive
Counteroffensive,
  Phase VII

DECORATIONS

Presidential Unit Citation (Army), Streamer embroidered **CHERBOURG**

Presidential Unit Citation (Army), Streamer embroidered **HAGUE PENINSULA**

Presidential Unit Citation (Army), Streamer embroidered **ROETGEN, GERMANY**

Presidential Unit Citation (Army), Streamer embroidered **NOTHBERG, GERMANY** (1st Battalion, 47th Infantry cited)

Presidential Unit Citation (Army), Streamer embroidered **FREUZENBERG CASTLE**

Presidential Unit Citation (Army), Streamer embroidered **REMAGEN, GERMANY** (47th Infantry cited)

Presidential Unit Citation (Army), Streamer embroidered **OBERKIRCHEN, GERMANY**

Valorous Unit Award, Streamer embroidered **LONG BINH–BIEN HOA** (2d Battalion, 47th Infantry cited)

Valorous Unit Award, Streamer embroidered **SAIGON** (2d Battalion, 47th Infantry cited)

French Croix de Guerre with Palm, World War II, Streamer embroidered **CHERBOURG** (47th Infantry cited)

Belgian Fourragere 1940 (47th Infantry cited)

Cited in the Order of the Day of the Belgian Army for action at the **MEUSE RIVER** (47th Infantry cited)

Cited in the Order of the Day of the Belgian Army for action in the **ARDENNES** (47th Infantry cited)

Vietnamese Cross of Gallantry with Palm, Streamer embroidered **VIETNAM 1967–1968** (2d Battalion, 47th Infantry cited)

Vietnamese Cross of Gallantry with Palm, Streamer embroidered **VIETNAM 1968** (2d Battalion, 47th Infantry cited)

Vietnamese Cross of Gallantry with Palm, Streamer embroidered **VIETNAM 1969** (2d Battalion, 47th Infantry cited)

Vietnamese Civil Action Honor Medal, First Class, Streamer embroidered **VIETNAM 1967–1969** (2d Battalion, 47th Infantry cited)

3D BATTALION, 47TH INFANTRY

LINEAGE

| 1917 | Constituted 15 May as Company C, 47th Infantry, Regular Army; organized 1 June at Syracuse, NY, and assigned 19 November to the 4th Division |

Company lineage follows that of 47th Infantry from 1917 through 1947 activation at Fort Dix, NJ

| 1957 | Inactivated 1 December at Fort Carson, CO, relieved from assignment to 9th Infantry Division, and redesignated as Headquarters and Headquarters Company, 3d Battle Group, 47th Infantry |
| 1959 | Withdrawn 10 April from the Regular Army, allotted to Army Reserve, and assigned to 81st Infantry Division; Battle Group activated 1 May at Atlanta, GA |

1963	Inactivated 1 April at Atlanta, GA, and relieved from assignment to the 81st Infantry Division
1966	Redesignated 1 February as the 3d Battalion, 47th Infantry, withdrawn from Army Reserve, and allotted to Regular Army; assigned to the 9th Infantry Division and activated at Fort Riley, KS
1969	Inactivated 1 August at Fort Riley, KS

CAMPAIGN PARTICIPATION

World War I

Aisne-Marne
St. Mihiel
Meuse-Argonne
Lorraine 1918
Champagne 1918

World War II

Algeria-French Morocco
 (with arrowhead)
Tunisia
Sicily
Normandy
Northern France
Rhineland
Ardennes-Alsace
Central Europe

Vietnam

Counteroffensive,
 Phase II
Counteroffensive,
 Phase III
Tet Counteroffensive
Counteroffensive,
 Phase IV
Counteroffensive,
 Phase V
Counteroffensive,
 Phase VI
Tet 69 Counteroffensive
Summer-Fall 1969

DECORATIONS

Presidential Unit Citation (Army), Streamer embroidered **CHERBOURG**

Presidential Unit Citation (Army), Streamer embroidered **HAGUE PENINSULA**

Presidential Unit Citation (Army), Streamer embroidered **ROETGEN, GERMANY**

Presidential Unit Citation (Army), Streamer embroidered **NOTHBERG, GERMANY** (1st Battalion, 47th Infantry cited)

Presidential Unit Citation (Army), Streamer embroidered **FREUZENBERG CASTLE**

Presidential Unit Citation (Army), Streamer embroidered **REMAGEN, GERMANY** (47th Infantry cited)

Presidential Unit Citation (Army), Streamer embroidered **OBERKIRCHEN, GERMANY**

Presidential Unit Citation (Army), Streamer embroidered **MEKONG DELTA** (3d Battalion, 47th Infantry cited)

Meritorious Unit Commendation, Streamer embroidered **VIETNAM 1968** (3d Battalion, 47th Infantry cited)

French Croix de Guerre with Palm, World War II, Streamer embroidered **CHERBOURG** (47th Infantry cited)

Belgian Fourragere 1940 (47th Infantry cited)

Cited in the Order of the Day of the Belgian Army for action at the **MEUSE RIVER** (47th Infantry cited)

Cited in the Order of the Day of the Belgian Army for action in the **ARDENNES** (47th Infantry cited)

Vietnamese Cross of Gallantry with Palm, Streamer embroidered **VIETNAM 1967–1968** (3d Battalion, 47th Infantry cited)

Vietnamese Cross of Gallantry with Palm, Streamer embroidered **VIETNAM 1969** (3d Battalion, 47th Infantry cited)

Vietnamese Civil Action Honor Medal, First Class, Streamer embroidered **VIETNAM 1967–1969** (3d Battalion, 47th Infantry cited)

4TH BATTALION, 47TH INFANTRY

LINEAGE

1917	Constituted 15 May as Company D, 47th Infantry, Regular Army; organized 1 June at Syracuse, NY, and assigned 19 November to the 4th Division

Company lineage follows that of 47th Infantry from 1917 through 1947 activation at Fort Dix, NJ

1957	Inactivated 1 December at Fort Carson, CO, relieved from assignment to 9th Infantry Division, and redesignated as Headquarters and Headquarters Company, 4th Battle Group, 47th Infantry

1966	Redesignated 1 February as Headquarters and Headquarters Company, 4th Battalion, 47th Infantry, and assigned to 9th Infantry Division; activated at Fort Riley, KS
1969	Inactivated 1 August at Fort Riley, KS

CAMPAIGN PARTICIPATION

World War I

Aisne-Marne
St. Mihiel
Meuse-Argonne
Lorraine 1918
Champagne 1918

World War II

Algeria-French Morocco
(with arrowhead)
Tunisia
Sicily
Normandy
Northern France
Rhineland
Ardennes-Alsace
Central Europe

Vietnam

Counteroffensive,
Phase II
Counteroffensive,
Phase III
Tet Counteroffensive
Counteroffensive,
Phase IV
Counteroffensive,
Phase V
Counteroffensive,
Phase VI
Tet 69 Counteroffensive
Summer-Fall 1969

DECORATIONS

Presidential Unit Citation (Army), Streamer embroidered **CHERBOURG**

Presidential Unit Citation (Army), Streamer embroidered **HAGUE PENINSULA**

Presidential Unit Citation (Army), Streamer embroidered **ROETGEN, GERMANY**

Presidential Unit Citation (Army), Streamer embroidered **NOTHBERG, GERMANY** (1st Battalion, 47th Infantry cited)

Presidential Unit Citation (Army), Streamer embroidered **FREUZENBERG CASTLE**

Presidential Unit Citation (Army), Streamer embroidered **REMAGEN, GERMANY** (47th Infantry cited)

Presidential Unit Citation (Army), Streamer embroidered **OBERKIRCHEN, GERMANY**

French Croix de Guerre with Palm, World War II, Streamer embroidered **CHERBOURG** (47th Infantry cited)

Belgian Fourragere 1940 (47th Infantry cited)

Cited in the Order of the Day of the Belgian Army for action at the **MEUSE RIVER** (47th Infantry cited)

Cited in the Order of the Day of the Belgian Army for action in the **ARDENNES** (47th Infantry cited)

Vietnamese Cross of Gallantry with Palm, Streamer embroidered **VIETNAM 1967–1968** (4th Battalion, 47th Infantry cited)

Vietnamese Cross of Gallantry with Palm, Streamer embroidered **VIETNAM 1969** (4th Battalion, 47th Infantry cited)

Vietnamese Civil Action Honor Medal, First Class, Streamer embroidered **VIETNAM 1967–1969** (4th Battalion, 47th Infantry cited)

Company C additionally entitled to: Presidential Unit Citation (Army), Streamer embroidered **MEKONG DELTA** (Company C, 4th Battalion, 47th Infantry cited)

48TH INFANTRY

COAT OF ARMS

Motto: Dragoons

Symbolism: The colors blue and white are the present and former infantry colors. Black and gold are the colors of the Belgian coat of arms from which the Belgian lion is adapted. The wavy chevron on the canton is for descent from personnel of the 9th Infantry. The Belgian lion represents the organization's actions in the Ardennes and at St. Vith, for which it was cited twice in the Order of the Day of the Belgian Army.

The crest, consisting of Teutonic hunting horns, alludes to the German battle honors of World War II.

DISTINCTIVE INSIGNIA

The distinctive insignia is the shield and motto of the coat of arms.

LINEAGE

1917 Constituted 15 May as 48th Infantry, Regular Army; organized 1 June at Syracuse, NY, as an element of the 20th Division

1919 Relieved 28 February from assignment to 20th Division

1921 Inactivated 14 October at Camp Travis, TX

1922 Demobilized 31 July

1942 Reconstituted 27 February as the 48th Armored Infantry, Regular Army, an element of the 7th Armored Division; and activated 2 March at Camp Polk, LA

1943 Regiment broken up 20 September and its elements reorganized and redesignated as elements of the 7th Armored Division as follows: 48th Armored Infantry (less 1st and 2d Battalions) formed the 48th Armored Infantry Battalion; 1st Battalion formed the 38th Armored Infantry Battalion; 2d Battalion formed the 23d Armored Infantry Battalion

1945 Battalions inactivated 8–11 October at Camp Myles Standish, MA; Camp Shanks, NY; and Camp Kilmer, NJ

1950 Activated 24 November at Camp Roberts, CA

1953 Inactivated 15 November at Camp Roberts, CA

1957 The 48th, 38th, and 23d Armored Infantry Battalions relieved 15 February from assignment to 7th Armored Division and consolidated to form the 48th Infantry, a parent regiment under CARS

CAMPAIGN PARTICIPATION

World War II

Northern France
Rhineland
Ardennes-Alsace
Central Europe

DECORATIONS

Presidential Unit Citation (Army), Streamer embroidered **ST. VITH** (38th and 23d Infantry Battalions cited)

Belgian Fourragere 1940 (48th, 38th, and 23d Armored Infantry Battalions cited)

Cited in the Order of the Day of the Belgian Army for action in the **ARDENNES** (48th, 38th, and 23d Armored Infantry Battalions cited)

Cited in the Order of the Day of the Belgian Army for action at **ST. VITH** (48th, 38th, and 23d Armored Infantry Battalions cited)

1ST BATTALION, 48TH INFANTRY

LINEAGE

1917 Constituted 15 May as Company A, 48th Infantry, Regular Army; organized 1 June at Syracuse, NY, as an element of the 20th Division

Company lineage follows that of 48th Infantry from 1917 through 1942 activation at Camp Polk, LA

1943 Reorganized and redesignated 20 September as Company A, 38th Armored Infantry Battalion, an element of the 7th Armored Division

1945 Inactivated 11 October at Camp Shanks, NY

1950 Activated 24 November at Camp Roberts, CA

1953 Inactivated 15 November

1957 Redesignated 15 February as Headquarters and Headquarters Company, 1st Armored Rifle Battalion, 48th Infantry, relieved from assignment to 7th Armored Division, and assigned to the 1st Armored Division; activated at Fort Polk, LA, and inactivated 23 December

1958 Relieved 25 February from assignment to 1st Armored Division and activated 1 April in Germany

1963 Reorganized and redesignated 1 September as 1st Battalion, 48th Infantry, and assigned to 3d Armored Division

CAMPAIGN PARTICIPATION

World War II

Northern France
Rhineland
Ardennes-Alsace
Central Europe

DECORATIONS

Presidential Unit Citation (Army), Streamer embroidered **ST. VITH** (38th Armored Infantry Battalions cited)

Belgian Fourragere 1940 (38th Armored Infantry Battalion cited)

Cited in the Order of the Day of the Belgian Army for action in the **ARDENNES** (38th Armored Infantry Battalion cited)

Cited in the Order of the Day of the Belgian Army for action at **ST. VITH** (38th Armored Infantry Battalion cited)

2D BATTALION, 48TH INFANTRY

LINEAGE

1917   Constituted 15 May as Company B, 48th Infantry, Regular Army; organized 1 June at Syracuse, NY, as an element of the 20th Division

Company lineage follows that of 48th Infantry from 1917 through 1942 activation at Fort Polk, LA

1943   Reorganized and redesignated 20 September as Company B, 38th Armored Infantry Battalion, an element of the 7th Armored Division

1945   Inactivated 11 October at Camp Shanks, NY

1950   Activated 24 November at Camp Roberts, CA

1953   Inactivated 15 November at Camp Roberts, CA

1957   Relieved 15 February from assignment to 7th Armored Division, redesignated 1 October as Headquarters and Headquarters Company, 2d Armored Rifle Battalion, 48th Infantry, and assigned to the 3d Armored Division and activated in Germany

1963   Reorganized and redesignated 1 September as 2d Battalion, 48th Infantry

CAMPAIGN PARTICIPATION

World War II

Northern France
Rhineland
Ardennes-Alsace
Central Europe

DECORATIONS

Presidential Unit Citation (Army), Streamer embroidered **ST. VITH** (38th Armored Infantry Battalions cited)

Belgian Fourragere 1940 (38th Armored Infantry Battalion cited)

Cited in the Order of the Day of the Belgian Army for action in the **ARDENNES** (38th Armored Infantry Battalion cited)

Cited in the Order of the Day of the Belgian Army for action at **ST. VITH** (38th Armored Infantry Battalion cited)

50TH INFANTRY

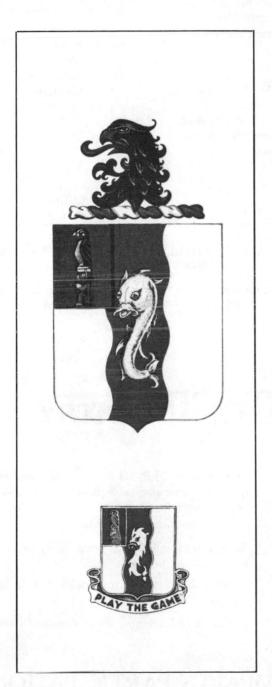

COAT OF ARMS

Motto: Play the Game

Symbolism: The regiment was originally organized at Syracuse, NY, with personnel from the 23d Infantry. The shield is in the former and present colors of the infantry (white and blue). The dolphin is the device of Syracuse, and the totem pole in the canton is taken from the crest of the 23d Infantry. The pale with wavy edges indicates the regiment's occupation duty in the Rhine Province after World War I. At the time of the armistice on 11 November 1918 the 50th had been under orders for Silesia. The crest is the eagle's head of these two provinces.

DISTINCTIVE INSIGNIA

The distinctive insignia is the shield and motto of the coat of arms.

LINEAGE

1917	Constituted 15 May at 50th Infantry, Regular Army; organized 1 June at Syracuse, NY
1918	Assigned 31 July to 20th Division
1919	Relieved 28 February from assignment to 20th Division
1921	Inactivated 31 December in Germany
1922	Demobilized 31 July
1942	Reconstituted 8 January as 50th Armored Infantry, Regular Army, and assigned to 6th Armored Division; activated 15 February at Fort Knox, KY
1943	Regiment broken up 20 September and elements reorganized and redesignated as an element of the 6th Armored division as follows: 50th Armored Infantry (less 1st and 2d Battalions) formed 50th Armored Infantry Battalion; 1st Battalion formed 44th Armored Infantry Battalion; 2d Battalion formed 9th Armored Infantry Battalion
1945	Battalions inactivated 18–19 September at Camp Shanks, NY
1950	Activated 5 September at Fort Leonard Wood, MO
1956	Inactivated 16 March
1957	Relieved 1 July from assignment to 6th Armored Division
1959	The 50th, 44th and 9th Armored Infantry Battalions consolidated 1 July to form 50th Infantry, a parent regiment under CARS

CAMPAIGN PARTICIPATION

World War II

Normandy
Northern France
Rhineland
Ardennes-Alsace
Central Europe

Vietnam

Counteroffensive, Phase III
Tet Counteroffensive
Counteroffensive, Phase IV
Counteroffensive, Phase V
Counteroffensive, Phase VI
Tet 69 Counteroffensive
Summer–Fall 1969
Winter–Spring 1970
Sanctuary Counteroffensive
Counteroffensive, Phase VII

DECORATIONS

Valorous Unit Award, Streamer embroidered **BINH DUONG PROVINCE** (Company F, 50th Infantry cited)

French Croix de Guerre with Palm, World War II, Streamer embroidered **BREST** (50th Armored Infantry Battalion cited)

1st Battalion, 50th Infantry

LINEAGE

1917	Constituted 15 May as Company A, 50th Infantry, Regular Army; organized 1 June at Syracuse, NY
	Company lineage follows that of 50th Infantry from 1917 through 1943 reorganization
1943	Reorganized and redesignated 20 September as Company A, 44th Armored Infantry Battalion, an element of the 6th Armored Division
1945	Inactivated 19 September at Camp Shanks, NY
1950	Activated 5 September at Fort Leonard Wood, MO
1956	Inactivated 16 March
1957	Redesignated 1 July as Headquarters and Headquarters Company, 1st Armored Rifle Battalion, and relieved from assignment to 6th Armored Division and activated in Germany
1963	Reorganized and redesignated 1 July as 1st Battalion, 50th Infantry
1967	Relieved 1 September from assignment to 2d Armored Division
1970	Assigned 16 December to 2d Armored Division

CAMPAIGN PARTICIPATION

World War II

Normandy

Northern France
Rhineland

Ardennes-Alsace
Central Europe

Vietnam

Counteroffensive,
    Phase III
Tet Counteroffensive
Counteroffensive,
    Phase IV
Counteroffensive,
    Phase V

Counteroffensive,
    Phase VI
Tet 69 Counteroffensive
Summer–Fall 1969
Winter–Spring 1970
Sanctuary
    Counteroffensive
Counteroffensive,
    Phase VII

DECORATIONS

None.

2D BATTALION, 50TH INFANTRY

LINEAGE

1917   Constituted 15 May as Company B, 50th Infantry, Regular Army; organized 1 June at Syracuse, NY

         Company lineage follows that of 50th Infantry from 1917 through 1943 reorganization

1943   Reorganized and redesignated 20 September as Company B, 44th Armored Infantry Battalion, an element of the 6th Armored Division

1945   Inactivated 19 September at Camp Shanks, NY

1950   Activated 5 September at Fort Leonard Wood, MO

1956   Inactivated 16 March

1957   Redesignated 1 April as Headquarters and Headquarters Company, 2d Armored Rifle Battalion, 50th Infantry, and relieved from assignment to 6th Armored Division; assigned to 4th Armored Division and activated at Fort Hood, TX

1963   Reorganized and redesignated 1 July as 2d Battalion, 50th Infantry, relieved from assignment to 4th Armored Division and assigned to 2d Armored Division

CAMPAIGN PARTICIPATION

World War II

    Normandy
    Northern France
    Rhineland
    Ardennes-Alsace
    Central Europe

DECORATIONS

None.

3D ARMORED RIFLE BATTALION, 50TH INFANTRY

LINEAGE

1917   Constituted 15 May as Company C, 50th Infantry, Regular Army; organized 1 June at Syracuse, NY

Company lineage follows that of 50th Infantry from 1917 through 1943 reorganization

1943   Reorganized and redesignated 20 September as Company C, 44th Armored Infantry Battalion, an element of the 6th Armored Division

1945   Inactivated 19 September at Camp Shanks, NY

1950   Activated 5 September at Fort Leonard Wood, MO

1956   Inactivated 16 March

1958   Redesignated 25 February as Headquarters and Headquarters Company, 3d Armored Rifle Battalion, 50th Infantry; and relieved from assignment to 6th Armored Division and activated 1 April in Germany

1963   Inactivated 15 July in Germany

CAMPAIGN PARTICIPATION

World War II
- Normandy
- Northern France
- Rhineland
- Ardennes-Alsace
- Central Europe

DECORATIONS

None.

COMPANY E, 50TH INFANTRY

LINEAGE

1917   Constituted 15 May as Company E, 50th Infantry, Regular Army; organized 1 June at Syracuse, NY

Company lineage follows that of 50th Infantry from 1917 through 1943 reorganization

1943   Reorganized and redesignated 20 September as Company B, 9th Armored Infantry Battalion, an element of the 6th Armored Division

1945   Inactivated 18 September at Camp Shanks, NY

1950   Activated 5 September at Fort Leonard Wood, MO

1956   Inactivated 16 March

1957   9th Armored Infantry Battalion relieved 1 July from assignment to 6th Armored Division

1959   Redesignated 1 July as Headquarters and Headquarters Company, 5th Battle Group, 50th Infantry

1967   Redesignated 20 December as Company E, 50th Infantry, and activated in Vietnam

1969   Inactivated 1 February in Vietnam

CAMPAIGN PARTICIPATION

World War II-EAME
- Normandy
- Northern France
- Rhineland
- Ardennes-Alsace
- Central Europe

Vietnam
- Counteroffensive, Phase III
- Tet Counteroffensive
- Counteroffensive, Phase IV
- Counteroffensive, Phase V
- Counteroffensive, Phase VI

DECORATIONS

French Croix de Guerre with Palm, World War II, Streamer embroidered **CHAMBREY** (9th Armored Infantry Battalion cited)

Vietnamese Cross of Gallantry with Palm, Streamer embroidered **VIETNAM 1967–1968** (Company E, 50th Infantry cited)

Vietnamese Cross of Gallantry with Palm, Streamer embroidered **VIETNAM 1969** (Company E, 50th Infantry cited)

Vietnamese Civil Action Honor Medal, First Class, Streamer embroidered **VIETNAM 1967–1969** (Company E, 50th Infantry cited)

COMPANY F, 50TH INFANTRY

LINEAGE

1917   Constituted 15 May as Company F, 50th Infantry, Regular Army; organized 1 June at Syracuse, NY

Company lineage follows that of 50th Infantry from 1917 through 1943 reorganization

1943   Reorganized and redesignated 20 September as Company C, 9th Armored Infantry Battalion, an element of the 6th Armored Division

1945   Inactivated 18 September at Camp Shanks, NY

1950   Activated 5 September at Fort Leonard Wood, MO

1956   Inactivated 16 March

1957   9th Armored Infantry Battalion relieved 1 July from assignment to 6th Armored Division

1959   Redesignated 1 July as Headquarters and Headquarters Company, 6th Battle Group, 50th Infantry

1967   Redesignated 20 December as Company F, 50th Infantry, and activated in Vietnam

1969   Inactivated 1 February in Vietnam

CAMPAIGN PARTICIPATION

World War II-EAME

Normandy
Northern France
Rhineland
Ardennes-Alsace
Central Europe

Vietnam

Counteroffensive, Phase III
Tet Counteroffensive
Counteroffensive, Phase IV
Counteroffensive, Phase V
Counteroffensive, Phase VI
Tet 69 Counteroffensive
Consolidation I
Consolidation II
Cease-Fire

DECORATIONS

Valorous Unit Award, Streamer embroidered **BINH DUONG PROVINCE** (Company F, 50th Infantry cited)

French Croix de Guerre with Palm, World War II, Streamer embroidered **CHAMBREY** (9th Armored Infantry Battalion cited)

Vietnamese Cross of Gallantry with Palm, Streamer embroidered **VIETNAM 1967–1968** (Company F, 50th Infantry cited)

Vietnamese Cross of Gallantry with Palm, Streamer embroidered **VIETNAM 1969** (Company F, 50th Infantry cited)

51ST INFANTRY

COAT OF ARMS

Motto: I Serve

Symbolism: The shield is blue for infantry, with the bend taken from the coat of arms of Alsace. The ragged tree trunk symbolizes the Meuse-Argonne campaign of World War I.

DISTINCTIVE INSIGNIA

The distinctive insignia is the shield and motto of the coat of arms.

LINEAGE

1917   Constituted 15 May as 51st Infantry, Regular Army; organized 16 June at Chickamauga Park, GA; and assigned 16 November to 6th Division

1921   Inactivated 22 September at Camp Grant, IL

1927   Relieved 15 August from assignment to 6th Division and assigned to 9th Division

1933   Relieved 1 October from assignment to 9th Division and assigned to 6th Division

1940   Relieved 16 December from assignment to 6th Division

1941   Activated 15 April at Pine Camp, NY, as 51st Infantry (Armored), an element of 4th Armored Division

1942   Redesignated 1 January as 51st Armored Infantry

1943   Regiment broken up 10 September and elements reorganized and redesignated as elements of the 4th Armored Division as follows: 51st Armored Infantry (less 1st and 2d Battalions) formed 51st Armored Infantry Battalion; 1st Battalion formed 53d Armored Infantry Battalion; 2d Battalion formed 10th Armored Infantry Battalion

1946   51st Armored Infantry Battalion converted and redesignated 1 May as 51st Constabulary Squadron, relieved from assignment to 4th Armored Division, and assigned to 11th Constabulary Regiment

1948   Inactivated 20 December in Germany, relieved from assignment to 11th Constabulary Regiment, converted and redesignated as 51st Armored Infantry Battalion, and assigned to 4th Armored Division

1954   Activated 15 June at Fort Hood, TX

1957   Inactivated and relieved from assignment to 4th Armored Division

1959   The 51st, 553d, and 510th Armored Infantry Battalions consolidated 1 July to form 51st Infantry, a parent regiment under CARS

CAMPAIGN PARTICIPATION

World War I

  Meuse-Argonne
  Alsace 1918

World War II

  Normandy
  Northern France
  Rhineland
  Ardennes-Alsace
  Central Europe

Vietnam

  Counteroffensive, Phase II
  Counteroffensive, Phase III
  Tet Counteroffensive
  Counteroffensive, Phase IV
  Counteroffensive, Phase V
  Counteroffensive, Phase VI
  Tet 69 Counteroffensive
  Summer–Fall 1969
  Winter–Spring 1970
  Sanctuary Counteroffensive
  Counteroffensive, Phase VII
  Consolidation I
  Consolidation II
  Cease-Fire

DECORATIONS

Presidential Unit Citation (Army), Streamer embroidered **ARDENNES** (4th Armored Division cited)

Valorous Unit Award, Streamer embroidered **SAIGON-LONG BINH** (Company F, 51st Infantry cited)

Meritorious Unit Commendation, Streamer embroidered **VIETNAM 1967–1968** (Company D, 51st Infantry cited)

Meritorious Unit Commendation, Streamer embroidered **VIETNAM 1968–1969** (Company E, 51st Infantry cited)

French Croix de Guerre with Palm, World War II, Streamer embroidered **NORMANDY** (51st, 53d, and 10th Armored Infantry Battalions cited)

French Croix de Guerre with Palm, World War II, Streamer embroidered **MOSELLE RIVER** (51st, 53d, and 10th Armored Infantry Battalions cited)

French Croix de Guerre, World War II, Fourragere (51st, 53d, and 10th Armored Infantry Battalions cited)

1ST BATTALION, 51ST INFANTRY

LINEAGE

1917   Constituted 15 May as Company A, 51st Infantry, Regular Army; organized 16 June at Chickamauga Park, GA; and assigned 16 November to 6th Division

Company lineage follows that of 51st Infantry from 1917 through 1943 reorganization

1946   Converted and redesignated 1 May as Troop A, 53d Constabulary Squadron, an element of the 6th Constabulary Regiment

1948   53d Constabulary Squadron relieved 16 November from assignment to 6th Constabulary Regiment and assigned to U.S. Constabulary

1949   Inactivated 20 May in Germany, converted and redesignated as Company A, 53d Armored Infantry Battalion, an element of the 4th Armored Division

1953   Redesignated 25 February as Company A, 553d Armored Infantry Battalion, an element of 4th Armored Division

1954   Activated 15 June at Fort Hood, TX

1957   Inactivated 1 April, relieved from assignment to 4th Armored Division, redesignated 1 July as Headquarters and Headquarters Company, 1st Armored Rifle Battalion, 51st Infantry; assigned to 2d Armored Division and activated in Germany

1963   Reorganized and redesignated 1 July as 1st Battalion, 51st Infantry, relieved from assignment to 2d Armored Division, and assigned to 4th Armored Division

CAMPAIGN PARTICIPATION

World War I
   Meuse-Argonne
   Alsace 1918

World War II
   Normandy
   Northern France
   Rhineland
   Ardennes-Alsace
   Central Europe

DECORATIONS

Presidential Unit Citation (Army), Streamer embroidered **ARDENNES** (4th Armored Division cited)

French Croix de Guerre with Palm, World War II, Streamer embroidered **NORMANDY** (53d Armored Infantry Battalion cited)

French Croix de Guerre with Palm, World War II, Streamer embroidered **MOSELLE RIVER** (53d Armored Infantry Battalion cited)

French Croix de Guerre, World War II, Fourragere (53d Armored Infantry Battalion cited)

2D BATTALION, 51ST INFANTRY

LINEAGE

1917   Constituted 15 May as Company B, 51st Infantry, Regular Army; organized 16 June at Chickamauga Park, GA; and assigned to the 6th Division

Company lineage follows that of 51st Infantry from 1917 through 1943 reorganization

1946   Converted and redesignated 1 May as Troop B, 53d Constabulary Squadron, an element of the 6th Constabulary Regiment

1948   Relieved 16 November from assignment to 6th Constabulary Regiment, and assigned to U.S. Constabulary

1949   Inactivated 20 May in Germany, converted and redesignated as Company B, 53d Armored Infantry Battalion, an element of the 4th Armored Division

1953   Redesignated 25 February as Company B, 553d Armored Infantry Battalion, an element of 4th Armored Division

1954   Activated 15 June at Fort Hood, TX

| 1957 | Reorganized and redesignated 1 April as Headquarters and Headquarters Company, 2d Armored Rifle Battalion, 51st Infantry and assigned to 4th Armored Division |
| 1963 | Reorganized and redesignated 1 August as 2d Battalion, 51st Infantry |

CAMPAIGN PARTICIPATION

World War I

Meuse-Argonne
Alsace 1918

World War II

Normandy
Northern France
Rhineland
Ardennes-Alsace
Central Europe

DECORATIONS

Presidential Unit Citation (Army), Streamer embroidered **ARDENNES** (4th Armored Division cited)

French Croix de Guerre with Palm, World War II, Streamer embroidered **NORMANDY** (53d Armored Infantry Battalion cited)

French Croix de Guerre with Palm, World War II, Streamer embroidered **MOSELLE RIVER** (53d Armored Infantry Battalion cited)

French Croix de Guerre, World War II, Fourragere (53d Armored Infantry Battalion cited)

3D BATTALION, 51ST INFANTRY

LINEAGE

| 1917 | Constituted 15 May as Company C, 51st Infantry, Regular Army; organized 16 June at Chickamauga Park, GA; and assigned to the 6th Division |

Company lineage follows that of 51st Infantry from 1917 through 1943 reorganization

1946	Converted and redesignated 1 May as Troop C, 53d Constabulary Squadron, an element of the 6th Constabulary Regiment
1948	Relieved 16 November from assignment to 6th Constabulary Regiment and assigned to U.S. Constabulary
1949	Inactivated 20 May in Germany, converted and redesignated as Company C, 53d Armored Infantry Battalion, an element of the 4th Armored Division
1953	Redesignated 25 February as Company C, 553d Armored Infantry Battalion, an element of 4th Armored Division
1954	Activated 15 June at Fort Hood, TX
1957	Inactivated 1 April and relieved from assignment to 4th Armored Division
1958	Redesignated 25 February as Headquarters and Headquarters Company, 3d Armored Rifle Battalion, 51st Infantry, and activated 1 April in Germany

| 1963 | Assigned 1 April to 4th Armored Division and reorganized and redesignated 15 August as 3d Battalion, 51st Infantry |

CAMPAIGN PARTICIPATION

World War I

Meuse-Argonne
Alsace 1918

World War II

Normandy
Northern France
Rhineland
Ardennes-Alsace
Central Europe

DECORATIONS

Presidential Unit Citation (Army), Streamer embroidered **ARDENNES** (4th Armored Division cited)

French Croix de Guerre with Palm, World War II, Streamer embroidered **NORMANDY** (53d Armored Infantry Battalion cited)

French Croix de Guerre with Palm, World War II, Streamer embroidered **MOSELLE RIVER** (53d Armored Infantry Battalion cited)

French Croix de Guerre, World War II, Fourragere (53d Armored Infantry Battalion cited)

COMPANY D, 51ST INFANTRY

LINEAGE

1917   Constituted 15 May as Company D, 51st Infantry, Regular Army; organized 16 June at Chickamauga Park, GA; and assigned 16 November to the 6th Division

Company lineage follows that of 51st Infantry from 1917 through 1943 reorganization

1946   Converted and redesignated 1 May as Troop A, 10th Constabulary Squadron, an element of the 14th Constabulary Regiment

1948   Inactivated 20 December in Germany, converted and redesignated as Company A, 10th Armored Infantry Battalion, an element of the 4th Armored Division

1953   Redesignated 25 February as Company A, 510th Armored Infantry Battalion, an element of 4th Armored Division

1954   Activated 15 June at Fort Hood, TX

1957   Inactivated 1 April at Fort Hood, TX, and relieved from assignment to 4th Armored Division

1959   Redesignated 1 July as Headquarters and Headquarters Company, 4th Battle Group, 51st Infantry

1966   Redesignated 23 March as Company D, 51st Infantry, and activated 1 June at Fort Lewis, WA

CAMPAIGN PARTICIPATION

World War I

Meuse-Argonne
Alsace 1918

World War II-EAME

Normandy
Northern France
Rhineland
Ardennes-Alsace
Central Europe

Vietnam

Counteroffensive, Phase II
Counteroffensive, Phase III
Tet Counteroffensive
Counteroffensive, Phase IV
Counteroffensive, Phase V
Counteroffensive, Phase VI
Tet 69 Counteroffensive
Summer-Fall 1969
Winter-Spring 1970
Sanctuary Counteroffensive
Counteroffensive, Phase VII
Consolidation I
Consolidation II
Cease-Fire

DECORATIONS

Presidential Unit Citation (Army), Streamer embroidered **ARDENNES** (4th Armored Division cited)

Meritorious Unit Commendation, Streamer embroidered **VIETNAM 1967-1968** (Company D, 51st Infantry cited)

French Croix de Guerre with Palm, World War II, Streamer embroidered **NORMANDY** (10th Armored Infantry Battalion cited)

French Croix de Guerre with Palm, World War II, Streamer embroidered **MOSELLE RIVER** (10th Armored Infantry Battalion cited)

French Croix de Guerre, World War II, Fourragere (10th Armored Infantry Battalion cited)

Company E, 51st Infantry

LINEAGE

1917   Constituted 15 May as Company E, 51st Infantry, Regular Army; organized 16 June at Chickamauga Park, GA; and assigned 16 November to 6th Division

Company lineage follows that of 51st Infantry from 1917 through 1943 reorganization

1946   Converted and redesignated 1 May as Troop B, 10th Constabulary Squadron, an element of the 14th Constabulary Regiment

1948   Inactivated 20 December in Germany, converted and redesignated as Company B, 10th Armored Infantry Battalion, an element of the 4th Armored Division

1953   Redesignated 25 February as Company B, 510th Armored Infantry Battalion, an element of 4th Armored Division

1954   Activated 15 June at Fort Hood, TX

1957   Inactivated 1 April at Fort Hood, TX, and relieved from assignment to 4th Armored Division

1959   Redesignated 1 July as Headquarters and Headquarters Company, 5th Battle Group, 51st Infantry

1967   Redesignated 20 December as Company E, 51st Infantry, and activated in Vietnam

1969   Inactivated 1 February in Vietnam

CAMPAIGN PARTICIPATION

World War I
> Meuse-Argonne
> Alsace 1918

World War II-EAME
> Normandy
> Northern France
> Rhineland
> Ardennes-Alsace
> Central Europe

Vietnam
> Counteroffensive, Phase III
> Tet Counteroffensive
> Counteroffensive, Phase IV
> Counteroffensive, Phase V
> Counteroffensive, Phase VI

DECORATIONS

Presidential Unit Citation (Army), Streamer embroidered **ARDENNES** (4th Armored Division cited)

Meritorious Unit Commendation, Streamer embroidered **VIETNAM 1968–1969** (Company E, 51st Infantry cited)

French Croix de Guerre with Palm, World War II, Streamer embroidered **NORMANDY** (10th Armored Infantry Battalion cited)

French Croix de Guerre with Palm, World War II, Streamer embroidered **MOSELLE RIVER** (10th Armored Infantry Battalion cited)

French Croix de Guerre, World War II, Fourragere (10th Armored Infantry Battalion cited)

Company F, 51st Infantry

LINEAGE

1917   Constituted 15 May as Company F, 51st Infantry, Regular Army; organized 16 June at Chickamauga Park, GA; and assigned 16 November to 6th Division

Company lineage follows that of 51st Infantry from 1917 through 1943 reorganization

1946   Converted and redesignated 1 May as Troop C, 10th Constabulary Squadron, an element of the 14th Constabulary Regiment

1948   Inactivated 20 December in Germany, converted and redesignated as Company C, 10th Armored Infantry Battalion, an element of the 4th Armored Division

1953   Redesignated 25 February as Company C, 510th Armored Infantry Battalion, an element of 4th Armored Division

1954   Activated 15 June at Fort Hood, TX

1957   Inactivated 1 April and relieved from assignment to 4th Armored Division

1959	Redesignated 1 July as Headquarters and Headquarters Company, 6th Battle Group, 51st Infantry
1967	Redesignated 11 August as Company F, 51st Infantry, and activated 25 September in Vietnam
1968	Inactivated 26 December in Vietnam

CAMPAIGN PARTICIPATION

World War I

Meuse-Argonne
Alsace 1918

World War II-EAME

Normandy
Northern France
Rhineland
Ardennes-Alsace
Central Europe

Vietnam

Counteroffensive, Phase III
Tet Counteroffensive
Counteroffensive, Phase IV
Counteroffensive, Phase V
Counteroffensive, Phase VI

DECORATIONS

Presidential Unit Citation (Army), Streamer embroidered **ARDENNES** (4th Armored Division cited)

Valorous Unit award, Streamer embroidered **SAIGON-LONG BINH** (Company F, 51st Infantry cited)

French Croix de Guerre with Palm, World War II, Streamer embroidered **NORMANDY** (10th Armored Infantry Battalion cited)

French Croix de Guerre with Palm, World War II, Streamer embroidered **MOSELLE RIVER** (10th Armored Infantry Battalion cited)

French Croix de Guerre, World War II, Fourragere (10th Armored Infantry Battalion cited)

Vietnamese Cross of Gallantry with Palm, Streamer embroidered **VIETNAM 1968** (Company F, 51st Infantry cited)

52D INFANTRY
(Ready Rifles)

COAT OF ARMS

Motto: *Fortis et Certus* (Brave and True)

Symbolism: The shield is blue for infantry. The charges on the canton represent the 11th Infantry from whose personnel this regiment was organized. Its first combat service was in the Gérardmer Sector in the province of Alsace, a short distance west of Colmar; therefore, a mace taken from the arms of Colmar has been used for the crest. The bend from the arms of Alsace is charged with the 6th Division shoulder sleeve insignia to show that the regiment was with that division in France during World War I.

DISTINCTIVE INSIGNIA

The distinctive insignia is the shield and motto of the coat of arms.

LINEAGE

1917	Constituted 15 May as 52d Infantry, Regular Army; organized 16 June at Chickamauga Park, GA, and assigned 16 November to 6th Division
1921	Inactivated 1 September at Camp Grant, IL
1927	Relieved 15 August from assignment to 6th Division and assigned to 9th Division
1933	Relieved 1 October from assignment to 9th Division and assigned to 6th Division
1940	Relieved 1 October from assignment to 6th Division
1942	Redesignated 15 July as 52d Armored Infantry, assigned to 9th Armored Division, and activated at Fort Riley, KS
1943	Regiment broken up 9 October and elements reorganized and redesignated as elements of the 9th Armored Division as follows: 52d Armored Infantry (less 1st, 2d, and 3d Battalions) formed 52d Armored Infantry Battalion; 1st Battalion formed 60th Armored Infantry Battalion; 2d Battalion formed 27th Armored Infantry Battalion; 3d Battalion disbanded
1945	Battalions inactivated 13 October at Camp Patrick Henry, VA
1950	Relieved 14 September from assignment to 9th Armored division and consolidated to form 52d Infantry, an element of the 71st Infantry Division
1953	Relieved 25 February from assignment to 71st Infantry Division, regiment broken up and elements redesignated as elements of the 9th Armored Division as follows: 52d Infantry (less 1st, 2d, and 3d Battalions) formed 52d Infantry Battalion; 1st Battalion formed 560th Armored Infantry Battalion; 2d Battalion formed 527th Armored Infantry Battalion; former 3d Battalion reconstituted as 528th Armored Infantry Battalion
1956	Relieved 23 July from assignment to 9th Armored Infantry and activated 15 August at Vicenza, Italy
1957	The 560th, 527th, and 528th Armored Infantry Battalions relieved 1 March from assignment to 9th Armored Division
1958	Inactivated 24 June at Vicenza, Italy
1959	The 52d, 560th, 527th, and 528th Armored Infantry Battalions consolidated 1 July to form 52d Infantry, a parent regiment under CARS

CAMPAIGN PARTICIPATION

World War I

Meuse-Argonne
Alsace 1918

World War II

Rhineland
Ardennes-Alsace
Central Europe

Vietnam

Counteroffensive,
Phase II
Counteroffensive,
Phase III
Tet Counteroffensive
Counteroffensive,
Phase IV
Counteroffensive,
Phase V
Counteroffensive,
Phase VI
Tet 69 Counteroffensive
Summer–Fall 1969
Winter–Spring 1970
Sanctuary
Counteroffensive
Counteroffensive,
Phase VII
Consolidation I
Consolidation II
Cease-Fire

DECORATIONS

Presidential Unit Citation (Army), Streamer embroidered **BASTOGNE** (52d Armored Infantry Battalion cited)

Presidential Unit Citation (Army), Streamer embroidered **REMAGEN BRIDGEHEAD** (52d and 27th Armored Infantry Battalions cited)

Presidential Unit Citation (Army), Streamer embroidered **SAIGON–TET OFFENSIVE** (Company C, 52d Infantry cited)

Meritorious Unit Commendations, Streamer embroidered **VIETNAM 1967** (Company D, 52d Infantry cited)

Meritorious Unit Commendation, Streamer embroidered **VIETNAM 1968** (Company C and Company D, 52d Infantry cited)

Meritorious Unit Commendation, Streamer embroidered **VIETNAM 1968–1969** (Company C, 52d Infantry cited)

Belgian Croix de Guerre 1940 with Palm, Streamer embroidered **BASTOGNE**; cited in the Order of the Day of the Belgian Army for action at **BASTOGNE** (52d Armored Infantry Battalion cited)

1st Battalion, 52d Infantry
(Ready Rifles)

LINEAGE

1917   Constituted 15 May as Company A, 52d Infantry, Regular Army

Company lineage follows that of 52d Infantry from 1917 through 1943 reorganization

1943   Reorganized and redesignated 9 October as Company A, 60th Armored Infantry Battalion, an element of the 9th Armored Division

1945   Inactivated 13 October at Camp Patrick Henry, VA

1950   Redesignated 14 September as Company A, 52d Infantry, an element of the 71st Infantry Division

1953   Redesignated 25 February as Company A, 560th Armored Infantry Company, an element of the 9th Armored division

1957   Redesignated 1 March as Headquarters and Headquarters Company, 1st Armored Rifle Battalion, 52d Infantry; relieved from assignment to 9th Armored Division and activated at Fort Hood, TX

1962   Reorganized and redesignated 3 February as 1st Battalion, 52d Infantry, and assigned to 1st Armored Division

1967   Relieved 12 May from assignment to 1st Armored Division and assigned to 198th Infantry Brigade

1969   Relieved 15 February from assignment to 198th Infantry Brigade and assigned to 23d Infantry Division

CAMPAIGN PARTICIPATION

World War I
Meuse-Argonne
Alsace 1918

World War II
Rhineland
Ardennes-Alsace
Central Europe

Vietnam
Counteroffensive, Phase III
Tet Counteroffensive
Counteroffensive, Phase IV
Counteroffensive, Phase V
Counteroffensive, Phase VI
Tet 69 Counteroffensive
Summer–Fall 1969
Winter–Spring 1970
Sanctuary Counteroffensive
Counteroffensive, Phase VII
Consolidation I

DECORATIONS

Presidential Unit Citation (Army), Streamer embroidered **BASTOGNE**

Presidential Unit Citation (Army), Streamer embroidered **REMAGEN BRIDGEHEAD**

2d Battalion, 52d Infantry
(Ready Rifles)

LINEAGE

1917   Constituted 15 May as Company A, 52d Infantry, Regular Army

Company lineage follows that of 52d Infantry from 1917 through 1943 reorganization

1943   Reorganized and redesignated 9 October as Company B, 60th Armored Infantry Battalion, an element of the 9th Armored Division

1945   Inactivated 13 October at Camp Patrick Henry, VA

1950   Redesignated 14 September as Company B, 52d Infantry, an element of the 71st Infantry Division

1953	Redesignated 25 February as Company B, 560th Infantry Battalion, an element of the 9th Armored division
1957	Relieved 1 March from assignment to 9th Armored Division, redesignated 30 August as Headquarters and Headquarters Company, 2d Armored Rifle Battalion, 52d Infantry; activated 1 October in Germany and assigned to 3d Armored Division
1962	Reorganized and redesignated 3 February as 2d Battalion, 52d Infantry; relieved from assignment to 3d Armored Division and assigned to 1st Armored Division
1963	Inactivated 10 September at Ford Hood, TX
1967	Inactivated 12 May at Fort Hood, TX

CAMPAIGN PARTICIPATION

World War I

Meuse-Argonne
Alsace 1918

World War II

Rhineland
Ardennes-Alsace
Central Europe

DECORATIONS

Presidential Unit Citation (Army), Streamer embroidered **BASTOGNE**

Presidential Unit Citation (Army), Streamer embroidered **REMAGEN BRIDGEHEAD**

COMPANY C, 52D INFANTRY
(Ready Rifles)

LINEAGE

1917	Constituted 15 May as Company C, 52d Infantry
	Company lineage follows that of 52d Infantry from 1917 through 1943 reorganization
1943	Reorganized and redesignated 9 October as Company C, 60th Armored Infantry Battalion, an element of the 9th Armored Division
1945	Inactivated 13 October at Camp Patrick Henry, VA
1950	Redesignated 14 September as Company C, 52d Infantry, an element of the 71st Infantry Division
1953	Redesignated 25 February as Company C, 560th Infantry Battalion, an element of the 9th Armored division
1957	Relieved 1 March from assignment to 9th Armored Division
1959	Redesignated 1 July as Headquarters and Headquarters Company, 3d Battle Group, 52d Infantry
1966	Redesignated 23 March as Company C, 52d Infantry, and activated 1 June at Fort Lewis, WA

CAMPAIGN PARTICIPATION

World War I

Meuse-Argonne
Alsace 1918

World War II-EAME

Rhineland
Ardennes-Alsace
Central Europe

Vietnam

Counteroffensive, Phase II
Counteroffensive, Phase III
Tet Counteroffensive

Counteroffensive, Phase IV
Counteroffensive, Phase V
Counteroffensive, Phase VI
Tet 69 Counteroffensive
Summer–Fall 1969
Winter–Spring 1970
Sanctuary Counteroffensive
Counteroffensive, Phase VII
Consolidation I
Consolidation II
Cease-Fire

DECORATIONS

Presidential Unit Citation (Army), Streamer embroidered **SAIGON–TET OFFENSIVE** (Company C, 52d Infantry cited)

Meritorious Unit Commendation, Streamer embroidered **VIETNAM 1968** (Company C, 52d Infantry cited)

Meritorious Unit Commendation, Streamer embroidered **VIETNAM 1968–1969** (Company C, 52d Infantry cited)

COMPANY D, 52D INFANTRY
(Ready Rifles)

LINEAGE

1917   Constituted 15 May as Company D, 52d Infantry, Regular Army

Company lineage follows that of 52d Infantry from 1917 through 1943 reorganization

1943   Reorganized and redesignated 9 October as Company A, 27th Armored Infantry Battalion, an element of the 9th Armored Division

1945   Inactivated 13 October at Camp Patrick Henry, VA

1950   Redesignated 14 September as Company E, 52d Infantry, an element of the 71st Infantry Division

1953   Redesignated 25 February as Company A, 527th Infantry Battalion, an element of the 9th Armored Division

1957   Relieved 1 March from assignment to 9th Armored Division

1959   Redesignated 1 July as Headquarters and Headquarters Company, 4th Battle Group, 52d Infantry

1966   Redesignated 23 March as Company D, 52d Infantry, and activated 1 June at Fort Lewis, WA

1969   Inactivated 22 November in Vietnam

CAMPAIGN PARTICIPATION

World War I
   Meuse-Argonne
   Alsace 1918

World War II-EAME
   Rhineland
   Ardennes-Alsace
   Central Europe

Vietnam
   Counteroffensive,
    Phase II

Counteroffensive,
  Phase III
Tet Counteroffensive
Counteroffensive,
  Phase IV
Counteroffensive,
  Phase V
Counteroffensive,
  Phase VI
Tet 69 Counteroffensive
Summer–Fall 1969
Winter–Spring 1970

DECORATIONS

Presidential Unit Citation (Army), Streamer embroidered REMAGEN BRIDGEHEAD (27th Armored Infantry Battalion cited)

Meritorious Unit Commendation, Streamer embroidered VIETNAM 1967 (Company D, 52d Infantry cited)

Meritorious Unit Commendation, Streamer embroidered VIETNAM 1968 (Company D, 52d Infantry cited)

Cited in the Order of the Day of the Belgian Army for action in the ARDENNES (27th Armored Infantry Battalion cited)

COMPANY E, 52D INFANTRY
(Ready Rifles)

LINEAGE

1917   Constituted 15 May as Company E, 52d Infantry, Regular Army

Company lineage follows that of 52d Infantry from 1917 through 1943 reorganization

1943   Reorganized and redesignated 9 October as Company B, 27th Armored Infantry Battalion, an element of the 9th Armored Division

1945   Inactivated 13 October at Camp Patrick Henry, VA

1950   Redesignated 14 September as Company F, 52d Infantry, an element of the 71st Infantry Division

1953   Redesignated 25 February as Company B, 527th Infantry Battalion, an element of the 9th Armored Division

1957	Relieved 1 March from assignment to 9th Armored division
1959	Redesignated 1 July as Headquarters and Headquarters Company, 5th Battle Group, 52d Infantry
1967	Redesignated 20 December as Company E, 52d Infantry, and activated in Vietnam
1969	Inactivated 1 February in Vietnam

CAMPAIGN PARTICIPATION

World War I

Meuse-Argonne
Alsace 1918

World War II-EAME

Rhineland
Ardennes-Alsace
Central Europe

Vietnam

Counteroffensive,
Phase III
Tet Counteroffensive
Counteroffensive,
Phase IV
Counteroffensive,
Phase V
Counteroffensive,
Phase VI

DECORATIONS

Presidential Unit Citation (Army), Streamer embroidered **REMAGEN BRIDGEHEAD** (27th Armored Infantry Battalion cited)

Cited in the Order of the Day of the Belgian Army for action in the **ARDENNES** (27th Armored Infantry Battalion cited)

Vietnamese Cross of Gallantry with Palm, Streamer embroidered **VIETNAM 1967–1969** (Company E, 52d Infantry cited)

COMPANY F, 52D INFANTRY
(Ready Rifles)

LINEAGE

1917	Constituted 15 May as Company F, 52d Infantry, Regular Army
	Company lineage follows that of 52d Infantry from 1917 through 1943 reorganization
1943	Reorganized and redesignated 9 October as Company C, 27th Armored Infantry Battalion, an element of the 9th Armored Division
1945	Inactivated 13 October at Camp Patrick Henry, VA
1950	Redesignated 14 September as Company G, 52d Infantry, an element of the 71st Infantry Division
1953	Redesignated 25 February as Company C, 527th Infantry Battalion, an element of the 9th Armored division
1957	Relieved 1 March from assignment to 9th Armored division
1959	Redesigned 1 July as Headquarters and Headquarters Company, 6th Battle Group, 52d Infantry
1967	Redesignated 20 December as Company F, 52d Infantry, and activated in Vietnam
1969	Inactivated 1 February in Vietnam

CAMPAIGN PARTICIPATION

World War I

Meuse-Argonne
Alsace 1918

World War II-EAME

Rhineland
Ardennes-Alsace
Central Europe

Vietnam

Counteroffensive,
Phase III
Tet Counteroffensive
Counteroffensive,
Phase IV
Counteroffensive,
Phase V
Counteroffensive,
Phase VI

DECORATIONS

Presidential Unit Citation (Army), Streamer embroidered **REMAGEN BRIDGEHEAD** (27th Armored Infantry Battalion cited)

Cited in the Order of the Day of the Belgian Army for action in the **ARDENNES** (27th Armored Infantry Battalion cited)

Vietnamese Cross of Gallantry with Palm, Streamer embroidered **VIETNAM 1967–1968** (Company F, 52d Infantry cited)

54TH INFANTRY

COAT OF ARMS

Motto: I Will Cast My Shoe Over It

Symbolism: This regiment was originally organized with personnel from the 6th Infantry, which is represented on the canton. The shield is blue for infantry with a gold bend taken from the arms of Alsace where the regiment saw its first combat service. The ragged tree trunk is for the Meuse-Argonne campaign.

The crest is the insignia of the 6th Division, with which the regiment served during World War I, charged with a mailed foot to commemorate the march from the Vosges to the Argonne and back to southern France.

DISTINCTIVE INSIGNIA

The distinctive insignia is the shield of the coat of arms.

LINEAGE

1917   Constituted 15 May as 54th Infantry, Regular Army; organized 16 June at Chickamauga Park, Georgia and assigned 16 November to 6th Division

1922   Inactivated 24 October at Fort Wayne, Michigan

1923   Relieved 24 March from assignment to 6th Division and assigned to 7th Division

1940   Relieved 1 October from assignment to 7th Division

1942   Redesignated 14 June as 54th Armored Infantry and activated 15 July at Fort Benning, Georgia as an element of the 10th Armored Division

1943   Regiment broken up 20 September and elements reorganized as elements of the 10th Armored Division as follows: 54th Armored Infantry (less 1st, 2d, and 3d Battalions) formed 54th Armored Infantry Battalion; 1st Battalion formed 61st Armored Infantry Battalion; 2d Battalion formed 20th Armored Infantry Battalion; 3d Battalion disbanded

1945   Battalions inactivated 13–23 October at Camp Patrick Henry, VA

1950   Relieved 14 September from assignment to 10th Armored Division and consolidated to form 54th Infantry, an element of the 71st Infantry Division

1953   Relieved 25 February from assignment to 71st Infantry Division; regiment broken up and elements redesignated as elements of the 90th Armored Division as follows: 54th Infantry (less 1st, 2d, and 3d Battalions) formed 54th Armored Infantry Battalion; 1st Battalion formed 561st Armored Infantry Battalion; 2d Battalion formed 520th Armored Infantry Battalion; former 3d Battalion reconstituted as 554th Armored Infantry Battalion

1957   Battalions relieved 1 April from assignment to 10th Armored Division

1959   The 54th, 561st, 520th, and 554th Armored Infantry Battalions consolidated 1 July to form 54th Infantry, a parent regiment under CARS

CAMPAIGN PARTICIPATION

World War I
    Meuse-Argonne
    Alsace 1918

World War II
    Rhineland
    Ardennes-Alsace
    Central Europe

Vietnam
    Counteroffensive, Phase II
    Counteroffensive, Phase III
    Tet Counteroffensive
    Counteroffensive, Phase IV
    Counteroffensive, Phase V
    Counteroffensive, Phase VI
    Tet 69 Counteroffensive
    Summer-Fall 1959
    Winter-Spring 1970
    Sanctuary Counteroffensive
    Counteroffensive, Phase VII
    Consolidation I
    Consolidation II
    Cease-Fire

DECORATIONS

Presidential Unit Citation (Army), Streamer embroidered **BASTOGNE** (54th Armored Infantry Battalion [less Companies A and C] and 20th Armored Infantry Battalion [less Company A] cited)

Meritorious Unit Commendation, Streamer embroidered **VIETNAM 1967–1968** (Company C, 54th Infantry cited)

Belgian Croix de Guerre 1940 with Palm, Streamer embroidered **BASTOGNE**; cited in the Order of the Day of the Belgian Army for action at **BASTOGNE** (54th Armored Infantry Battalion [less Companies A and C] and 20th Armored Infantry Battalion [less Company A] cited)

1st Battalion, 54th Infantry

LINEAGE

1917   Constituted 15 May as Company A, 54th Infantry, Regular Army

    Company lineage follows that of 54th Infantry from 1917 through 1943 reorganization

1943   Reorganized and redesignated 20 September as Company A, 61st Armored Infantry Battalion, an element of 10th Armored Division

1945   Inactivated 23 October at Camp Patrick Henry, VA

1950	Redesignated 14 September as Company A, 54th Infantry, an element of the 71st Infantry Division
1953	Redesignated 25 February as Company A, 561st Armored Infantry Battalion, an element of the 10th Armored Division
1957	Redesignated as Headquarters and Headquarters Company, 1st Armored Rifle Battalion, 54th Infantry; relieved from assignment to 10th Armored Division, assigned to the 4th Armored Division and activated at Fort Hood, TX
1963	Reorganized and redesignated 5 June as 1st Battalion, 54th Infantry

CAMPAIGN PARTICIPATION

World War I

Meuse-Argonne
Alsace 1918

World War II

Rhineland
Ardennes-Alsace
Central Europe

DECORATIONS

Presidential Unit Citation (Army), Streamer embroidered **BASTOGNE**

2D BATTALION, 54TH INFANTRY

LINEAGE

1917	Constituted 15 May as Company A, 54th Infantry, Regular Army
	Company lineage follows that of 54th Infantry from 1917 through 1943 reorganization
1943	Reorganized and redesignated 20 September as Company B, 61st Armored Infantry Battalion, an element of the 10th Armored Division
1945	Inactivated 23 October at Camp Patrick Henry, VA
1950	Redesignated 14 September as Company B, 54th Infantry, an element of the 71st Infantry Division
1953	Redesignated 25 February as Company B, 561st Armored Infantry Battalion, an element of the 10th Armored Division
1957	Relieved 1 April from assignment to 10th Armored Division, redesignated 29 August as Headquarters and Headquarters Company, 2d Armored Rifle Battalion, 54th Infantry, and activated 23 September at Fort Knox, KY
1963	Reorganized and redesignated 15 July as 2d Battalion, 54th Infantry, and assigned to 4th Armored Division

CAMPAIGN PARTICIPATION

World War I

Meuse-Argonne
Alsace 1918

World War II

Rhineland
Ardennes-Alsace
Central Europe

DECORATIONS

Presidential Unit Citation (Army), Streamer embroidered **BASTOGNE**

COMPANY C, 54TH INFANTRY

LINEAGE

1917   Constituted 15 May as Company C, 54th Infantry

Company lineage follows that of 54th Infantry from 1917 through 1943 reorganization

1943   Reorganized and redesignated 20 September as Company C, 61st Armored Infantry Battalion, an element of the 10th Armored Division

1945   Inactivated 23 October at Camp Patrick Henry, VA

1950   Redesignated 14 September as Company C, 54th Infantry, an element of the 71st Infantry Division

1953   Redesignated 25 February as Company C, 561st Armored Infantry Battalion, an element of the 10th Armored Division

1959   Redesignated 1 July as Headquarters and Headquarters Company, 3d Battle Group, 54th Infantry

1966   Redesignated 23 March as Company C, 54th Infantry, and activated 1 June at Fort Lewis, WA

CAMPAIGN PARTICIPATION

World War I
Meuse-Argonne
Alsace 1918

World War II-EAME
Rhineland
Ardennes-Alsace
Central Europe

Vietnam
Counteroffensive, Phase II
Counteroffensive, Phase III
Tet Counteroffensive
Counteroffensive, Phase IV
Counteroffensive, Phase V
Counteroffensive, Phase VI
Tet 69 Counteroffensive
Summer-Fall 1959
Winter-Spring 1970
Sanctuary Counteroffensive
Counteroffensive, Phase VII
Consolidation I
Consolidation II
Cease-Fire

DECORATIONS

Meritorious Unit Commendation, Streamer embroidered **VIETNAM 1967–1968** (Company C, 54th Infantry cited)

4TH BATTALION, 54TH INFANTRY

LINEAGE

1917   Constituted 15 May as Company D, 54th Infantry, Regular Army

Company lineage follows that of 54th Infantry from 1917 through 1943 reorganization

1943   Reorganized and redesignated 20 September as Company A, 20th Armored Infantry Battalion, an element of the 10th Armored Division

1945   Inactivated 23 October at Camp Patrick Henry, VA

1950   Redesignated 14 September as Company E, 54th Infantry, an element of the 71st Infantry Division

1953   Redesignated 25 February as Company A, 520th Armored Infantry Battalion, an element of the 10th Armored Division

1957   Relieved 1 April from assignment to 10th Armored Division

1959   Redesignated 1 July as Headquarters and Headquarters Company, 4th Battle Group, 54th Infantry

1963   Redesignated 18 April as Headquarters and Headquarters Company, 4th Armored Rifle Battalion, 54th Infantry; activated 15 July at Fort Knox, KY, and reorganized and redesignated 24 September as 4th Battalion, 54th Infantry

1968   Assigned 15 April to 194th Armored Brigade

CAMPAIGN PARTICIPATION

World War I

Meuse-Argonne
Alsace 1918

World War II

Rhineland
Ardennes-Alsace
Central Europe

DECORATIONS

Presidential Unit Citation (Army), Streamer embroidered **BASTOGNE**

COMPANY E, 54TH INFANTRY

LINEAGE

1917   Constituted 15 May as Company E, Regular Army

Company lineage follows that of 54th Infantry from 1917 through 1943 reorganization

1943   Reorganized and redesignated 20 September as Company B, 20th Armored Infantry Battalion, an element of the 10th Armored Division

1945   Inactivated 23 October at Camp Patrick Henry, VA

1950   Redesignated 14 September as Company F, 54th Infantry, an element of the 71st Infantry Division

1953   Redesignated 25 February as Company B, 520th Armored Infantry Battalion, an element of the 10th Armored Division

1957   Relieved 1 April from assignment to 10th Armored Division

1959   Redesignated 1 July as Headquarters and Headquarters Company, 5th Battle Group, 54th Infantry

1967   Redesignated 25 July as Company E, 54th Infantry and activated at Fort Stewart, GA

CAMPAIGN PARTICIPATION

World War I

Meuse-Argonne
Alsace 1918

World War II—EAME

Rhineland
Ardennes-Alsace
Central Europe

DECORATIONS

Presidential Unit Citation (Army), Streamer embroidered **BASTOGNE** (20th Armored Infantry Battalion [less Company A] cited)

Belgian Croix de Guerre 1940 with Palm, Streamer embroidered **BASTOGNE**; cited in the Order of the Day of the Belgian Army for action at **BASTOGNE** (20th Armored Infantry Battalion [less Company A] cited)

58TH INFANTRY
(The Patriots)

COAT OF ARMS

Motto: Love of Country

Symbolism: The field is blue for infantry. The regiment was originally organized with personnel from the 4th Infantry, as shown by the small shield. The broken chevron commemorates the piercing of the German line during World War I between Soissons and Rheims, which are represented by the silver and gold fleurs-de-lis taken from the arms of those cities, respectively.

The torpedo in the crest commemorates the first losses of the regiment on 23 May 1918, when the troop ship *Moldavia* carrying part of the unit was torpedoed by the Germans. World War I service in France as an element of the 4th Division is shown by the ivy leaf from the divisional shoulder sleeve insignia.

DISTINCTIVE INSIGNIA

The distinctive insignia is the shield and motto of the coat of arms.

LINEAGE

1917	Constituted 15 May as the 58th Infantry, Regular Army; organized 5 June at Gettysburg National Park, PA, and assigned 19 November to the 4th Division
1922	Inactivated 21 June at Fort George Wright, WA, demobilized 31 July and relieved from assignment to 4th Division
1942	Reconstituted 8 April as the 58th Infantry, Regular Army; activated 24 April at Fort Lewis, WA
1944	Regiment broken up 26 January and its elements reorganized and redesignated as follows: Headquarters disbanded; 1st Battalion formed the 203d Infantry Battalion, 2d Battalion formed the 204th Infantry Battalion; 3d Battalion formed the 205th Infantry Battalion
1959	The 58th, 43d, and 45th Armored Infantry Battalions consolidated 1 July to form the 58th Infantry, a parent regiment under CARS

CAMPAIGN PARTICIPATION

World War I
Aisne-Marne
St. Mihiel
Meuse-Argonne
Champagne 1918
Lorraine 1918

World War II
Aleutian Islands
Rhineland
Ardennes-Alsace
Central Europe

Vietnam
Counteroffensive,
  Phase II
Counteroffensive,
  Phase III
Tet Counteroffensive
Counteroffensive,
  Phase IV
Counteroffensive,
  Phase V
Counteroffensive,
  Phase VI
Tet 69 Counteroffensive
Summer-Fall 1969
Winter-Spring 1970
Sanctuary
  Counteroffensive
Counteroffensive, Phase
  VII
Consolidation I
Consolidation II
Cease-Fire

DECORATIONS

Meritorious Unit Commendation, Streamer embroidered **VIETNAM 1967–1968** (Company D, 58th Infantry cited)

1ST BATTALION, 58TH INFANTRY
(The Patriots)

LINEAGE

1917	Constituted 15 May as Company A, 58th Infantry, Regular Army; organized 5 June at Gettysburg National Park, PA, and assigned 19 November to the 4th Division
	Company lineage follows that of 58th Infantry from 1917 through 1942 activation at Fort Lewis, WA
1944	Reorganized and redesignated 26 January as Company A, 203d Infantry Battalion
1945	Inactivated 2 March at Camp Shelby, MS
1951	Consolidated 10 July with Company A, 58th Armored Infantry Battalion; consolidated unit designated Company A, 58th Armored Infantry Battalion

Company A, 58th Armored Infantry Battalion lineage differs from that of Company A, 203d Infantry Battalion from its constitution through 1951 consolidation as follows:

1917	*Constituted 15 May as Company A, 49th Infantry, Regular Army; organized 1 June at Syracuse, NY*
1921	*Inactivated 18 November at Fort Snelling, MN*
1922	*Demobilized 31 July*
1942	*Reconstituted 1 April as Company A, 49th Armored Infantry, and activated at Fort Knox, KY, as an element of the 8th Armored Division*
1943	*Reorganized and redesignated 20 September as Company A, 58th Armored Infantry Battalion, an element of the 8th Armored Division*
1945	*Inactivated 11 November at Camp Kilmer, NJ*

1956	Relieved 23 July from assignment to 8th Armored Division and activated 15 August in Germany
1957	Inactivated 9 August in Germany
1959	Redesignated 1 July as Headquarters and Headquarters Company, 1st Battle Group, 58th Infantry
1960	Redesignated 18 March as Headquarters and Headquarters Company, 1st Armored Rifle Battalion, 58th Infantry, and activated 16 May at Fort Benning, GA, an element of the 1st Infantry Brigade
1962	Relieved 20 September from assignment to 1st Infantry Brigade and assigned to the 197th Infantry Brigade; reorganized and redesignated 24 September as 1st Battalion, 58th Infantry

CAMPAIGN PARTICIPATION

World War I
Aisne-Marne
St. Mihiel
Meuse-Argonne
Champagne 1918
Lorraine 1918

World War II
Aleutian Islands
Rhineland
Ardennes-Alsace
Central Europe

DECORATIONS

None.

2D ARMORED RIFLE BATTALION, 58TH INFANTRY
(The Patriots)

LINEAGE

1917	Constituted 15 May as Company B, 58th Infantry, Regular Army; organized 5 June at Gettysburg National Park, PA, and assigned 19 November to the 4th Division
	Company lineage follows that of 58th Infantry from 1917 through 1942 activation at Fort Lewis, WA
1944	Reorganized and redesignated 26 January as Company B, 203d Infantry Battalion
1945	Inactivated 2 March at Camp Shelby, MS
1951	Consolidated 10 July with Company B, 58th Armored Infantry Battalion; consolidated unit designated Company B, 58th Armored Infantry Battalion, an element of the 8th Armored Division
	Company B, 58th Armored Infantry Battalion lineage differs from that of Company B, 203d Infantry Battalion from its constitution through 1951 consolidation as follows:
1917	*Constituted 15 May as Company B, 49th Infantry, Regular Army; organized 1 June at Syracuse, NY*

1921	*Inactivated 18 November at Fort Snelling, MN*
1922	*Demobilized 31 July*
1942	*Reconstituted 1 April as Company B, 49th Armored Infantry, and activated at Fort Knox, KY, as an element of the 8th Armored Division*
1943	*Reorganized and redesignated 20 September as Company B, 58th Armored Infantry Battalion, an element of the 8th Armored Division*
1945	*Inactivated 11 November at Camp Kilmer, NJ*
1956	Relieved 23 July from assignment to 8th Armored Division and activated 15 August in Germany
1957	Reorganized and redesignated 1 July as Headquarters and Headquarters Company, 2d Armored Rifle Battalion, 58th Infantry, and assigned to the 2d Armored Division
1963	Inactivated 1 July at Fort Hood, TX, and relieved from assignment to 2d Armored Division

CAMPAIGN PARTICIPATION

World War I

Aisne-Marne
St. Mihiel
Meuse-Argonne
Champagne 1918
Lorraine 1918

World War II

Aleutian Islands
Rhineland
Ardennes-Alsace
Central Europe

DECORATIONS

None.

COMPANY C, 58TH INFANTRY
(The Patriots)

LINEAGE

1917	Constituted 15 May as Company C, 58th Infantry, Regular Army; organized 5 June at Gettysburg National Park, PA, and assigned 19 November to the 4th Division

Company lineage follows that of 58th Infantry from 1917 through 1942 activation at Fort Lewis, WA

1944	Reorganized and redesignated 26 January as Company C, 203d Infantry Battalion
1945	Inactivated 2 March at Camp Shelby, MS
1951	Consolidated 10 July with Company C, 58th Armored Infantry Battalion; consolidated unit designated Company C, 58th Armored Infantry Battalion, an element of the 8th Armored Division

Company C, 58th Armored Infantry Battalion lineage differs from that of Company C, 203d Infantry Battalion from its constitution through 1951 consolidation as follows:

1917	Constituted 15 May as Company C, 49th Infantry, Regular Army; organized 1 June at Syracuse, NY
1921	Inactivated 18 November at Fort Snelling, MN
1922	Demobilized 31 July
1942	Reconstituted 1 April as Company C, 49th Armored Infantry, Regular Army; activated at Fort Knox, KY, as an element of the 8th Armored Division
1943	Reorganized and redesignated 20 September as Company C, 58th Armored Infantry Battalion, an element of the 8th Armored Division

1945	Inactivated 11 November at Camp Kilmer, NJ
1956	Relieved 23 July from assignment to 8th Armored Division and activated 15 August in Germany
1957	Inactivated 9 August in Germany
1959	Redesignated 1 July as Headquarters and Headquarters Company, 3d Battle Group, 58th Infantry
1962	Redesignated 2 October as Company C, 58th Infantry, and assigned to the 194th Armored Brigade and activated 21 December at Fort Ord, CA
1964	Inactivated 15 May at Fort Ord, CA, and relieved from assignment to the 194th Armored Brigade
1965	Activated 15 May in Germany
1969	Inactivated 10 February at Fort Carson, CO

CAMPAIGN PARTICIPATION

World War I

Aisne-Marne
St. Mihiel
Meuse-Argonne
Champagne 1918
Lorraine 1918

World War II—EAME

Rhineland
Ardennes-Alsace
Central Europe

DECORATIONS

None.

265

COMPANY D, 58TH INFANTRY
(The Patriots)

LINEAGE

1917   Constituted 15 May as Company D, 58th Infantry, Regular Army; organized 5 June at Gettysburg National Park, PA, and assigned 19 November to the 4th Division

Company lineage follows that of 58th Infantry from 1917 through 1942 activation at Fort Lewis, WA

1944   Reorganized and redesignated 26 January as Company D, 203d Infantry Battalion

1945   Inactivated 2 March at Camp Shelby, MS

1951   Consolidated 10 July with Service Company, 58th Armored Infantry Battalion, to form Company D, 58th Armored Infantry Battalion, an element of the 8th Armored Division

Service Company, 58th Armored Infantry Battalion lineage differs from that of Company D, 203d Infantry Battalion from its constitution through 1951 consolidation as follows:

1943   *Constituted 15 September as Service Company, 58th Armored Infantry Battalion, Regular Army; activated 20 September at Camp Polk, LA, as an element of the 8th Armored Division*

1945   *Inactivated 11 November at Camp Kilmer, NJ*

1956   Relieved 26 July from assignment to 8th Armored Division and activated 15 July in Germany

1957   Inactivated 9 August in Germany

1959   Redesignated 1 July as Headquarters and Headquarters Company, 13th Battle Group, 58th Infantry

1966   Redesignated 23 March as Company D, 58th Infantry, and activated 1 June at Fort Lewis, WA

CAMPAIGN PARTICIPATION

World War I
Aisne-Marne
St. Mihiel
Meuse-Argonne
Champagne 1918
Lorraine 1918

World War II—EAME
Rhineland
Ardennes-Alsace
Central Europe

Vietnam
Counteroffensive, Phase II
Counteroffensive, Phase III
Tet Counteroffensive
Counteroffensive, Phase IV
Counteroffensive, Phase V
Counteroffensive, Phase VI
Tet 69 Counteroffensive
Summer-Fall 1969
Winter-Spring 1970
Sanctuary Counteroffensive
Counteroffensive, Phase VII
Consolidation I
Consolidation II
Cease-Fire

DECORATIONS

Meritorious Unit Commendation, Streamer embroidered **VIETNAM 1967–1968** (Company D, 58th Infantry cited)

COMPANY E, 58TH INFANTRY
(The Patriots)

LINEAGE

1917   Constituted 15 May as Company E, 58th Infantry, Regular Army; organized 5 June at Gettysburg National Park, PA, and assigned 19 November to the 4th Division

Company lineage follows that of 58th Infantry from 1917 through 1942 activation at Fort Lewis, WA

1944   Reorganized and redesignated 26 January as Company A, 204th Infantry Battalion

1945   Inactivated 8 March at Camp Shelby, MS

1948   Redesignated 30 September as Company A, 43d Armored Infantry Battalion

1949   Activated 28 January at Fort Sill, OK, as an element of the 2d Armored Division

1957	Inactivated 1 July in Germany and relieved from assignment to 2d Armored Division
1959	Redesignated 1 July as Headquarters and Headquarters Company, 4th Battle Group, 58th Infantry
1967	Redesignated 20 December as Company E, 58th Infantry and activated in Vietnam
1969	Inactivated 1 February in Vietnam

CAMPAIGN PARTICIPATION

World War I

Aisne-Marne
St. Mihiel
Meuse-Argonne
Champagne 1918
Lorraine 1918

World War II—AP

Aleutian Islands

Vietnam

Counteroffensive, Phase III
Tet Counteroffensive
Counteroffensive, Phase IV
Counteroffensive, Phase V
Counteroffensive, Phase VI

DECORATIONS

Vietnamese Cross of Gallantry with Palm, Streamer embroidered **VIETNAM 1967–1969** (Company E, 58th Infantry cited)

Vietnamese Civil Action Honor Medal, First Class, Streamer embroidered **VIETNAM 1967–1969** (Company E, 58th Infantry cited)

COMPANY F, 58TH INFANTRY
(The Patriots)

LINEAGE

| 1917 | Constituted 15 May as Company F, 58th Infantry, Regular Army; organized 5 June at Gettysburg National Park, PA, and assigned 19 November to the 4th Division |

Company lineage follows that of 58th Infantry from 1917 through 1942 activation at Fort Lewis, WA

1944	Reorganized and redesignated 26 January as Company B, 204th Infantry Battalion
1945	Inactivated 8 March at Camp Shelby, MS
1948	Redesignated 30 September as Company B, 43d Armored Infantry Battalion
1949	Activated 28 January at Fort Sill, OK, as an element of the 2d Armored Division
1957	Inactivated 1 July in Germany and relieved from assignment to 2d Armored Division
1959	Redesignated 1 July as Headquarters and Headquarters Company, 5th Battle Group, 58th Infantry
1968	Redesignated 10 January as Company F, 58th Infantry, and activated in Vietnam
1969	Inactivated 1 February in Vietnam

CAMPAIGN PARTICIPATION

World War I

Aisne-Marne
St. Mihiel
Meuse-Argonne
Champagne 1918
Lorraine 1918

World War II—AP

Aleutian Islands

Vietnam

Counteroffensive, Phase III
Tet Counteroffensive
Counteroffensive, Phase IV
Counteroffensive, Phase V
Counteroffensive, Phase VI

DECORATIONS

Vietnamese Cross of Gallantry with Palm, Streamer embroidered **VIETNAM 1968–1969** (Company F, 58th Infantry cited)

60TH INFANTRY

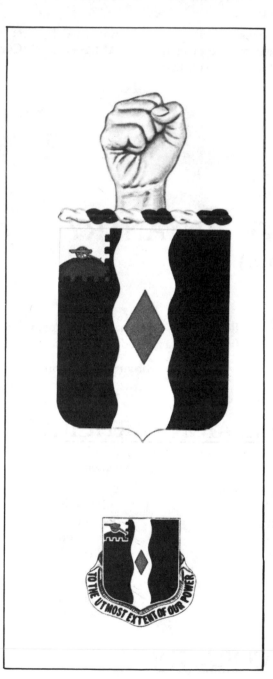

COAT OF ARMS

Motto: To the Utmost Extent of Our Power

Symbolism: This regiment was originally organized with personnel from the 7th Infantry, which is represented on the canton. It participated in World War I as an element of the 5th Division, the insignia of which is carried on the shield. Black, white, and red show engagements against Germany, and the wavy pale is for the Meuse River, the crossing of which near Dun in November 1918 was an outstanding operation of the regiment.

The crest and motto symbolize the spirit of the regiment during the Meuse crossing and are guides for the future conduct of the organization.

DISTINCTIVE INSIGNIA

The distinctive insignia is the shield and motto of the coat of arms.

LINEAGE

1917	Constituted 15 May as 60th Infantry, Regular Army; organized 10 June at Gettysburg National Park, PA, and assigned 17 November to the 5th Division
1921	Inactivated 2 September at Camp Jackson, SC
1927	Relieved 15 August from assignment to 5th Division and assigned to 8th Division
1933	Relieved 1 October from assignment to 8th Division and assigned to 5th Division
1939	Relieved 16 October from assignment to 5th Division
1940	Assigned 1 August to the 9th Division and activated 10 August at Fort Bragg, NC
1946	Inactivated 30 November–28 December in Germany
1947	Activated 15 July at Fort Dix, NJ
1957	Relieved 1 December from assignment to 9th Infantry Division and reorganized as a parent regiment under CARS

CAMPAIGN PARTICIPATION

World War I

St. Mihiel
Meuse-Argonne
Alsace 1918
Lorraine 1918

World War II

Algeria-French Morocco (with arrowhead)
Tunisia
Sicily
Normandy
Northern France
Rhineland
Ardennes-Alsace
Central Europe

Vietnam

Counteroffensive, Phase II
Counteroffensive, Phase III
Tet Counteroffensive
Counteroffensive, Phase IV
Counteroffensive, Phase V
Counteroffensive, Phase VI
Tet 69 Counteroffensive
Summer-Fall 1959
Winter-Spring 1970
Sanctuary Counteroffensive
Counteroffensive, Phase VII

DECORATIONS

Presidential Unit Citation (Army), Streamer embroidered **STE. COLOMBE** (2d Battalion, 60th Infantry cited)

Presidential Unit Citation (Army), Streamer embroidered **SCHWAM-MANAUEL DAMS** (2d Battalion, 60th Infantry cited)

Presidential Unit Citation (Army), Streamer embroidered **SEDJENANE VALLEY** (2d Battalion, 60th Infantry cited)

Presidential Unit Citation (Army), Streamer embroidered **DINH TUONG PROVINCE** (2d Battalion, 60th Infantry cited)

Presidential Unit Citation (Army), Streamer embroidered **MEKONG DELTA** (3d Battalion, 60th Infantry cited)

Valorous Unit Award, Streamer embroidered **SAIGON** (5th Battalion, 60th Infantry cited)

French Croix de Guerre with Palm, World War II, Streamer embroidered **COTENTIN PENINSULA** (60th Infantry cited)

Belgian Fourragere 1940 (60th Infantry cited)

Cited in the Order of the Day of the Belgian Army for action at the **MEUSE RIVER** (60th Infantry cited)

Cited in the Order of the Day of the Belgian Army for action in the **ARDENNES** (60th Infantry cited)

1ST BATTALION, 60TH INFANTRY

LINEAGE

1917	Constituted 15 May as Company A, 60th Infantry, Regular Army; organized 10 June at Gettysburg National Park, PA, and assigned 17 November to the 5th Division
	Company lineage follows that of 60th Infantry from 1917 through 1947 activation at Fort Dix, NJ
1957	Reorganized and redesignated 1 December as Headquarters and Headquarters Company, 1st Battle Group, 60th Infantry, and assigned to the 9th Infantry Division
1962	Inactivated 31 January at Fort Carson, CO
1963	Redesignated 20 May as 1st Battalion, 60th Infantry, relieved from assignment to the 172d Infantry Brigade and activated 1 July in Alaska

CAMPAIGN PARTICIPATION

World War I

St. Mihiel
Meuse-Argonne
Alsace 1918
Lorraine 1918

World War II

Algeria-French Morocco
  (with arrowhead)
Tunisia
Sicily
Normandy
Northern France
Rhineland
Ardennes-Alsace
Central Europe

DECORATIONS

Presidential Unit Citation (Army), Streamer embroidered **STE. COLOMBE**

Presidential Unit Citation (Army), Streamer embroidered **SCHWAM-MANAUEL DAMS**

Presidential Unit Citation (Army), Streamer embroidered **SEDJENANE VALLEY**

French Croix de Guerre with Palm, World War II, Streamer embroidered **COTENTIN PENINSULA** (60th Infantry cited)

Belgian Fourragere 1940 (60th Infantry cited)

Cited in the Order of the Day of the Belgian Army for action at the **MEUSE RIVER** (60th Infantry cited)

Cited in the Order of the Day of the Belgian Army for action in the **ARDENNES** (60th Infantry cited)

2D BATTALION, 60TH INFANTRY

LINEAGE

1917	Constituted 15 May as Company B, 60th Infantry, Regular Army; organized 10 June at Gettysburg National Park, PA, and assigned 17 November to the 5th Division
	Company lineage follows that of 60th Infantry from 1917 through 1947 activation at Fort Dix, NJ
1957	Inactivated 1 December in Germany and relieved from assignment to 9th Infantry Division
1958	Redesignated 12 February as Headquarters and Headquarters Company, 2d Battle Group, 60th Infantry, and activated 15 February at Fort Devens, MA, an element of the 2d Infantry Brigade
1962	Inactivated 19 February at Fort Devens, MA, and relieved 20 April from assignment to 2d Infantry Brigade
1966	Redesignated 1 February as 2d Battalion, 60th Infantry, assigned to the 9th Infantry Division, and activated at Fort Riley, KS
1970	Inactivated 13 October at Fort Lewis, WA

CAMPAIGN PARTICIPATION

World War I

St. Mihiel
Meuse-Argonne
Alsace 1918
Lorraine 1918

World War II

Algeria-French Morocco
  (with arrowhead)
Tunisia
Sicily
Normandy
Northern France

Rhineland
Ardennes-Alsace
Central Europe

Vietnam

Counteroffensive,
  Phase II
Counteroffensive,
  Phase III
Tet Counteroffensive
  (other campaigns to be
  determined)

DECORATIONS

Presidential Unit Citation (Army), Streamer embroidered **STE. COLOMBE**

Presidential Unit Citation (Army), Streamer embroidered **SCHWAM-MANAUEL DAMS**

Presidential Unit Citation (Army), Streamer embroidered **SEDJENANE VALLEY**

Presidential Unit Citation (Army), Streamer embroidered **GERMANY** (Company B, 60th Infantry cited)

Presidential Unit Citation (Army), Streamer embroidered **DINH TUONG PROVINCE** (2d Battalion, 60th Infantry cited)

French Croix de Guerre with Palm, World War II, Streamer embroidered **COTENTIN PENINSULA** (60th Infantry cited)

Belgian Fourragere 1940 (60th Infantry cited)

Cited in the Order of the Day of the Belgian Army for action at the **MEUSE RIVER** (60th Infantry cited)

Cited in the Order of the Day of the Belgian Army for action in the **ARDENNES** (60th Infantry cited)

Vietnamese Cross of Gallantry with Palm, Streamer embroidered **VIETNAM 1966–1968** (2d Battalion, 60th Infantry cited)

Vietnamese Cross of Gallantry with Palm, Streamer embroidered **VIETNAM 1968** (2d Battalion, 60th Infantry cited)

Vietnamese Cross of Gallantry with Palm, Streamer embroidered **VIETNAM 1969** (2d Battalion, 60th Infantry cited)

Vietnamese Civil Action Honor Medal, First Class, Streamer embroidered **VIETNAM 1966–1969** (2d Battalion, 60th Infantry cited)

Company B additionally entitled to: Valorous Unit Award, Streamer embroidered **BEN TRE CITY** (Company B, 2d Battalion, 60th Infantry cited)

3D BATTALION, 60TH INFANTRY

LINEAGE

1917   Constituted 15 May as Company C, 60th Infantry, Regular Army, organized 10 June at Gettysburg National Park, PA, and assigned 17 November to the 5th Division

Company lineage follows that of 60th Infantry from 1917 through 1947 activation at Fort Dix, NJ

1957   Inactivated 1 December in Germany, relieved from assignment to 9th Infantry Division, redesignated as Headquarters and Headquarters Company, 3d Battle Group, 60th Infantry

1966   Redesignated 1 February as Headquarters and Headquarters Company, 3d Battalion, 60th Infantry; assigned to the 9th Infantry Division and activated at Fort Riley, KS

1969   Inactivated 1 August at Fort Riley, KS

CAMPAIGN PARTICIPATION

World War I

St. Mihiel
Meuse-Argonne
Alsace 1918
Lorraine 1918

World War II

Algeria-French Morocco
  (with arrowhead)
Tunisia
Sicily
Normandy
Northern France
Rhineland
Ardennes-Alsace
Central Europe

Vietnam

Counteroffensive,
  Phase II
Counteroffensive,
  Phase III
Tet Counteroffensive
Counteroffensive,
  Phase IV

Counteroffensive,
  Phase V
Counteroffensive,
  Phase VI
Tet 69 Counteroffensive
Summer-Fall 1969

DECORATIONS

Presidential Unit Citation (Army), Streamer embroidered **STE. COLOMBE**

Presidential Unit Citation (Army), Streamer embroidered **SCHWAM-MANAUEL DAMS**

Presidential Unit Citation (Army), Streamer embroidered **SEDJENANE VALLEY**

Presidential Unit Citation (Army), Streamer embroidered **MEKONG DELTA** (3d Battalion, 60th Infantry cited)

French Croix de Guerre with Palm, World War II, Streamer embroidered **COTENTIN PENINSULA** (60th Infantry cited)

Belgian Fourragere 1940 (60th Infantry cited)

Cited in the Order of the Day of the Belgian Army for action at the **MEUSE RIVER** (60th Infantry cited)

Cited in the Order of the Day of the Belgian Army for action in the **ARDENNES** (60th Infantry cited)

Vietnamese Cross of Gallantry with Palm, Streamer embroidered **VIETNAM 1966–1968** (3d Battalion, 60th Infantry cited)

Vietnamese Cross of Gallantry with Palm, Streamer embroidered **VIETNAM 1969** (3d Battalion, 60th Infantry cited)

Vietnamese Civil Action Honor Medal, First Class, Streamer embroidered **VIETNAM 1966–1969** (3d Battalion, 60th Infantry cited)

5TH BATTALION, 60TH INFANTRY

LINEAGE

1917	Constituted 15 May as Company E, 60th Infantry, Regular Army; organized 10 June at Gettysburg National Park, PA, and assigned 17 November to the 5th Division
	Company lineage follows that of 60th Infantry from 1917 through 1947 activation at Fort Dix, NJ
1957	Inactivated 1 December in Germany and relieved from assignment to 9th Infantry Division, and redesignated as Headquarters and Headquarters Company, 5th Battle Group, 60th Infantry
1966	Redesignated 1 February as Headquarters and Headquarters Company, 5th Battalion, 60th Infantry, and assigned to the 9th Infantry Division and activated at Fort Riley, KS
1970	Inactivated 13 October at Fort Lewis, WA

CAMPAIGN PARTICIPATION

World War I

St. Mihiel
Meuse-Argonne
Alsace 1918
Lorraine 1918

World War II

Algeria-French Morocco
  (with arrowhead)
Tunisia
Sicily
Normandy
Northern France
Rhineland
Ardennes-Alsace
Central Europe

Vietnam

Counteroffensive,
  Phase II
Counteroffensive,
  Phase III
Tet Counteroffensive
Counteroffensive,
  Phase IV
Counteroffensive,
  Phase V
Counteroffensive,
  Phase VI
Tet 69 Counteroffensive
Summer-Fall 1969
Winter-Spring 1970
Sanctuary
  Counteroffensive
Counteroffensive
  Phase VII

DECORATIONS

Presidential Unit Citation (Army), Streamer embroidered **STE. COLOMBE** (2d Battalion, 60th Infantry cited)

Presidential Unit Citation (Army), Streamer embroidered **SCHWAM-MANAUEL DAMS** (2d Battalion, 60th Infantry cited)

Presidential Unit Citation (Army), Streamer embroidered **SEDJANANE VALLEY** (2d Battalion, 60th Infantry cited)

Valorous Unit Award, Streamer embroidered **SAIGON** (5th Battalion, 60th Infantry cited)

French Croix de Guerre with Palm, World War II, Streamer embroidered **COTENTIN PENINSULA** (60th Infantry cited)

Belgian Fourragere 1940 (60th Infantry cited)

Cited in the Order of the Day of the Belgian Army for action at the **MEUSE RIVER** (60th Infantry cited)

Cited in the Order of the Day of the Belgian Army for action in the **ARDENNES** (60th Infantry cited)

Vietnamese Cross of Gallantry with Palm, Streamer embroidered **VIETNAM 1966–1968** (5th Battalion, 60th Infantry cited)

Vietnamese Cross of Gallantry with Palm, Streamer embroidered **VIETNAM 1968** (5th Battalion, 60th Infantry cited)

Vietnamese Cross of Gallantry with Palm, Streamer embroidered **VIETNAM 1969** (5th Battalion, 60th Infantry cited)

Vietnamese Civil Action Honor Medal, First Class, Streamer embroidered **VIETNAM 1966–1969** (5th Battalion, 60th Infantry cited)

Company B and Company C each additionally entitled to: Valorous Unit Award, Streamer embroidered **CHOLON-SAIGON** (Company B and Company C, 5th Battalion, 60th Infantry cited)

61ST INFANTRY

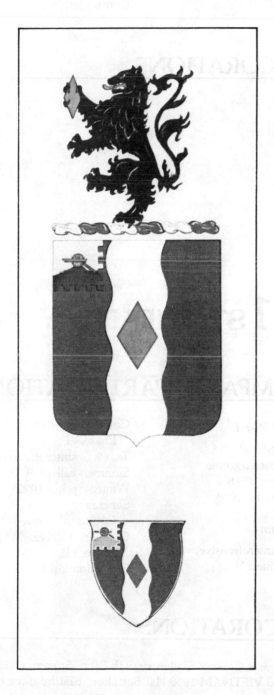

COAT OF ARMS

Motto: The Best Lead the Rest

Symbolism: This regiment was originally organized with personnel from the 7th Infantry, which is represented on the canton. It participated in World War I as an element of the 5th Division, the insignia of which is carried on the shield and also in the crest. The wavy pale represents the Meuse River, the crossing of which near Dun in November 1918 was an outstanding operation of the regiment. The lion of the crest is taken from the arms of Montmédy, the nearest place to Dun having a coat of arms

DISTINCTIVE INSIGNIA

The distinctive insignia is the shield of the coat of arms.

LINEAGE

1917   Constituted 15 May as 61st Infantry, Regular Army; organized 10 June at Gettysburg National Park, PA, and assigned 17 November to the 5th Division

1921   Inactivated 2 September at Camp Jackson, SC

1927   Relieved 15 August from assignment to 5th Division and assigned to 8th Division

1933   Relieved 1 October from assignment to 8th Division and assigned to 5th Division

1939   Relieved 16 October from assignment to 5th Division

1944   Disbanded 11 November

1950   Reconstituted 10 August as an element of 8th Infantry Division, Regular Army, and activated 17 August at Fort Jackson, SC

1956   Inactivated 1 September at Fort Carson, CO, and relieved from assignment to 8th Infantry Division

1962   Reorganized 17 January as a parent regiment under CARS

CAMPAIGN PARTICIPATION

World War I

St. Mihiel
Meuse-Argonne
Alsace 1918
Lorraine 1918

Vietnam

Counteroffensive,
  Phase V

Counteroffensive,
  Phase VI
Tet 69 Counteroffensive
Summer–Fall 1969
Winter–Spring 1970
Sanctuary
  Counteroffensive
Counteroffensive,
  Phase VII
Consolidation I

DECORATIONS

None.

1ST BATTALION, 61ST INFANTRY

LINEAGE

1917   Constituted 15 May as Company A, 61st Infantry, Regular Army; organized 10 June at Gettysburg National Park, PA, and assigned 17 November to the 5th Division

Company lineage follows that of 61st Infantry from 1917 through 1956 relief from assignment to 8th Infantry Division

1962   Redesignated 17 January as Headquarters and Headquarters Company, 1st Battalion, 61st Infantry, and activated 19 February at Fort Carson, CO, as an element of the 5th Infantry Division

CAMPAIGN PARTICIPATION

World War I

St. Mihiel
Meuse-Argonne
Alsace 1918
Lorraine 1918

Vietnam

Counteroffensive,
  Phase V

Counteroffensive,
  Phase VI
Tet 69 Counteroffensive
Summer–Fall 1969
Winter–Spring 1970
Sanctuary
  Counteroffensive
Counteroffensive,
  Phase VII
Consolidation I

DECORATIONS

Vietnamese Cross of Gallantry with Palm, Streamer embroidered **VIETNAM 1968** (1st Battalion, 61st Infantry cited)

2D BATTALION, 61ST INFANTRY

LINEAGE

1917   Constituted 15 May as Company B, 61st Infantry, Regular Army; organized 10 June at Gettysburg National Park, PA, and assigned 17 November to the 5th Division

Company lineage follows that of 61st Infantry from 1917 through 1956 relief from assignment to 8th Infantry Division

1962   Redesignated 17 January as Headquarters and Headquarters Company, 2d Battalion, 61st Infantry, and activated 19 February at Fort Carson, CO, as an element of the 5th Infantry Division

1970   Relieved 15 December from assignment to 5th Infantry Division and assigned to the 4th Infantry Division

CAMPAIGN PARTICIPATION

World War I

  St. Mihiel
  Meuse-Argonne
  Alsace 1918
  Lorraine 1918

DECORATIONS

None.

3D BATTALION, 61ST INFANTRY

LINEAGE

1917   Constituted 15 May as Company C, 61st Infantry, Regular Army; organized 10 June at Gettysburg National Park, PA, and assigned 17 November to the 5th Division

Company lineage follows that of 61st Infantry from 1917 through 1956 relief from assignment to 8th Infantry Division

1962   Redesignated 17 January as Headquarters and Headquarters Company, 3d Battalion, 61st Infantry

1969   Activated 15 November at Fort Carson, CO, as an element of the 5th Infantry Division

1970   Inactivated 15 December at Fort Carson, CO

CAMPAIGN PARTICIPATION

World War I

  St. Mihiel
  Meuse-Argonne
  Alsace 1918
  Lorraine 1918

DECORATIONS

None.

75TH INFANTRY
(Merrill's Marauders)

COAT OF ARMS

Motto: *Sua Sponte* (Of Their Own Accord)

Symbolism: The colors blue, white, red, and green represent four of the original six combat teams of the 5307th Composite Unit (Provisional), commonly referred to as "Merrill's Maurauders," which were identified by color. (To avoid confusion, the other two colors, khaki and orange, were not represented in the design.) The unit's close co-operation with the Chinese forces in the China-Burma-India theater is represented by the sun symbol from the Chinese flag. The white star represents the Star of Burma, the country in which the Marauders campaigned during World War II. The lightning bolt is symbolic of the strike characteristics of the Marauders' behind-the-line activities.

DISTINCTIVE INSIGNIA

The distinctive insignia is the shield of the coat of arms.

LINEAGE

1943	Organized 3 October in the Army of the United States, China-Burma-India Theater of Operations, as the 5307th Composite Unit (Provisional)
1944	Consolidated 10 August with the 475th Infantry to form the 475th Infantry
1945	Inactivated 1 July in China
1954	Redesignated 21 June as the 75th Infantry, allotted 26 October to the Regular Army and activated 20 November on Okinawa
1956	Inactivated 21 March on Okinawa
1969	Reorganized 1 January as a parent regiment under CARS and companies activated as follows: Company A activated 21 February at Fort Benning, GA; Company B activated 10 February at Fort Carson, CO; Company C activated 1 February in Vietnam; Company D activated 20 November in Vietnam; Company E activated 1 February in Vietnam, inactivated 23 August at Fort Lewis, WA, activated 1 October in Vietnam and inactivated 12 October 1970; Company F activated 1 February in Vietnam; Company G activated 1 February in Vietnam; Company H activated 1 February in Vietnam; Company I activated 1 February in Vietnam, inactivated 7 April; Company K activated 1 February in Vietnam, inactivated 10 December 1970; Company L activated 1 February in Vietnam; Company M activated 1 February in Vietnam, inactivated 12 October 1970; Company N activated 1 February in Vietnam; Company O activated 1 February in Vietnam, inactivated 20 November, activated 4 August in Alaska; Company P activated 1 February in Vietnam

CAMPAIGN PARTICIPATION

World War II

India-Burma
Central Burma

Vietnam

Counteroffensive,
  Phase VI
Tet 69 Counteroffensive

Summer–Fall 1969
Winter–Spring 1970
Sanctuary
  Counteroffensive
Counteroffensive,
  Phase VII
Consolidation I
Consolidation II
Cease-Fire

DECORATIONS

Presidential Unit Citation (Army), Streamer embroidered **MYITKYINA** (5307th Composite Unit cited)

Valorous Unit Award, Streamer embroidered **BINH DUONG PROVINCE** (Company F, 75th Infantry cited)

Valorous Unit Award, Streamer embroidered **THUA THIEN–QUANG TRI** (Company L, 75th Infantry cited)

Meritorious Unit Commendation, Streamer embroidered **VIETNAM 1969** (Company G, 75th Infantry cited)

Meritorious Unit Commendation, Streamer embroidered **VIETNAM 1969–1970** (Company M, 75th Infantry cited)

Company E additionally entitled to: Vietnamese Cross of Gallantry with Palm, Streamer embroidered **VIETNAM 1969** (Company E, 75th Infantry cited); Vietnamese Civil Action Honor Medal, First Class, Streamer embroidered **VIETNAM 1969** (Company E, 75th Infantry cited)

Company F additionally entitled to: Vietnamese Cross of Gallantry with Palm, Streamer embroidered **VIETNAM 1969** (Company F, 75th Infantry cited)

Company H additionally entitled to: Vietnamese Cross of Gallantry with Palm, Streamer embroidered **VIETNAM 1969** (Company H, 75th Infantry cited)

Company I additionally entitled to: Vietnamese Civil Action Honor Medal, First Class, Streamer embroidered **VIETNAM 1969–1970** (Company I, 75th Infantry cited)

Company K additionally entitled to: Vietnamese Cross of Gallantry with Palm, Streamer embroidered **VIETNAM 1969** (Company K, 75th Infantry cited); Vietnamese Civil Action Honor Medal, First Class, Streamer embroidered **VIETNAM 1969** (Company K, 75th Infantry cited)

Company L additionally entitled to: Vietnamese Cross of Gallantry with Palm, Streamer embroidered **VIETNAM 1969** (Company L, 75th Infantry cited)

Company O additionally entitled to: Vietnamese Cross of Gallantry with Palm, Streamer embroidered **VIETNAM 1969** (Company O, 75th Infantry cited)

87TH INFANTRY

COAT OF ARMS

Motto: *Vires Montesque Vincimus* (We Conquer Power and Mountains)

Symbolism: The shield bears a snow capped mountain to represent both the region where the organization first received its specialized training and the normal home of mountain troops. The crossed ski pole and ice axe are symbolic of the tools used by mountain troops, while the horseshoe indicates the pack elements of the organization. The fact that the 87th Infantry was the first organization of its kind is indicated by the single red horseshoe.

The red castle tower is reminiscent of the battle of Castel d'Aiano in Northern Italy, a bloody struggle against prepared positions, rough terrain, heavily mined areas, and enemy artillery fire; its three battlements stand for campaigns in the Aleutians, North Apennines, and Po Valley. The fountain (wavy white and blue-striped disc) represents the crossing of the Po River which brought the 87th

(continued on next page)

DISTINCTIVE INSIGNIA

The distinctive insignia is the shield and motto of the coat of arms.

(continued from previous page)

to the foothills of the Alps. The cata-mountain or wildcat personifies the fighting spirit, cunning, and aggressiveness of the mountain infantry, and the lance and pennant allude to the arms of the province of Bologna where the unit emerged after fighting its way out of the Apennine Mountains.

LINEAGE

1941	Constituted 15 November in the Army of the United States as 87th Infantry Mountain Regiment
1942	Redesignated 12 May as 87th Mountain Infantry and activated 25 May at Fort Lewis, WA
1944	Reorganized and redesignated 22 February as 87th Infantry; assigned to the 10th Light Division and redesignated 6 November as 87th Mountain Infantry
1945	Inactivated 21 November at Camp Carson, CO
1948	Redesignated 18 June as 87th Infantry, allotted 25 June to the Regular Army, and activated 1 July at Fort Riley, KS
1957	Relieved 1 July from assignment to 10th Infantry Division and reorganized as a parent regiment under CARS

CAMPAIGN PARTICIPATION

World War II

Aleutian Islands
North Apennines
Po Valley

Vietnam

Counteroffensive, Phase II
Counteroffensive, Phase III
Tet Counteroffensive
Counteroffensive, Phase IV
Counteroffensive, Phase V
Counteroffensive, Phase VI
Tet 69 Counteroffensive
Summer–Fall 1969
Winter–Spring 1970
Sanctuary Counteroffensive
Counteroffensive, Phase VII
Consolidation I
Consolidation II
Cease-Fire

DECORATIONS

Meritorious Unit Commendation, Streamer embroidered **SAIGON AREA 1966–1967** (Company C, 87th Infantry cited)

Meritorious Unit Commendation, Streamer embroidered **VIETNAM 1967** (Company D, 87th Infantry cited)

Meritorious Unit Commendation, Streamer embroidered **VIETNAM 1967–1968** (Company C, 87th Infantry cited)

Meritorious Unit Commendation, Streamer embroidered **VIETNAM 1968** (Company D, 87th Infantry cited)

1ST BATTALION, 87TH INFANTRY

LINEAGE

1941	Constituted 15 November in the Army of the United States as Company A, 87th Infantry Mountain Regiment, and activated at Fort Lewis, WA
	Company lineage follows that of 87th Infantry from 1941 through 1948 activation at Fort Riley, KS
1957	Reorganizaed and redesignated 1 July as Headquarters and Headquarters Company, 1st Battle Group, 87th Infantry; remained assigned to 10th Infantry Division
1958	Relieved 14 June from assignment to 10th Infantry Division and assigned to 2d Infantry Division
1963	Reorganized and redesignated 15 February as 1st Battalion, 87th Infantry; relieved 4 September from assignment to 2d Infantry Division and assigned to 8th Infantry Division

CAMPAIGN PARTICIPATION

World War II

Aleutian Islands
North Apennines
Po Valley

DECORATIONS

None.

2D Battalion, 87th Infantry

LINEAGE

1941 Constituted 15 November in the Army of the United States as Company B, 87th Infantry Mountain Regiment

Company lineage follows that of 87th Infantry from 1941 through 1948 activation at Fort Riley, KS

1957 Inactivated 1 July in Germany, relieved from assignment to 10th Infantry Division, and redesignated as Headquarters and Headquarters Company, 2d Battle Group, 87th Infantry

1963 Redesignated 25 January as Headquarters and Headquarters Company, 2d Battalion, 87th Infantry, and assigned to 2d Infantry Division; activated 15 February at Fort Benning, GA, relieved 4 September from assignment to 2d Infantry Division and assigned to 8th Infantry Division

1966 Inactivated 1 May in Germany

CAMPAIGN PARTICIPATION

World War II

 Aleutian Islands
 North Apennines
 Po Valley

DECORATIONS

None.

Company C, 87th Infantry

LINEAGE

1941 Constituted 15 November in the Army of the United States as Company C, 87th Infantry Mountain Regiment

Company lineage follows that of 87th Infantry from 1941 through 1948 activation at Fort Riley, KS

1957 Inactivated 1 July in Germany, relieved from assignment to 10th Infantry Division, and redesignated as Headquarters and Headquarters Company, 3d Battle Group, 87th Infantry

1966 Redesignated 23 March as Company C, 87th Infantry, and activated 1 June at Fort Lewis, WA

CAMPAIGN PARTICIPATION

World War II-AP

 Aleutian Islands

World War II-EAME

 North Apennines
 Po Valley

Vietnam

 Counteroffensive, Phase II
 Counteroffensive, Phase III
 Tet Counteroffensive
 Counteroffensive, Phase IV
 Counteroffensive, Phase V
 Counteroffensive, Phase VI
 Tet 69 Counteroffensive
 Summer–Fall 1969
 Winter–Spring 1970
 Sanctuary Counteroffensive
 Counteroffensive, Phase VII
 Consolidation I
 Consolidation II
 Cease-Fire

COMPANY D, 87TH INFANTRY

LINEAGE

1941 Constituted 15 November in the Army of the United States as Company D, 87th Infantry Mountain Regiment

1942 Redesignated 12 May as Company D, 87th Mountain Infantry and activated 25 May at Fort Lewis, WA

1944 Absorbed 22 February by the regiment, assigned to the 10th Infantry Division, and reorganized 6 November at Camp Swift, TX, as Company D, 87th Infantry

1945 Inactivated 21 November at Camp Carson, CO

1948 Redesignated 18 June as Company D, 87th Infantry, allotted 25 June to the Regular Army, and activated 1 June at Fort Riley, KS

1957 Inactivated 1 July in Germany, relieved from assignment to 10th Infantry Division, and redesignated as Headquarters and Headquarters Company, 4th Battle Group, 87th Infantry

1966 Redesignated 23 March as Company D, 87th Infantry, activated 1 June at Fort Lewis, WA

1969 Inactivated 8 November in Vietnam

CAMPAIGN PARTICIPATION

World War II-AP
  Aleutian Islands

World War II-EAME
  North Apennines
  Po Valley

Vietnam
  Counteroffensive, Phase II
  Counteroffensive, Phase III

  Tet Counteroffensive
  Counteroffensive, Phase IV
  Counteroffensive, Phase V
  Counteroffensive, Phase VI
  Tet 69 Counteroffensive
  Summer–Fall 1969
  Winter–Spring 1970

DECORATIONS

Meritorious Unit Commendation, Streamer embroidered **VIETNAM 1967** (Company D, 87th Infantry cited)

Meritorious Unit Commendation, Streamer embroidered **VIETNAM 1968** (Company D, 87th Infantry cited)

187TH INFANTRY
(Rakkasans)

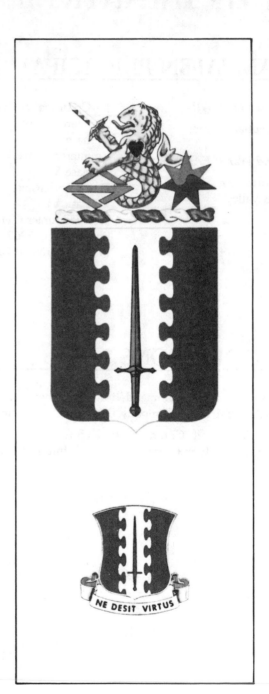

COAT OF ARMS

Motto: *Ne Desit Virtus* (Let Valor Not Fail)

Symbolism: The blue is for the infantry. The partition line of the pale representing clouds and the double handed sword, an ancient infantry weapon, symbolize the character of the organization as an airborne infantry unit.

The golden sea lion, adapted from the seal of the President of the Philippines, represents the award of the Philippine Presidential Unit Citation. The heart on the lion's shoulder points out the action on Purple Heart Hill. The winged sword with three notches in the blade signifies the unit's amphibious assault landing in the Philippines and its two combat jumps in Korea. The red diamond shape is the insignia of the city of Yokohama, Japan, where the 187th began four years of occupation duty. The seven-pointed star, divided in the manner of the Korean Tae-Guk, stands for the unit's participation in the Korean War.

DISTINCTIVE INSIGNIA

The distinctive insignia is the shield and motto of the coat of arms.

LINEAGE

1942   Constituted 12 November in the Army of the United States as 187th Glider Infantry

1943   Activated 25 February at Camp Mackall, NC, as an element of the 11th Airborne Division

1948   Allotted 15 November to the Regular Army

1949   Reorganized and redesignated 30 June as 187th Airborne Infantry

1951   Relieved 1 February from assignment to 11th Airborne Division

1956   Assigned 1 July to 101st Airborne Division

1957   Relieved 25 April from assignment to 101st Airborne Division and reorganized and redesignated as 187th Infantry, a parent regiment under CARS

CAMPAIGN PARTICIPATION

World War II	Korean War
New Guinea	UN offensive (with arrowhead)
Leyte	CCF intervention
Luzon (with arrowhead)	First UN counteroffensive (with arrowhead)
	CCF spring offensive
	Korea, summer–fall 1952
	Korea, summer 1953

Vietnam

Counteroffensive, Phase III
Tet Counteroffensive
Counteroffensive, Phase IV
Counteroffensive, Phase V
Counteroffensive, Phase VI
Tet 69 Counteroffensive
Summer–Fall 1969
Winter–Spring 1970
Sanctuary Counteroffensive
Counteroffensive, Phase VII
Consolidation I
Consolidation II

DECORATIONS

Presidential Unit Citation (Army), Streamer embroidered **TAGAYTAY RIDGE** (1st Battalion, 187th Glider Infantry cited)

Presidential Unit Citation (Army), Streamer embroidered **SUKCHON** (3d Battalion, 187th Airborne Infantry and attached units cited)

Presidential Unit Citation (Navy), Streamer embroidered **INCHON** (3d Battalion, 187th Airborne Infantry cited)

Valorous Unit Award, Streamer embroidered **THUA THIEN PROVINCE** (3d Battalion, 187th Infantry cited)

Philippine Presidential Unit Citation, Streamer embroidered **17 OCTOBER 1944 TO 4 JULY 1945** (187th Glider Infantry cited)

Republic of Korea Presidential Unit Citation, Streamer embroidered **KOREA 1950–1952** (187th Airborne Infantry cited)

Republic of Korea Presidential Unit Citation, Streamer embroidered **KOREA 1952–1953** (187th Airborne Infantry cited)

1ST BATTALION, 187TH INFANTRY
(Rakkasans)

LINEAGE

1942   Constituted 12 November in the Army of the United States as Company A, 187th Glider Infantry

Company lineage follows that of 187th Infantry from 1942 through 1956 assignment to 101st Airborne Division

1957   Reorganized and redesignated 1 March as Headquarters and Headquarters Company, 1st Airborne Battle Group, 187th Infantry; relieved from assignment to 101st Airborne Division and assigned to 11th Airborne Division

1958   Relieved 1 July from assignment to 11th Airborne Division and assigned to 24th Infantry Division

1959   Relieved 8 February from assignment to 24th Infantry Division and assigned to 82d Airborne Division

1964 Relieved 6 March from assignment to 82d Airborne Division, inactivated 25 May at Fort Bragg, NC, and consolidated with 1st Battalion, 187th Infantry, to form 1st Battalion, 187th Infantry, an element of 11th Air Assault Division

1965 Inactivated 30 June at Fort Benning, GA

CAMPAIGN PARTICIPATION

World War II

New Guinea
Leyte
Luzon (with arrowhead)

Korean War

UN offensive (with arrowhead)

CCF intervention
First UN counteroffensive (with arrowhead)
CCF spring offensive
Korea, summer–fall 1952
Korea, summer 1953

DECORATIONS

Presidential Unit Citation (Army), Streamer embroidered **TAGAYTAY RIDGE** (1st Battalion, 187th Glider Infantry cited)

Presidential Unit Citation (Army), Streamer embroidered **SUKCHON**

Presidential Unit Citation (Navy), Streamer embroidered **INCHON**

Philippine Presidential Unit Citation, Streamer embroidered **17 OCTOBER 1944 TO 4 JULY 1945** (187th Glider Infantry cited)

Republic of Korea Presidential Unit Citation, Streamer embroidered **KOREA 1950–1952** (187th Airborne Infantry cited)

Republic of Korea Presidential Unit Citation, Streamer embroidered **KOREA 1952–1953** (187th Airborne Infantry cited)

2D BATTALION, 187TH INFANTRY
(Rakkasans)

LINEAGE

1942 Constituted 12 November in the Army of the United States as Company B, 187th Glider Infantry

Company lineage follows that of 187th Infantry from 1942 through 1956 assignment to 101st Airborne Division

1957 Reorganized and redesignated 25 April as Headquarters and Headquarters Company, 2d Airborne Battle Group, 187th Infantry; remained assigned to 101st Airborne Division

1964 Relieved 1 February from assignment to 101st Airborne Division and inactivated 3 February at Fort Campbell, KY

CAMPAIGN PARTICIPATION

World War II

New Guinea
Leyte
Luzon (with arrowhead)

Korean War

UN offensive (with arrowhead)
CCF intervention
First UN counteroffensive (with arrowhead)

CCF spring offensive
Korea, summer–fall 1952
Korea, summer 1953

DECORATIONS

Presidential Unit Citation (Army), Streamer embroidered **TAGAYTAY RIDGE** (1st Battalion, 187th Glider Infantry cited)

Presidential Unit Citation (Army), Streamer embroidered **SUKCHON**

Presidential Unit Citation (Navy), Streamer embroidered **INCHON**

Philippine Presidential Unit Citation, Streamer embroidered **17 OCTOBER 1944 TO 4 JULY 1945** (187th Glider Infantry cited)

Republic of Korea Presidential Unit Citation, Streamer embroidered **KOREA 1950–1952** (187th Airborne Infantry cited)

Republic of Korea Presidential Unit Citation, Streamer embroidered **KOREA 1952-1953** (187th Airborne Infantry cited)

3D BATTALION, 187TH INFANTRY
(Rakkasans)

LINEAGE

1942   Constituted 12 November in the Army of the United States as Company C, 187th Glider Infantry

Company lineage follows that of 187th Infantry from 1942 through 1956 assignment to 101st Airborne Division

1957   Inactivated 25 April at Fort Campbell, KY, and relieved from assignment to 101st Airborne Division; redesignated as Headquarters and Headquarters Company, 3d Airborne Battle Group, 187th Infantry

1963   Redesignated 1 February as Headquarters and Headquarters Company, 3d Battalion, 187th Infantry, assigned to 11th Air Assault Division and activated 7 February at Fort Benning, GA

1964   Relieved 1 February from assignment to 11th Air Assault Division and assigned to 101st Airborne Division

CAMPAIGN PARTICIPATION

World War II
- New Guinea
- Leyte
- Luzon (with arrowhead)

Korean War
- UN offensive (with arrowhead)
- CCF intervention
- First UN counteroffensive (with arrowhead)
- CCF spring offensive
- Korea, summer-fall 1952
- Korea, summer 1953

Vietnam
- Counteroffensive, Phase III
- Tet Counteroffensive
- Counteroffensive, Phase IV
- Counteroffensive, Phase V
- Counteroffensive, Phase VI
- Tet 69 Counteroffensive
- Summer-Fall 1969
- Winter-Spring 1970
- Sanctuary Counteroffensive
- Counteroffensive, Phase VII
- Consolidation I
- Consolidation II

DECORATIONS

Presidential Unit Citation (Army), Streamer embroidered **TAGAYTAY RIDGE** (1st Battalion, 187th Glider Infantry cited)

Presidential Unit Citation (Army), Streamer embroidered **SUKCHON**

Presidential Unit Citation (Navy), Streamer embroidered **INCHON**

Valorous Unit Award, Streamer embroidered **THUA THIEN PROVINCE** (3d Battalion, 187th Infantry cited)

Philippine Presidential Unit Citation, Streamer embroidered **17 OCTOBER 1944 TO 4 JULY 1945** (187th Glider Infantry cited)

Republic of Korea Presidential Unit Citation, Streamer embroidered **KOREA 1950-1952** (187th Airborne Infantry cited)

Republic of Korea Presidential Unit Citation, Streamer embroidered **KOREA 1952-1953** (187th Airborne Infantry cited)

Vietnamese Cross of Gallantry with Palm, Streamer embroidered **VIETNAM 1968-1969** (3d Battalion, 187th Infantry cited)

188TH INFANTRY

COAT OF ARMS

Motto:　　　Winged Attack

Symbolism:　The principal colors of the shield are the present and old colors of infantry. The eagle's wing is symbolic of the method of vertical attack and striking power of the airborne forces. The golden sword of freedom severing the chain is symbolic of the organization's participation in the liberation of 2000 prisoners of war at the Los Baños prison camp in Luzon, Philippine Islands. The three red roundels (torteaux) on the wing represent the organization's three campaigns: New Guinea, Luzon, and Leyte.

The golden sun, adapted from the Philippine Presidential Seal, represents the award of the Philippine Presidential Unit Citation. The blue arrowhead bearing a scallop shell denotes the unit's participation in the amphibious assault landing on Nasugbu Point, Luzon. This unit's claim to the first landing in Japan (at Atsugi Airfield) is symbolized by the red mountain.

DISTINCTIVE INSIGNIA

The distinctive insignia is the shield and motto of the coat of arms.

LINEAGE

1942   Constituted 12 November in the Army of the United States as 188th Glider Infantry

1943   Activated 25 February at Camp Mackall, NC, as an element of the 11th Airborne Division

1945   Reorganized and redesignateed 20 July as 188th Parachute Infantry

1948   Allotted 15 November to the Regular Army

1949   Redesignated 30 June as 188th Airborne Infantry and inactivated at Camp Campbell, KY

1950   Activated 16 November at Fort Campbell, KY

1957   Inactivated 1 March in Germany and relieved from assignment to 11th Airborne Division

1963   Reorganized and redesignated 15 May as 188th Infantry, a parent regiment under CARS

CAMPAIGN PARTICIPATION

World War II

    New Guinea
    Leyte
    Luzon (with arrowhead)

DECORATIONS

Presidential Unit Citation (Army), Streamer embroidered **LUZON** (Regimental Headquarters and Headquarters Company and 1st and 2d Battalions, 188th Infantry cited)

Philippine Presidential Unit Citation, Streamer embroidered **17 OCTOBER 1944 TO 4 JULY 1945** (188th Glider Infantry cited)

1st Battalion, 188th Infantry

LINEAGE

1942   Constituted 12 November in the Army of the United States as Company A, 188th Glider Infantry

    Company lineage follows that of 188th Infantry from 1942 through 1957 relief from assignment to 11th Airborne Division

1963   Redesignated 17 July as Headquarters and Headquarters Company, 1st Battalion, 188th Infantry, assigned to 11th Air Assault Division and activated 18 July at Fort Benning, GA

1965   Inactivated 30 June

CAMPAIGN PARTICIPATION

World War II

    New Guinea
    Leyte
    Luzon (with arrowhead)

DECORATIONS

Presidential Unit Citation (Army), Streamer embroidered **LUZON** (1st Battalion, 188th Glider Infantry cited)

Philippine Presidential Unit Citation, Streamer embroidered **17 OCTOBER 1944 TO 4 JULY 1945** (188th Glider Infantry cited)

COMPANY E, 188TH INFANTRY

LINEAGE

1942   Constituted 12 November in the Army of the United States as Company E, 188th Glider Infantry

Company lineage follows that of 188th Infantry from 1942 through 1957 relief from assignment to 11th Airborne Division

1963   Redesignated 15 May as Headquarters and Headquarters Company, 4th Battalion, 188th Infantry

1965   Redesignated 25 August as Company E, 188th Infantry; activated 2 November at Fort Benning, GA, and inactivated 16 November

CAMPAIGN PARTICIPATION

World War II

New Guinea
Leyte
Luzon (with arrowhead)

DECORATIONS

Presidential Unit Citation (Army), Streamer embroidered **LUZON** (2d Battalion, 188th Glider Infantry cited)

Philippine Presidential Unit Citation, Streamer embroidered **17 OCTOBER 1944 TO 4 JULY 1945** (188th Glider Infantry cited)

325TH INFANTRY

COAT OF ARMS

Motto: Let's Go

Symbolism: The shield is white with a blue fess, the old and present infantry colors. The blue disc is from the shoulder sleeve insignia of the 82d Division and the white temple is from the seal of the state of Georgia. The blue Lorraine cross indicates the service of the regiment in World War I in the province of that name.

As the 325th Infantry was a glider unit during World War II, the wings are an adaption of those used on the Glider Qualification Badge. The red six-pointed star (from the arms of Cherbourg) alludes to the glider landing on the Cherbourg Peninsula and, with the red erect lion, to the glider landing at Nijmegen in the Netherlands. The trident alludes to Operation NEPTUNE

(continued on next page)

DISTINCTIVE INSIGNIA

The distinctive insignia is the shield and motto of the coat of arms.

(continued from previous page)

which launched the invasion of Normandy, and the three tines of the trident refer to North Africa and action in Sicily and Italy prior to the Normandy assault. The truncated pyramid simulates a type of tank obstacle (dragon's tooth) with protected the Siegfried Line, the linden leaf alluding to the fact that the regiment pierced and overran its defenses. (According to Teutonic mythology, Siegfried bathed in the blood of the dragon, Fafnir, and as a result was said to be invulnerable; only between the shoulders where a leaf had settled could he be overcome and killed.) The linden leaf also refers to the subsequent occupation of Berlin.

LINEAGE

1917	Constituted 5 August as the 325th Infantry, an element of the 8th Division; organized 1 September at Camp Gordon, GA
1919	Demobilized 18–25 May at Camp Upton, NY
1921	Reconstituted 24 June in the Organized Reserves as the 325th Infantry, an element of the 82d Division
1922	Organized in January at Columbus, GA
1942	Ordered into active military service 25 March, reorganized at Camp Claiborne, LA, and reorganized and redesignated 15 August as 325th Glider Infantry
1947	Reorganized and redesignated 15 December as 325th Infantry
1948	Allotted 15 November to Regular Army, reorganized and redesignated 15 December as 325th Airborne Infantry

1957	Relieved 1 September from assignment to 82d Airborne Division and reorganized and redesignated as 325th Infantry, a parent regiment under CARS

CAMPAIGN PARTICIPATION

World War I
St. Mihiel
Meuse-Argonne
Lorraine 1918

World War II
Sicily

Naples-Foggia
Normandy (with arrowhead)
Rhineland (with arrowhead
Ardennes-Alsace
Central Europe

DECORATIONS

Presidential Unit Citation (Army), Streamer embroidered **STE. MERE EGLISE** (325th Glider Infantry cited)

French Croix de Guerre with Palm, World War II, Streamer embroidered **STE. MERE EGLISE** (325th Glider Infantry cited)

French Croix de Guerre with Palm, World War II, Streamer embroidered **COTENTIN** (325th Glider Infantry cited)

French Croix de Guerre, World War II, Fourragere (325th Glider Infantry cited)

Military Order of William (Degree of the Knight of the Fourth Class), Streamer embroidered **NIJMEGEN 1944** (325th Glider Infantry cited)

Netherlands Orange Lanyard (325th Glider Infantry cited)

Belgian Fourragere 1940 (325th Glider Infantry cited)

Cited in the Order of the Day of the Belgian Army for action in the **ARDENNES** (325th Glider Infantry cited)

Cited in the Order of the Day of the Belgian Army for action in **BELGIUM AND GERMANY** (325th Glider Infantry cited)

1ST BATTALION, 325TH INFANTRY

LINEAGE

1917	Constituted 5 August as the Company A, 325th Infantry, an element of the 82d Division; organized 1 September at Camp Gordon, GA

Company lineage follows that of 325th Infantry from 1917 through 1948 redesignation

1957	Reorganized and redesignated 1 September as Headquarters and Headquarters Company, 1st Airborne Battle Group, 325th Infantry; remained assigned to the 82d Airborne Division

1964   Reorganized and redesignated 25 May as 1st Battalion, 325th Infantry

CAMPAIGN PARTICIPATION

World War I

St. Mihiel
Meuse-Argonne
Lorraine 1918

World War II

Sicily
Naples-Foggia
Normandy (with
    arrowhead)
Rhineland (with
    arrowhead
Ardennes-Alsace
Central Europe

DECORATIONS

Presidential Unit Citation (Army), Streamer embroidered **STE. MERE EGLISE** (325th Glider Infantry cited)

French Croix de Guerre with Palm, World War II, Streamer embroidered **STE. MERE EGLISE** (325th Glider Infantry cited)

French Croix de Guerre with Palm, World War II, Streamer embroidered **COTENTIN** (325th Glider Infantry cited)

French Croix de Guerre, World War II, Fourragere (325th Glider Infantry cited)

Military Order of William (Degree of the Knight of the Fourth Class), Streamer embroidered **NIJMEGEN 1944** (325th Glider Infantry cited)

Netherlands Orange Lanyard (325th Glider Infantry cited)

Belgian Fourragere 1940 (325th Glider Infantry cited)

Cited in the Order of the Day of the Belgian Army for action in the **ARDENNES** (325th Glider Infantry cited)

Cited in the Order of the Day of the Belgian Army for action in **BELGIUM AND GERMANY** (325th Glider Infantry cited)

2D BATTALION, 325TH INFANTRY

LINEAGE

1917   Constituted 5 August as the Company B, 325th Infantry, an element of the 82d Division; organized 1 September at Camp Gordon, GA

Company lineage follows that of 325th from 1917 through 1948 redesignation

1957   Inactivated 1 September at Fort Bragg, NC, relieved from assignment to 82d Airborne Division, and redesignated as Headquarters and Headquarters Company, 2d Airborne Battle Group, 325th Infantry

1964   Redesignated 6 March as Headquarters and Headquarters Company, 2d Battalion, 325th Infantry, assigned to 82d Airborne Division and activated 25 May at Fort Bragg, NC

CAMPAIGN PARTICIPATION

World War I

St. Mihiel
Meuse-Argonne
Lorraine 1918

World War II

Sicily
Naples-Foggia
Normandy (with
    arrowhead)
Rhineland (with
    arrowhead
Ardennes-Alsace
Central Europe

DECORATIONS

Presidential Unit Citation (Army), Streamer embroidered **STE. MERE EGLISE** (325th Glider Infantry cited)

French Croix de Guerre with Palm, World War II, Streamer embroidered **STE. MERE EGLISE** (325th Glider Infantry cited)

French Croix de Guerre with Palm, World War II, Streamer embroidered **COTENTIN** (325th Glider Infantry cited)

French Croix de Guerre, World War II, Fourragere (325th Glider Infantry cited)

Military Order of William (Degree of the Knight of the Fourth Class), Streamer embroidered NIJMEGEN 1944 (325th Glider Infantry cited)

Netherlands Orange Lanyard (325th Glider Infantry cited)

Belgian Fourragere 1940 (325th Glider Infantry cited)

Cited in the Order of the Day of the Belgian Army for action in the ARDENNES (325th Glider Infantry cited)

Cited in the Order of the Day of the Belgian Army for action in BELGIUM AND GERMANY (325th Glider Infantry cited)

3D BATTALION, 325TH INFANTRY

LINEAGE

1917   Constituted 5 August as the Company C, 325th Infantry, an element of the 82d Division; organized 1 September at Camp Gordon, GA

Company lineage follows that of 325th Infantry from 1917 through 1948 redesignation

1918   Another company constituted 23 July as 2d Battalion, 401st Infantry, an element of the 101st Division, demobilized 30 November

2d Battalion, 401st Infantry lineage differs from that of 325th Infantry from its constitution to 1945 consolidation as follows:

1921   *Reconstituted 24 June in the Organized Reserves as an element of the 101st Division; organized in November at Milwaukee, WI*

1942   *Disbanded 15 August, reconstituted in the Army of the United States as 2d Battalion, 401st Glider Infantry, an element of the 101st Airborne Division and activated at Camp Claiborne, LA*

1945   *Disbanded 1 March in France, relieved from assignment to 101st Airborne Division, reconstituted 6 April and consolidated with the 3d Battalion, 325th Glider Infantry; consolidated unit designated 3d Battalion, 325th Glider Infantry*

1957   Company C, 325th Airborne Infantry inactivated 1 September at Fort Bragg, NC, relieved from assignment to 82d Airborne Division, and redesignated as Headquarters and Headquarters Company, 3d Airborne Battle Group, 325th Infantry

1964   Redesignated 6 March as Headquarters and Headquarters Company, 3d Battalion, 325th Infantry, assigned to 82d Airborne Division and activated 25 May at Fort Bragg, NC

CAMPAIGN PARTICIPATION

World War I
St. Mihiel
Meuse-Argonne
Lorraine 1918

World War II
Sicily
Naples-Foggia
Normandy (with arrowhead)
Rhineland (with arrowhead)
Ardennes-Alsace
Central Europe

DECORATIONS

Presidential Unit Citation (Army), Streamer embroidered STE. MERE EGLISE (325th Glider Infantry cited)

French Croix de Guerre with Palm, World War II, Streamer embroidered STE. MERE EGLISE (325th Glider Infantry cited)

French Croix de Guerre with Palm, World War II, Streamer embroidered COTENTIN (325th Glider Infantry cited)

French Croix de Guerre, World War II, Fourragere (325th Glider Infantry cited)

Military Order of William (Degree of the Knight of the Fourth Class), Streamer embroidered NIJMEGEN 1944 (325th Glider Infantry cited)

Netherlands Orange Lanyard (325th Glider Infantry cited)

Belgian Fourragere 1940 (325th Glider Infantry cited)

Cited in the Order of the Day of the Belgian Army for action in the ARDENNES (325th Glider Infantry cited)

Cited in the Order of the Day of the Belgian Army for action in BELGIUM AND GERMANY (325th Glider Infantry cited)

4TH BATTALION, 325TH INFANTRY

LINEAGE

1917   Constituted 5 August as the Company D, 325th Infantry, an element of the 82d Division; organized 1 September at Camp Gordon, GA

Company lineage follows that of 325th Infantry from 1917 through 1942 reorganization at Camp Claiborne, LA

1945   Reorganized 1 March in France (Company D shares history and honors of the 325th Glider Infantry during the period from 15 August 1942 to 1 March 1945)

1947   Reorganized and redesignated 15 December as Company D, 325th Infantry

1948   Allotted 15 November to Regular Army, reorganized and redesignated 15 December as Company D, 325th Airborne Infantry

1957   Inactivated 1 September at Fort Bragg, NC, relieved from assignment to 82d Airborne Division, and redesignated as Headquarters and Headquarters Company, 4th Airborne Battle Group, 325th Infantry

1968   Redesignated 3 July as Headquarters and Headquarters Company, 4th Battalion, 325th Infantry; activated 15 July at Fort Bragg, NC, and assigned to 82d Airborne Division

1969   Inactivated 15 December and relieved from assignment to 82d Airborne Division

CAMPAIGN PARTICIPATION

World War I
St. Mihiel
Meuse-Argonne
Lorraine 1918

World War II
Sicily
Naples-Foggia
Normandy (with arrowhead)
Rhineland (with arrowhead
Ardennes-Alsace
Central Europe

DECORATIONS

Presidential Unit Citation (Army), Streamer embroidered **STE. MERE EGLISE** (325th Glider Infantry cited)

French Croix de Guerre with Palm, World War II, Streamer embroidered **STE. MERE EGLISE** (325th Glider Infantry cited)

French Croix de Guerre with Palm, World War II, Streamer embroidered **COTENTIN** (325th Glider Infantry cited)

French Croix de Guerre, World War II, Fourragere (325th Glider Infantry cited)

Military Order of William (Degree of the Knight of the Fourth Class), Streamer embroidered **NIJMEGEN 1944** (325th Glider Infantry cited)

Netherlands Orange Lanyard (325th Glider Infantry cited)

Belgian Fourragere 1940 (325th Glider Infantry cited)

Cited in the Order of the Day of the Belgian Army for action in the **ARDENNES** (325th Glider Infantry cited)

Cited in the Order of the Day of the Belgian Army for action in **BELGIUM AND GERMANY** (325th Glider Infantry cited)

327TH INFANTRY
(Bastogne Bulldogs)

COAT OF ARMS

Motto: Honor and Country

Symbolism: The shield is blue for infantry. Blue is also the color of the state flag of South Carolina, the location of the 327th infantry between World Wars I and II. The palmetto tree also alludes to South Carolina. The red bend is taken from the arms of the ancient province of Lorraine, and the fleurs-de-lis indicate the regiment's three World War I campaigns.

The nebuly delineation, a heraldic simulation for clouds, represents the regiment's service as the 327th Glider Infantry in World War II. The two spearheads surmounting the nebuly pierced disc indicate the unit's combat glider landings and its aggressive action in Normandy and in the Rhineland. The oak leaves and acorn connote Bastogne in the Ardennes. The pierced white disc

(continued on next page)

DISTINCTIVE INSIGNIA

The distinctive insignia is the shield and motto of the coat of arms.

(continued from previous page)

further alludes to the snow and to encircled Bastogne during the Battle of the Bulge, for which the organization was awarded the Presidential Unit Citation (Army). The colors red and green refer to the regiment's French and Belgian decorations.

LINEAGE

1917	Constituted 5 August at 327th Infantry, an element of the 82d Division; organized 17 September at Camp Gordon, GA
1919	Demobilized 26 May at Camp Upton, NY
1921	Reconstituted 24 June in the Organized Reserves as 327th Infantry, an element of the 82d Division and organized in December at Greenville, SC
1942	Ordered into active military service 25 March, reorganized at Camp Claiborne, LA, reorganized and redesignated 15 August as 327th Glider Infantry, relieved from assignment to 82d Airborne Division, and assigned to 101st Airborne Division
1945	Activated 6 July at Auxerre, France
1948	Redesignated 18 June as 516th Airborne Infantry, allotted 25 June to Regular Army, and activated 6 July at Camp Breckinridge, KY
1949	Inactivated 22 April
1950	Activated 25 August
1953	Inactivated 1 December
1954	Relieved 27 April from assignment to 101st Airborne Division and activated 15 May at Fort Jackson, SC
1956	Reorganized and redesignated 1 July as 327th Airborne Infantry and assigned to 101st Airborne Division
1957	Relieved 25 April from assignment to 101st Airborne Division, reorganized and redesignated as 327th Infantry, a parent regiment under CARS

CAMPAIGN PARTICIPATION

World War I
St. Mihiel
Meuse-Argonne
Lorraine 1918

World War II
Normandy (with arrowhead)
Rhineland (with arrowhead)
Ardennes-Alsace
Central Europe

Vietnam
Defense
Counteroffensive
Counteroffensive, Phase II
Counteroffensive, Phase III
Tet Counteroffensive
Counteroffensive, Phase IV
Counteroffensive, Phase V
Counteroffensive, Phase VI
Tet 69 Counteroffensive
Summer–Fall 1969
Winter–Spring 1970
Sanctuary Counteroffensive
Counteroffensive, Phase VII
Consolidation I
Consolidation II
Cease-Fire

DECORATIONS

Presidential Unit Citation (Army), Streamer embroidered **BASTOGNE** (101st Airborne Division cited)

Presidential Unit Citation (Army), Streamer embroidered **DAK TO, VIETNAM 1966** (1st Battalion and Company B, 2d Battalion, 327th Infantry cited)

Presidential Unit Citation (Army), Streamer embroidered **TRUNG LUONG** (2d Battalion, 327th Infantry cited)

Valorous Unit Award, Streamer embroidered **TUY HOA** (1st and 2d Battalions, 327th Infantry cited)

Meritorious Unit Commendation, Streamer embroidered **VIETNAM 1965–1966** (1st and 2d Battalions, 327th Infantry cited)

French Croix de Guerre with Palm, World War II, Streamer embroidered **NORMANDY** (327th Glider Infantry cited)

Netherlands Orange Lanyard (327th Glider Infantry cited)

Belgian Croix de Guerre 1940 with Palm, Streamer embroidered **BASTOGNE**; cited in the Order of the Day of the Belgian Army for action at **BASTOGNE** (327th Glider Infantry cited)

Belgian Fourragere 1940 (327th Glider Infantry cited)

Cited in the Order of the Day of the Belgian Army for action in **FRANCE AND BELGIUM** (327th Glider Infantry cited)

1st Battalion, 327th Infantry
(Bastogne Bulldogs)

LINEAGE

1917   Constituted 5 August as Company A, 327th infantry, an element of the 82d Division and organized 17 September at Camp Gordon, GA

Company lineage follows that of 327th Infantry from 1917 through 1956 assignment to 101st Airborne Division

1957   Reorganized and redesignated 25 April as Headquarters and Headquarters Company, 1st Airborne Battle Group, 327th Infantry and remained assigned to the 101st Airborne Division

1964   Reorganized and redesignated 3 February as 1st Battalion, 327th Infantry

CAMPAIGN PARTICIPATION

World War I

St. Mihiel
Meuse-Argonne
Lorraine 1918

World War II

Normandy (with arrowhead)
Rhineland (with arrowhead)
Ardennes-Alsace
Central Europe

Vietnam

Defense
Counteroffensive
Counteroffensive, Phase II
Counteroffensive, Phase III
Tet Counteroffensive
Counteroffensive, Phase IV
Counteroffensive, Phase V
Counteroffensive, Phase VI
Tet 69 Counteroffensive
Summer–Fall 1969
Winter–Spring 1970
Sanctuary Counteroffensive
Counteroffensive, Phase VII
Consolidation I
Consolidation II
Cease-Fire

DECORATIONS

Presidential Unit Citation (Army), Streamer embroidered **BASTOGNE** (101st Airborne Division cited)

Presidential Unit Citation (Army), Streamer embroidered **DAK TO, VIETNAM 1966** (1st Battalion, 327th Infantry cited)

Valorous Unit Award, Streamer embroidered **TUY HOA** (1st Battalion, 327th Infantry cited)

Meritorious Unit Commendation, Streamer embroidered **VIETNAM 1965–1966** (1st Battalion, 327th Infantry cited)

French Croix de Guerre with Palm, World War II, Streamer embroidered **NORMANDY** (327th Glider Infantry cited)

Netherlands Orange Lanyard (327th Glider Infantry cited)

Belgian Croix de Guerre 1940 with Palm, Streamer embroidered **BASTOGNE**; cited in the Order of the Day of the Belgian Army for action at **BASTOGNE** (327th Glider Infantry cited)

Belgian Fourragere 1940 (327th Glider Infantry cited)

Cited in the Order of the Day of the Belgian Army for action in **FRANCE AND BELGIUM** (327th Glider Infantry cited)

Vietnamese Cross of Gallantry with Palm, Streamer embroidered **VIETNAM 1966-1967** (1st Battalion, 327th Infantry cited)

Vietnamese Cross of Gallantry with Palm, Streamer embroidered **VIETNAM 1968-1969** (1st Battalion, 327th Infantry cited)

2D BATTALION, 327TH INFANTRY
(Bastogne Bulldogs)

LINEAGE

1917   Constituted 5 August as Company B, 327th infantry, an element of the 82d Division and organized 17 September at Camp Gordon, GA

Company lineage follows that of 327th Infantry from 1917 through 1956 assignment to 101st Airborne Division

1957   Inactivated 25 april at Fort Campbell, KY, relieved from assignment to 101st Airborne Division and redesignated Headquarters and Headquarters Company, 2d Airborne Battle Group, 327th Infantry

1964   Redesignated 21 January as Headquarters and Headquarters Company, 2d Battalion, 327th Infantry, assigned to 101st Airborne Division and activated 3 February at Fort Campbell, KY

CAMPAIGN PARTICIPATION

World War I

St. Mihiel
Meuse-Argonne
Lorraine 1918

World War II

Normandy (with arrowhead)
Rhineland (with arrowhead)
Ardennes-Alsace
Central Europe

Vietnam

Defense
Counteroffensive
Counteroffensive, Phase II
Counteroffensive, Phase III
Tet Counteroffensive
Counteroffensive, Phase IV
Counteroffensive, Phase V
Counteroffensive, Phase VI
Tet 69 Counteroffensive
Summer–Fall 1969
Winter–Spring 1970
Sanctuary Counteroffensive
Counteroffensive, Phase VII
Consolidation I
Consolidation II
Cease-Fire

DECORATIONS

Presidential Unit Citation (Army), Streamer embroidered **BASTOGNE** (101st Airborne Division cited)

Presidential Unit Citation (Army), Streamer embroidered **TRUNG LUONG** (2d Battalion, 327th Infantry cited) Company B, 2d Battalion, 327th Infantry cited)

Valorous Unit Award, Streamer embroidered **TUY HOA** (2d Battalion, 327th Infantry cited)

Meritorious Unit Commendation, Streamer embroidered **VIETNAM 1965–1966** (2d Battalion, 327th Infantry cited)

French Croix de Guerre with Palm, World War II, Streamer embroidered **NORMANDY** (327th Glider Infantry cited)

Netherlands Orange Lanyard (327th Glider Infantry cited)

Belgian Croix de Guerre 1940 with Palm, Streamer embroidered **BASTOGNE**; cited in the Order of the Day of the Belgian Army for action at **BASTOGNE** (327th Glider Infantry cited)

Belgian Fourragere 1940 (327th Glider Infantry cited)

Cited in the Order of the Day of the Belgian Army for action in **FRANCE AND BELGIUM** (327th Glider Infantry cited)

Vietnamese Cross of Gallantry with Palm, Streamer embroidered **VIETNAM 1966–1967** (2d Battalion, 327th Infantry cited)

Vietnamese Cross of Gallantry with Palm, Streamer embroidered **VIETNAM 1968–1969** (2d Battalion, 327th Infantry cited)

Company B additionally entitled to: Presidential Unit Citation (Army), Streamer embroidered **DAK TO, VIETNAM 1966** (Company B, 2d Battalion, 327th Infantry cited)

501ST INFANTRY

COAT OF ARMS

Motto:	Geronimo
Symbolism:	The colors blue and white indicate the infantry nature of the organization. The thunderbird is an appropriate symbol for a parachute unit. The motto has its origin in a cry uttered in the maiden jump of the unit's test platoon and is now tradition with the 501st Infantry.

The blue and yellow standard is the official standard of the town of Veghel, Holland. It was presented by the town to the 501st in honor of its efforts in liberating the town from the enemy. The lion refers to the Belgian Croix de Guerre and the Citation in the Order of the Day of the Belgian Army for the unit's action as Bastogne, whose arms are suggested by the red and blue shield on the lion's shoulder. The key refers to the position of Bastogne as a focal point of the German counterattack.

DISTINCTIVE INSIGNIA

The distinctive insignia is the shield and motto of the coat of arms.

LINEAGE

1942   Constituted 24 February in the Army of the United States as the 501st Parachute Infantry and activated 15 November at Camp Taccoa, GA

1945   Disbanded 1 August in Germany

1946   Reconstituted 1 August in the Army of the United States as 501st Parachute Infantry Battalion and activated at Fort Benning, GA

1948   Inactivated 23 November

1951   Expanded and redesignated 21 April as 501st Airborne Infantry, allotted to Regular Army, and activated 10 May at Camp Breckinridge, KY

1953   Inactivated 1 December at Camp Breckinridge, KY

1954   Assigned 27 April to 101st Airborne Division and activated 15 May at Fort Jackson, SC

1957   Relieved 25 April from assignment to 101st Airborne Division, reorganized and redesignated as 501st Infantry, a parent regiment under CARS

CAMPAIGN PARTICIPATION

World War II
- Normandy (with arrowhead)
- Rhineland (with arrowhead)
- Ardennes-Alsace
- Central Europe
- Asiatic-Pacific Theater without inscription

Vietnam
- Counteroffensive, Phase III
- Tet Counteroffensive
- Counteroffensive, Phase IV
- Counteroffensive, Phase V
- Counteroffensive, Phase VI
- Tet 69 Counteroffensive
- Summer–Fall 1969
- Winter–Spring 1970
- Sanctuary Counteroffensive
- Counteroffensive, Phase VII
- Consolidation I
- Consolidation II
- Cease-Fire

DECORATIONS

Presidential Unit Citation (Army), Streamer embroidered **BASTOGNE** (501st Parachute Infantry cited)

Presidential Unit Citation (Army), Streamer embroidered **NORMANDY** (501st Parachute Infantry cited)

French Croix de Guerre with Palm, World War II, Streamer embroidered **NORMANDY** (501st Parachute Infantry cited)

Netherlands Orange Lanyard (501st Parachute Infantry cited)

Belgian Croix de Guerre 1940 with Palm, Streamer embroidered **BASTOGNE**; cited in the Order of the Day of the Belgian Army for action at **BASTOGNE** (501st Parachute Infantry cited)

Belgian Fourragere 1940 (501st Parachute Infantry cited)

Cited in the Order of the Day of the Belgian Army for action in **FRANCE AND BELGIUM** (501st Parachute Infantry cited)

1ST BATTALION, 501ST INFANTRY

LINEAGE

1940   Constituted 16 September in the Army of the United States as Company A, 501st Parachute Battalion, and activated 1 October at Fort Benning, GA

1942   Consolidated 24 February with Company A, 501st Parachute Infantry, inactivated 2 November in Australia and activated 15 November at Camp Taccoa, GA

Company lineage follows that of 501st Infantry from 1942 through 1954 activation at Fort Jackson, SC

1957   Reorganized and redesignated 25 April as Headquarters and Headquarters Company, 1st Airborne Battle Group, 501st Infantry; remained assigned to 101st Airborne Division

1964   Reorganized and redesignated 3 February as 1st Battalion, 501st Infantry

CAMPAIGN PARTICIPATION

World War II

Normandy (with
arrowhead)
Rhineland (with
arrowhead)
Ardennes-Alsace
Central Europe
Asiatic-Pacific Theater
without inscription

Vietnam

Counteroffensive,
Phase III
Tet Counteroffensive

Counteroffensive,
Phase IV
Counteroffensive,
Phase V
Counteroffensive,
Phase VI
Tet 69 Counteroffensive
Summer–Fall 1969
Winter–Spring 1970
Sanctuary
Counteroffensive
Counteroffensive,
Phase VII
Consolidation I
Consolidation II

DECORATIONS

Presidential Unit Citation (Army), Streamer embroidered **BASTOGNE** (501st Parachute Infantry cited)

Presidential Unit Citation (Army), Streamer embroidered **NORMANDY** (501st Parachute Infantry cited)

French Croix de Guerre with Palm, World War II, Streamer embroidered **NORMANDY** (501st Parachute Infantry cited)

Netherlands Orange Lanyard (501st Parachute Infantry cited)

Belgian Croix de Guerre 1940 with Palm, Streamer embroidered **BASTOGNE**; cited in the Order of the Day of the Belgian Army for action at **BASTOGNE** (501st Parachute Infantry cited)

Belgian Fourragere 1940 (501st Parachute Infantry cited)

Cited in the Order of the Day of the Belgian Army for action in **FRANCE AND BELGIUM** (501st Parachute Infantry cited)

Vietnamese Cross of Gallantry with Palm, Streamer embroidered **VIETNAM 1968** (1st Battalion, 501st Infantry cited)

Vietnamese Cross of Gallantry with Palm, Streamer embroidered **VIETNAM 1968–1969** (1st Battalion, 501st Infantry cited)

2D BATTALION, 501ST INFANTRY

LINEAGE

1940   Constituted 16 September in the Army of the United States as Company B, 501st Parachute Battalion; activated 1 October at Fort Benning, GA

1942   Consolidated 24 February with Company B, 501st Parachute Infantry, and consolidated unit designated Company B, 501st Parachute Infantry; inactivated 2 November in Australia and activated 15 November at Camp Taccoa, GA

Company lineage follows that of 501st Infantry from 1942 through 1954 activation at Fort Jackson, SC

1957   Inactivated 25 April at Fort Campbell, KY, and relieved from assignment to 101st Airborne Division; reorganized and redesignated 1 September as Headquarters and Headquarters Company, 2d Airborne Battle Group, 501st Infantry; assigned to the 82d Airborne Division and activated at Fort Bragg, NC

1964   Relieved 1 February from assignment to 82d Airborne Division, and assigned to 101st Airborne division; reorganized and redesignated 3 February as 2d Battalion, 501st Infantry

CAMPAIGN PARTICIPATION

World War II

Normandy (with
arrowhead)
Rhineland (with
arrowhead)
Ardennes-Alsace
Central Europe
Asiatic-Pacific Theater
without inscription

Vietnam

Counteroffensive,
Phase III
Tet Counteroffensive
Counteroffensive,
Phase IV
Counteroffensive,
Phase V
Counteroffensive,
Phase VI

Tet 69 Counteroffensive
Summer–Fall 1969
Winter–Spring 1970
Sanctuary
    Counteroffensive

Counteroffensive,
    Phase VII
Consolidation I
Consolidation II
Cease-Fire

DECORATIONS

Presidential Unit Citation (Army), Streamer embroidered **BASTOGNE** (501st Parachute Infantry cited)

Presidential Unit Citation (Army), Streamer embroidered **NORMANDY** (501st Parachute Infantry cited)

French Croix de Guerre with Palm, World War II, Streamer embroidered **NORMANDY** (501st Parachute Infantry cited)

Netherlands Orange Lanyard (501st Parachute Infantry cited)

Belgian Croix de Guerre 1940 with Palm, Streamer embroidered **BASTOGNE**; cited in the Order of the Day of the Belgian Army for action at **BASTOGNE** (501st Parachute Infantry cited)

Belgian Fourragere 1940 (501st Parachute Infantry cited)

Cited in the Order of the Day of the Belgian Army for action in **FRANCE AND BELGIUM** (501st Parachute Infantry cited)

Vietnamese Cross of Gallantry with Palm, Streamer embroidered **VIETNAM 1968** (2d Battalion, 501st Infantry cited)

Vietnamese Cross of Gallantry with Palm, Streamer embroidered **VIETNAM 1968–1969** (2d Battalion, 501st Infantry cited)

Company C additionally entitled to: Valorous Unit Award, Streamer embroidered **THUA THIEN PROVINCE** (Company C, 2d Battalion, 501st Infantry cited)

502D INFANTRY

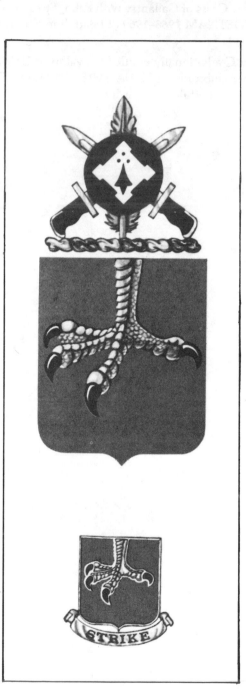

COAT OF ARMS

Motto: Strike

Symbolism: The blue of the shield is for infantry. The grasping eagle's claw is a representation of the airborne functions of the organization. The motto is expressive of the power of the organization.

The bayonets refer to the unit's bayonet charge at Carentan, Normandy. They are two in number in reference to the regiment's two Presidential Unit Citations (Army) and its two assault landings in World War II. The eagle's feather stands for the unit's airborne function; orange, the national color of the Netherlands, refers to the liberation of Best, Holland. The white four-bastioned fort encircled by a black background represents Bastogne, Belgium, surrounded by the German salient in the Battle of the Bulge. The ermine spot on the white fort refers to the snow which blanketed the battle's terrain.

DISTINCTIVE INSIGNIA

The distinctive insignia is the shield and motto of the coat of arms.

LINEAGE

1942	Constituted 24 February in the Army of the United States as the 502d Parachute Infantry; activated 2 March at Fort Benning, GA, and assigned 15 August to 101st Airborne Division
1945	Inactivated 30 November in France
1948	Redesignated 18 June as 502d Airborne Infantry, allotted 25 June to Regular Army, and activated 6 July at Camp Breckinridge, KY
1949	Inactivated 1 April
1950	Activated 25 August
1953	Inactivated 1 December
1954	Activated 15 May at Fort Jackson, SC
1957	Relieved 25 April from assignment to 101st Airborne Division; reorganized and redesignated as the 502d Infantry, a parent regiment under CARS

CAMPAIGN PARTICIPATION

World War II

Normandy (with arrowhead)
Rhineland (with arrowhead)
Ardennes-Alsace
Central Europe

Vietnam

Defense
Counteroffensive
Counteroffensive, Phase II
Counteroffensive, Phase III
Tet Counteroffensive
Counteroffensive, Phase IV
Counteroffensive, Phase V
Counteroffensive, Phase VI
Tet 69 Counteroffensive
Summer-Fall 1969
Winter-Spring 1970
Sanctuary Counteroffensive
Counteroffensive, Phase VII
Consolidation I
Consolidation II

DECORATIONS

Presidential Unit Citation (Army), Streamer embroidered **BASTOGNE** (101st Airborne Division cited)

Presidential Unit Citation (Army), Streamer embroidered **NORMANDY** (502d Parachute Infantry cited)

Presidential Unit Citation (Army), Streamer embroidered **AN KHE** (2d Battalion, 502d Infantry cited)

Presidential Unit Citation (Army), Streamer embroidered **DAK TO VIETNAM 1966** (2d Battalion, 502d Infantry cited)

Valorous Unit Award, Streamer embroidered **TUY HUA** (2d Battalion, 502d Infantry cited)

Valorous Unit Award, Streamer embroidered **QUANG THUONG DISTRICT** (1st Battalion, 502d Infantry cited)

Valorous Unit Award, Streamer embroidered **NAM HOA DISTRICT** (2d Battalion, 502d Infantry cited)

Valorous Unit Award, Streamer embroidered **BA LONG DISTRICT** (2d Battalion, 502d Infantry cited)

Meritorious Unit Commendation, Streamer embroidered **VIETNAM 1965-1966** (2d Battalion, 502d Infantry cited)

French Croix de Guerre with Palm, World War II, Streamer embroidered **NORMANDY** (502d Parachute Infantry cited)

Netherlands Orange Lanyard (502d Parachute Infantry cited)

Belgian Croix de Guerre 1940 with Palm, Streamer embroidered **BASTOGNE**; cited in the Order of the Day of the Belgian Army for action at **BASTOGNE** (502d Parachute Infantry cited)

Belgian Fourragere 1940 (502d Parachute Infantry cited)

Cited in the Order of the Day of the Belgian Army for action in **FRANCE AND BELGIUM** (502d Parachute Infantry cited)

1st Battalion, 502d Infantry

LINEAGE

1941   Constituted 14 March in the Army of the United States as Company A, 502d Parachute Battalion; activated 1 July at Fort Benning, GA

1942   Consolidated 24 February with Company A, 502d Parachute Infantry; consolidated unit designated Company A, 502d Parachute Infantry and assigned 15 August to 101st Airborne Division

Company lineage follows that of 502d Infantry from 1942 through 1954 activation at Fort Jackson, SC

1957   Reorganized and redesignated 25 April as Headquarters and Headquarters Company, 1st Airborne Battle Group, 502d Infantry; remained assigned to the 101st Airborne Division

1964   Reorganized and redesignated 3 February as 1st Battalion, 502d Infantry

CAMPAIGN PARTICIPATION

World War II

Normandy (with arrowhead)
Rhineland (with arrowhead)
Ardennes-Alsace
Central Europe

Vietnam

Counteroffensive, Phase III
Tet Counteroffensive
Counteroffensive, Phase IV
Counteroffensive, Phase V
Counteroffensive, Phase VI
Tet 69 Counteroffensive
Summer-Fall 1969
Winter-Spring 1970
Sanctuary Counteroffensive
Counteroffensive, Phase VII
Consolidation I
Consolidation II

DECORATIONS

Presidential Unit Citation (Army), Streamer embroidered **BASTOGNE** (101st Airborne Division cited)

Presidential Unit Citation (Army), Streamer embroidered **NORMANDY** (502d Parachute Infantry cited)

Valorous Unit Award, Streamer embroidered **QUANG THUONG DISTRICT** (1st Battalion, 502d Infantry cited)

French Croix de Guerre with Palm, World War II, Streamer embroidered **NORMANDY** (502d Parachute Infantry cited)

Netherlands Orange Lanyard (502d Parachute Infantry cited)

Belgian Croix de Guerre 1940 with Palm, Streamer embroidered **BASTOGNE**; cited in the Order of the Day of the Belgian Army for action at **BASTOGNE** (502d Parachute Infantry cited)

Belgian Fourragere 1940 (502d Parachute Infantry cited)

Cited in the Order of the Day of the Belgian Army for action in **FRANCE AND BELGIUM** (502d Parachute Infantry cited)

Vietnamese Cross of Gallantry with Palm, Streamer embroidered **VIETNAM 1968** (1st Battalion, 502d Infantry cited)

Vietnamese Cross of Gallantry with Palm, Streamer embroidered **VIETNAM 1968–1969** (1st Battalion, 502d Infantry cited)

2D BATTALION, 502D INFANTRY

LINEAGE

1941   Constituted 14 March in the Army of the United States as Company B, 502d Parachute Battalion; activated 1 July at Fort Benning, GA

1942   Consolidated 24 February with Company B, 502d Parachute Infantry to form Company B, 502d Parachute Infantry; assigned 15 August to 101st Airborne Division

Company lineage follows that of 502d Infantry from 1942 through 1954 activation at Fort Jackson, SC

1957   Reorganized and redesignated 1 March as Headquarters and Headquarters Company, 2d Airborne Battle Group, 502d Infantry; relieved from assignment to 101st Airborne Division and assigned to the 11th Airborne Division

1958   Inactivated 1 July in Germany

1964   Redesignated 21 January as 2d Battalion, 502d Infantry, relieved from assignment to 11th Airborne Division; assigned to 101st Airborne Division and activated 3 February at Fort Campbell, KY

CAMPAIGN PARTICIPATION

World War II

Normandy (with arrowhead)
Rhineland (with arrowhead)
Ardennes-Alsace
Central Europe

Vietnam

Defense
Counteroffensive
Counteroffensive, Phase III
Tet Counteroffensive
Counteroffensive, Phase IV
Counteroffensive, Phase V
Counteroffensive, Phase VI
Tet 69 Counteroffensive
Summer-Fall 1969
Winter-Spring 1970
Sanctuary Counteroffensive
Counteroffensive, Phase VII
Consolidation I
Consolidation II

DECORATIONS

Presidential Unit Citation (Army), Streamer embroidered **BASTOGNE** (101st Airborne Division cited)

Presidential Unit Citation (Army), Streamer embroidered **NORMANDY** (502d Parachute Infantry cited)

Presidential Unit Citation (Army), Streamer embroidered **AN KHE** (2d Battalion, 502d Infantry cited)

Presidential Unit Citation (Army), Streamer embroidered **DAK TO VIETNAM 1966** (2d Battalion, 502d Infantry cited)

Valorous Unit Award, Streamer embroidered **TUY HOA** (2d Battalion, 502d Infantry cited)

Valorous Unit Award, Streamer embroidered **NAM HOA DISTRICT** (2d Battalion, 502d Infantry cited)

Valorous Unit Award, Streamer embroidered **BA LONG DISTRICT** (2d Battalion, 502d Infantry cited)

Meritorious Unit Commendation, Streamer embroidered **VIETNAM 1965–1966** (2d Battalion, 502d Infantry cited)

French Croix de Guerre with Palm, World War II, Streamer embroidered **NORMANDY** (502d Parachute Infantry cited)

Netherlands Orange Lanyard (502d Parachute Infantry cited)

Belgian Croix de Guerre 1940 with Palm, Streamer embroidered **BASTOGNE**; cited in the Order of the Day of the Belgian Army for action at **BASTOGNE** (502d Parachute Infantry cited)

Belgian Fourragere 1940 (502d Parachute Infantry cited)

Cited in the Order of the Day of the Belgian Army for action in **FRANCE AND BELGIUM** (502d Parachute Infantry cited)

Vietnamese Cross of Gallantry with Palm, Streamer embroidered **VIETNAM 1966–1967** (2d Battalion, 502d Infantry cited)

Vietnamese Cross of Gallantry with Palm, Streamer embroidered **VIETNAM 1968–1969** (2d Battalion, 502d Infantry cited)

503D INFANTRY
(The Rock Regiment)

COAT OF ARMS

Motto: The Rock

Symbolism: The colors, blue and white, are the current and old colors of infantry. The inverted triangle terminating in the broken fort symbolizes the drop on Corregidor during the Luzon campaign, whereas the three parachutes represent the three other campaigns of the organization in World War II.

DISTINCTIVE INSIGNIA

The distinctive insignia is the shield and motto of the coat of arms.

LINEAGE

1942   Constituted 24 February in the Army of the United States as the 503d Parachute Infantry and Regiment (less 1st, 2d and 3d Battalions); activated 2 March at Fort Benning, GA (3d Battalion activated 8 June, 2d Battalion reorganized and redesignated 2 November as 2d Battalion, 509th Parachute Infantry—hereafter separate lineage; new 2d Battalion, 503d Infantry activated in Australia)

1945   Inactivated 24 December at Camp Anza, CA

1951   Redesignated 1 February as 503d Airborne Infantry, and allotted to Regular Army; assigned to 11th Airborne Division and activated 2 March at Fort Campbell, KY

1957   Relieved 1 March from assignment to 11th Airborne Division, reorganized and redesignated 503d Infantry, a parent regiment under CARS

CAMPAIGN PARTICIPATION

World War II

New Guinea
Leyte
Luzon (with arrowhead)
Southern Philippines

Vietnam

Defense
Counteroffensive
Counteroffensive, Phase II (with arrowhead)
Counteroffensive, Phase III
Tet Counteroffensive
Counteroffensive, Phase IV
Counteroffensive, Phase V
Counteroffensive, Phase VI
Tet 69 Counteroffensive
Summer-Fall 1969
Winter-Spring 1970
Sanctuary Counteroffensive
Counteroffensive, Phase VII
Consolidation I

DECORATIONS

Presidential Unit Citation (Army), Streamer embroidered **CORREGIDOR** (503d Parachute Infantry cited)

Presidential Unit Citation (Army), Streamer embroidered **BIEN HOA** (1st Battalion, 503d Infantry cited)

Presidential Unit Citation (Army), Streamer embroidered **PHOUC VINH** (2d Battalion, 503d Infantry cited)

Presidential Unit Citation (Army), Streamer embroidered **DAK TO** (173d Airborne Brigade [less 3d Battalion, 503d Infantry] cited)

Meritorious Unit Commendation, Streamer embroidered **VIETNAM 1965–1967** (1st, 2d, and 4th Battalions, 503d Infantry cited)

Philippine Presidential Unit Citation, Streamer embroidered **17 OCTOBER 1944 TO 4 JULY 1945** (503d Parachute Infantry cited)

1ST BATTALION, 503D INFANTRY
(The Rock Regiment)

LINEAGE

1941   Constituted 14 March in the Army of the United States as Company A, 503d Parachute Battalion; activated 22 August at Fort Benning, GA

1942   Consolidated 24 February with Company A, 503d Parachute Infantry to form Company A, 503d Parachute Infantry

Company lineage follows that of 503d Infantry from 1942 through 1951 activation at Fort Campbell, KY

1957   Reorganized and redesignated 1 March as Headquarters and Headquarters Company, 1st Airborne Battle Group, 503d Infantry; remained assigned to the 11th Airborne Division

1958   Relieved 1 July from assignment to the 11th Airborne Division and assigned to the 24th Infantry Division

1959   Relieved 7 January from assignment to the 24th Infantry Division and assigned to the 82d Airborne Division

1963   Relieved 26 March from assignment to 82d Airborne Division, assigned to the 173d Airborne Brigade; reorganized and redesignated 25 June as the 1st Battalion, 503d Infantry

CAMPAIGN PARTICIPATION

World War II

New Guinea
Leyte
Luzon (with arrowhead)
Southern Philippines

Vietnam

Defense
Counteroffensive
Counteroffensive,
  Phase II
Counteroffensive,
  Phase III

Tet Counteroffensive
Counteroffensive,
  Phase IV
Counteroffensive,
  Phase V
Counteroffensive,
  Phase VI
Tet 69 Counteroffensive
Summer-Fall 1969
Winter-Spring 1970
Sanctuary
  Counteroffensive
Counteroffensive, Phase
  VII
Consolidation I

DECORATIONS

Presidential Unit Citation (Army), Streamer embroidered **CORREGIDOR** (503d Parachute Infantry cited)

Presidential Unit Citation (Army), Streamer embroidered **BIEN HOA** (1st Battalion, 503d Infantry cited)

Presidential Unit Citation (Army), Streamer embroidered **DAK TO** (173d Airborne Brigade [less 3d Battalion, 503d Infantry] cited)

Meritorious Unit Commendation, Streamer embroidered **VIETNAM 1965–1967** (1st Battalion, 503d Infantry cited)

Philippine Presidential Unit Citation, Streamer embroidered **17 OCTOBER 1944 TO 4 JULY 1945** (503d Parachute Infantry cited)

2D BATTALION, 503D INFANTRY
(The Rock Regiment)

LINEAGE

1941	Constituted 14 March in the Army of the United States as Company B, 503d Parachute Battalion; activated 22 August at Fort Benning, GA
1942	Consolidated 24 February with Company B, 503d Parachute Infantry; consolidated unit designated Company B, 503d Parachute Infantry

Company lineage follows that of 503d Infantry from 1942 through 1951 activation at Fort Campbell, KY

1957	Inactivated 1 March in Germany and relieved from assignment to 11th Airborne Division, redesignated 1 September as Headquarters and Headquarters Company, 2d Airborne Battle Group, 503d Infantry; assigned to the 82d Airborne Division and activated at Fort Bragg, NC
1960	Relieved 24 June from assignment to 25th Infantry Division
1961	Relieved 1 July from assignment to 25th Infantry Division
1963	Assigned 26 March to the 173d Airborne Brigade and reorganized and redesignated 25 June as the 2d Battalion, 503d Infantry

CAMPAIGN PARTICIPATION

World War II

New Guinea
Leyte
Luzon (with arrowhead)
Southern Philippines

Vietnam

Defense
Counteroffensive
Counteroffensive,
  Phase II
  (with arrowhead)
Counteroffensive,
  Phase III

Tet Counteroffensive
Counteroffensive,
  Phase IV
Counteroffensive,
  Phase V
Counteroffensive,
  Phase VI
Tet 69 Counteroffensive
Summer-Fall 1969
Winter-Spring 1970
Sanctuary
  Counteroffensive
Counteroffensive, Phase
  VII
Consolidation I

DECORATIONS

Presidential Unit Citation (Army), Streamer embroidered **CORREGIDOR** (503d Parachute Infantry cited)

Presidential Unit Citation (Army), Streamer embroidered **PHUOC VINH** (2d Battalion, 503d Infantry cited)

Presidential Unit Citation (Army), Streamer embroidered **DAK TO** (173d Airborne Brigade [less 3d Battalion, 503d Infantry] cited)

Meritorious Unit Commendation, Streamer embroidered **VIETNAM 1965–1967** (2d Battalion, 503d Infantry cited)

Philippine Presidential Unit Citation, Streamer embroidered **17 OCTOBER 1944 TO 4 JULY 1945** (503d Parachute Infantry cited)

3D BATTALION, 503D INFANTRY
(The Rock Regiment)

LINEAGE

1941   Constituted 14 March in the Army of the United States as Company C, 503d Parachute Battalion; and activated 22 August at Fort Benning, GA

1942   Consolidated 24 February with Company C, 503d Parachute Infantry; consolidated unit designated Company C, 503d Parachute Infantry

Company lineage follows that of 503d Infantry from 1942 through 1951 activation at Fort Campbell, KY

1957   Inactivated 1 March in Germany, relieved from assignment to 11th Airborne Division, and redesignated as Headquarters and Headquarters Company, 3d Airborne Battle Group, 503d Infantry

1967   Redesignated 6 February as Headquarters and Headquarters Company, 3d Battalion, 503d Infantry; activated 1 April at Fort Bragg, NC, and assigned to the 173d Airborne Brigade

CAMPAIGN PARTICIPATION

World War II

New Guinea
Leyte
Luzon (with arrowhead)
Southern Philippines

Vietnam

Counteroffensive, Phase III
Tet Counteroffensive
Counteroffensive, Phase IV
Counteroffensive, Phase V
Counteroffensive, Phase VI
Tet 69 Counteroffensive
Summer-Fall 1969
Winter-Spring 1970
Sanctuary Counteroffensive
Counteroffensive, Phase VII
Consolidation I

DECORATIONS

Presidential Unit Citation (Army), Streamer embroidered **CORREGIDOR** (503d Parachute Infantry cited)

Philippine Presidential Unit Citation, Streamer embroidered **17 OCTOBER 1944 TO 4 JULY 1945** (503d Parachute Infantry cited)

4TH BATTALION, 503D INFANTRY
(The Rock Regiment)

LINEAGE

1942   Activated 2 November in the Army of the United States in Australia as Company D, 503d Parachute Infantry

1945   Inactivated 24 December at Camp Anza, CA

1951   Redesignated 1 February as Company D, 503d Airborne Infantry, an element of the 11th Airborne Division; allotted to Regular Army and activated 2 March at Fort Campbell, KY

1957   Inactivated 1 March in Germany and relieved from assignment to 11th Airborne Division; redesignated as Headquarters and Headquarters Company, 4th Airborne Battle Group, 503d Infantry

1966   Redesignated 26 March as Headquarters and Headquarters Company, 4th Battalion, 503d Infantry; assigned to 173d Airborne Brigade and activated 1 April at Fort Campbell, KY

CAMPAIGN PARTICIPATION

World War II

New Guinea
Leyte
Luzon (with arrowhead)
Southern Philippines

Vietnam

Counteroffensive
Counteroffensive, Phase II
Counteroffensive, Phase III
Tet Counteroffensive
Counteroffensive, Phase IV
Counteroffensive, Phase V
Counteroffensive, Phase VI
Tet 69 Counteroffensive
Summer-Fall 1969
Winter-Spring 1970
Sanctuary Counteroffensive
Counteroffensive, Phase VII
Consolidation I

DECORATIONS

Presidential Unit Citation (Army), Streamer embroidered **CORREGIDOR** (503d Parachute Infantry cited)

Presidential Unit Citation (Army), Streamer embroidered **DAK TO** (173d Airborne Brigade [less 3d Battalion, 503d Infantry] cited)

Meritorious Unit Commendation, Streamer embroidered **VIETNAM 1966–1967** (4th Battalion, 503d Infantry cited)

Philippine Presidential Unit Citation, Streamer embroidered **17 OCTOBER 1944 TO 4 JULY 1945** (503d Parachute Infantry cited)

504TH INFANTRY

COAT OF ARMS

Motto: Strike—Hold

Symbolism: The blue is the color of the infantry whose functions are represented by the sword, flaming through the sky, the flames symbolizing the zeal of the personnel in the performance of their duties. The motto is expressive of the determination of the personnel to strike swiftly and hold their ground at any cost; therefore, it is appropriate for the organization.

The wyvern and the bridge stand for the regiment's combat service in World War II at Anzio, Italy, and at Nijmegan, Holland, for each of which actions the Presidential Unit Citation (Army) was awarded. The wyvern is black in reference to the nickname "black-hearted devils in baggy pants" given to paratroopers of the regiment at Anzio. The bridge, orange for the Netherlands, further alludes to the attack on the bridges at Nijmegan. The three pheons stand for the regiment's three assault landings, in Sicily, at Anzio, and in the Rhineland.

DISTINCTIVE INSIGNIA

The distinctive insignia is the shield and motto of the coat of arms.

LINEAGE

1942   Constituted 24 February in the Army of the United States as the 504th Parachute Infantry; activated 1 May at Fort Benning, GA, and assigned 15 August to the 82d Airborne Division

1947   Reorganized and redesignated 15 December as 504th Airborne Infantry

1948   Allotted 15 November to Regular Army

1957   Relieved 1 September from assignment to the 82d Airborne Division and reorganized and redesignated as the 504th Infantry, a parent regiment under CARS

CAMPAIGN PARTICIPATION

World War II

Sicily (with arrowhead)
Naples-Foggia
Anzio (with arrowhead)

Rhineland (with arrowhead)
Ardennes-Alsace
Central Europe

DECORATIONS

Presidential Unit Citation (Army), Streamer embroidered **ANZIO BEACHHEAD** (3d Battalion, 504th Parachute Infantry cited)

Presidential Unit Citation (Army), Streamer embroidered **NIJMEGAN, HOLLAND** (1st and 3d Battalions, 504th Parachute Infantry cited)

Presidential Unit Citation (Army), Streamer embroidered **CHENEUX, BELGIUM** (1st Battalion [less Company A], 504th Parachute Infantry cited)

Military Order of William (Degree of the Knight of the Fourth Class), Streamer embroidered **NIJMEGEN 1944** (504th Parachute Infantry cited)

Netherlands Orange Lanyard (504th Parachute Infantry cited)

Belgian Fourragere 1940 (504th Parachute Infantry cited)

Cited in the Order of the Day of the Belgian Army for action in the **ARDENNES** (504th Parachute Infantry cited)

Cited in the Order of the Day of the Belgian Army for action in **BELGIUM AND GERMANY** (504th Parachute Infantry cited)

1ST BATTALION, 504TH INFANTRY

LINEAGE

1942   Constituted 24 February in the Army of the United States as Company A, 504th Parachute Infantry; activated 1 May at Fort Benning, GA, and assigned 15 August to 82d Airborne Division

Company lineage follows that of 504th Infantry from 1942 through 1948 allotment to Regular Army

1957   Reorganized and redesignated 1 September as Headquarters and Headquarters Company, 1st Airborne Battle Group, 504th Infantry; remained assigned to 82d Airborne Division

1958   Relieved 11 December from assignment to 82d Airborne Division and assigned to the 8th Infantry Division

1963   Relieved 1 April from assignment to the 8th Infantry Division and assigned to the 82d Airborne Division

1964   Reorganized and redesignated 25 May as 1st Battalion, 504th Infantry

CAMPAIGN PARTICIPATION

World War II

Sicily (with arrowhead)
Naples-Foggia
Anzio (with arrowhead)

Rhineland (with arrowhead)
Ardennes-Alsace
Central Europe

DECORATIONS

Presidential Unit Citation (Army), Streamer embroidered **ANZIO BEACHHEAD**

Presidential Unit Citation (Army), Streamer embroidered **NIJMEGAN, HOLLAND** (1st Battalion, 504th Parachute Infantry cited)

Presidential Unit Citation (Army), Streamer embroidered **CHENEUX, BELGIUM**

Presidential Unit Citation (Army), Streamer embroidered **RHINE RIVER** (Company A, 504th Parachute Infantry cited)

Military Order of William (Degree of the Knight of the Fourth Class), Streamer embroidered **NIJMEGEN 1944** (504th Parachute Infantry cited)

Netherlands Orange Lanyard (504th Parachute Infantry cited)

Belgian Fourragere 1940 (504th Parachute Infantry cited)

Cited in the Order of the Day of the Belgian Army for action in the **ARDENNES** (504th Parachute Infantry cited)

Cited in the Order of the Day of the Belgian Army for action in **BELGIUM AND GERMANY** (504th Parachute Infantry cited)

2D BATTALION, 504TH INFANTRY

LINEAGE

1942   Constituted 24 February in the Army of the United States as Company B, 504th Parachute Infantry; activated 1 May at Fort Benning, GA, and assigned 15 August to 82d Airborne Division

Company lineage follows that of 504th Infantry from 1942 through 1948 allotment to Regular Army

1957   Reorganized and redesignated 1 March as Headquarters and Headquarters Company, 2d Airborne Battle Group, 504th Infantry; relieved from assignment to the 82d Airborne Division and assigned to the 11th Airborne Division

1958   Inactivated 1 July in Germany

1960   Relieved 9 May from assignment to 11th Airborne Division, assigned to the 82d Airborne Division, and activated 1 July at Fort Bragg, NC

1964   Reorganized and redesignated 25 May as 2d Battalion, 504th Infantry

CAMPAIGN PARTICIPATION

World War II

Sicily (with arrowhead)
Naples-Foggia
Anzio (with arrowhead)

Rhineland (with arrowhead)
Ardennes-Alsace
Central Europe

DECORATIONS

Presidential Unit Citation (Army), Streamer embroidered **ANZIO BEACHHEAD**

Presidential Unit Citation (Army), Streamer embroidered **NIJMEGAN, HOLLAND** (1st Battalion, 504th Parachute Infantry cited)

Presidential Unit Citation (Army), Streamer embroidered **CHENEUX, BELGIUM** (1st Battalion [less Company A], 504th Parachute Infantry cited)

Military Order of William (Degree of the Knight of the Fourth Class), Streamer embroidered **NIJMEGEN 1944** (504th Parachute Infantry cited)

Netherlands Orange Lanyard (504th Parachute Infantry cited)

Belgian Fourragere 1940 (504th Parachute Infantry cited)

Cited in the Order of the Day of the Belgian Army for action in the **ARDENNES** (504th Parachute Infantry cited)

Cited in the Order of the Day of the Belgian Army for action in **BELGIUM AND GERMANY** (504th Parachute Infantry cited)

3D BATTALION, 504TH INFANTRY

LINEAGE

1942
Constituted 24 February in the Army of the United States as Company C, 504th Parachute Infantry; activated 1 May at Fort Benning, GA, and assigned 15 August to 82d Airborne Division

Company lineage follows that of 504th Infantry from 1942 through 1948 allotment to Regular Army

1957
Inactivated 1 September at Fort Bragg, NC, relieved from assignment to 82d Airborne Division, and redesignated as Headquarters and Headquarters Company, 3d Airborne Battle Group, 504th Infantry

1968
Redesignated 3 July as Headquarters and Headquarters Company, 3d Battalion, 504th Infantry, and activated 15 July at Fort Bragg, NC, as an element of the 82d Airborne Division

1969
Inactivated 15 December and relieved from assignment to 82d Airborne Division

CAMPAIGN PARTICIPATION

World War II

Sicily (with arrowhead)
Naples-Foggia
Anzio (with arrowhead)
Rhineland (with arrowhead)
Ardennes-Alsace
Central Europe

DECORATIONS

Presidential Unit Citation (Army), Streamer embroidered **ANZIO BEACHHEAD**

Presidential Unit Citation (Army), Streamer embroidered **NIJMEGAN, HOLLAND** (1st Battalion, 504th Parachute Infantry cited)

Presidential Unit Citation (Army), Streamer embroidered **CHENEUX, BELGIUM** (1st Battalion [less Company A], 504th Parachute Infantry cited)

Military Order of William (Degree of the Knight of the Fourth Class), Streamer embroidered **NIJMEGEN 1944** (504th Parachute Infantry cited)

Netherlands Orange Lanyard (504th Parachute Infantry cited)

Belgian Fourragere 1940 (504th Parachute Infantry cited)

Cited in the Order of the Day of the Belgian Army for action in the **ARDENNES** (504th Parachute Infantry cited)

Cited in the Order of the Day of the Belgian Army for action in **BELGIUM AND GERMANY** (504th Parachute Infantry cited)

505TH INFANTRY
(Panthers)

COAT OF ARMS

Motto: H-Minus

Symbolism: Blue and white are the old and present colors of infantry. The black panther symbolizes stealth, speed, and courage, all characteristics of a good parachutist. The wings are added to represent entry into combat via air, and the bendlets symbolize the unit's parachute drops into combat.

The winged red arrowhead in the crest is used to represent the regiment's first combat attack in Sicily during World War II.

DISTINCTIVE INSIGNIA

The distinctive insignia is the shield, crest, and motto of the coat of arms.

LINEAGE

1942   Constituted 24 June in the Army of the United States as the 505th Parachute Infantry and activated 6 July at Fort Benning, GA

1943   Assigned 10 February to 82d Airborne Division

1948   Reorganized and redesignated 15 December as 505th Airborne Infantry and allotted 15 December to Regular Army

1957   Relieved 1 September from assignment to 82d Airborne Division and reorganized and redesignated as the 505th Infantry, a parent regiment under CARS

CAMPAIGN PARTICIPATION

World War II

Sicily (with arrowhead)
Naples-Foggia
Normandy (with arrowhead)
Rhineland (with arrowhead)
Ardennes-Alsace
Central Europe

Vietnam

Tet Counteroffensive
Counteroffensive, Phase IV
Counteroffensive, Phase V
Counteroffensive, Phase VI
Tet 69 Counteroffensive
Summer–Fall 1969
Winter–Spring 1970

DECORATIONS

Presidential Unit Citation (Army), Streamer embroidered **STE. MERE EGLISE** (505th Parachute Infantry cited)

Presidential Unit Citation (Army), Streamer embroidered **NIJMEGEN** (2d Battalion, 505th Parachute Infantry cited)

French Croix de Guerre with Palm, World War II, Streamer embroidered **STE. MERE EGLISE** (505th Parachute Infantry cited)

French Croix de Guerre with Palm, World War II, Streamer embroidered **COTENTIN** (505th Parachute Infantry cited)

French Croix de Guerre, World War II, Fourragere (505th parachute Infantry cited)

Military Order of William (Degree of the Knight of the Fourth Class), Streamer embroidered **NIJMEGEN 1944** (505th Parachute Infantry cited)

Netherlands Orange Lanyard (505th Parachute Infantry cited)

Belgian Fourragere 1940 (505th Parachute Infantry cited)

Cited in the Order of the Day of the Belgian Army for action in the **ARDENNES** (505th Parachute Infantry cited)

Cited in the Order of the Day of the Belgian Army for action in **BELGIUM AND GERMANY** (505th Parachute Infantry cited)

1ST BATTALION, 505TH INFANTRY
(Panthers)

LINEAGE

1942   Constituted 24 June in the Army of the United States as Company A, 505th Parachute Infantry; activated 6 July at Fort Benning, GA

Company lineage follows that of 505th Infantry from 1942 through 1948 allottment to Regular Army

1957   Reorganized and redesignated 1 September as Headquarters and Headquarters Company, 1st Airborne Battle Group, 505th Infantry; remained assigned to 82d Airborne Division

1959   Relieved 15 January from assignment to 82d Airborne Division and assigned to 8th Infantry Division

1963   Relieved 1 April from assignment to 8th Infantry Division and assigned to 82d Airborne Division

1964   Reorganized and redesignated 25 May as 1st Battalion, 505th Infantry

CAMPAIGN PARTICIPATION

World War II

Sicily (with arrowhead)
Naples-Foggia
Normandy (with arrowhead)
Rhineland (with arrowhead)
Ardennes-Alsace
Central Europe

Vietnam

Tet Counteroffensive
Counteroffensive, Phase IV
Counteroffensive, Phase V
Counteroffensive, Phase VI
Tet 69 Counteroffensive
Summer–Fall 1969
Winter–Spring 1970

DECORATIONS

Presidential Unit Citation (Army), Streamer embroidered **STE. MERE EGLISE** (505th Parachute Infantry cited)

Presidential Unit Citation (Army), Streamer embroidered **NIJMEGEN**

French Croix de Guerre with Palm, World War II, Streamer embroidered **STE. MERE EGLISE** (505th Parachute Infantry cited)

French Croix de Guerre with Palm, World War II, Streamer embroidered **COTENTIN** (505th Parachute Infantry cited)

French Croix de Guerre, World War II, Fourragere (505th parachute Infantry cited)

Military Order of William (Degree of the Knight of the Fourth Class), Streamer embroidered **NIJMEGEN 1944** (505th Parachute Infantry cited)

Netherlands Orange Lanyard (505th Parachute Infantry cited)

Belgian Fourragere 1940 (505th Parachute Infantry cited)

Cited in the Order of the Day of the Belgian Army for action in the **ARDENNES** (505th Parachute Infantry cited)

Cited in the Order of the Day of the Belgian Army for action in **BELGIUM AND GERMANY** (505th Parachute Infantry cited)

Vietnamese Cross of Gallantry with Palm, Streamer embroidered **VIETNAM 1968-1969** (1st Battalion, 505th Infantry cited)

2D BATTALION, 505TH INFANTRY
(Panthers)

LINEAGE

1942   Constituted 24 June in the Army of the United States as Company B, 505th Parachute Infantry; activated 6 July at Fort Benning, GA

Company lineage follows that of 505th Infantry from 1942 through 1948 allottment to Regular Army

1957   Reorganized and redesignated 1 March as Headquarters and Headquarters Company, 2d Airborne Battle Group, 505th Infantry; relieved from assignment to 82d Airborne Division and assigned to the 11d Airborne Division

1958   Inactivated 1 July in Germany

1964   Redesignated 6 March as 2d Battalion, 505th Infantry; relieved from assignment to 11th Airborne division, assigned to 82d Airborne Division, and activated 25 May at Fort Bragg, NC

CAMPAIGN PARTICIPATION

World War II

Sicily (with arrowhead)
Naples-Foggia
Normandy (with arrowhead)
Rhineland (with arrowhead)
Ardennes-Alsace
Central Europe

Vietnam

Tet Counteroffensive
Counteroffensive, Phase IV
Counteroffensive, Phase V
Counteroffensive, Phase VI
Tet 69 Counteroffensive
Summer–Fall 1969
Winter–Spring 1970

DECORATIONS

Presidential Unit Citation (Army), Streamer embroidered **STE. MERE EGLISE** (505th Parachute Infantry cited)

Presidential Unit Citation (Army), Streamer embroidered **NIJMEGEN**

French Croix de Guerre with Palm, World War II, Streamer embroidered **STE. MERE EGLISE** (505th Parachute Infantry cited)

French Croix de Guerre with Palm, World War II, Streamer embroidered **COTENTIN** (505th Parachute Infantry cited)

French Croix de Guerre, World War II, Fourragere (505th Parachute Infantry cited)

Military Order of William (Degree of the Knight of the Fourth Class), Streamer embroidered **NIJMEGEN 1944** (505th Parachute Infantry cited)

Netherlands Orange Lanyard (505th Parachute Infantry cited)

Belgian Fourragere 1940 (505th Parachute Infantry cited)

Cited in the Order of the Day of the Belgian Army for action in the **ARDENNES** (505th Parachute Infantry cited)

Cited in the Order of the Day of the Belgian Army for action in **BELGIUM AND GERMANY** (505th Parachute Infantry cited)

Vietnamese Cross of Gallantry with Palm, Streamer embroidered **VIETNAM 1968–1969** (2d Battalion, 505th Infantry cited)

3D BATTALION, 505TH INFANTRY
(Panthers)

LINEAGE

1942   Constituted 24 June in the Army of the United States as Company C, 505th Parachute Infantry; activated 6 July at Fort Benning, GA

Company lineage follows that of 505th Infantry from 1942 through 1948 allottment to Regular Army

1957   Inactivated 1 September at Fort Bragg, NC, relieved from assignment to 82d Airborne Division, and redesignated as Headquarters and Headquarters Company, 3d Airborne Battle Group, 505th Infantry

1968   Redesignated 3 July as Headquarters and Headquarters Company, 3d Battalion, 505th Infantry, and activated 15 July at Fort Bragg, NC, as an element of the 82d Airborne Division

1969   Inactivated 15 December and relieved from assignment to 82d Airborne Division

CAMPAIGN PARTICIPATION

World War II

Sicily (with arrowhead)
Naples-Foggia
Normandy (with arrowhead)

Rhineland (with arrowhead)
Ardennes-Alsace
Central Europe

DECORATIONS

Presidential Unit Citation (Army), Streamer embroidered **STE. MERE EGLISE** (505th Parachute Infantry cited)

Presidential Unit Citation (Army), Streamer embroidered **NIJMEGEN**

French Croix de Guerre with Palm, World War II, Streamer embroidered **STE. MERE EGLISE** (505th Parachute Infantry cited)

French Croix de Guerre with Palm, World War II, Streamer embroidered **COTENTIN** (505th Parachute Infantry cited)

French Croix de Guerre, World War II, Fourragere (505th Parachute Infantry cited)

Military Order of William (Degree of the Knight of the Fourth Class), Streamer embroidered **NIJMEGEN 1944** (505th Parachute Infantry cited)

Netherlands Orange Lanyard (505th Parachute Infantry cited)

Belgian Fourragere 1940 (505th Parachute Infantry cited)

Cited in the Order of the Day of the Belgian Army for action in the **ARDENNES** (505th Parachute Infantry cited)

Cited in the Order of the Day of the Belgian Army for action in **BELGIUM AND GERMANY** (505th Parachute Infantry cited)

506TH INFANTRY
(Currahee)

COAT OF ARMS

Motto: *Currahee* (Stands Alone)

Symbolism: The blue field of the shield is for the infantry. The thunderbolt indicates the regiment's particular threat and technique of attack: striking with speed, power, and surprise from the sky. Six parachutes represent the fact that the 506th was the sixth parachute regiment constituted in the U.S. Army. The green silhouette represents Currahee Mountain—the cite of the regiment's activation (Camp Toccoa, GA)—and symbolizes the organization's strength, independence, and ability to stand alone for which paratroops are renowned. In fact *Currahee* is the American aboriginal Cherokee Indian equivalent for "Stands Alone."

The winged sword-breaker represents airborne troops. The conjoined caltraps stand for the enemy line of defense behind which paratroopers are dropped. They are two in number in reference to

(continued on next page)

DISTINCTIVE INSIGNIA

The distinctive insignia is the shield and motto of the coat of arms.

(continued from previous page)

the unit's two air assault landings. The fleur-de-lis is for the Normandy invasion and the bugle horn, from the arms of Eindhoven, Holland, refers to the organization's capture of that objective. The spikes of the caltraps stand for the unit's World War II decorations. The demi-roundel represents a section of the hub of a wheel. It stands for Bastogne, Belgium, strategic crossroads of highways and railways. The hub, surmounted by the winged sword-breaker, commemorates the organization's heroic defense of Bastogne in the Battle of the Bulge.

CAMPAIGN PARTICIPATION

World War II

Normandy (with arrowhead)
Rhineland (with arrowhead
Ardennes-Alsace
Central Europe

Vietnam

Counteroffensive, Phase III
Tet Counteroffensive
Counteroffensive, Phase IV
Counteroffensive, Phase V
Counteroffensive, Phase VI
Tet 69 Counteroffensive
Summer–Fall 1969
Winter–Spring 1970
Sanctuary Counteroffensive
Counteroffensive, Phase VII
Consolidation I
Consolidation II

LINEAGE

1942	Constituted 1 July in the Army of the United States as the 506th Parachute Infantry; activated 20 July at Camp Toccoa, GA
1945	Assigned 1 March to 101st Airborne Division and inactivated 30 November at Auxerre, France
1948	Redesignated 18 June as the 506th Airborne Infantry and allotted 25 June to the Regular Army; activated 6 July at Camp Breckinridge, KY
1949	Inactivated 1 April
1950	Activated 25 August
1953	Inactivated 1 December
1954	Activated 15 May at Fort Jackson, SC
1957	Relieved 25 April from assignment to 101st Airborne division; reorganized and redesignated as the 506th Infantry, a parent regiment under CARS

DECORATIONS

Presidential Unit Citation (Army), Streamer embroidered **BASTOGNE** (506th Parachute Infantry cited)

Presidential Unit Citation (Army), Streamer embroidered **NORMANDY** (506th Parachute Infantry cited)

Valorous Unit Award, Streamer embroidered **PHAN THIET** (3d Battalion, 506th Infantry cited)

French Croix de Guerre with Palm, World War II, Streamer embroidered **NORMANDY** (506th Parachute Infantry cited)

Netherlands Orange Lanyard (506th Parachute Infantry cited)

Belgian Croix de Guerre 1940 with Palm, Streamer embroidered **BASTOGNE**; cited in the Order of the Day of the Belgian Army for action at **BASTOGNE** (506th Parachute Infantry cited)

Belgian Fourragere 1940 (506th Parachute Infantry cited)

Cited in the Order of the Day of the Belgian Army for action in **FRANCE AND BELGIUM** (506th Parachute Infantry cited)

1ST BATTALION, 506TH INFANTRY
(Currahee)

LINEAGE

| 1942 | Constituted 1 July in the Army of the United States as Company A, 506th Parachute Infantry; activated 20 July at Camp Toccoa, GA |

Company lineage follows that of 506th Infantry from 1942 through 1954 activation at Fort Jackson, SC

| 1957 | Reorganized and redesignated 25 April as Headquarters and Headquarters Company, 1st Air- |

borne Battle Group, 506th Infantry; remained assigned to the 101st Airborne Division

1964   Reorganized and redesignated 3 February as 1st Battalion

CAMPAIGN PARTICIPATION

World War II

Normandy (with arrowhead)
Rhineland (with arrowhead
Ardennes-Alsace
Central Europe

Vietnam

Counteroffensive, Phase III
Tet Counteroffensive
Counteroffensive, Phase IV
Counteroffensive, Phase V
Counteroffensive, Phase VI
Tet 69 Counteroffensive
Summer–Fall 1969
Winter–Spring 1970
Sanctuary Counteroffensive
Counteroffensive, Phase VII
Consolidation I
Consolidation II

DECORATIONS

Presidential Unit Citation (Army), Streamer embroidered **BASTOGNE** (506th Parachute Infantry cited)

Presidential Unit Citation (Army), Streamer embroidered **NORMANDY** (506th Parachute Infantry cited)

French Croix de Guerre with Palm, World War II, Streamer embroidered **NORMANDY** (506th Parachute Infantry cited)

Netherlands Orange Lanyard (506th Parachute Infantry cited)

Belgian Croix de Guerre 1940 with Palm, Streamer embroidered **BASTOGNE**; cited in the Order of the Day of the Belgian Army for action at **BASTOGNE** (506th Parachute Infantry cited)

Belgian Fourragere 1940 (506th Parachute Infantry cited)

Cited in the Order of the Day of the Belgian Army for action in **FRANCE AND BELGIUM** (506th Parachute Infantry cited)

Vietnamese Cross of Gallantry with Palm, Streamer embroidered **VIETNAM 1968–1969** (1st Battalion, 506th Infantry cited)

2D BATTALION, 506TH INFANTRY
(Currahee)

LINEAGE

1942   Constituted 1 July in the Army of the United States as Company B, 506th Parachute Infantry; activated 20 July at Camp Toccoa, GA

Company lineage follows that of 506th Infantry from 1942 through 1954 activation at Fort Jackson, SC

1957   Inactivated 25 April at Fort Campbell, KY, relieved from assignment to 101st Airborne Division, and redesignated Headquarters and Headquarters Company, 2d Airborne Battle Group, 506th Infantry

1964   Redesignated 21 January as Headquarters and Headquarters Company, 2d Battalion, 506th Infantry, assigned to the 101st Airborne Division, and activated 3 February at Fort Campbell, KY

CAMPAIGN PARTICIPATION

World War II

Normandy (with arrowhead)
Rhineland (with arrowhead
Ardennes-Alsace
Central Europe

Vietnam

Counteroffensive, Phase III
Tet Counteroffensive
Counteroffensive, Phase IV
Counteroffensive, Phase V
Counteroffensive, Phase VI
Tet 69 Counteroffensive
Summer–Fall 1969
Winter–Spring 1970
Sanctuary Counteroffensive
Counteroffensive, Phase VII
Consolidation I
Consolidation II

DECORATIONS

Presidential Unit Citation (Army), Streamer embroidered **BASTOGNE** (506th Parachute Infantry cited)

Presidential Unit Citation (Army), Streamer embroidered **NORMANDY** (506th Parachute Infantry cited)

French Croix de Guerre with Palm, World War II, Streamer embroidered **NORMANDY** (506th Parachute Infantry cited)

Netherlands Orange Lanyard (506th Parachute Infantry cited)

Belgian Croix de Guerre 1940 with Palm, Streamer embroidered **BASTOGNE**; cited in the Order of the Day of the Belgian Army for action at **BASTOGNE** (506th Parachute Infantry cited)

Belgian Fourragere 1940 (506th Parachute Infantry cited)

Cited in the Order of the Day of the Belgian Army for action in **FRANCE AND BELGIUM** (506th Parachute Infantry cited)

Vietnamese Cross of Gallantry with Palm, Streamer embroidered **VIETNAM 1968–1969** (2d Battalion, 506th Infantry cited)

3D BATTALION, 506TH INFANTRY
(Currahee)

LINEAGE

1942   Constituted 1 July in the Army of the United States as Company C, 506th Parachute Infantry; activated 20 July at Camp Toccoa, GA

Company lineage follows that of 506th Infantry from 1942 through 1954 activation at Fort Jackson, SC

1957   Inactivated 25 April at Fort Campbell, KY, relieved from assignment to 101st Airborne Division, and redesignated as Headquarters and Headquarters Company, 3d Airborne Battle Group, 506th Infantry

1967   Redesignated 6 February as Headquarters and Headquarters Company, 3d Battalion, 506th Infantry; activated 1 April at Fort Campbell, KY, and assigned to the 101st Airborne Division

CAMPAIGN PARTICIPATION

World War II

Normandy (with arrowhead)
Rhineland (with arrowhead
Ardennes-Alsace
Central Europe

Vietnam

Counteroffensive, Phase III
Tet Counteroffensive
Counteroffensive, Phase IV
Counteroffensive, Phase V
Counteroffensive, Phase VI
Tet 69 Counteroffensive
Summer–Fall 1969
Winter–Spring 1970
Sanctuary Counteroffensive
Counteroffensive, Phase VII

DECORATIONS

Presidential Unit Citation (Army), Streamer embroidered **BASTOGNE** (506th Parachute Infantry cited)

Presidential Unit Citation (Army), Streamer embroidered **NORMANDY** (506th Parachute Infantry cited)

Valorous Unit Award, Streamer embroidered **PHAN THIET** (3d Battalion, 506th Infantry cited)

French Croix de Guerre with Palm, World War II, Streamer embroidered **NORMANDY** (506th Parachute Infantry cited)

Netherlands Orange Lanyard (506th Parachute Infantry cited)

Belgian Croix de Guerre 1940 with Palm, Streamer embroidered **BASTOGNE**; cited in the Order of the Day of the Belgian Army for action at **BASTOGNE** (506th Parachute Infantry cited)

Belgian Fourragere 1940 (506th Parachute Infantry cited)

Cited in the Order of the Day of the Belgian Army for action in **FRANCE AND BELGIUM** (506th Parachute Infantry cited)

Vietnamese Cross of Gallantry with Palm, Streamer embroidered **VIETNAM 1968–1969** (3d Battalion, 506th Infantry cited)

508TH INFANTRY

FURY FROM THE SKY

COAT OF ARMS

Motto: Fury From the Sky

Symbolism: The two principal colors of the shield (blue and white) are the current and old colors of infantry. The lion on the coat of arms is the same as the French leopard used in the arms of Normandy, and commemorates the organization's landing and campaign in that province. The silver bar, called a bend, is in honor of the organization's service in the Rhineland.

The wyvern in the crest is taken from the shoulder sleeve insignia of the 508th Airborne Regimental Combat Team in which the regiment was the primary element in the 1950s. The color red alludes to the unit's unofficial nickname, "Red Devils." The arrowhead divided in two colors, yellow and black, refers to the two assault landings made by the 508th in Normandy and in the Rhineland. The fourteen notches of the arrowhead allude to the regiment's overall honors in World War II—four campaigns and ten decorations.

DISTINCTIVE INSIGNIA

The distinctive insignia is the shield and motto of the coat of arms.

LINEAGE

1942	Constituted 6 October in the Army of the United States as the 508th Parachute Infantry; activated 20 October at Camp Blanding, FL
1946	Inactivated 25 November at Camp Kilmer, NJ
1951	Redesignated 16 April as the 508th Airborne Infantry, allotted to Regular Army, and activated at Fort Bragg, NC
1957	Inactivated 22 March at Fort Campbell, KY
1962	Reorganized and redesignated 15 July as 508th Infantry, a parent regiment under CARS

CAMPAIGN PARTICIPATION

World War II

Normandy (with arrowhead)
Rhineland (with arrowhead)
Ardennes-Alsace
Central Europe

Vietnam

Tet Counteroffensive
Counteroffensive, Phase IV
Counteroffensive, Phase V
Counteroffensive, Phase VI
Tet 69 Counteroffensive
Summer–Fall 1969
Winter–Spring 1970

DECORATIONS

Presidential Unit Citation (Army), Streamer embroidered **COTENTIN PENINSULA** (508th Parachute Infantry cited)

Valorous Unit Award, Streamer embroidered **HUE AND SAIGON** (1st Battalion, 508th Infantry cited)

French Croix de Guerre with Palm, World War II, Streamer embroidered **STE. MERE EGLISE** (508th Parachute Infantry cited)

French Croix de Guerre with Palm, World War II, Streamer embroidered **COTENTIN** (508th Parachute Infantry cited)

French Croix de Guerre, World War II, Fourragere (508th Parachute Infantry cited)

Military Order of William (Degree of the Knight of the Fourth Class), Streamer embroidered **NIJMEGEN 1944** (508th Parachute Infantry cited)

Netherlands Orange Lanyard (508th Parachute Infantry cited)

Belgian Fourragere 1940 (508th Parachute Infantry cited)

Cited in the Order of the Day of the Belgian Army for action in the **ARDENNES** (508th Parachute Infantry cited)

Cited in the Order of the Day of the Belgian Army for action in **BELGIUM AND GERMANY** (508th Parachute Infantry cited)

Cited in the Order of the Day of the Belgian Army for action at **ST. VITH** (508th Parachute Infantry cited)

1ST BATTALION, 508TH INFANTRY

LINEAGE

1942	Constituted 6 October in the Army of the United States as Company A, 508th Parachute Infantry; activated 20 October at Camp Blanding, FL
	Company lineage follows that of 508th Infantry from 1942 through 1957 inactivation at Fort Campbell, KY
1962	Redesignated 15 July as Headquarters and Headquarters Company, 1st Battalion, 508th Infantry
1964	Assigned 6 March to 82d Airborne Division and activated 25 May at Fort Bragg, NC

CAMPAIGN PARTICIPATION

World War II

Normandy (with arrowhead)
Rhineland (with arrowhead)
Ardennes-Alsace
Central Europe

Vietnam

Tet Counteroffensive
Counteroffensive, Phase IV
Counteroffensive, Phase V
Counteroffensive, Phase VI
Tet 69 Counteroffensive
Summer–Fall 1969
Winter–Spring 1970

DECORATIONS

Presidential Unit Citation (Army), Streamer embroidered **COTENTIN PENINSULA** (508th Parachute Infantry cited)

Valorous Unit Award, Streamer embroidered **HUE AND SAIGON** (1st Battalion, 508th Infantry cited)

French Croix de Guerre with Palm, World War II, Streamer embroidered **STE. MERE EGLISE** (508th Parachute Infantry cited)

French Croix de Guerre with Palm, World War II, Streamer embroidered **COTENTIN** (508th Parachute Infantry cited)

French Croix de Guerre, World War II, Fourragere (508th Parachute Infantry cited)

Military Order of William (Degree of the Knight of the Fourth Class), Streamer embroidered **NIJMEGEN 1944** (508th Parachute Infantry cited)

Netherlands Orange Lanyard (508th Parachute Infantry cited)

Belgian Fourragere 1940 (508th Parachute Infantry cited)

Cited in the Order ot the Day of the Belgian Army for action in the **ARDENNES** (508th Parachute Infantry cited)

Cited in the Order of the Day of the Belgian Army for action in **BELGIUM AND GERMANY** (508th Parachute Infantry cited)

Cited in the order of the Day of the Belgian Army for action at **ST. VITH** (508th Parachute Infantry cited)

Vietnamese Cross of Gallantry with Palm, Streamer embroidered **VIETNAM 1968–1969** (1st Battalion, 508th Infantry cited)

2D BATTALION, 508TH INFANTRY

LINEAGE

1942   Constituted 6 October in the Army of the United States as Company B, 508th Parachute Infantry; activated 20 October at Camp Blanding, FL

        Company lineage follows that of 508th Infantry from 1942 through 1957 inactivation at Fort Campbell, KY

1962   Redesignated 15 July as Headquarters and Headquarters Company, 2d Battalion, 508th Infantry

1964   Assigned 6 March to 82d Airborne Division and activated 25 May at Fort Bragg, NC

CAMPAIGN PARTICIPATION

World War II

  Normandy (with arrowhead)
  Rhineland (with arrowhead)
  Ardennes-Alsace
  Central Europe

DECORATIONS

Presidential Unit Citation (Army), Streamer embroidered **COTENTIN PENINSULA** (508th Parachute Infantry cited)

French Croix de Guerre with Palm, World War II, Streamer embroidered **STE. MERE EGLISE** (508th Parachute Infantry cited)

French Croix de Guerre with Palm, World War II, Streamer embroidered **COTENTIN** (508th Parachute Infantry cited)

French Croix de Guerre, World War II, Fourragere (508th Parachute Infantry cited)

Military Order of William (Degree of the Knight of the Fourth Class), Streamer embroidered **NIJMEGEN 1944** (508th Parachute Infantry cited)

Netherlands Orange Lanyard (508th Parachute Infantry cited)

Belgian Fourragere 1940 (508th Parachute Infantry cited)

Cited in the Order of the Day of the Belgian Army for action in the **ARDENNES** (508th Parachute Infantry cited)

Cited in the Order of the Day of the Belgian Army for action in **BELGIUM AND GERMANY** (508th Parachute Infantry cited)

Cited in the Order of the Day of the Belgian Army for action at **ST. VITH** (508th Parachute Infantry cited)

3D BATTALION, 508TH INFANTRY

LINEAGE

1942   Constituted 6 October in the Army of the United States as Company C, 508th Parachute Infantry; activated 20 October at Camp Blanding, FL

Company lineage follows that of 508th Infantry from 1942 through 1957 inactivation at Fort Campbell, KY

1962   Redesignated 15 July as Headquarters and Headquarters Company, 3d Battalion, 508th Infantry; assigned 3 August to 193d Infantry Brigade and activated 8 August at Ford Kobbe, Canal Zone

1968   Inactivated 26 June at Fort Kobbe, Canal Zone

CAMPAIGN PARTICIPATION

World War II

Normandy (with
    arrowhead)
Rhineland (with
    arrowhead)
Ardennes-Alsace
Central Europe

DECORATIONS

Presidential Unit Citation (Army), Streamer embroidered **COTENTIN PENINSULA** (508th Parachute Infantry cited)

French Croix de Guerre with Palm, World War II, Streamer embroidered **STE. MERE EGLISE** (508th Parachute Infantry cited)

French Croix de Guerre with Palm, World War II, Streamer embroidered **COTENTIN** (508th Parachute Infantry cited)

French Croix de Guerre, World War II, Fourragere (508th Parachute Infantry cited)

Military Order of William (Degree of the Knight of the Fourth Class), Streamer embroidered **NIJMEGEN 1944** (508th Parachute Infantry cited)

Netherlands Orange Lanyard (508th Parachute Infantry cited)

Belgian Fourragere 1940 (508th Parachute Infantry cited)

Cited in the Order of the Day of the Belgian Army for action in the **ARDENNES** (508th Parachute Infantry cited)

Cited in the Order of the Day of the Belgian Army for action in **BELGIUM AND GERMANY** (508th Parachute Infantry cited)

Cited in the order of the Day of the Belgian Army for action at **ST. VITH** (508th Parachute Infantry cited)

509TH INFANTRY

COAT OF ARMS

Motto: All the Way

Symbolism: The stylized yellow (gold) figure of a parachutist on a black ground is adapted from the device worn by the regiment during World War II and by which it was known throughout the Mediterranean Theater. The red field alludes to the red berets worn by the British 1st Airborne Division and the close association between it and the regiment during World War II in England and North Africa. The nebuly (heraldic delineation for water) white and blue bars (the colors blue and white are used for infantry) refer to the record breaking flight from England parachuting into North Africa on 8 November 1942. The two segments of the wavy blue bar simulate the streamers of the Presidential Unit Citations (Army) awarded for the

(continued on next page)

DISTINCTIVE INSIGNIA

The distinctive insignia is the shield and motto of the coat of arms.

(continued from previous page)

gallant actions at Carano, Italy, and Liege, Belgium, and in being a heraldic symbol of water refer to the amphibious landing on the Anzio-Nettuno beachhead on 22 January 1944. The black pile simulates a parachute jump and in also being a heraldic symbol used frequently for engineers (i.e., pile driving), the two sides refer to the ground defense the organization participated in during the Anzio and Ardennes-Alsace (Battle of the Bulge) campaigns. The five arrowheads are for the five assault landings made by the regiments in World War II.

The jackal and crescent are taken from the regimental badge of the French 3d Zouaves Regiment, and symbolize the parachute jump and seizure of the airfield at Youks-les-Bains near the border of Tunisia. One of the results of this hazardous operation on 15 November 1942 was the authority granted by the French Commander in Chief for personnel of the 509th Infantry to wear the badge of the 3d Zouaves Regiment. The rock and crescent allude to the subsequent successful action at Faid Pass in Tunisia.

LINEAGE

| 1941 | Constituted 14 March in the Army of the United States as the 504th Parachute Battalion; activated 5 October at Fort Benning, GA |
| 1942 | Reorganized and redesignated 24 February as 2d Battalion, 503d Parachute Infantry; reorganized and redesignated 2 November as 2d Battalion, 509th Parachute Infantry |

1943	Reorganized and redesignated 10 December as 509th Parachute Infantry Battalion
1945	Disbanded 1 March in France
1947	Reconstituted 12 May in the Regular Army as the 509th Parachute Infantry Battalion
1963	Reorganized and redesignated 1 April as the 509th Infantry, a parent regiment under CARS

CAMPAIGN PARTICIPATION

World War II

Algeria-French Morocco (with arrowhead)
Tunisia (with arrowhead)
Naples-Foggia (with arrowhead)

Anzio (with arrowhead)
Rome-Arno
Southern France (with arrowhead)
Rhineland
Ardennes-Alsace

DECORATIONS

Presidential Unit Citation (Army), Streamer embroidered **LIEGE, BELGIUM** (509th Parachute Infantry Battalion cited)

Presidential Unit Citation (Army), Streamer embroidered **CARANO, ITALY** (509th Parachute Infantry Battalion cited)

French Croix de Guerre with Silver Star, World War II, Streamer embroidered **MUY EN PROVENCE** (509th Parachute Infantry Battalion cited)

Cited in the Order of the Day of the Belgian Army for action in the **ARDENNES** (509th Parachute Infantry Battalion cited)

Cited in the Order of the Day of the Belgian Army for action at **ST. VITH** (509th Parachute Infantry Battalion cited)

Personnel authorized to wear the insignia of the French 3d Zouaves Regiment (2d Battalion, 503d Parachute Infantry cited); Letter Order 969, French Commanded in Chief, 6 February 1944, and DF, Comment 1, WD G-1, 27 December 1944)

1ST BATTALION, 509TH INFANTRY

LINEAGE

| 1941 | Constituted 14 March in the Army of the United States as Company A, 504th Parachute Battalion; activated 5 October at Fort Benning, GA |

| 1942 | Reorganized and redesignated 24 February as Company D, 503d Parachute Infantry; reorganized and redesignated 2 November as Company D, 509th Parachute Infantry |
| 1943 | Reorganized and redesignated 10 December as Company A, 509th Parachute Infantry Battalion |

1945   Disbanded 1 March in France

1947   Reconstituted 12 May in the Regular Army as Company A, 509th Parachute Infantry Battalion

1963   Redesignated 27 March as Headquarters and Headquarters Company, 1st Battalion, 509th Infantry; assigned to the 8th Infantry Division and activated 1 April in Germany

CAMPAIGN PARTICIPATION

World War II

Algeria-French Morocco (with arrowhead)
Tunisia (with arrowhead)
Naples-Foggia (with arrowhead)

Anzio (with arrowhead)
Rome-Arno
Southern France (with arrowhead)
Rhineland
Ardennes-Alsace

DECORATIONS

Presidential Unit Citation (Army), Streamer embroidered **LIEGE, BELGIUM** (509th Parachute Infantry Battalion cited)

Presidential Unit Citation (Army), Streamer embroidered **CARANO, ITALY** (509th Parachute Infantry Battalion cited)

French Croix de Guerre with Silver Star, World War II, Streamer embroidered **MUY EN PROVENCE** (509th Parachute Infantry Battalion cited)

Cited in the Order of the Day of the Belgian Army for action in the **ARDENNES** (509th Parachute Infantry Battalion cited)

Cited in the Order of the Day of the Belgian Army for action at **ST. VITH** (509th Parachute Infantry Battalion cited)

Personnel authorized to wear the insignia of the French 3d Zouaves Regiment (2d Battalion, 503d Parachute Infantry cited); Letter Order 969, French Commander in Chief, 6 February 1944, and DF, Comment 1, WD G-1, 27 December 1944)

2D BATTALION, 509TH INFANTRY

LINEAGE

1941   Constituted 14 March in the Army of the United States as Company B, 504th Parachute Battalion; activated 5 October at Fort Benning, GA

1942   Reorganized and redesignated 24 February as Company E, 503d Parachute Infantry; reorganized and redesignated 2 November as Company E, 509th Parachute Infantry

1943   Reorganized and redesignated 10 December as Company B, 509th Parachute Infantry Battalion

1963   Redesignated 27 March as Headquarters and Headquarters Company, 2d Battalion, 509th Infantry; assigned to the 8th Infantry Division and activated 1 April in Germany

CAMPAIGN PARTICIPATION

World War II

Algeria-French Morocco (with arrowhead)
Tunisia (with arrowhead)
Naples-Foggia (with arrowhead)

Anzio (with arrowhead)
Rome-Arno
Southern France (with arrowhead)
Rhineland
Ardennes-Alsace

DECORATIONS

Presidential Unit Citation (Army), Streamer embroidered **LIEGE, BELGIUM** (509th Parachute Infantry Battalion cited)

Presidential Unit Citation (Army), Streamer embroidered **CARANO, ITALY** (509th Parachute Infantry Battalion cited)

French Croix de Guerre with Silver Star, World War II, Streamer embroidered **MUY EN PROVENCE** (509th Parachute Infantry Battalion cited)

Cited in the Order of the Day of the Belgian Army for action in the **ARDENNES** (509th Parachute Infantry Battalion cited)

Cited in the Order of the Day of the Belgian Army for action at **ST. VITH** (509th Parachute Infantry Battalion cited)

Personnel authorized to wear the insignia of the French 3d Zouaves Regiment (2d Battalion, 503d Parachute Infantry cited); Letter Order 969, French Commander in Chief, 6 February 1944, and DF, Comment 1, WD G-1, 27 December 1944)

511TH INFANTRY

COAT OF ARMS

Motto: Strength From Above

Symbolism: Blue is the infantry color, and the blue and green signify the sky and the earth—the nebuly dividing line being the heraldic symbol for clouds. The white, wedge-shaped figure represents a parachute (for airborne infantry) and is also indicative of a wedge being driven from sky to earth, thus alluding to the regimental motto, "Strength From Above." The sun with rays is for service in the Philippines; the crossed kris and war club represent service in New Guinea; and the torii symbolizes service in Japan.

DISTINCTIVE INSIGNIA

The distinctive insignia is the shield and motto of the coat of arms.

LINEAGE

1942   Constituted 12 November in the Army of the United States as the 511th Parachute Infantry

1943   Activated 5 January at Camp Toccoa, GA, and assigned 25 February to the 11th Airborne Division

1948   Allotted 15 November to the Regular Army

1949   Reorganized and redesignated 30 June as 511th Airborne Infantry

1957   Inactivated 1 March in Germany and relieved from assignment to the 11th Airborne Division

1963   Reorganized and redesignated 15 May as the 511th Infantry, a parent regiment under CARS

CAMPAIGN PARTICIPATION

World War II

New Guinea
Leyte
Luzon (with arrowhead)

DECORATIONS

Presidential Unit Citation (Army), Streamer embroidered **MANILA** (Regimental Headquarters and Headquarters Company and 1st, 2d, and 3d Battalions, 511th Parachute Infantry cited)

Philippine Presidential Unit Citation, Streamer embroidered **17 OCTOBER 1944 TO 4 JULY 1945** (511th Parachute Infantry cited)

1ST BATTALION, 511TH INFANTRY

LINEAGE

1942   Constituted 12 November in the Army of the United States as Company A, 511th Parachute Infantry

1943   Activated 5 January at Camp Toccoa, GA, and assigned 25 February to the 11th Airborne Division

1948   Allotted 15 November to the Regular Army

1949   Reorganized and redesignated 30 June as Company A, 511th Airborne Infantry

1957   Inactivated 1 March in Germany and relieved from assignment to the 11th Airborne Division

1963   Redesignated 17 July as Headquarters and Headquarters Company, 1st Battalion, 511th Infantry; assigned to the 11th Air Assault Division and activated 18 July at Fort Benning, GA

1965   Inactivated 30 June at Fort Benning, GA, relieved from assignment to 11th Air Assault Division, and activated 2 November, and inactivated 16 November

CAMPAIGN PARTICIPATION

World War II

New Guinea
Leyte
Luzon (with arrowhead)

DECORATIONS

Presidential Unit Citation (Army), Streamer embroidered **MANILA** (1st Battalion, 511th Parachute Infantry cited)

Philippine Presidential Unit Citation, Streamer embroidered **17 OCTOBER 1944 TO 4 JULY 1954** (511th Parachute Infantry cited)

1ST SPECIAL FORCES

COAT OF ARMS

Motto: *De Oppresso Liber* (Liberate From Oppression)

Symbolism: The shield was originally approved for the 1st Special Service Force of World War II on 26 February 1943. The knife is of a distinctive shape and pattern and was issued only to the 1st Special Service Force.

The crest is the crossed arrow collar (branch) insignia of the 1st Special Service Force, World War II, changed from gold to silver for harmony with the shield and to make a difference from collar insignia. The motto more fully translated means "from oppression we will liberate them."

DISTINCTIVE INSIGNIA

The distinctive insignia is the crest and motto of the coat of arms combined with the fighting knife from the shield in the form of a badge.

LINEAGE

1942	Constituted 5 July in the Army of the United States as the 1st Special Service Force, a joint Canadian-American organization to consist of the 1st, 2d, and 3d Regiments and Service Battalion; activated 9 July at Fort William Henry Harrison, MT
1945	Disbanded 6 January in France
1960	Reconstituted 15 April in Regular Army and consolidated with the 1st, 3d, 4th, 5th, and 6th Ranger Infantry Battalions and the 2d Infantry Battalion to form the 1st Special Forces, a parent regiment under CARS

CAMPAIGN PARTICIPATION

World War II

Algeria-French Morroco (with arrowhead)
Tunisia
Sicily (with arrowhead)
Naples-Foggia (with arrowhead)
Anzio (with arrowhead)
Rome-Arno
Normandy (with arrowhead)
Northern France
Southern France (with arrowhead)
Rhineland
Ardennes-Alsace
Central Europe
Aleutian Islands
New Guinea
Leyte (with arrowhead)
Luzon

Vietnam

Advisory
Defense
Counteroffensive
Counteroffensive, Phase II
Counteroffensive, Phase III
Tet Counteroffensive
Counteroffensive, Phase IV
Counteroffensive, Phase V
Counteroffensive, Phase VI
Tet 69Counteroffensive
Summer-Fall 1969
Winter-Spring 1970
Sanctuary Counteroffensive
Counteroffensive, Phase VII

DECORATIONS

Presidential Unit Citation (Army), Streamer embroidered **EL GUETTAR** (1st Ranger Battalion cited)

Presidential Unit Citation (Army), Streamer embroidered **SALERNO** (1st and 3d Ranger Battalions cited)

Presidential Unit Citation (Army), Streamer embroidered **POINTE DU HOE** (2d and 5th Ranger Infantry Battalions cited)

Presidential Unit Citation (Army), Streamer embroidered **SAAR RIVER AREA** (5th Ranger Infantry Battalion cited)

Presidential Unit Citation (Army), Streamer embroidered **VIETNAM 1966–1968** (5th Special Forces Group, 1st Special Forces cited)

Meritorious Unit Commendation, Streamer embroidered **VIETNAM 1968** (5th Special Forces Group, 1st Special Forces cited)

1ST SPECIAL FORCES GROUP, 1ST SPECIAL FORCES

LINEAGE

1942	Constituted 5 July in the Army of the United States as the 1st Special Service Force
	Company lineage follows that of 1st Special Forces from its constitution through 1945
	Another company constituted 27 May in the Army of the United States as Company B, 1st Ranger Battalion; activated 19 June at Carrickfergus, Northern Ireland
1943	*Redesignated 1 August as Company B, 1st Ranger Infantry Battalion*
1944	*Disbanded 15 August in the United States*
1948	*Reconstituted 1 September in the Army of the United States as Company B, 1st Infantry Battalion; activated at Fort Gulick, Canal Zone*
1950	*Inactivated 4 January and redesignated 2 November as 5th Ranger Infantry Company, allotted to Regular Army, and activated 20 November at Fort Benning, GA*

1951	Inactivated 1 August in Korea
1952	Redesignated 24 November as Company B, 1st Ranger Infantry Battalion
1960	The 2d Company, 1st Battalion, 1st Regiment, 1st Special Service Force reconstituted 15 April and consolidated with Company B, 1st Ranger Infantry Battalion to form Headquarters and Headquarters Company, 1st Special Forces Group, 1st Special Forces; consolidated 30 September with Headquarters and Headquarters Group, 1st Special Forces Group, to form Headquarters and Headquarters Company 1st Special Forces Group, 1st Special Forces; activated 4 October on Okinawa

CAMPAIGN PARTICIPATION

World War II

Algeria-French Morroco (with arrowhead)
Tunisia
Sicily (with arrowhead)
Naples-Foggia (with arrowhead)
Anzio (with arrowhead)
Rome-Arno
Normandy (with arrowhead)
Northern France
Southern France (with arrowhead)
Rhineland
Ardennes-Alsace
Central Europe
Aleutian Islands
New Guinea
Leyte (with arrowhead)
Luzon

Korean War

First UN counteroffensive
CCF spring offensive
UN summer-fall offensive

DECORATIONS

Presidential Unit Citation (Army), Streamer embroidered **EL GUETTAR** (1st Ranger Battalion cited)

Presidential Unit Citation (Army), Streamer embroidered **SALERNO** (1st Ranger Battalion cited)

Presidential Unit Citation (Army), Streamer embroidered **POINTE DU HOE**

Presidential Unit Citation (Army), Streamer embroidered **SAAR RIVER AREA**

Republic of Korea Presidential Unit Citation, Streamer embroidered **KOREA** (5th Ranger Infantry Company cited)

2D SPECIAL FORCES GROUP, 1ST SPECIAL FORCES

LINEAGE

1942	Constituted 5 July in the Army of the United States as the Headquarters and Headquarters Detachment, 2d Battalion, 1st Regiment, 1st Special Service Force, a joint Canadian-American organization activated 9 July at Fort William Henry Harrison, MT
	Company lineage follows that of 1st Special Forces from its constitution through 1945
	Another company constituted 11 March in the Army of the United States as Headquarters and Headquarters Company, 2d Ranger Battalion; activated 1 April at Camp Forrest, TN, and redesignated 1 August as Headquarters and Headquarters Company, 2d Ranger Infantry Battalion
1945	*Inactivated 23 October at Camp Patrick Henry, VA*
1949	*Redesignated 29 July as Headquarters and Headquarters Company, 2d Infantry Battalion; activated 15 September at Fort Gulick, Canal Zone*
1950	*Inactivated 4 January*
1952	*Redesignated 24 November as Headquarters and Headquarters Company, 2d Ranger Infantry Battalion; allotted to Regular Army*
1955	*Redesignated 14 June as Headquarters, Headquarters and Service Company, 2d Infantry Battalion; activated 1 July in Iceland*
1960	*Inactivated 11 March at Fort Hamilton, NY*
1960	Reconstituted 15 April in Regular Army, and consolidated with Headquarters, Headquarters and Service Company, 2d Infantry Battalion to form Headquarters and Headquarters Company, 2d Special Forces Group, 1st Special Forces; withdrawn 14 December from Regular Army and allotted to Army Reserve

1961	Group activated 15 March at Columbus, OH
1966	Inactivated 31 January at Columbus, OH

CAMPAIGN PARTICIPATION

World War II

Algeria-French Morroco
(with arrowhead)
Tunisia
Sicily (with arrowhead)
Naples-Foggia (with
arrowhead)
Anzio (with arrowhead)
Rome-Arno
Normandy (with
arrowhead)

Northern France
Southern France (with
arrowhead)
Rhineland
Ardennes-Alsace
Central Europe
Aleutian Islands
New Guinea
Leyte (with arrowhead)
Luzon

DECORATIONS

Presidential Unit Citation (Army), Streamer embroidered **EL GUETTAR**

Presidential Unit Citation (Army), Streamer embroidered **SALERNO**

Presidential Unit Citation (Army), Streamer embroidered **POINTE DU HOE** (2d Ranger Infantry Battalion cited)

Presidential Unit Citation (Army), Streamer embroidered **SAAR RIVER AREA**

French Croix de Guerre with Silver-Gilt Star, World War II, Streamer embroidered **POINT DU HOE** (2d Ranger Infantry Battalion cited)

3D SPECIAL FORCES GROUP, 1ST SPECIAL FORCES

LINEAGE

1942	Constituted 5 July in Army of the United States as Headquarters and Headquarters Detachment, 1st Battalion, 2d Regiment, 1st Special Service Force
	Company lineage follows that of 1st Special Forces from its constitution through 1945
1943	*Another company organized 21 May as Headquarters and Headquarters Company, 3d Ranger Battalion (Provisional) in North Africa; constituted 21 July in the Army of the United States as Headquarters and Headquarters Company, 3d Ranger Battalion; redesignated 1 August as Headquarters and Headquarters Company, 3d Ranger Infantry Battalion*
1944	*Disbanded 15 August in the United States*
1952	*Reconstituted 24 November as Headquarters and Headquarters Company, 3d Ranger Infantry Battalion, Regular Army*
1960	Reconstituted 15 April in Regular Army, consolidated with Headquarters and Headquarters Company, 3d Ranger Infantry Battalion; designated as Headquarters and Headquarters Company, 3d Special Forces Group, 1st Special Forces

1963	Activated 5 December at Fort Bragg, NC
1969	Group inactivated 1 December

CAMPAIGN PARTICIPATION

World War II

Algeria-French Morroco
(with arrowhead)
Tunisia
Sicily (with arrowhead)
Naples-Foggia (with
arrowhead)
Anzio (with arrowhead)
Rome-Arno
Normandy (with
arrowhead)

Northern France
Southern France (with
arrowhead)
Rhineland
Ardennes-Alsace
Central Europe
Aleutian Islands
New Guinea
Leyte (with arrowhead)
Luzon

DECORATIONS

Presidential Unit Citation (Army), Streamer embroidered **EL GUETTAR**

Presidential Unit Citation (Army), Streamer embroidered **SALERNO** (3d Ranger Battalion cited)

Presidential Unit Citation (Army), Streamer embroidered **POINTE DU HOE**

Presidential Unit Citation (Army), Streamer embroidered **SAAR RIVER AREA**

5TH SPECIAL FORCES GROUP, 1ST SPECIAL FORCES

LINEAGE

1942   Constituted 5 July in Army of the United States as Headquarters and Headquarters Detachment, 1st Battalion, 3d Regiment, 1st Special Service Force

Company lineage follows that of 1st Special Forces from its constitution through 1945

1943   *Another company constituted 21 July in the Army of the United States as Headquarters and Headquarters Company, 5th Ranger Battalion; redesignated 1 August as Headquarters and Headquarters Company, 5th Ranger Infantry Battalion; activated 1 September at Camp Forrest, TN*

1945   *Inactivated 22 October at Camp Miles Standish, MA*

1960   Reconstituted 15 April in Regular Army, consolidated with Headquarters and Headquarters Company, 5th Ranger Infantry Battalion as Headquarters and Headquarters Company, 5th Special Forces Group, 1st Special Forces

1961   Activated 21 September at Fort Bragg, NC

CAMPAIGN PARTICIPATION

World War II

Algeria-French Morroco (with arrowhead)
Tunisia
Sicily (with arrowhead)
Naples-Foggia (with arrowhead)
Anzio (with arrowhead)
Rome-Arno
Normandy (with arrowhead)
Northern France
Southern France (with arrowhead)
Rhineland
Ardennes-Alsace
Central Europe
Aleutian Islands
New Guinea
Leyte (with arrowhead)
Luzon

Vietnam

Advisory
Defense
Counteroffensive
Counteroffensive, Phase II
Counteroffensive, Phase III
Tet Counteroffensive
Counteroffensive, Phase IV
Counteroffensive, Phase V
Counteroffensive, Phase VI
Tet 69 Counteroffensive
Summer-Fall 1969
Winter-Spring 1970
Sanctuary Counteroffensive
Counteroffensive, Phase VII

DECORATIONS

Presidential Unit Citation (Army), Streamer embroidered **EL GUETTAR**

Presidential Unit Citation (Army), Streamer embroidered **SALERNO**

Presidential Unit Citation (Army), Streamer embroidered **POINTE DU HOE** (5th Ranger Infantry Battalion cited)

Presidential Unit Citation (Army), Streamer embroidered **SAAR RIVER AREA** (5th Ranger Infantry Battalion cited)

Presidential Unit Citation (Army), Streamer embroidered **VIETNAM 1966–1968** (5th Special Forces Group, 1st Special Forces cited)

Meritorious Unit Commendation, Streamer embroidered **VIETNAM 1968** (5th Special Forces Group, 1st Special Forces cited)

French Croix de Guerre with Silver-Gilt Star, World War II, Streamer embroidered **POINT DU HOE** (5th Ranger Infantry Battalion cited)

Vietnamese Cross of Gallantry with Palm, Streamer embroiderd **VIETNAM 1964–1969** (5th Special Forces Group, 1st Special Forces cited)

6TH SPECIAL FORCES GROUP, 1ST SPECIAL FORCES

LINEAGE

1942   Constituted 5 July in the Army of the United States as Headquarters and Headquarters Detachment, 2d Battalion, 3d Regiment, 1st Special Service Force

Company lineage follows that of 1st Special Forces from its constitution through 1945

1940   Another company constituted 16 December in Regular Army as Headquarters and Headquarters Battalion, 98th Field Artillery Battalion

1941 .   Activated 20 January at Fort Lewis, WA

1944   Converted and redesignated 25 September as Headquarters and Headquarters Company, 6th Ranger Infantry Battalion

1945   Inactivated 30 December in Japan

1960   Reconstituted 15 April in Regular Army, and consolidated with Headquarters and Headquarters Company, 6th Ranger Infantry Battalion to form Headquarters and Headquarters Company, 6th Special Forces Group, 1st Special Forces

1963   Activated 1 May at Fort Bragg, NC

CAMPAIGN PARTICIPATION

World War II

Algeria-French Morroco (with arrowhead)
Tunisia
Sicily (with arrowhead)
Naples-Foggia (with arrowhead)
Anzio (with arrowhead)
Rome-Arno
Normandy (with arrowhead)

Northern France
Southern France (with arrowhead)
Rhineland
Ardennes-Alsace
Central Europe
Aleutian Islands
New Guinea
Leyte (with arrowhead)
Luzon

DECORATIONS

Presidential Unit Citation (Army), Streamer embroidered EL GUETTAR

Presidential Unit Citation (Army), Streamer embroidered SALERNO

Presidential Unit Citation (Army), Streamer embroidered POINTE DU HOE

Presidential Unit Citation (Army), Streamer embroidered SAAR RIVER AREA

Philippine Presidential Unit Citation (Army), Streamer embroidered 17 OCTOBER 1944 TO 4 JULY 1945 (6th Ranger Infantry Battalion cited)

7TH SPECIAL FORCES GROUP, 1ST SPECIAL FORCES

LINEAGE

1942   Constituted 5 July in Army of the United States as 1st Company, 1st Battalion, 1st Regiment, 1st Special Service Force

Company lineage follows that of 1st Special Forces from its constitution through 1945

1942   Another company constituted 27 May in the Army of the United States as Company A, 1st Ranger Battalion; activated 19 June at Carrickfergus, Northern Ireland

1943   Redesignated 1 August as Company A, 1st Ranger Infantry Battalion

1944   Disbanded 15 August in the United States

1948	Reconstituted 1 September in Army of the United States as Company A, 1st Infantry Battalion, and activated at Fort Gulick, Canal Zone
1950	Activated 4 January, redesignated 25 October as 1st Ranger Infantry Company, allotted to Regular Army, and activated 28 October at Fort Benning, GA
1951	Inactivated 1 August in Korea
1952	Redesignated 24 November as Company A, 1st Ranger Infantry Battalion
1960	Reconstituted 15 April in Regular Army; consolidated with Company A, 1st Ranger Infantry Battalion to form Headquarters and Headquarters Company, 7th Special Forces Group, 1st Special Forces; consolidated 6 June with Headquarters and Headquarters Company, 77th Special Forces Group to form Headquarters and Headquarters Company, 7th Special Forces Group, 1st Special Forces; activated at Fort Bragg, NC

CAMPAIGN PARTICIPATION

World War II

Algeria-French Morroco (with arrowhead)
Tunisia
Sicily (with arrowhead)
Naples-Foggia (with arrowhead)
Anzio (with arrowhead)
Rome-Arno
Normandy (with arrowhead)
Northern France
Southern France (with arrowhead)
Rhineland
Ardennes-Alsace
Central Europe
Aleutian Islands
New Guinea
Leyte (with arrowhead)
Luzon

Korean War

CCF intervention
First UN counteroffensive
CCF spring offensive
UN summer-fall offensive

DECORATIONS

Presidential Unit Citation (Army), Streamer embroidered **EL GUETTAR** (1st Ranger Battalion cited)

Presidential Unit Citation (Army), Streamer embroidered **SALERNO** (1st Ranger Battalion cited)

Presidential Unit Citation (Army), Streamer embroidered **POINTE DU HOE**

Presidential Unit Citation (Army), Streamer embroidered **SAAR RIVER AREA**

Presidential Unit Citation (Army), Streamer embroidered **HONG-CHON** (1st Ranger Infantry Company cited)

Presidential Unit Citation (Army), Streamer embroidered **CHIPYONG-NI** (1st Ranger Infantry Company cited)

8TH SPECIAL FORCES GROUP, 1ST SPECIAL FORCES

LINEAGE

1942	Constituted 5 July in the Army of the United States as Headquarters and Headquarters Detachment, 1st Battalion, 1st Regiment, 1st Special Service Force
	Company lineage follows that of 1st Special Forces from its constitution through 1945
1942	Another Company constituted 27 May in Army of the United States as Headquarters and Headquarters Company, 1st Ranger Battalion; activated 19 June at Carrickfergus, Northern Ireland
1943	Redesignated 1 August as Headquarters and Headquarters Company, 1st Ranger Infantry Battalion
1944	Disbanded 15 August in the United States
1948	Reconstituted 1 September in Army of the United States as Headquarters and Headquarters Company, 1st Infantry Battalion; activated at Fort Gulick, Canal Zone
1950	Inactivated 4 January at Fort Gulick, Canal Zone
1952	Redesignated 24 November as Headquarters and Headquarters Company, 1st Ranger Infantry Battalion, and allotted to Regular Army
1960	Reconstituted 15 April in Regular Army; consolidated with Headquarters and Headquarters Company, 1st Ranger Infantry Battalion to form Headquarters and Headquarters Company, 8th Special Forces Group, 1st Special Forces
1963	Activated 1 April at Fort Gulick, Canal Zone

CAMPAIGN PARTICIPATION

World War II

Algeria-French Morroco
(with arrowhead)
Tunisia
Sicily (with arrowhead)
Naples-Foggia (with
arrowhead)
Anzio (with arrowhead)
Rome-Arno
Normandy (with
arrowhead)

Northern France
Southern France (with
arrowhead)
Rhineland
Ardennes-Alsace
Central Europe
Aleutian Islands
New Guinea
Leyte (with arrowhead)
Luzon

DECORATIONS

Presidential Unit Citation (Army), Streamer embroidered EL
GUETTAR (1st Ranger Battalion cited)

Presidential Unit Citation (Army), Streamer embroidered
SALERNO (1st Ranger Battalion cited)

Presidential Unit Citation (Army), Streamer embroidered
POINTE DU HOE

Presidential Unit Citation (Army), Streamer embroidered
SAAR RIVER AREA

9TH SPECIAL FORCES GROUP, 1ST SPECIAL FORCES

LINEAGE

1942   Constituted 5 July in the Army of the United
States as the 3d Company, 1st Battalion, 1st Regiment, 1st Special Service Force

*Company lineage follows that of 1st Special
Forces from its constitution through 1945*

*Another company constituted 27 May in the
Army of the United States as Company C, 1st
Ranger Battalion, and activated 19 June at Car-
rickfergus, Northern Ireland*

1943   *Redesignated 1 August as Company C, 1st Ranger
Infantry Battalion*

1944   *Disbanded 15 August in the United States*

1948   *Reconstituted 1 September in Army of the United
States as Company C, 1st Infantry Battalion; activated at Fort Gulick, Canal Zone*

1950   *Inactivated 4 January*

1952   *Redesignated 24 November as Company C, 1st
Ranger Infantry Battalion and allotted to Regular
Army*

1960   Reconstituted 15 April in Regular Army; consoli-
dated with Company C, 1st Ranger Infantry Bat-
talion to form Headquarters and Headquarters
Company, 9th Special Forces Group, 1st Special
Forces; withdrawn 14 December from Regular
Army and allotted to Army Reserve

1961   Activated 1 February at Little Rock, AR

1966   Inactivated 31 January

CAMPAIGN PARTICIPATION

World War II

Algeria-French Morroco
(with arrowhead)
Tunisia
Sicily (with arrowhead)
Naples-Foggia (with
arrowhead)
Anzio (with arrowhead)
Rome-Arno
Normandy (with
arrowhead)

Northern France
Southern France (with
arrowhead)
Rhineland
Ardennes-Alsace
Central Europe
Aleutian Islands
New Guinea
Leyte (with arrowhead)
Luzon

DECORATIONS

Presidential Unit Citation (Army), Streamer embroidered EL
GUETTAR (1st Ranger Battalion cited)

Presidential Unit Citation (Army), Streamer embroidered
SALERNO (1st Ranger Battalion cited)

Presidential Unit Citation (Army), Streamer embroidered
POINTE DU HOE

Presidential Unit Citation (Army), Streamer embroidered
SAAR RIVER AREA

10TH SPECIAL FORCES GROUP, 1ST SPECIAL FORCES

LINEAGE

1942   Constituted 5 July in Army of the United States as the 4th Company, 2d Battalion, 1st Regiment, 1st Special Service Force

Company lineage follows that of 1st Special Forces from its constitution through 1945

1943   *Another company constituted 11 March in Army of the United States as Company A, 2d Ranger Battalion; activated 1 April at Camp Forrest, TN, and redesignated 1 August as Company A, 2d Ranger Infantry Battalion*

1945   *Inactivated 23 October at Camp Patrick Henry, VA*

1949   *Redesignated 29 July as Company A, 2d Infantry Battalion, and activated 15 September at Fort Gulick, Canal Zone*

1950   *Inactivated 4 January at Fort Gulick, Canal Zone; redesignated 25 October as 2d Ranger Infantry Company, and allotted to Regular Army; activated 28 October at Fort Benning, GA*

1951   Inactivated 1 August in Korea

1952   Redesignated 24 November as Company A, 2d Ranger Infantry Battalion

1955   Redesignated 14 June as Company A, 2d Infantry Battalion, and activated 1 July in Iceland

1960   Inactivated 11 March at Fort Hamilton, NY

1960   Reconstituted 15 April in Regular Army, and consolidated with Company A, 2d Infantry Battalion to form Headquarters and Headquarters Company, 10th Special Forces Group, 1st Special Forces; consolidated 30 September with Headquarters and Headquarters Company, 10th Special Forces Group to form Headquarters and Headquarters Company, 10th Special Forces Group, 1st Special Forces

CAMPAIGN PARTICIPATION

World War II

Algeria-French Morroco (with arrowhead)
Tunisia
Sicily (with arrowhead)
Naples-Foggia (with arrowhead)
Anzio (with arrowhead)
Rome-Arno
Normandy (with arrowhead)
Northern France
Southern France (with arrowhead)
Rhineland
Ardennes-Alsace
Central Europe
Aleutian Islands
New Guinea
Leyte (with arrowhead)
Luzon

Korean War

CCF intervention
First UN counteroffensive (with arrowhead)
CCF spring offensive
UN summer-fall offensive

DECORATIONS

Presidential Unit Citation (Army), Streamer embroidered **EL GUETTAR**

Presidential Unit Citation (Army), Streamer embroidered **SALERNO**

Presidential Unit Citation (Army), Streamer embroidered **POINTE DU HOE** (2d Ranger Infantry Battalion cited)

Presidential Unit Citation (Army), Streamer embroidered **SAAR RIVER AREA**

French Croix de Guerre with Silver-Gilt Star, World War II, Streamer embroidered **POINTE DU HOE** (2d Ranger Infantry Battalion cited)

11TH SPECIAL FORCES GROUP, 1ST SPECIAL FORCES

LINEAGE

1942   Constituted 5 July in Army of the United States as the 5th Company, 2d Battalion, 1st Regiment, 1st Special Service Force

Company lineage follows that of 1st Special Forces from its constitution through 1945

1943   *Another company constituted 11 March in Army of the United States as Company B, 2d Ranger Battalion; activated 1 April at Camp Forrest, TN, and redesignated 1 August as Company B, 2nd Ranger Infantry Battalion*

1945   *Inactivated 23 October at Camp Patrick Henry, VA*

1949   *Redesignated 29 July as Company B, 2nd Infantry Battalion, and activated 15 September at Fort Gulick, Canal Zone*

1950   *Inactivated 4 January at Fort Gulick, Canal Zone; redesignated 2 November as the 6th Ranger Infantry Battalion, allotted to Regular Army, and activated 20 November at Fort Benning, GA*

1951   *Inactivated 1 December in Germany*

1952   *Redesignated 24 November as Company B, 2d Ranger Infantry Battalion*

1955   *Redesignated 14 June as Company B, 2d Infantry Battalion; activated 1 July in Iceland*

1960   *Inactivated 11 March at Fort Hamilton, NY*

1960   Reconstituted 15 April in Regular Army, and consolidated with Company B, 2d Infantry Battalion, to form Headquarters and Headquarters Company, 11th Special Forces Group, 1st Special Forces; withdrawn 14 December from Regular Army and allotted to Army Reserve

1961   Activated 1 March at Boston, MA

1963   Location changed 22 March to Staten Island, NY

CAMPAIGN PARTICIPATION

World War II

Algeria-French Morroco (with arrowhead)
Tunisia
Sicily (with arrowhead)
Naples-Foggia (with arrowhead)
Anzio (with arrowhead)
Rome-Arno
Normandy (with arrowhead)
Northern France
Southern France (with arrowhead)
Rhineland
Ardennes-Alsace
Central Europe
Aleutian Islands
New Guinea
Leyte (with arrowhead)
Luzon

DECORATIONS

Presidential Unit Citation (Army), Streamer embroidered EL GUETTAR

Presidential Unit Citation (Army), Streamer embroidered SALERNO

Presidential Unit Citation (Army), Streamer embroidered POINTE DU HOE (2d Ranger Infantry Battalion cited)

Presidential Unit Citation (Army), Streamer embroidered SAAR RIVER AREA

French Croix de Guerre with Silver-Gilt Star, World War II, Streamer embroidered POINTE DU HOE (2d Ranger Infantry Battalion cited)

12TH SPECIAL FORCES GROUP, 1ST SPECIAL FORCES

LINEAGE

1942   Constituted 5 July in Army of the United States as the 6th Company, 2d Battalion, 1st Regiment, 1st Special Service Force

Company lineage follows that of 1st Special Forces from its constitution through 1945

1943   *Another company constituted 11 March in Army of the United States as Company C, 2d Ranger Battalion; activated 1 April at Camp Forrest, TN, and redesignated 1 August as Company C, 2nd Ranger Infantry Battalion*

1945   *Inactivated 23 October at Camp Patrick Henry, VA*

1949   *Redesignated 29 July as Company C, 2nd Infantry Battalion, and activated 15 September at Fort Gulick, Canal Zone*

1950   *Inactivated 4 January*

1951   *Redesignated 27 February as 14th Ranger Infantry Company, allotted to Regular Army, activated at Fort Benning, GA, and inactivated 27 October at Camp Carson, CO*

1952   *Redesignated 24 November as Company C, 2d Ranger Infantry Battalion*

1955   *Redesignated 14 June as Company C, 2d Infantry Battalion; activated 1 July in Iceland*

1960   *Inactivated 11 March at Fort Hamilton, NY*

1960   Reconstituted 15 April in Regular Army, consolidated with Company C, 2d Infantry Battalion, to form Headquarters and Headquarters Company, 12th Special Forces Group, 1st Special Forces; withdrawn 14 December from Regular Army and allotted to Army Reserve

1961   Activated 1 March at Chicago, IL

1964   Location changed 19 January to Oak Park, IL

CAMPAIGN PARTICIPATION

World War II
- Algeria-French Morroco (with arrowhead)
- Tunisia
- Sicily (with arrowhead)
- Naples-Foggia (with arrowhead)
- Anzio (with arrowhead)
- Rome-Arno
- Normandy (with arrowhead)
- Northern France
- Southern France (with arrowhead)
- Rhineland
- Ardennes-Alsace
- Central Europe
- Aleutian Islands
- New Guinea
- Leyte (with arrowhead)
- Luzon

DECORATIONS

Presidential Unit Citation (Army), Streamer embroidered **EL GUETTAR**

Presidential Unit Citation (Army), Streamer embroidered **SALERNO**

Presidential Unit Citation (Army), Streamer embroidered **POINTE DU HOE** (2d Ranger Infantry Battalion cited)

Presidential Unit Citation (Army), Streamer embroidered **SAAR RIVER AREA**

French Croix de Guerre with Silver-Gilt Star, World War II, Streamer embroidered **POINTE DU HOE** (2d Ranger Infantry Battalion cited)

13TH SPECIAL FORCES GROUP, 1ST SPECIAL FORCES

LINEAGE

1942   Constituted 5 July in Army of the United States as the 1st Company, 1st Battalion, Second Regiment, 1st Special Service Force

Company lineage follows that of 1st Special Forces from its constitution through 1945

1943   *Another company constituted 21 May in North Africa as Company A, 3d Ranger Battalion (Provisional); designated 21 July as Company A, 3d Ranger Battalion, and redesignated 1 August as Company A, 3d Ranger Infantry Battalion*

1944   *Disbanded 15 August in the United States*

1950   *Reconstituted 25 October in Regular Army as 3d Ranger Infantry Company; activated 28 October at Fort Benning, GA*

1951   *Inactivated 1 August in Korea*

1952   *Redesignated 24 November as Company A, 3d Ranger Infantry Battalion*

1960   Reconstituted 15 April in Regular Army; consolidated with Company A, 3d Ranger Infantry Battalion, to form Headquarters and Headquarters Company, 13th Special Forces Group, 1st Special Forces; withdrawn 14 December from Regular Army and allotted to Army Reserve

1961   Activated 1 March at Jacksonville, FL

1963   Inactivated 15 April

CAMPAIGN PARTICIPATION

World War II

Algeria-French Morroco (with arrowhead)
Tunisia
Sicily (with arrowhead)
Naples-Foggia (with arrowhead)
Anzio (with arrowhead)
Rome-Arno
Normandy (with arrowhead)
Northern France
Southern France (with arrowhead)
Rhineland
Ardennes-Alsace
Central Europe
Aleutian Islands
New Guinea
Leyte (with arrowhead)
Luzon

Korean War

First UN counteroffensive
CCF spring offensive
UN summer-fall offensive

DECORATIONS

Presidential Unit Citation (Army), Streamer embroidered **EL GUETTAR**

Presidential Unit Citation (Army), Streamer embroidered **SALERNO** (3rd Ranger Battalion cited)

Presidential Unit Citation (Army), Streamer embroidered **POINTE DU HOE**

Presidential Unit Citation (Army), Streamer embroidered **SAAR RIVER AREA**

Republic of Korea Presidential Unit Citation, Streamer embroidered **UIJONGBU CORRIDOR** (3d Ranger Infantry Company cited)

Republic of Korea Presidential Unit Citation, Streamer embroidered **KOREA** (3d Ranger Infantry Company cited)

17TH SPECIAL FORCES GROUP, 1ST SPECIAL FORCES

LINEAGE

1942 Constituted 5 July in the Army of the United States as the 5th Company, 2d Battalion, Second Regiment, 1st Special Service Force

Company lineage follows that of 1st Special Forces from its constitution through 1945

1943 *Another company organized 29 May in North Africa as Company B, 4th Ranger Battalion (Provisional); constituted 21 July in the Army of the United States as Company B, 4th Ranger Battalion; redesignated 1 August as Company B, 4th Ranger Infantry Battalion*

1944 *Disbanded 24 October at Camp Butner, NC*

1950 *Reconstituted 2 November in Regular Army as the 8th Ranger Infantry Company; activated 20 November at Fort Benning, GA*

1951 *Inactivated 1 August in Korea*

1952 *Redesignated 24 November as Company B, 4th Ranger Infantry Battalion*

1960 Reconstituted 15 April in Regular Army, and consolidated with Company B, 4th Ranger Infantry Battalion, to form Headquarters and Headquarters Company, 17th Special Forces Group, 1st Special Forces; withdrawn 14 December from Regular Army and allotted to Army Reserve

1961 Activated 3 April at Boise, ID; location changed 1 September to Seattle, WA

1966 Inactivated 31 January

CAMPAIGN PARTICIPATION

World War II
Algeria-French Morroco (with arrowhead)
Tunisia
Sicily (with arrowhead)
Naples-Foggia (with arrowhead)
Anzio (with arrowhead)
Rome-Arno
Normandy (with arrowhead)
Northern France
Southern France (with arrowhead)
Rhineland
Ardennes-Alsace
Central Europe
Aleutian Islands
New Guinea
Leyte (with arrowhead)
Luzon

Korean War
First UN counteroffensive
CCF spring offensive
UN summer-fall offensive

DECORATIONS

Presidential Unit Citation (Army), Streamer embroidered **EL GUETTAR**

Presidential Unit Citation (Army), Streamer embroidered **SALERNO**

Presidential Unit Citation (Army), Streamer embroidered **POINTE DU HOE**

Presidential Unit Citation (Army), Streamer embroidered **SAAR RIVER AREA**

Republic of Korea Presidential Unit Citation, Streamer embroidered **KOREA** (8th Ranger Infantry Company cited)

24TH SPECIAL FORCES GROUP, 1ST SPECIAL FORCES

LINEAGE

1942   Constituted 5 July in Army of the United States as the 6th Company, 2d Battalion, Third Regiment, 1st Special Service Force

Company lineage follows that of 1st Special Forces from its constitution through 1945

1940   *Another company constituted 16 December in the Regular Army as Battery C, 98th Field Artillery Battalion*

1941   *Activated 20 January at Fort Lewis, WA*

1944   *Converted and redesignated 25 September as Company C, 6th Ranger Infantry Battalion*

1945   *Inactivated 30 December in Japan*

1960   Reconstituted 15 April in Regular Army, consolidated with Company C, 6th Ranger Infantry Battalion to form Headquarters and Headquarters Company, 24th Special Forces Group, 1st Special Forces; withdrawn 14 December from Regular Army and allotted to Army Reserve

1961   Activated 6 January at Fort DeRussy, Hawaii

1966   Inactivated 30 December in Japan

CAMPAIGN PARTICIPATION

World War II

Algeria-French Morroco (with arrowhead)
Tunisia
Sicily (with arrowhead)
Naples-Foggia (with arrowhead)
Anzio (with arrowhead)
Rome-Arno
Normandy (with arrowhead)
Northern France
Southern France (with arrowhead)
Rhineland
Ardennes-Alsace
Central Europe
Aleutian Islands
New Guinea
Leyte (with arrowhead)
Luzon

DECORATIONS

Presidential Unit Citation (Army), Streamer embroidered **EL GUETTAR**

Presidential Unit Citation (Army), Streamer embroidered **SALERNO**

Presidential Unit Citation (Army), Streamer embroidered **POINTE DU HOE**

Presidential Unit Citation (Army), Streamer embroidered **SAAR RIVER AREA**

Presidential Unit Citation (Army), Streamer embroidered **CABU, LUZON** (Company C, 6th Ranger Infantry Battalion cited)

Philippine Presidential Unit Citation, Streamer embroidered **17 OCTOBER 1944 TO 4 JULY 1945** (6th Ranger Infantry Battalion cited)

MEDAL OF HONOR RECIPIENTS

We have listed regiment by regiment the Medal of Honor winners. Our principal source is *Medal of Honor Regiments, 1863-1973* (Washington: Government Printing Office, 1973) published by the Senate Committee on Veterans Affairs. Medal of Honor citations are listed by the number or title the recipient unit bore at the time of the award, regardless of subsqent changes. In the case of units renumbered after the Civil War or armored infantry units temporarily renumbered during World War II, we have listed the recipient under the current U. S. Army designation.

Certain World War II Medal of Honor recipients from the 7th, 15th, and 30th Infantry are listed in government sources only by division. We have passed their regimental identification on the excellent Medal of Honor section in Taggart, Donald G., *History of the Third Infantry Division in World War II.* (Washington: Infantry Journal Press,1947).

Our guiding principle has been to recognize as many Medal of Honor winners associated with the Regular Army infantry regiments as possible. We apologize in advance for any errors or omissions that may have occurred.

1st INFANTRY

Maus, Marion P. 1886
McMahon, Thomas J. 1969

2d INFANTRY

Burke, Daniel W. 1862
Bondsteel, James Leroy 1969

3d INFANTRY

Fegan, James 1868
Herron, Leander 1868
Holland, Michael Fleming 1969

4th INFANTRY

Greer, Allen J. 1901
Van Schaick, Louis J. 1901
Barkley, Frank J. 1918

5th INFANTRY

Kyle, John 1869
DeArmond, Willian 1874
Hay, Fred S. 1874

James, John 1874
Kelly, John J.H. 1874
Kelly, Thomas 1874
Knox, John W. 1874
Koelpin, William 1874
Mitchell, John 1874
Baker, John 1876-77
Burke, Richard 1876-77
Byrne, Denis 1876-77
Cable, Joseph A. 1876-77
Calvert, James S. 1876-77
Coonrod, Aquilla 1876-77
Donelly, John S. 1876-77
Freemeyer, Christopher 1876-77
Haddo, John 1876-77
Haddoo, John 1876-77
Hogan, Henry 1876-77
Holland, David 1876-77
Hunt, Fred O. 1876-77
Johnston, Edward 1876-77
Kennedy, Philip 1876-77
Kreher, Wendelin 1876-77
McCormick, Michael 1876-77
McGar, Owen 1876-77
McHugh, John 1876-77
McLoughlin, Michael 1876-77
McPhelan, Robert 1876-77
Miller, George 1876-77
Montrose, Charles H. 1876-77
Roche, David 1876-77
Rodenburg, Henry 1876-77
Rooney, Edward 1876-77
Ryan, David 1876-77
Sheppard, Charles 1876-77
Wallace, William 1876-77
Whitehead, Patton G. 1876-77
Wilson, Charles 1876-77
Baird, George W. 1877
Butler, Edmond 1877
Carter, Mason 1877
Casey, James S. 1877
Long, Oscar T. 1877
McDonald, Robert 1877
Romeyn, Henry 1877
Woodfill, Samuel 1918
DeGlopper, Charles N. 1944
Handrich, Melvin O. 1950

Dodd, Carl H. 1951
Ferandez, Daniel 1966
Young, Marvin R. 1968
Doahe, Stephen Holden 1969

6th INFANTRY

Byrne, Bernard A. 1899
Minue, Nicholas 1943
McCleery Finnis D. 1968

7th INFANTRY

O'Neill, Stephen 1863
Bell, James 1875
Evans, William 1876
Brown, Lorenzo D. 1877
Edwards, William D. 1877
McLennon, John 1877
Rogan, Patrick 1877
Wilson, Milden H. 1877
Lindstrom, Floyd K. 1943
Bender, Stanley 1944
Connor, James P. 1944
Maxwell, Robert P. 1944
Olson, Truman O. 1944
Valdez, Jose T. 1945
Crump, Jerry K. 1951
Essebagger, John, Jr. 1951
Gilliland, Charles L. 1951
Goodblood, Claire 1951
Knight, Noah O. 1951
Kyle, Darwin K. 1951
Mendonca, Leroy A. 1951
Miyamura, Hiroshi H. 1951
Wilson, Benjamin T. 1951

8th INFANTRY

Weld, Seth L. 1906
Mabry, George L., Jr. 1944
Ray, Bernard J. 1944
Bellrichard, Leslie Allen 1967
Grandstoff, Bruce Alan 1967
McNerney, David H. 1967
Molnar, Frankie Zoly 1967
Smith, Elmelindo R. 1967

9th INFANTRY

Wellborn, Ira C. 1898
Wallace, George W. 1900
Bart, Frank J. 1918
VanIersel, Ludovicus M.M. 1918
Soderman, William A. 1944
Kaufman, Loren R. 1950
Ouellette, Joseph R. 1950
Smith, David M. 1950
Story, Luther H. 1950
Watkins, Travis E. 1950
Krzyzowski, Edward C. 1951

Sargent, Rupert L. 1967
Yabes, Maximo 1967
Cutinha, Nicholas J. 1968

10th INFANTRY

Schwan, Theodore 1864
Cantrell, Charles P. 1898
Cummins, Andrew J. 1898
Keller, William 1898
Nash, James J. 1898
Polond, Alfred 1898

11th INFANTRY

Cutts, James M. 1864
Patterson, John H. 1864
McDonald, Franklin M. 1872

12th INFANTRY

Younker, John L. 1862
Evans, Donald W., Jr. 1967
Willett, Louis E. 1967
Olson, Kenneth L. 1968
Roark, Anund D. 1968
Hartstock, Robert W. 1969
Penry, Richard A. 1970

13th INFANTRY

Kephart, James 1863
Quinn, Alexander M. 1898
Prussman, Ernest W. 1944
Wetzel, Walter C. 1945

14th INFANTRY

Wood, H. Clay 1861
Williams, George C. 1862
Wright, Robert 1864
Porter, Donn T. 1952
West, Ernest E. 1952
Womack, Bryant E. 1952
Belcher, Ted 1966
Grant, Joseph Xavier 1966
McDonald, Phill G. 1968
Bennett, Thomas W. 1969

15th INFANTRY

Carson, William J. 1863
Craig, Robert 1943
Olson, Arlo L. 1943
Antolak, Sylvester 1944
Christian, Herbert T. 1944
Johnson, Elden H. 1944
Kandle, Victor L. 1944
Kefurt, Gus 1944
Mills, James H. 1944
Schauer, Henry 1944
Tominac, John J. 1944

Ware, Keith L. 1944
Whiteley, Eli 1944
Burke, Frank 1945
Daly, Michael J. 1945
Merrell, Joseph T. 1945
Murphy, Andie L. 1945
Bennett, Emory L. 1951
Mize, Ola L. 1953
Pendleton, Charles T. 1953

16th INFANTRY

Barry, Augustus 1863-65
Schroeder, Henry T. 1900
Henry, Robert T. 1944
Lindsey, Jake W. 1944
Monteith, Jimmie W., Jr. 1944
Pinder, John J., Jr. 1944
Robinson, James W. 1966
Leonard, Matthew 1967

17th INFANTRY

Berg, George 1898
Brookin, Oscar 1898
Buzzard, Ulysses G. 1898
Graves, Thomas J. 1898
Hardaway, Benjamin T. 1898
Ressler, Norman W. 1898
Roberts, Charles D. 1898
Shepherd, Warren J. 1898
Wende, Bruno 1898
Brostrom, Leonard c. 1944
Thorson, John T. 1944
Harvey, Raymond 1951
Ingman, Einar H. Jr., 1951
Lyell, William T. 1951
Rodriguez, Joseph C. 1951
Barker, Charles H. 1953
Shea, Richard T. 1953

18th INFANTRY

Freeman, Henry B. 1862
Phistever, Frederick 1862
Grant, George 1867
Barrett, Carlton W. 1944
Brown, Bobbie, E. 1944
Ehlers, Walter D. 1944
Merli, Gino J. 1944
Schaefer, Joseph E. 1944
Thompson, Max 1944
Peterson, George 1945
Will, Walter J. 1945

19th INFANTRY

Prentice, Joseph R. 1862
Stewart, George E. 1899
Gedeon, louis 1900
Cecil, Josephus S. 1906

Adams, Stanley T. 1951
Brittin, Nelson V. 1951
Red Cloud, Mitchell 1951

20th INFANTRY

Mayfield, Melvin 1945
Rudolph, Donald E. 1945
Stone, Lester R., Jr. 1969

21st INFANTRY

DeSwan, John T. 1898
Doherty, Thomas M. 1898
Fournia, Frank O. 1898
Kelly, Thomas 1898
Nee, George H. 1898
Pfisterer, Herman 1898
Diamond, James H. 1945
Duke, Ray E. 1951
Jordan, Mack A. 1951
Bacon, Nicky Daniel 1968
Shea, Daniel J. 1969

22d INFANTRY

Schou, Julins 1870
McCann, Bernard 1876-77
Pierce, Charles H. 1899
Ray, Charles W. 1899
Garcia, Marcario 1944
Warren, John E., Jr. 1969

23d INFANTRY

Allen, William 1873
Heyl, Charles H. 1876
Leonard, Patrick 1876
Lylton, Jeptha L. 1876
Sage, William H. 1899

Shelton, George M. 1900
Cowan, Richard Eller 1944
Lopez, Jose M. 1944
McVeigh, John J. 1944
Edwards, Junior D. 1951
Lee, Hubert L. 1951
Pililaau, Herbert K. 1951
Sitman, William S. 1951

26th INFANTRY

Reese, James W. 1943
McGraw, Francis X. 1944
Warner, Henry T. 1944
Stryker, Robert T. 1967

27th INFANTRY

George C. Shaw
Davis, Charles W. 1943
Cooley, Raymond H. 1945
Collier, John W. 1950
Desiderio, Reginald B. 1950
Millett, Lewis L. 1951
Sudut, Jerome A. 1951
Martinez, Benito 1952
Baker, John T., Jr. 1966
Foley, Robert T. 1966
Fleek, Charles Clinton 1967
Pitts, Riley L. 1967
Lambers, Paul Ronald 1968

28th INFANTRY

Ellis, Michael B. 1918
Morelock, Sterling 1918
Parker, Samuel I. 1918
Henry, Frederick T. 1950
Hibbs, Robert John 1966
Rubis, Euripides 1966
Miller, Gary L. 1969

30th INFANTRY

Britt, Mannee L. 1943
Adams, Lucian 1944
Dutko, John W. 1944
Gibson, Eric G. 1944
Hawks, Lloyd C. 1944
Kessler, Patrick L. 1944
Knappenberger, Alton W. 1944
Messerschmidt, Harold O. 1944
Murray, Charles P., Jr. 1944
Ross, Wilburn K. 1944
Squires, John C. 1944

31st INFANTRY

Pomeroy, Ralph E. 1952
Schowalter, Edward R., Jr. 1952
Crescenz, Michael J. 1968

32nd INFANTRY

Martinez, Joe P. 1943
Faith, Don C., Jr. 1950

34th INFANTRY

Moon, Harold H., Jr. 1944
Mower, Charles E. 1944

35th INFANTRY

Fournier, William G. 1943
Hall, Lewis 1943
McGaha, Charles L. 1945
Jecelin, William R. 1950
Kanell, Billie G. 1951
Moyer, Donald R. 1951
Ray, Ronald Eric 1966
Karopczyc, Stephen Edward 1967
Stumpf, Kenneth E. 1967

38th INFANTRY

Carey, Alvin P. 1944
Burris, Tony K. 1951
Long, Charles R. 1951
Rosser, Ronald E. 1952

39th INFANTRY

DeVore, Edward A., Jr. 1968
Nash, David P. 1968
Jenknins, Don J. 1969

41st INFANTRY

Albee, George E. 1869
Whittington, Hulon B. 1944

46th INFANTRY

Dunagan, Kern W. 1969

47th INFANTRY

Sheridan, Carl V. 1944
Fous, James W. 1968
Lang, George C. 1969

48th INFANTRY

Dietz, Robert H. 1945
Kelly, Thomas J. 1945

50th INFANTRY

Gammon, Archer T. 1945

51st INFANTRY

Fields, James H. 1944
Hendrix, James R. 1944

60th INFANTRY

Allworth, Edward G. 1918
Nelson, William L. 1943
Butts, John E. 1944
Keller, Leonard B. 1967
Wright, Raymond R. 1967
Kinsman, Thomas James 1968
Sasser, Clarence E. 1968

75th INFANTRY

Law, Robert D. 1969
Pruden, Robert J. 1969

187th INFANTRY

Bucha, Paul W. 1968
Wilson, Richard G. 1950
Hernandez, Rodolfo P. 1951
Hammond, Lester, Jr. 1952

325 INFANTRY

DeGlopper, Charles N. 1944

327th INFANTRY

Gardner, James A. 1966

501st INFANTRY

Hooper, Joe R. 1968
Sims, Clifford C. 1968

502d INFANTRY

Cole, Robert G. 1944
Mann, Joe E. 1944
Wayrymen, Dale E. 1967
Lee, Milton A. 1968

503d INFANTRY

Eubanks, Ray E. 1944
McCarter, Lloyd G. 1945
Joel, Lawrence 1965
Olive, Milton L. 1965
Pierce, Larry s. 1965
Morris, Charles B. 1966
Barnes, John A. 1967
Lozada, Carlos J. 1967
Michael, Don L. 1967
Robel, Laszlo 1968
Blanchfield, Michael R. 1969

504th INFANTRY

Towle, John R. 1944

506th INFANTRY

Guenette, Peter M. 1968
Herda, Frank A. 1968
Roberts, Gordon R. 1969
Kays, Kenneth M. 1970

508th INFANTRY

Funk, Leonard A., Jr. 1945

509th INFANTRY

Huff, Paul B. 1944

511th INFANTRY

Fryar, Elmer E. 1944
Perez, Manuel, Jr. 1945

1st SPECIAL FORCES

Donlon, Roger Hugh C. 1964

24th INFANTRY*

* Although not currently a part of the Combat Arms Regimental System, we have included information on the old 24th and 25th Infantry regiments. In a similar manner to the better-known 9th and 10th Cavalry, the 24th and 25th Infantry were formed after the Civil War from freed slaves and veterans of the U.S. Colored Troops. They gave many years of distinguished service, most notable during the Indian Wars, to a nation which seldom gave them the recognition they deserved. Disbanded during the Korean War as part of the integration of the Armed Forces, they were not selected for CARS in 1957 despite their seniority and campaign credits. It is to be hoped that U.S. Army reorganizations of the future will find a place for one or both of these units. We feel that no historical treatment of the U.S. Infantry would be complete without some mention of them.

COAT OF ARMS

Motto: *Semper Paratus* (Always Prepared)

Symbolism: This regiment uses a regimental badge in lieu of a coat of arms. The badge is blue for infantry. The blockhouse and scroll commemorate service in the Santiago campaign of 1898, particularly the action at San Juan Hill.

DISTINCTIVE INSIGNIA

The badge of the regiment with a scroll or bearing the motto *Semper Paratus* (Always Prepared) in blue letters.

LINEAGE

1866	Organized as the 38th and 41st Infantry by the Act of Congress of July 28 to provide military careers for freed slaves; 38th Infantry organized at Jefferson Barracks, MO; 41st Infantry at Baton Rouge, LA
1869	The 38th and 41st Infantry reorganized as 24th Infantry
1898	The 24th Infantry assigned to 3d Brigade, 1st Division
1947	Assigned to the 25th Infantry Division 1 February
1951	Relieved from the 25th Infantry Division 1 August; inactivated 1 October at Pusan, Korea

CAMPAIGN PARTICIPATION

Indian Wars
Comanches

War With Spain
Santiago

Philippine Insurrection
San Isidro
Luzon 1900
Luzon 1901

Korean War
UN Defensive
UN Offensive
CCF Intervention
First UN Counteroffensive
CCF Spring Offensive
UN Summer-Fall Offensive

DECORATIONS

Republic of Korea Presidential Unit Citation. Streamer embroidered **MASAN-CHINJU** (24th Infantry cited)

MEDAL OF HONOR WINNERS

Brown, Benjamin 1889
Mays, Isaiah 1889
Thompson, William 1950
Charlton, Cornelius H. 1951

25TH INFANTRY*

*Although not currently a part of the Combat Arms Regimental System, we have included information on the old 24th and 25th Infantry regiments. In a similar manner to the better-known 9th and 10th Cavalry, the 24th and 25th Infantry were formed after the Civil War from freed slaves and veterans of the U.S. Colored Troops. They gave many years of distinguished service, most notable during the Indian Wars, to a nation which seldom gave them the recognition they deserved. Disbanded during the Korean War as part of the integration of the Armed Forces, they were not selected for CARS in 1957 despite their seniority and campaign credits. It is to be hoped that U.S. Army re-organizations of the future will find a place for one or both of these units. We feel that no historical treatment of the U.S. Infantry would be complete without some mention of them.

COAT OF ARMS

Motto: Onward

Symbolism: The shield is azure for infantry. The blockhouse represents the regiment's service in Cuba and the royal palm is from the coat of arms of that republic. The arrow in the iron gauntlet symbolizes Indian service in the frontier days and is indicative of the steadfastness of the regiment. The bolo indicates the Philippine campaigns.

DISTINCTIVE INSIGNIA

The insignia is the shield and motto of the coat of arms.

LINEAGE

1866 Organized as the 39th and 40th Infantry by the Act of Congress of July 28 to provide military careers for freed slaves; 39th Infantry organized at Greenville, LA; 40th Infantry organized at Washington, DC, with Nelson A. Miles as its first colonel

1869 The 39th and 40th Infantry consolidated to form the 25th Infantry at New Orleans, LA, 20 April

1898 The 25th Infantry first U.S. unit mobilized for War with Spain; assigned to 2d Brigade, 2d Division

1942 Assigned to the 93d Division (subsequently the 93d Infantry Division) 1 January

1946 Inactivated at Camp Stoneman, CA, 5 February, and relieved from the 93d Infantry Division; reactivated at Fort Benning, GA, 27 February to 7 May

1949 Regiment Headquarters inactivated at Fort Benning, GA, 20 May; 1st Battalion at Fort Lewis, WA, 31 May; and 2d Battalion at Fort Benning, GA, 10 February

1950 Regimental elements redesignated 20 October with Regimental Headquarters as the 25th Infantry Battalion, 1st Battalion as the 94th Infantry Battalion, and 2d Battalion as the 95th Infantry Battalion

CAMPAIGN PARTICIPATION

Indian Wars
Comanches
Pine Ridge

War With Spain
Santiago

Philippine Insurrection
Luzon 1899
Luzon 1900

World War II
New Guinea
Northern Solomons
Bismarck Archipelago

DECORATIONS

None to date.

351